UNDECLARED

UNDECLARED

A PHILOSOPHY OF FORMATIVE HIGHER EDUCATION

CHRIS HIGGINS

The MIT Press
Cambridge, Massachusetts
London, England

The MIT Press would like to thank the anonymous peer reviewers who provided comments on drafts of this book. The generous work of academic experts is essential for establishing the authority and quality of our publications. We acknowledge with gratitude the contributions of these otherwise uncredited readers.

This book was set in Bembo Book MT Pro by Westchester Publishing Services. Printed and bound in the United States of America.

Library of Congress Cataloging-in-Publication Data

Names: Higgins, Chris, 1967– author.
Title: Undeclared : a philosophy of formative higher education / Chris Higgins.
Description: Cambridge, Massachusetts : The MIT Press, 2024. | Includes bibliographical references and index.
Identifiers: LCCN 2023028597 (print) | LCCN 2023028598 (ebook) |
    ISBN 9780262547499 (paperback) | ISBN 9780262377614 (epub) |
    ISBN 9780262377607 (pdf)
Subjects: LCSH: Education, Higher—Aims and objectives.
Classification: LCC LB2322.2 .H487 2024 (print) | LCC LB2322.2 (ebook) |
    DDC 378/.01—dc23/eng/20230814
LC record available at https://lccn.loc.gov/2023028597
LC ebook record available at https://lccn.loc.gov/2023028598

10 9 8 7 6 5 4 3

For Annabel and Zoe, two beautifully undeclared human beings coming into their own.

CONTENTS

Philosophical reflection is recognized as the adventure of one who seeks to understand. . . . Its most appropriate expression is an essay where the character of the utterance (a traveller's tale) matches the character of the engagement, an intellectual adventure which has a course to follow but no destination. A philosophical essay leaves much to the reader, often saying too little for fear of saying too much; its attention is concentrated but it does not cross all of the ts of the argument; its mood is cautious without being defensive; it is personal but never merely "subjective"; it does not dissemble about the conditionality of the conclusions it throws up and although it may enlighten it does not instruct. It is, in short, a well-considered intellectual adventure recollected in tranquility.
—Michael Oakeshott[1]

Undeclared explores a territory I am calling "formative higher education." The phrase is intentionally ambiguous: "higher education" suggests an institutional frame, a formal process occurring in colleges and universities; "formative education" evokes a broader existential task, the quest to understand, cultivate, and enact ourselves in lives worth living. To what extent such soulcraft still has a place in the university is one of the book's driving questions. To this end, I inspect the corporatization, instrumentalization, and privatization of the contemporary university; search for the ghost of the whole person in the machinery of Gen Ed; examine the miseducation of the professoriate; and expose the reduction of vocational formation to technical training and credentialing.

Ultimately, though, my aim is recuperative, not suspicious. The goal is to make contact with estranged aspects of ourselves and unearth forgotten dimensions of learning. I want us to get reacquainted with our inner sophomores (whether one graduated some time ago or is in fact currently a sophomore). I attempt to pry open a space for *skholê* in the midst of the grind and to recover a humane conception of vocation from the shell game of credentialing. *Undeclared* offers a picture of personhood as dynamic integrity and a vision of higher education as a quest for meaning and purpose. I ask us to imagine college as a community of persons-in-process, supporting each other's efforts to make sense of ourselves, to clarify what matters, to carve out meaningful projects, and to organize our talents in the service of something worthwhile.

The book is composed of three long essays, punctuated by three shorter interludes. The first essay, "Soul Action: The Search for Integrity in General Education," considers what it would mean to take holistic higher education seriously. Hidden in the platitude to "educate the whole person" are four tasks as electrifying as they are daunting: to discover what you are made of, judge what aspects of yourself are most important to cultivate, develop each to some fullness, and integrate these separate lines of development into a unity of character and outlook. Our formalistic approach to general education trivializes some of this work and ignores the rest. Students encounter not live invitations to explore and integrate, but fossilized requirements for "scattering and smattering."[2] But we cannot ask of students something that we do not ask of ourselves. We scholars struggle even to bridge disciplines in meaningful ways, let alone to model how one might integrate fact and value, knowing and doing, thinking and feeling, mind and body, living and learning. Exploring how we face up to, flee from, and live with the tensions constitutive of our all-too-human (second) nature, I develop an account of character as complex coherence, of personhood as ongoing soul action.

What would it look like to build a college from the ground up to stimulate and support such soul action for students and teachers alike? To answer this question, the second essay, "Wide Awake: Aesthetic Education at Black Mountain College," revisits one of the great experiments in the history of higher education. At Black Mountain, we find not perfunctory distribution requirements but an entire communal life—from classroom learning to college governance, from dining hall to dorm room, from theater rehearsal to work shift—devoted to general education. The arts were center stage in this (extra)curriculum, but not exactly as we have seen them before. Black Mountain treated art neither as an object of veneration nor as a vehicle for self-expression but as medium, as enabling constraints in which one can work out the terms and direction of one's freedom. Black Mountain

College offers not a dusty artifact but a living reminder, not a scalable model but a proof of concept that general education need not be scattered and hollow. Sitting in on the Socratic seminars of John Andrew Rice, the design studio of Josef Albers, the writing workshop of Charles Olson, and the makings and happenings of MC Richards, Buckminster Fuller, Merce Cunningham, and John Cage testifies to the possibility of higher education as vibrant and resonant, as integrated and integrating.

When asked to defend their practicality, the liberal arts vacillate between two apologies: the old one that there is more to college than vocational preparation and the new one that humanities graduates actually fare well on the job market. The final essay, "Job Prospects: Vocational Formation as Humane Learning," blazes a trail out of this lose-lose situation. The typical humanistic complaint about the second apology is that it cheapens the humanities. By contrast, I show how both strategies make a mockery of vocation itself, leaving unquestioned the vertiginous reduction of vocational education to training and credentialing. This excludes, I argue, no fewer than four essential aspects of vocational formation: finding a worthy form of work to which you are suited, becoming aware of the ethical geography in and around your practice, finding in that work sources of your ongoing self-cultivation, and preparing to leave the practice if and when it begins to stunt your growth. What this expanded vision makes clear is that humane learning is in fact central to vocational enactment. Indeed, vocational life is itself a continuation of our effort to form ourselves. Through a series of philosophical engagements and literary cases, I offer a phenomenology of vocational experience, tracing the lines of formation from college into the worlds of work.

In this way, the three essays work to expand the higher educational imagination, recovering ideals that have been shoved aside or replaced by counterfeits. But talk of educational aims rings hollow without a clear-eyed recognition of conditions on the ground in contemporary universities. While the essays also attend to material conditions, the interludes offer targeted desublimations, intervening where we are prone to lapse into romanticization. The first, "Campus Tour," offers a survey of the deformations of the corporatized university. The second, "New Student Orientation," acknowledges the powerful push to instrumentalize learning and probes the possibilities for reorientation. The third, "Public Hearing," explores how the defunding of public universities proceeds hand in hand with the vitiation of the arts and humanities.

The organization of the essays is thematic, not analytic. These are, in the words of Michael Oakeshott, traveler's tales. Each follows a path where it leads, paying careful attention at every turn. And of course the most interesting part of travel is who you bump into. To stage the most direct and vivid encounter with the question at hand, I engage an eclectic cast of characters. I turn not only to standard figures in philosophy of education (Plato, Rousseau, Dewey, Oakeshott) and philosophers of meaning and value (Gadamer, Arendt, MacIntyre, Walzer), but also to essayists who simultaneously discuss and enact formation (Montaigne, Emerson, Thoreau, Nietzsche, Berger), novelists (Woolf, Salinger, Ishiguro), higher education experimentalists (Rice, Albers, Olson), songwriters (Waters and Biafra), and various figures of biographical interest (Robert Oppenheimer, Ruth Bader Ginsburg, Piet Oudolf).

This belletrist approach may seem strange now that scholarly writing is dominated by the journal article and the monograph.[3] And one can certainly write a monograph on the displacement of formative higher education in the performative university. However, the normalization of this mode of writing is one of the forces working to marginalize humane learning. The research report positions authors as distanced from both their subjects and themselves, imagining an audience that is somehow both intramural and adversarial (confederates of a scholarly tribe, ready to turn on their own). The article deploys its pawns (citations) to defend its king (the thesis). The essayist stands up from the board and sets out in search of interesting interlocutors.

If our aim is to recenter formative aims in higher education, then we are better served by reclaiming the rich and varied tradition of humane letters (poetry and prose; the dialogue and the bildungsroman; the epigram, the letter, and the autobiography; the consolation, the meditation, and the thought experiment). It is no coincidence that many of the great treatments of formative experience have taken the form of essays.[4] The essay is itself a formative genre, staging the attempt of the author to make something of their experience, in dialogue with others who, as Ezra Pound puts it, have "taken the risk of printing the results of their own personal inspection and survey."[5] The essay reunites knowledge and self-knowledge, situating both in the quest to make something of oneself. Unlike the research report, the essay is both voiced and addressed, written from one soul to others. It implies, it enacts, a community of searchers.

ACKNOWLEDGMENTS

The seed of my interest in educational philosophy and experimentation was planted during my middle school years at the Newark Center for Creative Learning, where I encountered two of my first formative educators, Mike Edwards and Ray Magnani. It sprouted a few years later when I opened my copy of the Yale *Blue Book* to find an essay on the purposes of liberal learning. This interest became a calling during my doctoral work at Columbia under the supervision of René Arcilla, a sophisticated thinker who nonetheless always kept faith with his inner sophomore. René not only helped shape my thinking about humane learning, but also introduced me to the texts and contexts that spurred me to deepen my own liberal education. I am grateful to René and others, including Maxine Greene, Robbie McClintock, and David Blacker, for providing living proof that scholarship can and should be a voiced expression of one's provisional judgments and ongoing searches. Though David, René, and I have not yet launched our Black Mountain, the exciting turn in David's work—and his timely posing to me of Billy Bragg's question—helped me peek out of the matrix and transform my experience of the university. Watching René, Maxine, Robbie, and David, in their different ways, gather and maintain the courage of their convictions has helped me learn to better detect and stand behind my own gleams of light.

I began this book at the University of Illinois at Urbana-Champaign (UIUC) and completed it at Boston College (BC). Arriving in Urbana in 2006, I could not imagine that I would go on to develop such pride in and loyalty to Illinois. UIUC boasts the rare college of education with an unbroken commitment to humanistic educational scholarship (constantly renewed by the efforts of stalwarts such as Jim Anderson, Nick Burbules, and Yoon Pak). Through the Unit for Criticism and Interpretive Theory, the Illinois Program for Research in the Humanities, and the Campus Faculty Association, I also found a warm welcome into a vibrant, interdisciplinary, faculty community. I was fortunate to be able to talk and teach, imagine and organize with colleagues such as (the late) Nancy Abelmann, Liora Bresler, Tim Bretl, Chip Bruce, Antoinette Burton, Wally Feinberg, Dan Gilbert, Lauren Goodlad, Rochelle Gutierrez, Chris Lubienski, Anke Pinkert, and Valleri Robinson. And it was at UIUC that I rediscovered my love of undergraduate education. Even as Illinois gave me a good look at the pathologies of the modern multiversity, it restored my faith in institutions.

I came to BC in 2019 to join its effort to re-center questions of meaning, purpose, and value in the educational conversation. I found a university truly committed to the holistic development of its students, faculty, and staff, one eager to unfold new dimensions of its rich Ignatian tradition in response to a changing world. It has been cheering to work alongside such formative fellow-travelers as Andrew Basler, Biz Bracher, Cristiano Casalini, Sam Deane, David Goodman, Tomeu Estelrich, Greg Fried, Burt Howell, Micah Lott, Erik Owens, Mike Sacco, Martin Scanlan, Scott Seider, Dennis Shirley, and Elizabeth Shlala. The Lynch School of Education and Human Development (LSEHD), led by Dean Stanton Wortham, catalyzes and supports work that has intellectual depth, moral integrity, and creative life. In 2020, we created a new undergraduate major, Transformative Educational Studies, that attempts to embody the experiential and experimental ethos outlined in *Undeclared*; and in 2022, we launched a new Department of Formative Education to advance the interdisciplinary, humane study of the education of whole persons for lives of meaning and purpose. I want to thank LSEHD and BC not only for this spur to innovate but also for supporting my scholarship, including with a semester sabbatical that was crucial to the completion of *Undeclared*.

During the book's long gestation, opportunities to share work in progress were invaluable. I developed the kernel of the book (what grew into "Campus Tour," "Soul Action," and "New Student Orientation") across a series of presentations. Thanks to Joseph McAlhany and the Great Ideas program for the invitation to present a first sketch at Carthage College in 2013 (unfortunately, as if to illustrate my argument, Carthage has since shut the door on Great Ideas, along with the Departments of Classics and Philosophy). The 2015 AERA Philosophy of Education SIG Invited Lecture was the perfect occasion to flesh out the argument, which I further developed in presentations at two BC conferences: "Tracking Development Toward Living a Life of Meaning and Purpose" (2017) and "Formative Education: Mapping the Terrain" (2019) (thanks to Henry Braun, Stanton Wortham,

Cristiano Casalini, and Dennis Shirley, for these invitations). I got to test out my critique of Gen Ed in a presentation to UIUC's Higher Education Collaborative in 2019 (thanks to Jennifer Delaney). And I was excited to share a finished portion of "Soul Action" at the 2021 Psychology and the Other conference (thanks to David Goodman).

"Public Hearing" is a distillation and revision of an earlier paper, "The Death Spiral of Contemporary Public Higher Education," which I had the opportunity to workshop at Illinois State University and to present at Eastern Illinois University (thanks to Gina Schouten and the Spencer Foundation; and to C. C. Wharram and the EIU Humanities Center). This version was published as Chris Higgins, "The Death Spiral of Contemporary Public Higher Education," *Thresholds in Education* 41, no. 3 (2018) (thanks to guest editors Jess Heybach and Eric Sheffield).

I was able to test out the argument of "Job Prospects" in two presentations, one at Loyola University Chicago in 2018 (thanks to Amy Shuffelton) and the other at LSEHD in 2019. The kind invitation to keynote the 2019 meeting of the North Eastern Philosophy of Education Society gave me the chance to refine it.

I first wrote about Black Mountain College in a short piece that framed up some of the main themes of *Undeclared*: Chris Higgins, "From the Editor: Undeclared," *Educational Theory* 67, no. 3 (2017). I am grateful for the invitation to present portions of "Wide Awake" as keynotes at the 2021 Simposio Internacional de Filosofía de la Educación at the University of Navarra and at the 2022 Korean Philosophy of Education Society meeting at Seoul National University. Thanks also to Paul Standish for inviting me to share this work in the PESGB Wednesday Seminar Series in 2023. A Spanish translation of the first keynote was published as Chris Higgins, "Renovando la imaginación educativa en el Black Mountain College," trans. T. Alonso-Sainz, in *Retos actuales de la acción educativa: Carácter y personalidad*, ed. J. A. Ibáñez-Martín & C. Naval (Narcea, 2022) (thanks to Tania Alonso for her attention to the text).

I also owe a big thanks to those who have helped to move *Undeclared* into print: my wonderful editor at the MIT Press, Susan Buckley; sharp copyeditor, Susan Campbell; and attentive project manager, Rashmi Malhotra. Thanks also to Harrison Mullen for his labors in framing up the first draft of the index, and to Bella Otoka for proofing it.

Finally, I want to thank my advance readers and interlocutors, including my three hiking companions, Tim Bretl, David Goodman, and Amy

Shuffelton, who all read sections/versions of "Soul Action." I lost my most loyal hiking companion, Betty Nella Biscuit Burns Higgins, right as the book moved into production—as I hint in the text, it was Betty who taught me the meaning of *le sentiment de l'existence*. I am grateful to four friends of my work—René Arcilla, Kevin Gary, Megan Laverty, and Rachel Wahl—who generously read and commented on a complete draft. More recently, Kathleen Knight-Abowitz, Chris Martin, Susan Verducci Sandford, and Bryan Warnick dove in to the proofs to help craft a panel proposal. Working through aspects of *Undeclared*—and my struggles to complete it—with Alexandra Woods was invaluable. And I could not have written this book without Jennifer Burns. Jen supports my writing in many ways, including always serving as my first reader. For decades, she has been a true friend to my search for and enactment of vocation.

PROLOGUE

A quest is not . . . a search for something already adequately characterized, as miners search for gold or geologists for oil. It is in the course of the quest and only through encountering and coping with the various particular harms, dangers, temptations and distractions which provide any quest with its episodes and incidents that the goal of the quest is finally to be understood. A quest is always an education both as to the character of that which is sought and in self-knowledge.
—Alasdair MacIntyre[1]

One fall, several years ago, when I was teaching at a flagship public university, an undergraduate student followed me back to my office after lecture. We had been discussing Michael Oakeshott's classic essay on liberal education, "A Place of Learning," and I assumed that the student had come to continue the conversation.[2] And in a way he had. But I could tell that there was something he wanted to get off his chest. He fidgeted in his chair. He glanced at the door, which was partly open. Then he lowered his voice and told me, "I am . . ." I couldn't make out the final word. Worried, I leaned in and asked him to repeat what he had said. Then he told me his shameful secret: "I am undeclared."

I don't know how moments like this still manage to surprise me. I am well aware of the stigma. In the modern multiversity, Gen Ed is just a toll booth on the credential highway. Students get the message, loud and clear: pick a lane and step on the gas! But listening to this particular student, I couldn't help but feel amazed at the efficiency of our miseducation. Here he was, beginning his sophomore year, and he was already miscategorizing the virtue of the quest as the vice of indecision.[3] What sprang to mind were the famous lines from Yeats:

The blood-dimmed tide is loosed, and everywhere
The ceremony of innocence is drowned;
The best lack all conviction, while the worst
Are full of passionate intensity.[4]

Fortunately, something told me that it was probably a bit early in the day for talk of drowning in a sea of blood, so I downshifted to Tolkien's more palatable one-liner, "Not all who wander are lost." And, truly, this student had not yet even begun to wander. He had entered (like many universities, mine admitted students directly into a school and a program) as a computer engineering major.[5] It was only recently that he had, as it were, hit force quit.

As we discussed his experience, we found our way back to one of Oakeshott's characteristically lyrical passages:

Each of us is born in a corner of the earth and at a particular moment in historic time, lapped round with locality. But school and university are places apart where a declared learner is emancipated from the limitations of his local circumstances and from the wants he may happen to have acquired, and is moved by intimations of what he has never yet dreamed.[6]

We were struck by the irony of this phrase, "a declared learner." Oakeshott is not talking about picking a lane in the credential race. What he wants us to declare is precisely our intention to engage in a form of learning that is uncoerced and unscripted:

It is, in the first place, an adventure in which an individual consciousness confronts the world he inhabits, responds to what Henry James called "the ordeal of consciousness," and thus enacts and discloses himself. This engagement is an adventure in a precise sense. It has no pre-ordained course to follow: with every thought and action a human being lets go a mooring and puts out to sea on a self-chosen but largely unforeseen course.[7]

Oakeshott's words had resonated with this undeclared sophomore. He had come to university hoping for something different from his earlier schooling. Instead, grinding from exam to exam and from pre-req to pre-req, he found himself caught up in what was just a more advanced version of the same old game of "studenting."[8] The irony was, only now that he was "undeclared" was he starting to approach his studies as a "declared learner." Why, we wondered, do we attach a negative prefix to this period of exploration when it was his freshman year that had felt *dis*connected, *un*integrated, and *in*significant?

It wasn't "relevance" he was after, if that means a rush to translate into familiar languages and practical applications. He was interested in expanded vocabularies and was game to follow ideas wherever they might lead. All he was asking for was a chance to explore how the core ideas in various classes interconnect and link up with the project of becoming an educated person. In fact, he had come to office hours to ask what I thought of an idea he had. He was thinking of starting an organization where groups of students from a given major could investigate, synthesize, and present to each other some of the core ideas in their discipline, and where students from different disciplines could explore overlaps and divergences in these ideas and talk about what it means to be educated.

It sounds like an institution of higher education, I said. I think we should try it.

CAMPUS TOUR

We have to recognize that the University is a *ruined institution*, while thinking what it means to dwell in those ruins without recourse to romantic nostalgia.
—Bill Readings[1]

First, let's make a quick stop at the University of California, Los Angeles, to gather some information. Since 1966, UCLA has conducted a nationwide survey of incoming freshmen about their goals for college and life. One survey question gives us a fascinating glimpse into changing values, asking the freshmen to indicate "to you personally the importance" of a variety of goals such as "becoming an authority in my field," "raising a family," "keeping up to date with political affairs," and "improving my understanding of other . . . cultures." Given our faith in the young to recall us to our ideals when we drift toward cynicism, two items on this question stand out: "developing a meaningful philosophy of life" and "being very well-off financially." The changing priorities tell the story of the last half century (see table 1).

The trend lines draw an indelible X, the cynical chiasmus that is the signature of late capitalism. The desire to be *very* well-off (comfortable is not enough) rises steadily; the meaning of life plummets, wallowing in the mid-forties since the reelection of Ronald Reagan.

Unsurprisingly, these value shifts are mirrored in the changing popularity of college majors. In 1971, there were more humanities majors (16.6%) than business majors (13.7%); in 2020, there were almost three times as many business majors (19%) as humanities majors (6.9%).[3] Or consider the relative number of majors in these five fields in 2020:

1. Business (387,851)
2. Engineering (128,322)

3. Homeland security, law enforcement, and firefighting (57,044)
4. Parks, recreation, leisure, fitness studies, and kinesiology (53,749)
5. Philosophy and religious studies (11,889)[4]

Perhaps the meaning of life is clear after all.

As college education comes to resemble professional training, and training itself devolves into mere credentialing, branding becomes difficult. How do you dress up a labor market queue in the garb of higher learning? Thus, Cornell recently found itself uneasy with its double identity as both an Ivy League institution and a "farm school," that is a large land-grant university with strong agricultural programs.[5] To deal with this ironic case of "Ivy envy," an "image committee" was formed and the university bookstore unveiled "a new line of hats and sweatshirts that looked vintage and emphasized Cornell's Ivy tradition. A blue fitted hat with a simple red C became a big seller, as did a red hooded sweatshirt with a small C on the front."[6]

Readings offers another vivid example of this double bind in action, from his days at Syracuse University in the late eighties. At the time, Syracuse was rethinking itself "as an aggressive institution that modeled itself on the corporation rather than clinging to ivy-covered walls."[7] The problem is that the university is a very particular kind of corporation, "one of whose functions (products?) is the granting of degrees with a cultural cachet."[8] This tension revealed itself in Syracuse's visual rebranding process. A new "explicitly 'corporate' logo" was designed, sidelining the traditional seal bearing the Latin motto "Suos Cultores Scientia Coronat" (Science crowns those who seek her).[9] However, Syracuse retained the traditional seal "for official academic documents such as degree certificates."[10] There have been several rebrandings since this time. The current logo is a simple block "S" (orange on white or vice versa), which the Division of Marketing and Communication describes as "bold and dynamic, reflecting how

Table 1

Students by decade deeming stated goal "very important" or "essential"[2]

	1966–1969	1970s	1980s	1990s	2000s	2010s
Developing a meaningful philosophy of life	85.2%	67.8%	47.9%	45.8%	44.7%	46.6%
Being very well-off financially	41.5%	47.6%	69.2%	72.4%	74.5%	81.6%

we connect exploration and action to go beyond what's possible."[11] Just as Readings predicts, the brand guidelines add this note: "While our primary logo should be applied in most contexts, the heritage logo can be a powerful way to elevate our prowess and prestige."[12]

Our next stop is the University of Virginia. As the story goes, Jefferson was so proud of his founding of UVA that he chose it as one of three accomplishments to be inscribed on his gravestone, leaving off such minor accomplishments as governor of Virginia and president of the United States.[13] At the heart of Jefferson's vision for UVA was its main quad or "academical village," at once a literal and educational architecture designed to create a conversational community of learners.[14] The early curriculum was varied in content and public-minded in its aims. Jefferson requested professorships in ten areas: ancient and natural languages, pure and applied mathematics, physical and life sciences, law and medicine, government and humane letters.[15] Jefferson wanted UVA to offer a "higher grade of education," forming in students "reasoning faculties" and "habits of reflection," to "enlarge their minds" and "cultivate their morals," "rendering them examples of virtue to others & of happiness within themselves," all of this in order to "provide for the good . . . of their country."[16] But times have changed and universities have evolved. Has this pedagogical architecture become outmoded?

As it happens, there was an attempted coup in Charlottesville in 2012 that turned on this very question. UVA's first female president, Teresa Sullivan, was just concluding her second year in office. By all accounts, things were going well. Sullivan was well liked by both faculty and students, a fact that became apparent in the vocal protests triggered by her temporary ouster.[17] So what led UVA to try to remove a popular president who had just begun to serve? The Sullivan ouster was spearheaded by the chair ("Rector") of the board of trustees ("Board of Visitors"), the real-estate developer Helen Dragas.[18] Dragas and her allies were pressing for structural changes, hoping to shift resources away from "obscure academic departments" such as German and Classics and to get in on the ground floor of the MOOC (massive open online course) revolution.[19]

Sullivan is no rabid humanist, mind you, but a quantitative demographer by training, whose leadership style has been described as "technocratic."[20] Indeed, one of her first moves in office was to shift UVA to an RCM (responsibility center management) budget model, the hallmark of the corporate university.[21] However, Sullivan made the mistake of urging a cautious approach to launching the academical village into cyberspace. According to Dragas, Sullivan was wedded to a problematic "model of incremental, marginal change."[22] By contrast, Dragas was preaching the gospel according to Clayton Christensen: disrupt or be disrupted.[23] And lo: Betamax begat VHS which begat the DVD which begat Blu-ray which begat Netflix. And Christensen saw that it was good. "All that is solid melts into air," Marx and Engels observed ambivalently; "all that is holy is profaned."[24] MELT IT!, the Christensenians chant. According to Dragas, UVA (with its traditional baggage of quads, departments, and classrooms) was facing an "existential threat" and a clear choice: pivot into this brave new world of MOOCs or become the Betamax of higher ed.[25]

Emails from the weeks leading up to the failed ouster show Dragas and Vice-Rector Mark Kington feeding off of the growing hype around MOOCs and Education 2.0. On May 4, Kington sent Dragas a David Brooks editorial from the *Times*, "The Campus Tsunami," quoting Christensen and hyping Coursera (the for-profit MOOC provider launched earlier that April, announcing partnerships with Penn, Princeton, Stanford, and Michigan). On May 31, Dragas sent Kington an email with the header "good piece in WSJ today—why we can't afford to wait," containing a link to "Higher Education's Online Revolution," a commentary by John Chubb and Terry Moe with the subhead "The substitution of technology (which is cheap) for labor (which is expensive) can vastly increase access to an elite-caliber education."[26]

Even while Dragas was building consensus on the board, she was working with two powerful alumni to build a public case for the removal of Sullivan.[27] One was Peter Kiernan, a graduate, like Dragas and Kington, of UVA's Darden School of Business and chair of Darden's Foundation Board. Kiernan had been introduced to Dragas by his billionaire buddy, Paul Tudor Jones.[28] As resistance to the removal of Sullivan grew, Kiernan and Jones were there, ready to provide Christensenesque ideological cover. Kiernan emailed Darden trustees, stressing the principles of RCM ("many of the schools will face the notion of self sufficiency") and the need for a leader more disruptive than Sullivan.[29] "The governance of the University was not sufficiently tuned to the dramatic changes" faced by universities, he suggested: "These are matters for strategic dynamism rather than strategic planning."[30] Meanwhile, Jones offered his spin on the attempted coup in the form of an op-ed dubbing Jefferson the original "change agent," applauding the board's

"bold action" and hoping for a new president who could "chart an innovative path" for UVA in the "world of academia" as it might be in 2032. "Why
be good," Jones asked, "when there is outstanding to be had?"[31]

The story has a curious ending as, while Sullivan was reinstated, Dragas
was also reappointed by Governor McDonnell for another term as rector.
And despite the outcry caused by the revelation that a real estate developer
and a pair of hedge fund operators from Greenwich were trying to "disrupt" Jefferson's university after a peek into Christensen's crystal ball, UVA
signed on to Coursera anyway, less than a month after Sullivan's reinstatement. In a statement released on the occasion, Sullivan offered an excellent
impression of Dragas and her consiglieres, justifying the decision by saying,
"It's critical for UVA to be in on the ground floor so that we can learn along
with our peers what the future holds."[32] These new online courses, Sullivan
wrote, "will in no way diminish the value of a UVA degree, but rather
enhance our brand and allow others to experience the learning environment of Jefferson's Academical Village."[33]

We are told that public relations is an art, and perhaps it's true. Even in
this single measure, we see Sullivan's skill as a composer. Notice the use of
counterpoint: the left hand carries the rumbling bass of the uncertain future;
the right, the rising tones of certain success. Left hand: the storm clouds of
technological change are approaching; the building you are in will likely
collapse; you had better get in on the ground floor of the new one! Right
hand: rest assured, there are blue skies ahead; your old building will be just as
grand as ever. This FOMO counterpoint resolves in a crescendo: Buy now!

While it is risky to press any harder on a PR soundbite, let us be brave.
In particular, let's look more closely at Sullivan's reassurance that expanding
occupancy in the academical village will only enhance UVA's brand. This is
a perfect example of what epistemologists call "bullshit": it is conceivably
true, very likely false, and ultimately truth and falsity are beside the point.
What Sullivan declines to discuss is what sort of curtain will be drawn
between the first- and second-class cabins in this new hybrid university.
For she is surely aware that "the value of a UVA degree" is directly related
to the percentage of students denied admissions—this is the cruel but perfectly transparent law of exchange-value governing the market that higher
education has become.[34]

The whole point of ideology—the narratives and images that smooth
over our social contradictions—is to blend in. It is this fact that leads Louis

Althusser to describe ideology as a screen of "tenacious obviousnesses."[35]
The phrase "massively open" does this work in the case of MOOCs. It
eases us into magical thinking: as if problems of access in higher education stemmed merely from the fact that our classrooms were too small. But
the contradictions show through when Sullivan conjures up the MOOAV
(massively open online academical village). If there were two things Jefferson cared about in his design of UVA, they were scale and materiality. The
academical village had to be small enough to foster sustained relationships
and some degree of intimacy. When Sullivan insists that the new online
audiences will get to "experience the learning environment" that Jefferson
designed, she is clearly protesting too much. MOOCs obviously do not
transport students to campus; they provide a platform through which professors may "deliver" something we are now told to call "content." Jefferson would, and we should, flatly reject this alchemical conceit of Education
2.0, that educational form and content can be severed.

The academical village is not transposable content: it is a medium in
its own right. The lawn, encircled by the freestanding pavilions and connecting colonnades, embodies what A. Bartlett Giamatti describes as a key
phenomenological aspect of liberal learning, the experience of "a free and
ordered space."[36] The UVA Coursera page is like a warped version of Jefferson's village: at the top is a photographic header, showing a corner of the
lawn—underneath a list of courses in no discernible order, represented by
mostly clip-art icons.[37] By contrast, the colonnaded gaps between pavilions
on Jefferson's lawn make palpable the differences among and connections
between the disciplines. At the center of the academical village is its secular
church, the gorgeous Rotunda that Jefferson modeled on the Pantheon.
Here the contrast between Charlottesville and cyberspace is intense. Imagine looking for a book in a space that embodies the aspiration to become
citizens of a republic of letters; now imagine double clicking on a pdf.

Jefferson's lawn also offers a reminder that one need not choose between
culture and utility. The idea of the academical village was eminently practical. Jefferson saw too many colleges "overbuilding themselves," erecting
one large building "sufficient to contain the whole institution."[38] Such a
building could too easily become "a common den of noise, of filth, and
of fetid air" and would be overly "exposed to accident of fire, and . . . bad
cases of infection."[39] And as for the beautiful linking colonnades? What

could be more practical than, having separated the pavilions housing each professor, providing covered walkways "under which [the students] may go dry from school to school"?[40] Jefferson's distributed pavilions were also fiscally practical, as he "shrewdly realized that the parsimonious state legislators would be more willing to fund a university consisting of modest units rather than a single monumental building."[41]

In both plan and elevation, Jefferson's pavilions embody key educational ideas. The plan features living quarters above a ground-floor classroom. The entry hallways, with their beautiful arched doorways separating and connecting the two spaces, stage the connection of living and learning.[42] In the elevations, Jefferson sought "a variety of appearance, no two alike."[43] While UVA would not add a professional school of architecture until 1919, from the start the lawn itself was conceived as a standing classroom for experiential architectural learning.[44] Jefferson carefully composed the pavilions and colonnades as a study in contrasts across the Doric, Ionic, Corinthian, and Tuscan orders. In the end, to learn is to *live* ideas, and a human life is an embodied one.

Having evoked the importance of materiality and scale, two caveats are in order. First, I do not mean to suggest that interactions in brick-and-mortar settings are inherently more educative than those in online spaces. It is not hard to imagine pseudo learning on a leafy campus or genuine transformations online. What matters is the creation of a thoughtful architecture to support inquiry, reflection, conversation, and so on. The ratio of brick to click—as education is increasingly hybrid now in any case—is not the deciding factor.[45]

Second, to deflate the fantasy that democratic higher education is just a hyperlink away is neither to deny the importance of access nor to pretend that traditional campuses have been good at providing it. Indeed, turning our attention to the material conditions of educational experience helps concretize the facts of exclusion and subordination. Consider first the history of racial inequality. As Craig Steven Wilder has documented with devastating matter-of-factness, the rise of American universities was intertwined with ideas of racial superiority and purification and was dependent on the economics of slavery.[46] Jefferson's university was no exception. UVA did not admit its first African American undergraduate until 1950, and indeed Jefferson himself reports that Charlottesville was chosen for its "centrality to the white population of the state."[47] Even as UVA's architecture embodies the idea of ordered liberty, it indexes the dialectic of freedom and servitude. The initial construction of Jefferson's academical village was performed by enslaved Black men rented out by local slave owners to the university, which agreed merely to cover the costs of "feeding and maintaining" the slaves and returning them to their masters with "fresh outer- and undergarments."[48]

Class is an equally reliable marker of unequal access, at least if we are talking about access to genuinely higher education.[49] A recent study found stark differences between the college prospects of rich and poor students:

- The 1% are seventy-seven times more likely to attend an "Ivy-Plus" college than the bottom 20%.[50]
- Thirty-eight US Colleges enroll more students from the 1% than from the bottom 60%.[51]

At the ostensibly public UVA, to stick with our example, the median family income of undergraduates is $155,500; at nearby Piedmont Community College, it is $42,700. The academical village has been and continues to be a gated community.

It is nonetheless surprising that the inheritors of a flawed but evolving tradition of practice, reflectively shaped for nearly two centuries after Jefferson (who himself was working within a tradition of liberal arts education stretching back for two millennia), would simply hand the reins over to Coursera.[52] "A university," Michael Oakeshott observes, "is not like a dinghy which can be jiggled about to catch every transient breath of wind."[53] Because "time is limited," Herbert Spencer pointed out, educators cannot escape that "question of questions": "What knowledge is of most worth?"[54] But perhaps Spencer never considered the power of donors to preempt this question. In the same year that German and classics were rumored to be on the chopping block, UVA was cultivating a new $100 million gift from Jones whose previous $100 million had included $35 million to build a basketball facility named after his son.[55] The first step in securing the new gift was acceding to a request by Jones and his wife, a devotee of Ashtanga Yoga, to launch a yoga-related center at UVA. Though $15 million was secured to create a new Contemplative Sciences Center, the rest of the nine-figure ask was apparently shelved after the backlash suffered by Dragas and the reinstatement of Sullivan.

Again, the point is not that older subjects are better and newer ones are to be distrusted, only that some thought must be given to the overall shape of the curriculum, to the relation of the different branches of learning. This is what, theoretically, distinguishes a university from Amazon.com. "If the university is to be more than a skillfully coordinated department store," Grant and Riesman write, "it must somewhere demonstrate that its connections are deeper than the aisles through which consumer preferences are demonstrated."[56] Perhaps, after deliberation, a neuroscientific approach to yoga would make the cut (it might even help drum up interest in the meaning of life!). Nonetheless, a university cannot maintain its integrity if it is adding and dropping programs at the whims of donors or perceived consumer appeal. Enter the brave new world of the corporate university: while "hot yoga" is hot, classics and German have to fight it out in a budgetary cage match.[57]

At some point, hedge-fund higher education will realize that it can sell tickets to such bloodsport. For now, the mess is hidden behind "responsibility center management," a phrase which repackages trend-chasing and the abandonment of cross-subsidization as the sensible request to balance your check-book. Indeed, once we are speaking of "cross-subsidization," the jig is up, as we have already begun to think of academic units as separate shops and the university as nothing but a tax collector. And it turns out that UVA's Darden School was a trailblazer in the world of RCM. As David Kirp chronicles, in the late 1990s, UVA was looking for a new dean for Darden, finally finding their man in Ted Snyder, "who combines the calm demeanor of a scholar with the shark's instinct for the jugular."[58] After an offer was made, it took eighteen months for Snyder and UVA to come to terms. The sticking point, it turns out, was the "franchise fee," the percentage of Darden's tuition that would have to be coughed up to the university.[59] Snyder bounced to Yale three years later, but he left Darden in a sweet spot, paying an "internal tax rate" of 10%, "with side payments as a sweetener," and paying nothing on its "lucrative executive education programs or other private sources."[60] UVA's business school alone now boasts an endowment ($808 million) larger than that of twelve state flagships.[61]

Let's head next to Harvard Yard to find out how our oldest and richest university distributes resources. In fact, Harvard has practiced a homely version of RCM, "Every tub on its own bottom," for two centuries.[62] However, given its unique brand and stupendous endowment, there is usually no need to select tributes for an academic hunger games. Even "obscure" areas of study such as the humanities have a long established place on the quad. But perhaps the unpopularity of the meaning of life has reached even Cambridge. In 2006, facing a projected one hundred million dollar budget deficit, the Faculty of Arts and Sciences was offered a way to avoid foreclosure: sell off Massachusetts Hall (the oldest surviving building at Harvard, where hundreds of Continental Army soldiers were quartered during the siege of Boston) to the university's central administration.[63]

This is ironic, given that one documented budget pressure on the contemporary university is administrative bloat.[64] While the faculty-to-student ratio has remained constant, there has been a marked growth in the number of administrative and demi-administrative positions and a ballooning of top administrative salaries. During a period (1976–2018) in which the number of students grew by 78% and the number of faculty by 92%, the number of administrators and demi-administrators increased by 339%.[65] Meanwhile, from 2009 to 2012, in the aftermath of the worst recession since the Great Depression, average pay for *public* university presidents increased 14%, to $544,554. The gains were even more obscene at the twenty-five highest-paying publics, where presidential pay increased 34% to an average of $974,006.[66]

Well, here we are at Massachusetts Hall. Built in 1720, it was originally a dormitory, counting among its inhabitants Samuel Adams, John Adams, and John Hancock. Now it houses the offices of the university president, provost, treasurer, and vice presidents. Actually, fourteen freshmen are still housed on the fourth floor of Mass Hall, in the eaves of the academical village.[67]

The last stop on our tour is UC Berkeley. The year is 1964. There seems to be a protest going on at the administration building, Sproul Hall. At the time, there were still philosophy majors, and one of them, Mario Savio, has just grabbed the microphone. Let's hear what he has to say:

> I ask you to consider: If this is a firm, and if the board of regents are the board of directors; and if President Kerr in fact is the manager; then I'll tell you something. The faculty are a bunch of employees, and we're the raw material! But we're a bunch of raw materials that don't mean to be—have any process upon us. Don't mean to be made into any product. . . . Don't mean to end up being

bought by some clients of the University, be they the government, be they industry, be they organized labor, be they anyone! We're human beings!

There's a time when the operation of the machine becomes so odious, makes you so sick at heart, that you can't take part! You can't even passively take part! And you've got to put your bodies upon the gears and upon the wheels . . . upon the levers, upon all the apparatus, and you've got to make it stop! And you've got to indicate to the people who run it, to the people who own it, that unless you're free, the machine will be prevented from working at all![68]

The one thing in the world, of value, is active soul. This every man is entitled to; this every man contains within him, although, in almost all men, obstructed, and as yet unborn.
—Ralph Waldo Emerson[1]

SOUL ACTION: THE SEARCH FOR INTEGRITY
IN GENERAL EDUCATION

I call this the "corruption" of consciousness; because consciousness permits itself to be bribed or corrupted in the discharge of its function, being distracted from a formidable task towards an easier one.
—R. G. Collingwood[2]

For when all combine in every way to make everything easier, there remains only one possible danger, namely, that the ease becomes so great that it becomes altogether too great; then there is only one want left, though it is not yet a felt want, when people will want difficulty.
—Johannes Climacus (Søren Kierkegaard)[3]

THE FORMIDABLE TASK OF FORMATION

Anyone who doubts the power of language to shape thought has never looked closely at the linguistic specimen known as the truism. The tricky part is catching one, since truisms are masters of disguise. Indeed, a good truism trap is a work of art. It takes artful reframing—I am thinking of works such as Gustave Flaubert's "Dictionary of Received Ideas" and Jenny Holzer's installation series *Truisms*—to reveal the unstable and uncanny mix of ideas hidden under each cloak of the commonplace. Truisms are miraculous suspensions of the most disparate and ordinarily reactive cognitive ingredients: truths and half-truths, hopes and fears, facts and fancies, conjectures and contradictions. Somehow the appealing and the objectionable, the obvious and the absurd, the unexplored and the well-trodden all combine to form a bland and soothing bromide.

Found everywhere, truisms are especially concentrated in spheres where recipe-following is preferred to question-posing, where doubt is discouraged and hope cheerfully mandated. Case in point: education. A powerful magnet for kitsch and cliché, few spheres are better than education at rendering recipes, canning controversies, and serving up pieties. In the discussion that follows, I want to look at one particular educational bromide, the call to "educate the whole person."[4] This is virtuoso ventriloquism. What should arrest like the voice of the oracle announcing to you alone an enigmatic and difficult task sounds instead like someone reading the minutes of the Committee on Vaguely Appealing Ideas. When someone suggests educating the whole person, we nod assent. After all, who wants to argue for a fragmentary or lopsided education? What sort of educational scrooge would object to the aim of "well-roundedness"? To do so somehow just feels, well, unwholesome.

I am not suggesting that we abandon the holistic ideal, trading unthinking endorsement for easy dismissal. It is precisely the difficulty we want to recover: its force as a living idea, its fundamental and formidable challenge. But to do so we will need to topple it from its pedestal. This turns out to be rather easy since, to serve its function of making discourse safe from thought, a truism must pull off a delicate balancing act. Lean too far in one direction, and it collapses into an outright tautology; lean too far the other way, and the truism settles into a clearly controversial claim. Balance is achieved only by freezing dynamic thinking into fixed ideas.

Let's give our holistic truism a nudge by posing a basic question: Is wholeness an aspiration or, as it were, a preexisting condition? What it means to educate the whole person changes dramatically depending on our answer. Many holistic educators hold that wholeness is a given feature of our nature. But they tend to downplay the implications of this claim. If the various parts of us are inevitably interconnected, then we are always educating the whole person whether we know it or not. Even a lesson designed with the narrow aim of transmitting specific information will, for better or worse, inevitably ramify along other lines of intellectual development (reasoning, understanding, self-knowledge, and so on) and into our capacities for perceiving and imagining, feeling and relating, valuing and judging, willing and doing. Here's the rub: if all education is whole-person education, then our truism collapses into a tautology. Remove the redundancy, and the call to educate the whole person becomes simply a call to educate. More charitably, it is a call for greater awareness of the inevitable, indirect effects of educational interventions. Thus, we might become more curious about the hidden civics curriculum of the pep rally or more troubled by the anesthetic quality of so many literature courses. Though this is a worthy reminder, it lends little substance to the slogan to educate the whole person. It says, in effect, "educate well."

Nor does it take much to push the truism in the other direction, revealing not an empty or underdeveloped proposition but a frightening one. For critics of mass compulsory schooling, the narrowness of the enterprise may be its only saving grace—it is when the schools begin to target the whole person that you really need to worry. For testimonial evidence on this point, we have innumerable rock songs, from the classic countercultural—

> We don't need no education
> We don't need no thought control
> No dark sarcasm in the classroom
> Teacher, leave them kids alone[5]

—to the punk counter-countercultural:

> Your kids will meditate in school [twice]
> California Über Alles [twice]
> Über Alles California [twice]
> Zen fascists will control you
> Hundred percent natural
> You will jog for the master race
> And always wear the happy face . . .
> Mellow out or you will pay [twice][6]

In one of these sonic dystopias, schooling serves establishment culture; in the other, it serves an ascendant counterculture. Whether it is the old-school repression of the stiff upper lip or the repressive desublimation of Jerry Brown's California, the "thought control" of the schoolmaster or the "zen fascism" of progressive education, the accusation remains the same.[7] It is precisely as education forms the ambition to shape the whole person that it begins to take on a sinister cast. Holistic initiatives such as character education and authentic engagement are unmasked as cover stories for the real business of schooling: conformity and control.

Obviously, these are not educational treatises, but pop protests overstated for effect. However, they do succeed in opening imaginative space for genuine insights. Jello Biafra is on point with his spirited send-up of the mindlessness in mindfulness, and Roger Waters is right to object to the "dark sarcasm in the classroom." Every school has its share—one is more than enough—of teachers who, pushed around in the larger society, become petty dictators of their classroom worlds. This is not to bash teachers: every profession has its pathologies. Still, I don't think Waters overdramatizes the monstrousness of playing psychological games—manipulating tone, rationing recognition, currying favorites, cultivating insecurity—with a captive audience of young people placed in your care.

In this light, even Waters's famous refrain works as a statement of refusal. As an educational theory, however, "we don't need no education" leaves much to be desired. The *when*, *where*, *how*, and *why* of education are all debatable, but not the *whether*. For even shielding the young from influence amounts to guiding growth in light of a desired end. The idea that socialization itself is "thought control" rests on an untenably romantic, libertarian, and atomistic philosophical anthropology. To find our voices, we need to learn languages; to freely choose our different paths, we need practices that mark out fields of endeavor; to forge distinctive selves, we need interlocutors, models, and foils.[8] As Richard Rorty puts it,

> There is no such thing as human nature, in the deep sense. . . . Nor is there such a thing as alienation from one's essential humanity due to societal repression, in the deep sense made familiar by Rousseau and the Marxists. There is only the shaping of an animal into a human being by a process of socialization, followed (with luck) by the self-individualization and self-creation of that human being through his or her own later revolt against that very process.[9]

For Rorty, we are essentially essenceless. We are creatures possessing only the "second natures" of our historically, linguistically, and axiologically contingent cultures. However, it is not only songwriters who overstate their points for effect. In his effort to debunk essentialism and deflate the romantic notion of alienation, Rorty here elides an important point. Socialization and individualization are not distinct temporal phases, one passive and the other active. They are dialectically knotted from the start. Ironically, this is a point made by Hans-Georg Gadamer and Michael Oakeshott, the very thinkers Rorty invokes in his famous turn from epistemology to hermeneutics, from the quest for privileged representations to philosophy as edifying conversation.[10] While both Gadamer and Oakeshott would endorse Rorty's critique of essentialism, they would balk at his implication that we are passively socialized into our *Lebensformen*.[11] "Education is self-education," Gadamer observes, not because we go it alone but for the same reason Oakeshott thinks that human beings have an inalienable kind of freedom: namely that we inevitably play a role in the selection, interpretation, and synthesis of our "influences."[12] There is agency in influence.[13]

This suggests a way to salvage the core insight of our sonic dystopias without endorsing their "Don't tread on me!" theory of education. What I have in mind is brought out nicely by Robbie McClintock in his study of, simultaneously, Ortega y Gasset's intellectual formation and formative ideas.[14] "Ortega's personal genius," McClintock argues, was his "tremendous educability."[15] On the default view, in which agency and influence are contrasted, it sounds strange to compliment someone for their educability, like praising a sponge. However, like Gadamer and Oakeshott, Ortega challenged this default view, envisioning a dialectic of agency and influence, freedom and circumstance.[16] To motivate this untimely idea, McClintock contrasts two views of education: the modern idea that we are products of our circumstances and the Platonic conception of education as an active quest impelled from within by *eros*, the longing fueled by our sense of incompleteness. The former has a scientific aura; the latter sounds antiquarian and mystical. However, it is the Platonic view that has the greater explanatory power, at least when it comes to one interesting feature of formative experience: the feeling that we have yet to find our true teacher. If we were mere products of our local influences, how would this feeling of mismatch ever arise? This suggests that we are not passive objects of conditioning but active subjects, agents of our own education. Education then becomes, as McClintock puts it, "the sustained, skeptical search for the unknown teacher who can set forth that which one intuits to be possible, but which one has yet to encounter."[17] McClintock's claim is that all of us can recognize this impulse, not that all of us will complete such a search. Indeed, he stresses just how difficult it is to sustain one's skepticism without fetishizing it:

> Many youths, tired of their quest, stop looking too soon and accept as a prize that which happens to be at hand; and others, hardened to skeptical scoffing, pass by their true goal without responding.[18]

However, there remain the lucky "few who recognize their teacher" in a moment that exemplifies the interplay of agency and influence:

> Without giving up their powers of criticism, they let their teacher immerse them in influence, for they know that the influence is wholesome and that in time they can organize, edit, and perfect their acquirements. Thus, learning begins in a restless search and culminates in a decisive commitment. What but love could direct such delicate maneuvers?[19]

With this, we are now ready to reformulate the objection to holistic education. It is true that conceiving of education as transmission of detachable knowledge and skills shows a remarkable lack of ambition. Such learning, John Dewey rightly observed, is superficial and short-lived compared to that which "is transmuted into character . . . [existing] with the depth of meaning that attaches to its coming within urgent daily interests."[20] That is all very well and good, Waters and Biafra retort, but if you are going to try to shape me as a whole person, at least get to know me first. In other words, what is potentially sinister is not when education targets the whole person but when holistic education is grafted onto compulsory, one-size-fits-all, formalistic schooling. To say that whole-person education cannot be imposed from without is not to simply to call for "learner-centered education," as least not as this phrase is ordinarily used. It is not enough to make a concession to individuality and choice within an essentially heteronomous program. This engagement, whether we call it "whole-person education," formation, self-cultivation, or simply education, must be understood as the student's own existential project.

Education, then, is not about shaping a thing but rather about fostering conditions for self-formation (in the double sense of self-driven and cultivating selfhood). Whereas (modern mass) schooling begins with compulsion, formative education begins by awakening agency and orienting the student to the task of formation.[21] Whereas schooling must resort to batch processing, formative education offers a space for genuine exercise of agency, providing substantive alternatives through which students can pursue their individualizing quests. Whereas schooling tends toward the fragmented, arranging elements according to a logic of instruction (learn to add and subtract, then to multiply and divide; read Poe, then Hawthorne, then Melville, then Whitman, then Dickinson), formative education involves a logic of encounter, with phases of unsettling and reintegration.

Some might use the word "curriculum" expansively to name these facilitative conditions, but this courts an overemphasis on the narrowly academic and risks relocating agency to the teacher as curriculum designer. It may be more instructive simply to say that what is provided is a campus and a faculty. A campus, by which I mean not only an architecture but also the ethos embodied in that architecture, represents a standing effort to reunite living and learning and a standing invitation to take up the task of one's formation. A faculty includes stewards of formative resources, veterans of various practices of inquiry, and examples of individuals who pursue their formative tasks with integrity.

Let us review our progress so far. We set out to recover the dynamism and difficulty of the call to educate the whole person. Our hunch was that an enigmatic and formidable task lies hidden in our facile phrases and inert truisms. Whole-person education comes preapproved not because the ideal is so easy to understand and endorse, but because we are afraid to put any weight on it. The truism is too delicately balanced between tipping into the tautological or slipping into the sentimental. However, with this initial foray into the analysis of whole-person education, we have begun the dismount. We have reopened a basic question (Is wholeness a given of our nature, an aspiration, or perhaps somehow both?), recovered the crucial notion of the learner's agency, and recalibrated the role of the teacher (and facilitating environment) in formative education. But we have not yet stuck the landing, since we have only a vague sense of the key concept of wholeness. This is unsurprising, as holistic discourse suffers from a chronic case of fuzziness, stemming from a reluctance to make distinctions, as if it were a contradiction to articulate the dimensions and diremptions of wholeness. However, a well-drawn distinction enlarges thought, and it is a more capacious vision of the human we are after, not a blurry image.

Indeed, as soon as we sharpen our focus, it is clear that wholeness is not a simple but a compound concept, whose multiple meanings include both *completeness* and *undividedness*.[22] If, for example, we lack the whole shopping list, it may be because we have forgotten to list certain items or because the list has been torn in two. This distinction immediately broadens our view, revealing that we have been conflating these two senses of the term and defaulting to the idea of wholeness as completeness. We were not wrong to see well-roundedness, the aim of cultivating all aspects of oneself, as central to holistic education. However, the idea of wholeness as undividedness suggests that we have overlooked a second task, that of integrating these various cultivars into a unified character or coherent outlook. Thus, in the call to educate the whole person, we find not one but two formidable tasks, well-roundedness and integration. Let us do some further work recovering the difficulty of the overly familiar concept of well-roundedness before turning to the equally difficult, less familiar, process of integration.

The concept of well-roundedness is itself well-rounded, too much so, like Nietzsche's famous blank-rubbed coin:

> What, then, is truth? A mobile army of metaphors, metonyms, and anthropo-morphisms—in short, a sum of human relations which have been enhanced, transposed, and embellished poetically and rhetorically, and which after long use seem firm, canonical, and obligatory to a people: truths are illusions about which one has forgotten that this is what they are; metaphors which are worn out and without sensuous power; coins which have lost their pictures and now matter only as metal, no longer as coins.[23]

Nietzsche vividly captures how our tentative figurations of the world harden into self-evident truths, how our expressive metaphors degenerate into blank linguistic tokens. All ideas begin as live insights (or missteps) in particular movements of thought. However, once formulated in handy phrases and passed from speaker to speaker, this dynamic quality begins to fade from view. The conversations in which the ideas appeared as rejoinders are effaced; the questions to which they were proposed as answers go begged. Well-roundedness is just such a token. Whatever live question it once proposed to answer is now replaced by the rhetorical question, Is it better to be well-rounded or over-specialized? The contingency, contentiousness, and dynamism—the jagged edges—of this idea have been rubbed smooth through overuse. The injunction to be well-rounded no longer enjoins. It simply asks us to whisper down the lane.

In order to defamiliarize this linguistic token and reconnect with its "sensuous power," consider these questions to which well-roundedness might be the answer: What is the ideal shape of a soul? Is it better to have a symmetrical self? Does a bad character have rough edges? If these questions border on the nonsensical, it is not because it is incoherent to describe the mind in spatial terms. Mind is embodied: our knowings and feelings are closely related to our taking up and navigating three-dimensional space. Indeed, in one leading theory, consciousness emerged precisely as a way of mapping what is going on in the body.[24] Gut feelings, cluttered minds, deep experiences, shallow people: these are more than figures of speech. Insofar as they are metaphors, they are, in Lakoff and Johnson's phrase, "metaphors we live by."[25] We not only *have* the idea of the self as interior space—a screening room for mental images, a sanctuary from intrusion, a room furnished with ideas, an arena for conflicts—we *live* it.[26] That said, we should find it stranger than we do that one of our dominant spatial tropes in education has its roots in furniture-making. Before we spoke of well-rounded persons, we spoke of well-rounded or well-turned speech and writing, and before that, "well-turned" referred to material objects that had been "skillfully formed, shaped, or rounded, especially on a lathe."[27] The idea seems to be that one's self (mind, character, talents, interests) ought not be pitted or lopsided but evenly filled out and balanced. It is an odd metaphor, but not without interest. It suggests that we experience evenly developed characters as pleasing and overdeveloped capacities as jagged intrusions, that the evenly developed can handle the varied situations in life with greater balance, and so on. Still, it is a little hard to see why this particular metaphor became handy linguistic currency. In any case, the point is not to restore the image on the coin but to recover the conversations it ended and the questions it begs.

Luckily for us, the presumptuousness of the idea is not very well hidden. The ideal of well-roundedness is this: educate all of the parts of yourself. This sounds eminently reasonable. There is only one small problem. It requires that we know what we are made of, that we understand what it is in us that requires balanced cultivation. Perhaps we are trying to balance mind and body or to develop both reason and emotion. Perhaps the goal is to cultivate both self-knowledge and interpersonal awareness, or both worldly and spiritual vocation. What is it that we are trying to round evenly: our interests, talents, faculties, virtues, capabilities, sensitivities? Hidden inside the modest-sounding request to be well-rounded is a huge ask: know thyself! As Heraclitus (captured in a recent, playful translation), puts it, "Applicants for wisdom / do what I have done: / inquire within."[28] Nor is this inquiry likely to be quick and tidy. Heraclitus, again, "You could not discover the limits of soul, even if you traveled every road to do so: such is the depth of its meaning."[29]

What makes this interior search challenging is the need to navigate between two extremes. We must assume neither that we are unique, and thus can safely ignore the findings of other soul-searchers, nor that we are generic, and thus possess some uniform thing called human nature. As Alasdair MacIntyre argues, our selves are narrative constructions, built from the contingent tales, tropes, and *teloi* we happen to find in the time and place in which we have landed.[30] Switching to a visual metaphor, Iris Murdoch puts it this way: a human being is "the kind of creature who makes pictures of himself and then comes to resemble the picture."[31] Nor is this some recent, "narrative turn" in philosophical anthropology. At the dawn of Western philosophy, Heraclitus offered this epigram: "Soul is a self-proliferating account."[32]

In other words, if well-roundedness is to be more than a slogan, we need to engage in some serious soul-searching. What are my true talents and interests? What are the different dimensions of my nature? What are the fundamental human capabilities? Am I oblivious to certain aspects of the world or myself? As even this brief initial list makes clear, we must not only plumb the treacherous depths of individual self-knowledge (treacherous both because we lack distance and impartiality and because the "object of knowledge" changes through being understood) but also wade into the wider waters of philosophical anthropology, searching for insight into our nature, condition, and humanity. In order to develop the parts of the soul, we need an account of the soul, articulating its elements, mapping its precincts. We need a *logos* of the *psyche*. (Before "psychology" came to refer to a specific modern, empirical tradition within philosophical anthropology, it meant simply this: a reasoned account of the soul.)[33]

This is not the only demand the ideal of well-roundedness presses upon us. As finite creatures we need not only self-knowledge but ethical judgment. However we parse ourselves, we will find more in us than we can do justice to. Depth in one area will necessitate leaving others less developed. Just as scarcity of social resources prompt questions of distributive justice, McClintock explains,

> Problems of formative justice arise because persons . . . , always facing the future, find more possibilities and potentialities before them than they have the energy, time, ability, and wherewithal to fulfill. They must choose among these and in doing so they are struggling to form their unfolding lives.[34]

When we slip into facile talk of educating the whole person, the implicit fantasy is that we have all the time in the world. We can pursue all of our potentials, develop all of our dimensions. As if! Our lives are "unfolding" in real time. The fantasy version of formation is like the fantasy version of architecture: time stops and we confront a blank page; what complete structure shall we design? Forming oneself is more like rehabbing a haphazardly designed kitchen on a shoestring budget.[35] Or perhaps a medical metaphor better captures the stakes: even as you commit to growing some aspects of yourself, others will die off. Triage is required. What MacIntyre says about conduct applies equally well to self-cultivation. Life hands us not contrived dilemmas with preferred solutions but "tragic situations" involving multiple, authentic goods: "Whatever I do, I shall have left undone what I ought to have done."[36]

Thus, it is not enough to know what one is made of. What is required is not an impartial inventory but a normative reckoning: Which are my most valuable talents? What are my deepest, most satisfying interests? What is the core of my character? What makes me distinctive? In this way, the homely exhortation to well-roundedness opens onto fundamental ethical questions about leading a good life: To what should I devote my attention and efforts? What are the sources of meaning and growth? What is worthwhile to achieve and admirable to become? What is of highest value? What is human flourishing? Instead of calling for the cultivation of the whole person, we would do better to invert the injunction: Starve no *important* part of yourself! Stunt no *essential* dimension of your humanity! With this, we have begun to trade the facile phrase "well-rounded" for something stranger and more austere. To form ourselves as whole persons requires self-knowledge, ethical judgment, and existential triage.

As if wholeness-as-completeness were not challenging enough, holistic education confronts us with another equally challenging task: to integrate our various lines of development into a coherent character, unified outlook, and workable life-plan. To fully understand the necessity and difficulty of integration, we would need to commit to and explore a particular account of personhood and self-cultivation. We need an analysis of the soul before we can understand the compatibilities and tensions among its aspects. As we noted, well-roundedness may refer to a diversity of talents, a range of interests, a full complement of virtues. The aim may be to develop key faculties, essential capabilities, core domains of knowledge, major modes of responsiveness. The task of integration will vary accordingly. Our focus may be to reconcile freedom and circumstance, to mediate desire and conscience, or to reunite reason and emotion. Or we may focus in further on the conflicts internal to desire and emotion, the tensions among diverse interests, the pull of rival goods. The aim might be to unify mind, body, and spirit or to integrate self-knowledge, interpersonal intelligence, and attunement to nature. But it is not necessary to settle all debates in philosophical anthropology to make the case for integration, as many rival accounts agree on this point, that the soul is not only articulated but divided and discordant. To secure the claim that integration is necessary and difficult, we need only to canvas a few of the most famous geographies of the soul.

Let us look first at a famous moment in the Platonic dialogues, the chariot metaphor in the *Phaedrus*.[37] Here Plato's Socrates likens the psyche to
a chariot piloted by a charioteer and pulled by two steeds, one noble and
one ignoble. Each character represents a core human drive: truth-tracking
(charioteer), honor-loving (noble steed), and pleasure-seeking (ignoble
steed). The allegory's dramatic center is the pitched battle between reason
and appetite, as the charioteer, forced to throw all of his weight into the
wanton horse's bit, "bespatters his railing tongue and his jaws with blood,
and forces him down on his legs and haunches."[38] Moments like this lead
us toward the familiar conclusion that reason points us toward truth and
goodness while the appetites drag us off course. However, if this were the
moral of the story, Plato would have recommended simply cutting the
intemperate steed loose from its tack. The interest in Plato's metaphor lies
in its suggestion that the good life is not one of desire-free reason but one of
reason-shaped desire. Left to its own devices, desire tends to reduce the good
to simple pleasures; but the fact remains that it is desire that prods us into
contact with the good. As Giovanni Ferrari puts it, it is because "the charioteer actually learns from the fractious creature" that his "efforts to curb the
lustful horse merit the title of 'integration' rather than mere 'manipulation'
or 'repression.'"[39] For Plato, human flourishing involves "concern for all
voices in the soul," inflecting the "timbre" of each as they are integrated into
a "polyphonic song."[40] Even while highlighting the difficulty of integration,
Plato offers eloquent testimony on behalf of its necessity.

Rousseau's anthropology can be read as a modern departure from Plato's
account of the soul. The difference is that Rousseau gives a starring role
to the least important of the three characters in Plato's psychic drama, the
good horse, whom Plato describes as "a passionate lover of honor, tempered by restraint and modesty."[41] While Rousseau would not deny the
importance of reason or appetite, it is this "spirited" part of the soul, oriented toward social esteem, that most interests and worries Rousseau. We
could say that Rousseau zooms in on the honor-loving part of the soul,
which he calls "*amour propre*," to reveal its own internal divisions. That the
honor-loving part of the soul already involves integration is suggested in
Plato's phrase, "tempered by restraint and modesty." The idea seems to be
that, in an ideal polis, ideals of temperance will be woven into the fabric of social emotions such as pride and shame.[42] By contrast, Rousseau's
starting point is the pathologies of the soul that flourish in the actually

existing societies of eighteenth-century Europe. Here we find an inflamed and pernicious variant of *amour propre*. When we are well formed—and this is the point of the extended educational thought experiment that is *Emile*— then *amour propre* will be integrated with two other key components of the Rousseauian psyche, *pitie* and *amour de soi*.[43] *Pitie* is compassion for others. *Amour de soi* is the basic form of self-love that expresses itself in concern for and contentment in our independent existence in the world: it's good to be alive, to have this form, occupy this place, exercise these powers.[44] For Rousseau, individual and collective human flourishing hinges on how these parts of the soul grow together. *Amour de soi* may deepen as one discovers and actuates new dimensions of oneself through one's widening participation in social life. *Pitie* may likewise find wider expression as one's sense of humanity widens. The affirmative basis of personal existence—Hey, make room . . . I'm here! . . . I matter . . . Check out what I can do—may be harmonized with awareness of the predicament of others. And we could understand this harmony as the healthy form of *amour propre*, a desire to have a valued place in an equal network of recognition. However, if *amour propre* becomes inflamed and distorted, then self-love and concern for others may fuse in a manner that corrupts the individual's relation to both self and other. In the corrupt form of *amour propre*, self-affirmation becomes doubly alienated. I see my worth only in the eyes of others, and only as they see me comparing well to further others.[45] I become lost in the hall of mirrors that is social reputation. Meanwhile the innocent pleasure in being noticed degenerates into a more desperate demand (you must recognize me!). Gone is the ethos of *pitie*, replaced by an interest in others as tools of my own doomed effort to win a game of invidious comparisons (doomed, as thinkers such as G. W. F. Hegel and Jessica Benjamin have shown, because the imperious demand for recognition negates the locus of independent subjectivity and judgment that would lend that recognition meaning).[46]

Despite these interesting differences between their accounts, both Plato and Rousseau testify to the importance and difficulty of this second formative task. What worries Plato is the divorce of reason and appetite; what concerns Rousseau is the disconnection of self-love and compassion. They agree that it is not enough to cultivate the parts of the soul in isolation. Living well for each depends on a second, delicate process of integration.

Indeed, most geographers of the soul have located key boundary lines and border disputes, and some see us as fundamentally defined by polarities in our makeup and disconnects in our experience. Montaigne is one who took Heraclitus's advice to "inquire within." But his famous essays, his assayings of himself, lead to a surprising verdict: "Man is wholly and throughout but patchwork and motley."[47] Ultimately, Montaigne is so impressed by the "supple variations and contradictions so manifest in us" that he recommends against the "high and hazardous undertaking" of trying to "penetrate the very soul" to find its hidden unity.[48] Because generalizations so often lie—"Pope Boniface VIII, they say, entered office like a fox, behaved in it like a lion, and died like a dog"—Montaigne proudly declares that "'Distinguo' [I make a distinction] is the most universal member of my logic."[49] The unity of the self remains but a hypothesis; so far Montaigne has uncovered only heterogeneity:

> If I speak of myself in different ways, that is because I look at myself in different ways. All contradictions may be found in me by some twist and in some fashion. Bashful, insolent; chaste, lascivious; talkative, taciturn; tough, delicate; clever, stupid; surly, affable; lying, truthful; learned, ignorant; liberal, miserly, and prodigal: all this I see in myself to some extent according to how I turn; and whoever studies himself really attentively finds in himself, yes, even in his judgment, this gyration and discord. I have nothing to say about myself absolutely, simply, and solidly without confusion and without mixture, or in a word.[50]

Two later thinkers equally convinced of our essential contrariness but drawn nonetheless to the "high and hazardous" search for unity are Simone Weil and Sigmund Freud. Weil rejects the idea that we must choose between a unified and orderly soul or one ruled by discord and confusion. The order of the soul, Weil suggests, is found precisely in the dialectical pairing of our fundamental needs. We need, to choose three of her couplets, security *and* risk, order *and* liberty, equality *and* hierarchy.[51] Confusion enters in when, unable to view ourselves with this "both-and" logic, we disavow one half or the other of these defining ambivalences. Freud goes one step further in seeing disavowal itself as a fundamental need of the soul. The psyche is not, as it were, a container that just happens to include conflicts: it developed as a way to contain conflicts (between needs and world, between desires and norms, between associative and consecutive logics, among the rival relational voices we internalize, and so on). Psychic structure is like an architectural ruin, Freud suggests, a historical record of conflictual damage, patchwork, and reconstruction.[52] The coup de grace is our conflict over our conflictual nature itself. We feel compelled to simplify, compartmentalize, and minimize tension (*Thanatos*); and we are drawn toward new relationships and increased complexity (*Eros*).[53]

For us "patchwork" creatures, integrity is not given but forged. Ideals conflict with wants and needs; desires themselves pull in different directions; experience layers without knitting. The necessary work of personal integration is difficult, even harrowing. It requires tolerance of ambiguity, courage to face the unhandsome parts of ourselves, and creativity in finding novel harmonies. Even then, solutions are flawed. The work remains ongoing. And we should admit that while we are sometimes drawn to it, we are even more often repelled by this work. One feature of our inconsistent nature is our reluctance to plumb these inconsistent depths and "sift ourselves to the bottom."[54] We are wired to avoid cognitive dissonance and to seek comfort. We are drawn to disavow the inconvenient and unhandsome in ourselves. We prefer the simplicity of "either-or" to the complexity of "both-and." We edit out the bad side of good things and the good side of bad things; or, we settle for facile compromises or false syntheses. We look for conventional shortcuts to escape the task of creative integration. But the twofold task remains: to develop the worthy parts of ourselves into a livable unity. In the next section, we take a closer look at some of the ways in which we may fall short of and live up to this double demand of personal formation.

ROOTS AND BRANCHES

> And so the two precepts are perhaps not contradictory? Perhaps the first merely declares that man should have a center, the second that he should have a circumference?
> —Friedrich Nietzsche[55]

> What good are roots if you cannot take them with you?
> —Gertrude Stein[56]

The call to educate the whole person has a fairly prominent place in the museum of fine ideas. Docents usually stop to point it out and say a few words about the importance of well-roundedness. However, when the tour group moved on, we stayed behind to try an experiment: plug the injunction in to some live intellectual current and see if it still works. So far it seems to hold a pretty good charge, and, once we have it back in operation, it is clear that the museum didn't quite realize what they had: not a helpful reminder or finishing touch, but the very starting point of education; not a clear reading of north, but a conversation about how to build a compass; not a mildly appealing, impersonal policy proposal, but a direct personal injunction setting us two related tasks, each as intimidating as it is inescapable. To cultivate all of the important dimensions of yourself, you must strive to understand what you are made of and what you stand for. To integrate these diverse lines of development into a coherent character or outlook, you must engage in arduous and inventive soulcraft.

In one respect, these twin formative tasks are obviously complementary: if you don't develop multiple aspects of yourself, there is nothing to integrate; if you don't integrate, there is no coherent "you" to hold these separate interests. Here are the opening stanzas of a poem by Thoreau that speaks to this latter possibility:

(1)   I am a parcel of vain strivings tied
(2)   By a chance bond together,
(3)   Dangling this way and that, their links
(4)   Were made so loose and wide,
(5)   Methinks,
(6)   For milder weather.

(7)   A bunch of violets without their roots,
(8)   And sorrel intermixed,
(9)   Encircled by a wisp of straw
(10) Once coiled about their shoots,
(11) The law
(12) By which I'm fixed.

(13) A nosegay which Time clutched from out
(14) Those fair Elysian fields,
(15) With weeds and broken stems, in haste,
(16) Doth make the rabble rout
(17) That waste
(18) The day he yields.

(19) And here I bloom for a short hour unseen,
(20) Drinking my juices up,

(21) With no root in the land
(22) To keep my branches green,
(23) But stand
(24) In a bare cup.[57]

By the end of the first line, we realize that the opening phrase is more complicated than it seems. This is not the confident "I am" of first-person narration. This is a poem about the struggle for coherence and agency, a first-personal poem about the difficulty of achieving a first-person perspective. Clearly the narrator has projects, and the image of violets (line 7) leads us to believe that these projects have flowered. But apparently none of these sundry "strivings" is worth mentioning by name (1). The narrator is worried about what holds together these diverse inclinations, "dangling this way and that" (3). But the problem goes beyond the fact that the links between them are "so loose and wide" (4). The narrator fails to see himself in the linkages, in the act of linking, opting instead for the third-person description, "*their* links" (3, emphasis added). What makes a person distinctive is the way that they organize their aspirations and carry their commitments. Thoreau provides only generic collection and container words, such as "parcel," "bunch," and "cup" (1, 7, 24). What lends a person substance is the way that they lay claim to the history that birthed their enthusiasms. There is no personal history in this not-quite-a-self portrait, only the hazy "once" of myth (10).[58]

If autonomy means self-legislation, this narrator is very far from discovering a binding law of the self. What ties together his desires and ambitions is only a "wisp of straw" and even this is not knotted but only "encircled" or "coiled" (9–10). While the narrator's agency does eventually peek out in the final stanza's "I bloom" (19), the preceding stanzas offer a litany of manipulation and constraint verbs in the passive voice: "tied" (1), "bond together" (2), "made" (4); "encircled" (9), "coiled" (10), "fixed" (12), "clutched" (13). Nor does the narrator experience this as the hand of providence. While capital T "Time" is at work, it is not guiding him to heaven but precisely ripping— "with weeds and broken stems"—him from "Elysian fields" (13, 15, 14). This violent image suggests not only heteronomy but capriciousness. Forget a self-authored life-plan, there is no plan. His nosegay-self was made in "haste," representing only "a chance bond" (15, 2). And he pays a steep price for even this wisp-of-straw unity. Rather than find a taproot in the soil of experience, he stands, broken-stemmed, "in a bare cup" (24). "Drinking [his] juices up," his once green inclinations desiccate into "vain strivings" (20, 1). In this way, Thoreau captures well one possible dead-end in formative experience. Nascent interests develop, experience branches, but somewhere along the way we lose track of the fundamental human need for rooted integrity.

This complicates our initial assumption that our core formative tasks are obviously complementary. If Nietzsche is right to say that there is no logical contradiction between these precepts, Thoreau is right to remind us how difficult it can be in practice simultaneously to define a center and expand a circumference. The ideals of well-roundedness and integrity do not form a simple Venn diagram: their intersection inscribes an ethical ideal, a vision of the self as a differentiated unity or dynamic whole.[59] That such robust personhood is difficult to achieve is evident from our two characteristic ways of falling short of this ideal. True dynamic wholeness is rare; most of us sacrifice coherence to complexity or vice versa. Thus, we encounter *monomaniacs* who seek an axiological Rosetta stone that can translate the diversity of genuine goods into a single language of value and aspiration. The price of their unity is the winnowing of self, narrowing of experience, strain of disavowal, and hollowness of overspecialization. Their wholeness is not a dynamic equation, but a static remainder of their repeated factoring. And we encounter *compartmentalizers* who manage the heterogeneity of self and diversity of goods by dividing traits and experience into separate silos. The compartmentalizer purchases complexity at the price of incoherence and inauthenticity, as the unified person dissolves into a roster of role players.

If I am correct that differentiated, dynamic integrity is difficult to achieve, then we all know something about monomania or compartmentalization. However, to strengthen the argument that each represents a short-circuiting of the quest for robust personhood, let's put some flesh on the ideal types. To see how a person might trade complexity for unity or vice versa, we will need a working model of the dimensions of personhood. I will adopt the well-known division of formative labor into five domains: aesthetic, spiritual, civic, intellectual, and moral. First, let's consider the lives of monomaniacs, before turning to the character of the compartmentalizer.

Meet the Monas, a set of quintuplets distinguished only by their middle initials. Fearing a divided soul, all five found ways to unify their interests and development:

Mona A. had an epiphany that life is art and art is life. Now, the whole world is her gallery. Attending a town hall meeting is like watching a film. Moral dilemmas are material for her novel. Because she loves the beautiful stained glass windows and sublime organ, Mona A. sometimes goes to church with her sister, Mona S.

To be perfectly frank, though, Mona S. worries that Mona A. is going to hell. Back in her college days, Mona S. had enjoyed how different subjects brought out different sides of her. Later she decided that spirituality is empty if it only applies on Sundays and came to view secular subjects as the devil's diversions. Now Mona S. runs a blog criticizing liberal activists and godless scientists, including her sisters Mona C. and Mona I.

Mona C. is passionate about grassroots democracy and devotes all her energy to community organizing.

The egghead of the bunch, Mona I. is an empirical psychologist who studies how religious and political zealotry are rooted in basic personality factors. Mona S., Mona C., and Mona I. no longer speak to one another.

And none of the sisters have seen Mona M. for years: instead of attending the annual family reunion, she sends a card with a receipt for a carbon offset for the amount she would have spent on a plane ticket. It's the moral thing to do.

It should be clear that each Mona has paid a heavy price for her coherence, narrowing her sympathies and her world. Perhaps, though, this is the best we can do. After all, the jack-of-all-trades might end up with no pursuit deep enough to open up the interest of the world. At least each Mona has one rich vein of interest. Not so fast, says John Dewey, arguing that,

> as a man's vocation as artist is but the emphatically specialized phase of his diverse and variegated vocational activities, so his efficiency in it, in the humane sense of efficiency, is determined by its association with other callings. A person must have experience, he must live, if his artistry is to be more than a technical accomplishment. He cannot find the subject matter of his artistic activity within his art; this must be an expression of what he suffers and enjoys in other relationships—a thing which depends in turn upon the alertness and sympathy of his interests. What is true of an artist is true of any other special calling, . . . so that the scientific inquirer shall not be merely the scientist, the teacher merely the pedagogue, the clergyman merely one who wears the cloth, and so on.[60]

The prognosis is more dire than is commonly thought: it is not just a matter of missing out on the other things—the hyperspecialist misses out on their one thing!

Let us turn now to the second thought experiment. Meet Silas, the only person who manages to get along with all five Monas. Silas has been sure not to neglect any of these five aspects of his formation. He has developed adequately and proportionately his intellectual acuity, moral judgment, civic responsibility, aesthetic sensitivity, and spiritual awareness. However, Silas has constructed these not as interconnected and overlapping concerns but as separate silos. He relies on his intellect at work, attends the town meeting in a civic spirit, activates his aesthetic side at the museum, gets in touch with his spirituality at church, and weighs values in the face of dilemmas. This is a tidy solution for dealing with life's complexity—too tidy in fact. It turns out that Dewey's critique applies equally to Silas.[61] He is not an ordinary hyperspecialist, but his rigid compartmentalization makes him into a kind of serial monomaniac. Let's explore how sealing off these capacities distorts and impoverishes each.

Consider first the danger in Silas' compartmentalization of moral judgment. There is an important line of ethical thought suggesting that leading a good life is less about weighing dilemmas and more about waking up.[62] "The opposite of morality," Maxine Greene writes,

> is indifference—a lack of care, an absence of concern. Lacking wide-awakeness, I want to argue, individuals are likely to drift, to act on impulses of expediency. They are unlikely to identify situations as moral ones or to set themselves to assessing their demands. In such cases, it seems to me, meaningless to talk of obligation; it may be futile to speak of consequential choice.[63]

Indeed, this habit of dignifying as dilemmas selective moments from life's ceaseless flow of relation, valuation, and conduct may be one of our most effective sleep aids. When we commit the "mistake which makes morality a separate department of life," Dewey observes, "anxious solicitude for the few acts which are deemed moral is accompanied by edicts of exemption and baths of immunity for most acts. A moral moratorium prevails for everyday affairs."[64]

Now let's head to the museum, where we find poor Silas so tuned to the aesthetic that he misses the art. He is able to identify Yoko Ono as neo-Dadaist but unable to look in the moral mirror that is *Cut Piece*. He can tell you that Rothko's canvases are prepared with a sizing of rabbit-skin glue but is immune to the spiritual resonances of the color fields. He can engage in a debate over the site-specificity of Doris Salcedo's Untitled (2003), her Istanbul Biennial installation, but is unable to join her in civic mourning. Art suffocates when locked in a compartment, even—perhaps especially—when that compartment is a temple of art. As Claes Oldenburg puts it, "I am for an art that is political-erotical-mystical, that does something other than sit on its ass in a museum. I am for an art that grows up not knowing it is art at all."[65]

And so it goes, as Silas moves from sphere to sphere. To ensure the development of each of these five capacities, Silas planted each in a separate pot; in the process, he denied each its deeper roots in the soil of human experience. Silas's pursuits are varied but malnourished.

One might accept that a life splintered in this way would be impoverished while denying that anyone really is so divided. Perhaps the moral of the story is that these five experiential domains inevitably interpenetrate. After all, many have attested to the close connections among truth (intellectual and spiritual), goodness (moral and civic), and beauty. Are there any Silases out there? While Silas may seem bizarre, I contend that there is more than a little Silas in all of us. Western modernity is defined by distinctions—secular-religious, reason-tradition, reality-imagination, subjective-objective, fact-value, individual-social—that sever the connections between art, science, ethics, religion, and politics.[66] To be modern is to experience these as largely autonomous realms. Admittedly, this is not a flattering self-portrait. We saw how Silas's pigeonholing of the ethical and the aesthetic made him oblivious to the true nature of each. Are we really that bad off?

In the aesthetic realm, the answer is a decided yes. Following Hans-Georg Gadamer, we can see a distortion and enervation of aesthetic experience, more than two centuries in the making. This diagnostic history suggests that my depiction of Silas struggling to make genuine contact with Rothko, Ono, and Salcedo, while fictional, was hardly fanciful. Let me offer some anecdotal evidence on this score, before saying more about Gadamer's diagnosis.

When I lived in New York City, my subway route (what was then the 1/9) included a stop at Lincoln Center. Often, we would pull up just as a performance was letting out, and my subway car would fill up with people hanging on to a strap with one hand and a *Playbill* with the other. Crowded together as we were, I couldn't help but overhear their discussions of plays, symphonies, and operas (as someone interested in aesthetics, I had a duty to listen carefully!). What I found consistently missing in these discussions was any attempt to articulate what the artworks revealed about our world and ourselves. What I heard instead were endless variations on the same theme:

the difficulty of hitting that high F, the questionable casting of Ophelia, the virtuosity of the first violin, the poor pacing of the second act, and so on. Even without buying a ticket, I had a front-row seat for the performance of what Gadamer calls "aesthetic consciousness."

According to Gadamer, the modern aesthete is characterized by his selective attention and his sovereign bearing.[67] Sophisticates, such as those at Lincoln Center, have learned to focus on "what is supposed to be the work proper," differentiating proper aesthetic qualities from the supposedly "extra-aesthetic elements that cling to it, such as purpose, function, the significance of its content" (74). In order to further home in on "what is aesthetically intended," the modern aesthete then differentiates between "the original (play or musical composition) and its performance" (74). Thus, the focus on virtuosity that I witnessed on the 1/9.

Aesthetic consciousness not only differentiates but abstracts. Instead of meeting the artwork in the concrete world of unfolding experience, the aesthetic encounter is staged in "some alien universe into which we are magically transported for a time" (83). To ready it for transport, the artwork must be radically transformed. To enter the "timeless present" of aesthetic experience, its historicity must be erased (83). The audience will know that the work dates to a certain period but not that it is an "act of a mind and spirit that has collected and gathered itself historically" to find its voice anew in our own moment (83). Wrenched out of historical time, the work must also be abstracted from the social world, where it arose as one more human attempt to understand what is and identify what matters.

The arts are distinguished by their medium specificity, their interest in authenticity and style, and their stress on formal values such as clarity, economy, and freshness, but artistic intentions are hardly only aesthetic. Artists seek to map interior and exterior worlds; to document absences, witness presence, and capture "the music of what happens"; to expose impropriety and to question propriety; to fortify resolve, reckon with consequences, and mourn losses; to interest us in the workings of our souls and help us to get over ourselves; to behold the beautiful, befriend the abject, and honor the sacred; to disperse illusions and assemble hope; and so on.[68] These projects are intellectual, moral, civic, and spiritual. The attempt to sort them into separate buckets is a folly worthy of Erasmus or Borges (thus we must add one more artistic intention to our list: to dramatize folly).

The irony, as Gadamer explains, is that "abstracting down to the 'purely aesthetic' obviously eliminates it."[69] In bracketing off the elements that "situate the work in its world and thus determine the whole meaningfulness that it originally possessed," the modern aesthete "abstracts from all the conditions of a work's accessibility" (74). The aesthete is like someone who can measure every inch of a building's exterior without ever finding an entrance (just as Silas knows his way around Ono, Rothko, and Salcedo but can't access their moral, spiritual, and civic provocations).

What explains such obtuseness? Here is where Gadamer's critique of the "sovereignty of aesthetic consciousness" comes in (74). In an actual encounter with a work of art, we are drawn into the work. In effect, the work plays with us. As we are turned this way and that, we see our lives from new and perhaps disturbing angles. By contrast, aesthetic consciousness remains "the experiencing center from which everything considered art is measured."[70] The aesthete is not swept up. Having reduced the work to an aesthetic object, he turns it over in his hand, dissecting its intentions and judging its formal effects (just like Silas has a handle on Rothko, Ono, and Salcedo). In this way, Gadamer reads aesthetic consciousness as a form of self-protection, as a flight from true encounter.

It is not only the museums, theaters, and concert halls that are stuffed with Silases. Consider the world of science and technology, where we find a dangerous tendency to separate facts from values. The classic example here is Robert Oppenheimer. Eventually, Oppenheimer grew into the realization that he had "made a thing that by all the standards of the world we grew up in is an evil thing."[71] But it was too late. Like Silas, Oppenheimer and his colleagues on the Manhattan Project brought their intellects to work, sealing ethics in some other compartment. Oppenheimer describes their working mindset: "When you see something that is technically sweet, you go ahead and do it."[72] The Oppenheimer story is often treated as exceptional, with the early Oppenheimer seen as especially amoral or the later one as especially conscientious, or both. It is better read as illustrative of a general problem in our disjointed modernity. As Max Weber famously put it, we have become, "*Fachmenschen ohne Geist.*" While the alliteration in Parson's translation, "specialists without spirit," is nice, given that Weber casts his diagnosis in the form of a Zarathustra-like epigram, we might render *Fachmenschen* more expressively as "department men," "compartment creatures," or "pigeonhole people."[73] If the Silas case is an argument ad absurdum, then it is we moderns who are absurd.

In the previous section, we distinguished two tasks built into the call to form ourselves as whole persons: to cultivate the full range of our capacities and to integrate the diverse dimensions of ourselves into a coherence of character and outlook. Having identified some of the difficulties of each task, we turned to exploring the tension between them. We are tempted to take shortcuts, like the Monas and Silas, achieving coherence by winnowing the self or cultivating complexity by compartmentalizing it. Between these extremes lies the ideal of dynamic integrity. But what does this complex coherence look like?

In *The Waves,* Virginia Woolf provides a striking contrast with Thoreau's simultaneously immobilized and rootless parcel-self. In a pleasurable recognition of her own capaciousness, a confident avowal of her polychromatic, even contradictory, nature, Jinny declares, "I feel a thousand capacities spring up in me. I am arch, gay, languid, melancholy by turns. I am rooted, but I flow."[74] In this moment of, as it were, exuberant self-possession, we have a beautiful evocation of the ideal of personhood we have been tracking. Despite the tensions in her makeup, her myriad capacities, Jinny remains dynamically whole; even as she grows, and her energy flows along its branching paths, she remains rooted.

But should we take Jinny at her word, or is this just a sign of false consciousness? After all, Jinny makes this exuberant declaration at a dance, as her potential partners begin to approach her. Perhaps her flowing rootedness is simply an expression of internalized misogyny. Maybe she mistakes as a thousand capacities what are merely the many poses she must strike to attract and please; and mistakes as rooted integrity what is merely the coherence of the ritual in which she plays her part as one of the available women on display. Thus, as the guests begin to arrive, Jinny thinks,

> This is the prelude, this is the beginning. I glance, I peep, I powder. All is exact, prepared. My hair is swept in one curve. My lips are precisely red. I am ready now to join the men and women on the stairs, my peers. I pass them, exposed to their gaze, as they are to mine. Like lightning we look but do not soften or show signs of recognition. Our bodies communicate. This is my calling. This is my world.
>
> . . . This is what I have dreamt; this is what I have foretold. I am a native here. I tread naturally on thick carpets. I slide easily on smooth polished floors. (82)

We can point to the powder, lipstick, and upswept hair as signs that Jinny has been subordinated into an object of the male gaze. We can read Jinny as captive in an artificial world of "thick carpets" and "polished floors," thinking herself "native" only because she suffers from Stockholm syndrome.

While I agree that agency is key, I prefer a more recuperative, feminist reading. Jinny reports that she is in her element, feeling a sense of fit ("this is my calling"; "this is my world"; "I am a native here") and fluency ("I tread naturally"; "I slide easily"). Shall we believe her? Or do we know more about her than she herself does? Are we sure that virtuosity in navigating the social dance before the dance cannot be a true calling? Are powder and lipstick always signs of inauthenticity? Do we know that one cannot be rooted in an artificial environment of thick carpets and polished floors?

When we take Jinny at her word, we notice other details. Not once but twice in this short scene, Jinny stresses her equality with the assembled. In the passage above she refers to the "men and women on the stairs" as her "peers," noting that "she is exposed to their gaze, as they are to mine." A page later, she remarks, "My peers may look at me now. I look straight back at you, men and women" (83). Underlining the mutuality of the gaze, Jinny observes how the men nervously adjust their clothes, remarking that "They are very young. They are anxious to make a good impression" (82–83). Meanwhile, in addition to this imagery of artifice, there is also a notable use of natural imagery to capture the core idea of flowing rootedness. Right after mentioning the polished floors, she observes, "I now begin to unfurl, in this scent, in this radiance, as a fern when its curled leaves unfurl" (82).

Now let's look more closely at the key passage:

> I feel a thousand capacities spring up in me. I am arch, gay, languid, melancholy by turns. I am rooted, but I flow. All gold, flowing that way, I say to this one, "Come." Rippling black, I say to that one, "No." One breaks off from his station under the glass cabinet. He approaches. He makes toward me. This is the most exciting moment I have ever known. I flutter. I ripple. I stream like a plant flowing in the river, flowing this way, flowing that way but rooted, so that he may come to me. Come, I say, come. Pale, with dark hair, the one who is coming is melancholy, he is romantic. And I am arch and fluent and capricious; for he is melancholy, he is romantic. He is here; he stands at my side. (83)

This is not a portrait of objectification and subordination. True, Jinny changes her colors, but not like a chameleon. She shifts her feeling hues as part of asserting her agency, exercising her judgments of acceptance and rejection.[75] True, the men are mobile while the women must wait, but Jinny experiences this as bidding her suitor to come to her. True, Jinny shifts her mood to complement her suitor. If melancholy is one of her many moods, why must she cede the taciturn position and find the fluency and capriciousness to, in a word, chat him up? Again, this is unpersuasive, for why focus on melancholy alone? Jinny has just told us that she has a thousand capacities! And Woolf has taken the trouble to carry not only melancholy but also archness through from the one statement to the other. To make this work, the suspicious reading would have to conflate authenticity with a solipsism that says, "I never let the presence of others affect my mood or behavior." In that case, we reply, please keep to yourself! Jinny is not a sociopath. She is a social being who finds and activates different sides of herself in the dance of interpersonal interaction. With her melancholy suitor, she taps into her archness and ebullience. One of the reasons we seek out diverse others, as we saw above with Rousseau, is to learn more of our own nature and range and potential.

This recuperative, feminist reading takes Jinny at her word that hers is a "both-and" subjectivity. She experiences both diversity of capacity and unity of self. She manages both rootedness and flowing responsiveness, discovering and activating different of her myriad affective potentials in the shift of situation and dance of interlocution. With an old man, she feels that she "should be a child"; with "a great lady," she "should dissemble"; with girls her own age, she embraces the "drawn swords of an honorable antagonism" (84). Rather than read this as the "feminine" vice of people-pleasing inconstancy, we can see it as meeting the moment, as a form of virtuous responsiveness to a variegated universe along the lines of Homer's *metis* or Machiavelli's *virtú*.[76] We can only interpret such accommodations as evasions of authenticity if we ignore Jinny's own testimony that her shifting dance partners open her to her existential possibilities: "The door opens. The door goes on opening. . . . Here is my risk, here is my adventure."[77]

In Jinny, then, we have a portrait of the self as differentiated unity, of life as vibrantly rooted and branching. And we have a suggestion of how one might knit together some of the dialectics of experience (melancholy and gay, desiring subject and object of the gaze of others) with flowing grace. However, judging from this scene at least, there is something too easy about this. Silas could not maintain links across five capacities; Jinny flows effortlessly among a thousand. With Jinny, we are still dealing with something of an ideal type. While her dynamism is richly illustrated, we know too little about her experience of rootedness. Her integrity remains somewhat abstract. We need cases that capture more concretely the possibilities and peculiarities of soulcraft, that capture how character is forged and enacted in the very struggle to define a center and expand a circumference, in the uneasy search for roots we can take with us as we move to meet the offerings and demands of the world.

Somewhere between the idea of "having character" and that of "being a character" is a neglected, third conception of character. To "have character" is to exhibit moral integrity. In different cases, we are picking out the same moral trait, that of acting on worthy principles even when no one is looking. To "be a character" is to be unconventional. While some refusals of conformity and convention are principled and salutary, this is primarily an amoral concept. Case in point: the indie film, where only some of the characters are good but all them are quirky. What gets lost between the moral universalism of the former and the amoral particularism of the latter is the moral relevance of idiosyncratic feats of personal integration. Without denying that there may be universal features of psychic life, or at least common cultural patterns of psychological conflict, the puzzle of integrity ultimately differs for each individual, and there is even more room for divergence in the solutions. Each person is, if you will, a different way of holding oneself together.[78]

In indie films, distinctive features of personality are gimmicks of differentiation. This one carries a transistor radio; that one wrings his hands; this one wears track suits and headbands; that one always plays with his food. The quirks help differentiate the characters from each other and the genre as a whole from mainstream movies. And indeed people do have distinctive ways of inhabiting their bodies and navigating social space. All artful presentations (in film and literature, painting and photography) of human beings reveal such variegation, but it takes the patience of, as it were, a slow shutter speed in low light for the distinguishing features to develop. By contrast, indies are in a hurry. They raid the cultural shelves for a can of "neurotic tics" on their way to the acting class where they quickly grab some limps and strange voices. Far from being too imaginative, they end up using stock photos of "the distinctive individual." The other way in which indies go wrong is in their assumption that these distinguishing marks are all vectors of dissent from what is, again, a stock version of conformity. In actual fact, some of the lines most deeply etched in faces come precisely from the long work of joining and navigating the social order. Distinctive characters are not only found in strange hotels or rolling caravans. What is frustrating about indie films, then, is not that they turn the camera from the real to the fantastical, but that they point the camera at one of the most incredible features of reality and then forget to remove the lens cap.

People are strange, as the song goes, but strangeness is normal. It is interesting, and indeed moving, to see how each human magpie finds the materials to piece themselves together; how each bridges conflicts, lives with tensions, deals with disavowals. It is these work-arounds, evasions, and compromises that constitute character in this neglected, medial sense. The inner work of integrity, the ongoing effort to forge, live with, and modify a livable unity, betrays itself in outer signs: in subtleties of comportment (timber of voice, set of jaw, slope of shoulders); habits of behavior (throat clearing, leg bouncing, food gobbling); and patterns of interaction (dodging calls, falling on swords, holding court). These peculiar settlements of character are not moral universals (thou shalt grind your teeth at night), but they have an ethical charge that can attract, repel, inspire, and instruct. The other serves not as an example of how to be a good person but as a good example of how to be a person. We cannot impose the shape of their integrity onto the differing puzzle pieces in our soul, but we can take courage from the way that they have faced up to the task and inspiration from their successes in individualization. And in fact, such soulcraft does rely on some general virtues. We admire the honesty in rejecting off-the-shelf models and the courage of living through the construction; the ingenuity in synthesizing ideas from different worlds of discourse and the toughness to live with the remaining contradictions; the independent-mindedness to find one's own lane, and the grace to travel it. Witnessing the outer signs of these inward deeds can spur on our own efforts.

I have called the work "inward" because it involves self-examination and self-construction, adding that there are outward signs of this inward-facing work. However, the work itself is also outward facing, since character formation must be bound up with reality testing. One way to deny the tensions among our beliefs and values is to insulate them from what Max Weber called "inconvenient facts."[79] For example, in its investigation of the racial politics shaping a Brooklyn school district over time, the podcast *Nice White Parents* explores how privileged parents maintain their sense of themselves as progressive even as they continue to hoard resources. In the fifth and final episode, the host (Chana Joffe-Walt) is surprised by a parent (Amelia Costigan) who, finding herself face-to-face with a most inconvenient fact, manages to not close her eyes. Costigan had just learned that her twin boys had lucked into one of the three desirable middle schools in the district. Then something clicked:

JOFFE-WALT (VOICEOVER): Initially, Amelia was thrilled. She says her first thought was "we won." And then she stopped herself.

COSTIGAN: And I started to think about why I had been so self-absorbed about my own family. And I didn't think about the bigger picture. Like what does that mean for all the kids of color?

JOFFE-WALT: Wait, what made you—that seems like a really big leap. How did you make that transition?

COSTIGAN: Well, it's almost like—you know when you just kind of lose your path in life? And I think I just lost what was important to me. And then you know once I won, I started to realize this is really fucked up, you know? Like this is what I got. I mean, and it is a wonderful school. I'm glad that my children were able to have that. But then it was like, what does that mean?

JOFFE-WALT: Amelia got stuck on that word—winning. "She won" disturbed her. If her kids won, someone else's children lost.[80]

To be clear, this is but a flicker of avowal in a decades-long story of disavowal, whose moral is that nice White parents maintain the apparent coherence of their privileged progressivism by looking the other way.

With her portrait of Lee Sherman, Arlie Hochschild offers another nice illustration of the strain in deferring reality testing to preserve the coherence of our beliefs.[81] Lee is an avid outdoorsman from Louisiana who loves the bayou and the way of life that has grown up around it. His belief in local self-determination has made him a devoted member of the Tea Party, with its small-government, anti-regulatory platform. However, local industry is spewing highly toxic filth, poisoning wildlife, contaminating his community's food, and threatening the livelihood of all those who make their living off the bayou. So Lee faces a choice. If he wants to preserve the apparent harmony between his naturalism, communitarianism, and libertarianism, he will have to hide from the inconvenient facts that expose the tensions among these commitments. But this risks turning his ideals into mere husks. For what is naturalism if the fish and shellfish and birds and sugarcane are all dead? What is communitarianism if the community can no longer support itself? I suppose freedom from government control is maintained, but what of the positive freedom to fish and to attend a low-country boil? And isn't local industry treading on John's community, even if the Feds are not?

Lee's other option is to try to preserve these as living ideals, but that will require attending to nature, thinking about community, and wrestling with the nature of freedom. But then, no longer fixed in an abstract accordance, the tensions among his ideals will come to the fore. He may notice that his opposition to the EPA is in tension with his hatred of socialized medicine. The unregulated local industry has created a public health emergency, driving his neighbors to rely heavily on Medicare and other forms of public assistance. And Lee might come to question the Tea Party's equation of freedom with free-market fundamentalism, forging a different philosophy of self-determination, one that does not pretend that communitarianism and capitalism go hand in hand.

One day, Lee saw a bird drop out of the air, mid-flight, paralyzed from the chemical vapors sublimating from the swamp. While it is too late for Lee to unsee this, it is an open question whether he will acknowledge its implications. After all, opposable thumbs are nothing compared with the human ability to manipulate reality through disavowal.[82] Either way, there are consequences. To hide from the facts is to live with paper-thin ideals, forever risking that reality will bite you in the ass. But reality testing is taxing and leaves a mark.

Given our discussion of the different meanings of character, it is interesting how Weber vacillates in describing our acknowledgment of "inconvenient facts." To mark its importance and difficulty, he reaches for the phrase "moral achievement"; but he sets it off in scare quotes and adds the disclaimer that this "may sound too grandiose for something that should go without saying."[83] Certainly, facing difficult facts requires virtues such as humility, courage, and open-mindedness, but I am more interested in how this experience of facing up to reality shapes what I have been calling the medial sense of character. Earlier we cited Oppenheimer as an example of someone who had to face inconvenient facts. In a fascinating redefinition of style, he captures well the idea of character I have in mind:

> The problem of doing justice to the implicit, the imponderable, and the unknown is of course not unique to politics. It is always with us in science, it is with us in the most trivial of personal affairs, and it is one of the great problems of writing and all forms of art. The means by which it is solved is sometimes called style. It is style which complements affirmation with limitation and with humility; it is style which makes it possible to act effectively, but not absolutely; . . . it is style which is the deference that action pays to uncertainty.[84]

Here style is understood as an expression of, not as an alternative to, personal substance. Interestingly, though, Oppenheimer sees style not as simple affirmation, as the free flow of one's distinctive personality. It is instead the collision of "affirmation with limitation." As William James remarked of his writing, "I have to forge every sentence in the teeth of irreducible and stubborn facts."[85] Style is a particular pattern of disturbance, as fluency ripples over the resistances of the real.[86] Weber was right: the struggle to acknowledge inconvenient facts is a moral achievement, but not a rare feat of moral heroism to be marked by a statue in the town square. It is the sort of remarkable, everyday achievement revealed in the leaps and hesitations, the missions and omissions, the shortcuts and roundabouts—the awkward grace—of each forged form of fluency.

We have now seen several ways in which the inner work of integration reverberates beyond the self. First, we learn from each other's successes and failures as each works to define a center while pursuing a circumference. Character is instructive. Second, the search for dynamic integrity itself must engage the world. Soulcraft requires reality testing. And with Oppenheimer, we have just glimpsed a way of knitting these two ideas together. In the moral life, each of us not only speaks for a particular constellation of prizings and projects but also speaks with a voice whose distinctive timbre is an index of our ongoing effort to come to grips with inconvenient facts.

Soul action is outward facing in yet another way, as some feats of integration end up not only shaping the soul but also reshaping society. Here I think of the example of late Justice Ruth Bader Ginsburg. In numerous interviews, RBG shared an interesting account of her formative influences. The key figure in her development was her mother, whom RBG described as "the strongest and bravest person that I have ever known."[87]

Though RBG lost her mother when she was seventeen, she continued to draw on that strength throughout her life. In an interview about maternal loss, RBG described a daily ritual of remembrance: "I have her picture on the wall in my chambers, and it's where I can see her every day when I leave. I kind of smile when I look at it and say, 'she would have been proud of me.'"[88] This is a nice Hallmark moment, but we all know that parental pride is too complex an object to be captured in a medium-length, soft-focus shot. Parental pride can feel empty, as automatic enthusiasm fails to confer true recognition. Or it can feel overstuffed. As we unwrap the gift of pride, we find it packed in with a parent's own misplaced ambitions, with values forged in another time and place, with hopes too cramped to inhabit with one's full self.

It was no different in RBG's case. Her mother left her a very peculiar aspirational inheritance. She distilled her hopes for young Ruth into two tidy epigrams. The only problem was the glaring contradiction between them. In a conversation with Jeffrey Rosen, Dahlia Lithwick captured RBG's predicament nicely:

> Justice Ginsburg always talks about the advice that her mother gave her as a young girl. And at one level it sounds kind of trite; at another level I think it is actually very deep and kind of inherently contradictory. . . . Her mother always told her two things . . . : one, "be independent"; two, "be a lady." Now, bearing in mind that at the time "be a lady" meant "don't be independent," it is a life that she has actually crafted in which she has managed to do both.[89]

RBG's mother was offering this advice in the forties, two decades before the arrival of the pill and the publication of the *Feminine Mystique*, three decades before Roe, and three-quarters of a century before "me too." To be a lady, Lithwick suggests, meant to be proper and respectable, deferential and dependent. So RBG's mother bequeathed her a puzzle.

To many, the solution might seem obvious. Given two contradictory injunctions, one which seems like baggage from a bygone era and the other like a sign of changing times, we would not blame RBG for simply stowing the inconvenient part of this inheritance in the basement. And this is the narrative her new public prefers: "the Notorious RBG" began to throw off her decorous restraint in *Bush v. Gore*, continued to flex her independence in *Carhart* and *Ledbetter*, and finally claimed her full-throated voice as "gangsta" dissenter in *Shelby County* and *Hobby Lobby*.[90] However, as Lithwick explains, this narrative "disserves the part of her that is . . . very much a lady," that remains "very careful, very reserved."[91] Rosen agrees, describing RBG as an "apostle of judicial minimalism," who exemplifies both "jurisprudential as well as personal restraint."[92] In an interview with Rosen, RBG herself confirms that "what really changed was the composition of the court."[93] When the court became a vehicle for right-wing judicial activism with no concern for precedent, a "very small c conservative" such as RBG became a voice of dissent.[94]

So, instead of dropping the outdated half of her mother's contradictory advice, RBG took the harder path of, as Lithwick put it, crafting a life in which she could pursue both ideals. But we need to think about what this entails. It could mean that, Silas-like, she merely divides her life into two compartments, one for the expression of her independent spirit and another for her ladylike behavior. What she did instead was find a way to interpret the two ideals as not only compatible but completely interwoven. Her mother was telling her, "Be independent. Prepare for difficulty, and stand on your own two feet like Eleanor Roosevelt."[95] And the advice to be a lady was an extension, not a contradiction, of this first edict. RBG understood her mother to be talking not about polite decorum and gender subservience, but about another kind of modesty and restraint: "My mother's advice was don't lose time on useless emotions. Like, anger, resentment, remorse, envy."[96] When Rosen suggests that "it is that extraordinary self-mastery that is the advice of the great wisdom traditions of the *Bible and the Bhagavad Gita* and the Buddhist traditions to set aside your ego so that you can focus on achieving your true path," RBG agrees.[97] RBG wanted to stand on her two feet and occupy a place in the world. Ladylike deference would not achieve this, but if genteel restraint could be directed inward at what Buddhists call the "monkey brain," that could certainly help. RBG explains that she realized that "if I don't get past unproductive emotions, I'll just get bogged down and lose precious time from useful work."[98]

Here we might worry that RBG is diverting into self-restraint energy that might have been better directed against the patriarchy. But of course the work that RBG's self-mastery allowed her to do was deeply public, and indeed has helped to push forward gender equality in significant ways.[99] Thus, RBG's soulcraft was transformative in three distinct ways. First, for many, parental hopes remain something leaden and inert, a guilty pull from the past. RBG reworked her inheritance into a portable and livable form that she could carry into the times in which her life would unfold. For what good are roots if you cannot take them with you. Second, she continually reworked herself in light of this stoic aspiration. Third and finally, on the basis of this self-mastery, she rose to a position of influence in society where she was able to help us rework our cultural inheritance, transforming the terms "woman and independent" from antonyms to synonyms.

RBG's formative trajectory further illustrates that the inward, personal work of integration is anything but private. Each constellation of character—each individual's quest for rooted responsiveness to the diverse dimensions of self and world—bears witness to the perils and possibilities of personhood. Dynamic wholeness can collapse into monomania or compartmentalization. And yet the very effort to forge and sustain a differentiated integrity, to face up to inconvenient truths, to imaginatively rework one's inherited formative resources can inspire the efforts of others. Soul action resounds.

SCATTERING REQUIREMENTS

> Freedom is the catch-word of this new departure. It is a precious and an
> attractive word. But, O Liberty! what crimes and cruelties have been per-
> petuated in thy name!
> —James McCosh[100]

Given the complexity and importance of the task—educating a whole person—you would think we might have more patience for the idea of general education. Instead, our engagement is perfunctory, rushed, abbreviated. "Gen Ed": the phrase rolls right off the tongue and onto one's things-to-do-list. Do laundry: check. Take out trash: check. Satisfy Gen Ed requirements: check. When students at a large public university were recently asked how they choose Gen Ed classes, the most common response was "what best fits my schedule."[101] In another survey, only 7% of students at a state flagship disagreed with the idea that it would be better to replace Gen Ed coursework with more courses in the major.[102] Frustrating though it is, such student indifference only mirrors our own failure to invite students to think about college as something more than queuing for a credential and "paying for the party."[103]

Consider how the invitation to higher learning has evolved at one of the great land-grant universities, the University of Illinois at Urbana-Champaign

(UIUC).[104] Like the other institutions occasioned by the first Morrill Act of 1862, the Illinois Industrial University, as it was first called, began with nothing but a land scrip to be sold to endow the founding of

> at least one college where the leading object shall be, without excluding other scientific and classical studies and including military tactics, to teach such branches of learning as are related to agriculture and the mechanic arts . . . in order to promote the liberal and practical education of the industrial classes in the several pursuits and professions in life.[105]

In March 1867, the forty newly appointed trustees gathered in Springfield for an initial meeting devoted to electing officers and forming committees, including one charged with finding enough furniture to enable a second meeting to be held in Urbana.[106] At that second meeting, the Committee on Courses of Study and Faculty were ready to present a statement of aims and an initial plan of organization. The new university was to stand for the proposition that the "agricultural and mechanical arts" were themselves learned professions requiring systematic study and comprehension, "the peers of any others in their dignity, importance, and scientific scope." It would offer not superficial training but a "Pierian fount of learning" whose "unfailing flow" would enable "those whose thirst and whose capacities are large to drink their fill."

The committee sought not only depth but breadth, offering several arguments against "one-sided education." First, each trade itself demands a broad approach. If farmers and mechanics are also to be "investigators and inventors," they need something more than "simple knowledge of [their] art." They need scientific understanding and "the literary culture which will enable them to communicate . . . by public speech their knowledge and discoveries." Second, a broad education supports "movement and versatility," as graduates may go on to pursue "successive mastery of several vocations." Third, the university must prepare for "citizenship as well as for science and industry." When the time comes to leave "the harvest field for the forum," the "educated agriculturalist and mechanic" must be "broadbreasted, wise-hearted, clear-thinking." Rejecting the false choice between liberal and vocational education, the committee closed on this resounding note: "Let us educate for life, as well as for art, leaving genius free to follow its natural attractions, and lending to talent a culture fitting it for all of the emergencies of public or private duty."

Fast forward a century and a half, and we find a massive, comprehensive research university that more than fulfilled the first part of its mandate. UIUC helped lead the way as the mechanical arts proliferated and deepened into the modern STEM fields. However, something happened to this second idea of educating for life. The resounding call to educate the whole person decayed into the hum of bureaucratic machinery. When I taught at UIUC, here is how we invited students to cultivate themselves for private and public virtue: "The General Education (GenEd) requirements describe the core courses all students must take in order to graduate."[107] It is true that students who happened to read further would find some perfunctory language about exposure to disciplines and acquisition of thinking and communication skills—but talk about burying the lede! Incoming college students are already well-versed in *studenting*. They are well aware that requirements must be met, grades earned, credits accumulated. Here is a chance to announce that something else could and should be happening in one's undergraduate years, something of which all of this institutional machinery is but an indicator.

How about this for an alternative, *Onion*-style headline:

Archaeologists Discover Lost Concept of "Higher Education"

Evidence from the recent fossil record suggests that "higher education" may have once meant something other than an elaborate job screening process. While the work of excavation and interpretation is still under way, preliminary findings suggest that the phrase referred not to advanced schooling but to something that went beyond socialization, instruction, and training. Whatever this "higher education" was, it seems it could not be absorbed passively, as students themselves were apparently asked, according to a tentative translation of one inscription found at the site, "to take stock of what you have become and take a lead in your ongoing formation."

While I have presented this in a fanciful way, the idea is an earnest one. It is true that if universities are to remain solvent, the bursar must be paid. However, it is also true that if they are to remain *universities*, they must do more than admit and administrate students. They must hail those who arrive on campus as learners, summoning them to the formative tasks of higher education.

It is alarming how often this entirely fails to happen. I know because I teach undergraduate courses about educational aims. At first, students hold the material at arm's length. They believe that they are studying some distant object called "education." And part of this estrangement is by design. We teach texts that challenge the presentism, instrumentalism, and scholasticism that constrain the contemporary educational imagination, from Plato's famous allegory of socialization to Tara Westover's harrowing tale of emancipation.[108] However, each trip to a there and then returns to the here and now. We remind students that what we are discussing bears on what is happening right now, in this room. We prod them to connect the texts to their own educational trajectories and decisions. We ask them, in so many words, how they are shaping their college years in order to shape themselves. This seems to make an impact on a good number of students, and every semester one or two students—including juniors and seniors—make a point of coming to office hours to tell me, with a mix of excitement and dismay, that this is the first time anyone has talked with them about why we are here. They had been oriented to campus and advised about requirements, but no one had ever engaged them about the point of college.[109]

I don't mean to elevate telling over showing. These students surely had teachers who, without talking explicitly about the aims of education, provided compelling demonstrations of what is worth learning, doing, and becoming. Nonetheless, what I hear from undergraduates is that they look back on their schooling as a largely passive and bewildering experience, something done to them for reasons that were never truly or fully explained. I am reminded of a piece by the avant-garde doodler, David Shrigley, depicting a person sitting on a stool, milking a cow. The cow looks back over its shoulder and remarks, "What the hell are you doing?"[110] There is, after all, only so much milking you can take. I think that many students arrive on campus with a sense, however vague, that college could be and should be different. And they do find more freedom of choice. They get to pick a major, choose classes, and select from a wider variety of extracurricular activities. What they do not usually find are occasions to take stock of their education and shape their formative ideals. The purely negative freedom of the "elective" system begs the crucial question of where students will find the provocation and support, the resources and the reflective space, to cultivate their autonomy and make such election into a genuine act of agency. In my experience, undergraduates are more than eager to find their voices in the great conversation—at once educational and existential, ethical and political—about how to form ourselves and live our lives. They just need some models—for example, some noninstrumental language for discussing education—and some companions in the search.[111]

UIUC has updated their Gen Ed language, seemingly with the express purpose of remedying the cynical functionalism of the older version. But the new statement protests too much. After listing required areas of study and intended outcomes, it concludes, "General Education at Illinois is more than a set of required courses; it is a gateway into the Illinois experience."[112] I realize that verbal gimmicks are the stock-in-trade of websites everywhere, but this rhetorical sleight of hand is worth a closer look.[113] Of course we want Gen Ed to be something more than a "set of required courses," but wishing doesn't make it so. The hollowness and incoherence of Gen Ed is rooted in basic structural features of the modern multiversity.[114] Before we take a closer look at how the UIUC website pulls off this magic(al thinking) trick, let us examine one university structure that seems perfectly designed to derail any attempt to restore Gen Ed to substance.

The majority of leading universities now employ some version of RCM budgeting.[115] According to one early adopter (1990), Indiana University Bloomington, RCM is about "moving power" from central administration to academic units (this could be a school, department, or even a program) by giving them "ownership of their individual revenues and costs," which "allows them to be accountable for their own academic and financial planning and therefore encourages entrepreneurship, efficiency, and educationally sound choices."[116] Apparently, the authors had the "The Principles of Newspeak" close at hand: you are generously *allowed* to self-fund your activities (according to your shifting enrollments and success in the grant game) while becoming a proud *owner* of costs newly devolved to the unit level. In this way, each unit becomes a *responsibility center*, more commonly known as a franchise fighting for market share. IU Bloomington again: "Once the [individual units] have received their income, each pays a tax or assessment fee that goes back to a central unit at the university." It is doubtful that the entrepreneurialization of the academy has led to more "educationally sound choices." It is not even clear whether the new decentralized budgeting leads to greater efficiency. What is clear is that RCM threatens to make irreversible the trajectory of the modern university toward dis-integration.

This fragmentation was already well under way by 1963, when Clark Kerr, president of the University of California, Berkeley, coined the term "multiversity."[117] As Kerr points out, disunity was already a central theme in Abraham Flexner's famous survey, *Universities: American, English, German* (1930). Flexner argued that a university ought to be "characterized by a highness and definiteness of aim, unity of spirit and purpose."[118] What he found instead was something better described as a "federation," or even simply as "a line drawn about an enormous number of different institutions of heterogenous quality and purpose."[119] Kerr was not even the first university president to acknowledge the disunity he governed. He recalls how Robert Maynard Hutchins, who served as University of Chicago's president from 1930 to 1945, liked to quip that "the modern university [is] a series of separate schools and departments held together by a central heating system."[120] When Kerr tries to capture midcentury Berkeley in a snapshot, he does not focus nostalgically on some once-central quad or a statue of alma mater, but zooms way out to reveal a sprawling, Rube Goldberg-esque, academic-industrial machine, noting that midcentury Berkeley serves 100,000 students and another 200,000 through extension courses; lists over 10,000 courses in its catalogues; employs more people than IBM; operates in over a hundred locations in more than fifty countries; has "contact with nearly every industry [and] . . . level of government"; "is the world's largest purveyor of white mice"; and that "over 4000 babies were born in its hospitals."[121] Going Hutchins one better, Kerr remarks of Berkeley that, "in an area where heating is less important and the automobile more, I have sometimes thought of it as a series of individual faculty entrepreneurs held together by a common grievance over parking."[122] The multiversity, then, is a sprawling organism, with pseudopodia reaching into corporate R&D, government, health care, and other sectors. Campuses simultaneously serve as our culture's setting for our signature coming-of-age ritual, as epicenters of athletic entertainment, and as headhunters for multiple industries. Even within the category of education, broadly understood, there are competing mandates: instruction, socialization, sorting, credentialing. How could this hydra still have an eye on the core educational task of forming well-rounded and integrated persons? Amid this swirl of competing mandates, in the face of disciplinary divides entrenched in a rigid departmental structure, can faculty still work together to articulate an integral vision of undergraduate education?

The authors of the *Harvard Redbook* (1945) still managed to pull it off, though only with massive institutional support. Tellingly, the next major statement on general education, Daniel Bell's *The Reforming of General Education* (1966), was entrusted by design to "a committee of one."[123] With the rise of RCM in the last quarter of the twentieth century, it is no longer just a matter of incommensurable values and traditions in the curricular conversation. Units now come to the table driven by naked self-interest. And who can blame them, when capturing Gen Ed traffic has become a matter of survival? The curricular conversation has been replaced by an interdepartmental trade treaty: you recruit your students, and I'll recruit mine; I'll send students your way to fulfill a breadth requirement if you do the same for me. In this way, RCM serves as a powerful centripetal force, pulling our attention away from the roots of undergraduate education toward the ever-expanding branches of the tree of knowledge. At UIUC, for example, there are over three hundred majors and specializations. Here are a just a few from early in the alphabet: agri-accounting, behavioral neuroscience, companion animal and equine science, dance, French commercial studies, geophysics, health and aging.[124] The entrepreneurial university not only pits one side of the quad against the other but even sets up further battles between subspecialties.[125] Dance has to fight for room to move within fine and applied arts; a turf war breaks out in the ag school between agri-accounting and crop sciences; the growth of behavioral neuroscience threatens the growth of developmental psychology. Since these battles are often decided on the basis of enrollment, Gen Ed certification can make all the difference. And so RCM "efficiently" drives an endless proliferation of "core" courses, reducing general education to a vague directive to visit each corner of campus at least once. Such hollowing of educational substance is not new. "Education," Michael Oakeshott observes, "has had often to be rescued from the formalism into which it has degenerated."[126] The problem with RCM is that it creates a deep structural disincentive even to form a rescue party.

Now let us return to the rhetorical device of the gateway. Given that Gen Ed has become a cynical game of tax incentives and franchise fees, it is impossible to read UIUC's statement that "Gen Ed is more than a set of requirements" as anything other than magical thinking. The key to the trick is drawing our attention momentarily to the magician's assistant—the exciting but empty phrase "the Illinois experience"—so that the illusion can be carried off. And voila: gatekeeping is transformed into a gateway! Let us examine this magical gateway more closely. According to UIUC's not atypical requirements, students are required to take

- One of 3 "Composition 1" sequences (of 4, 6, or 8 credit hours)
- One of 57 "Advanced Composition" courses
- One of 144 "US Minority Cultures" courses
- One of 155 "Non-Western Cultures" courses
- One of 213 "Western/Comparative Cultures" courses
- Two of 493 "Humanities and the Arts" courses
- Two of 92 "Natural Sciences and Technology" courses
- One of 31 "Quantitative Reasoning 1" courses
- One of 77 remaining quantitative reasoning courses
- Two of 198 "Social and Behavioral Sciences" courses.[127]

Promised a point of entry, students instead discover a labyrinth of forking paths. Even this prescribed part of the curriculum preserves a dizzying amount of elective freedom, offering students something on the order of 10^{25} different ways to complete the requirements.[128] It turns out that there are nearly as many gateways to the "Illinois experience" as there are stars in the universe![129] Or perhaps it is better to say that this maze-walking is the Illinois experience. Either way, one half of the phrase tells a lie. Either there is no such thing as *the* Illinois experience, since there are as many different experiences as there are routes through the maze; or there is nothing distinctively Illinois about it, since major-plus-distribution-requirements has been the basic formula for US higher education for over a century.[130]

Doublespeak flourishes wherever institutional realities and ideals diverge, as we anxiously reach for signifiers that can cover up these gaps. We speak of "gateways" when the path into the curriculum has become a warren of checkpoints. We reach for phrases such as "the Illinois experience" because undergraduate education is somehow both disturbingly generic and impossibly multifarious. And what we find when we peel back the label "core courses" is a vast decentered universe of curricular possibilities in which the distinction between core and periphery is meaningless. Neither an orienting center nor well-marked path, Gen Ed classes are more like wormholes mysteriously transporting students from one corner of campus to another.

To this, one might respond that students define their own curricular centers through their choice of majors and that distribution requirements ensure that students explore their personal peripheries. The engineering major is forced to take some humanities and social science courses; the art major has to take some natural and social science; the psych major must try out the humanities and natural sciences. Isn't this a simple, flexible way to ensure well-roundedness and breadth of understanding? As I have already begun to suggest, I think the most honest answer is that we really have no idea what happens inside the black box of our distributed elective system. The only generalization we can make is that no student will graduate without some exposure to some different traditions and disciplines. In fact, even if we were looking at a particular transcript, I think we would be hard-pressed to say whether a student had become well-rounded.

Consider this hypothetical Gen Ed pathway at UIUC. Let's imagine a computer engineering (CE) major who completes one of the Comp 1 sequences and satisfies the science/technology and quantitative reasoning requirements through CE courses. That leaves eight requirements that, thanks to three "double dippers," can be met through five classes as follows:

1. Viking Sagas in Translation (Humanities/Arts; Western/Comparative Cultures)
2. Slavery and Identity (Humanities and the Arts; US Minority Cultures)
3. The Politics of the National Parks (Social/Behavioral Sciences)
4. Life in the Andes (Social/Behavioral Sciences; Non-Western Cultures)
5. Ethical Dilemmas of Business (Advanced Composition)[131]

Would these five classes help one explore what one is made of and cultivate the important parts of oneself? Will they provoke and support the work of personal integration? Will they broaden the student's outlook on the world? Will they reveal blind spots in CE and help the student appreciate rival ways of knowing? It's certainly possible, but it is hard to say without much more information. Will the student gain insight into Western culture during this semester with the Vikings? Will studying life in the Andes expose the contingency of the student's own culture? After final exams, will this student continue to think about the legacy of slavery, the politics of conservation, and the ethics of business? Will this student at all learn to think like a poet, historian, anthropologist, or philosopher? Transcripts are of no help in answering such questions.

Neither is a review of syllabi particularly helpful. Every couple of decades, a campus may conduct a searching discussion about what it means to be generally educated. In the meantime, Gen Ed committees just screen out clearly inappropriate courses and give the rest a pass. Mutually assured validation maintains détente in the RCM-budgeting cold war. Besides, the syllabus reflects only the *official* curriculum. What we need to understand is how the official curriculum is interpreted, embodied, and *enacted*. As an undergraduate, I took a course on Buddhism that satisfied a distribution requirement. Clearly the committee that approved this course had no idea how stultifying it would be. Buddhism appeared not as a contestable creed, living practice, or even as a dynamic movement of ideas across centuries and cultures, but as a series of inert facts: the number of characters in the Prajnaparamita Sutra (260), the date of the first Chinese translation of the Lotus Sutra (286 CE), and so on. Several years later, Richard Rorty gave me language for describing what I had experienced. In order for college courses to serve as "provocations to self-creation," we must find professors who are "not exclusively concerned with preparing people to be graduate students in their various specialities . . . and reproducing current disciplinary matrices."[132] I survived the Buddhism class unscathed. Indeed, as far as I can tell, no part of me was affected at all, aside from temporary information storage.

If the official curriculum is differentially enacted by teachers, the enacted curriculum itself is differentially *received* by students. If we really want to know whether a course is broadening, simply diverting, or even narrowing, we need to understand how students approach and make sense of the experience. The students in Introduction to Climate Science, for example, include freshmen and seniors and hail from a variety of majors including dance, communications, elementary ed, finance, and history. They chose the course because they heard it was the easiest course satisfying the natural science requirement; they are gravely concerned about global warming; it fit their schedule; it is a prerequisite for applying to the environmental studies major; they couldn't get into courses they wanted; their friend wanted to take it together; they have an uncle who is a climate change denier. Only when we consider these diverse trajectories can we start to answer key questions, such as, Are most students checked out from the start because they were just checking off a box? How many are finding a way to view the course material as possible answers to genuine questions? Do challenges to their worldviews even register, or are they filtered away by confirmation bias? Does the class offer the kind of space described by Michael Roth as "safe enough" from reprisal that students are able to "unfreeze" beliefs enough to modify them?[133] And what if these unfrozen beliefs are toxic for others? In Roth's "heterodox" classroom culture, the received curriculum will differ sharply for majoritarian and subaltern students.[134] Discussing general education without getting into such details of reception is just spitting in the wind.

Even unpacking the curriculum as enacted and received in particular classes is insufficient. In order to understand whether we are truly helping students become educated as whole persons, we need to expand our focus both temporally and spatially. Temporally, we must examine the entire trip from core to periphery and back again. Spatially, we must follow the student into informal educational spaces. With this wide-angle lens, two further dimensions come into view: the *hidden* curriculum (the lessons implied in the ways we position teachers and students and frame the act of learning) and the *null* curriculum (what we teach through our silences and omissions). As we have started to see, the hidden curriculum of Gen Ed is not very well hidden, barely papered over with this phrase "distribution requirements." Is Gen Ed an effort to distribute our time and energies in light of some ideal of formative justice? Or is this in fact what it sounds like, a logistical arrangement, a distribution of IUs across the ledgers of the multiversity? At first blush, the word "requirement" suggests unfreedom, and certainly students experience it as such. On closer inspection, Gen Ed is about not curtailing but channeling freedom. Steering your curricular shopping cart around the multiversity, selecting at least one item from each aisle, it becomes clear that what you are buying is the very idea of freedom as consumer choice.

Now let us look more closely at the beginning and end of the student's Gen Ed round trip. How do we frame the departure, and how do we receive the student upon their return? Here is where we find a series of instructive omissions. We do not tell students that they have come to a place devoted to preserving and animating the kinds of resources—practices, ideas, texts, works—that have proven useful in our efforts to understand and form ourselves. We do not point out that these crisscrossing paths worn into the quad are a physical representation of a centuries-old attempt to keep alive a thoughtful, dynamic conversation about how to live a life worth living. It would be nice if students encountered some productive framing of the project of general education as part of their recruitment, admission, and orientation. It would be even better if such ideas found reinforcement in their major courses. Does the art professor ever tell the art majors that it might be a good idea to make a serious study of economics or psychology?

Does the engineering professor testify to the importance of poetry or philosophy? Does the history professor recommend that history majors take an interest in biology or business? Every professor thinks that their own Gen Ed class is of supreme value. But how often do we signal the importance of the process as a whole? If Gen Ed is really just an interdepartmental trade pact among competing firms, why should we be surprised when students treat the process as an enigma, an annoyance, an educational excise tax?

Whereas we launch students in a problematic way, we pay virtually no attention to their return trip. And yet this is the most important phase of transformative education, which we can sequence as follows:

1. A student launches from Frame X to encounter unfamiliar Frame Y.
2. At first, the student has an almost entirely X-framed view of Y. Over time, it emerges that Y is not one more object to be framed by X, but a rival frame.
3. Eventually, the student might acquire not only a Y-framed view of Y but also a Y-framed view of X.

It is not clear how many Gen Ed experiences ever develop beyond phase 1. Even if someone does, in the course of a single semester, begin to get the hang of an alternate way of asking and answering, viewing and valuing, most campuses have no structures in place to support students to undertake the challenging work of phase 3, integrating their defamiliarizing experience into an expanded vision of their work, values, and world. Without a concerted effort, the novel ideas students encounter in their peripheries are likely to remain just that, peripheral. Trips to the national parks or the Andes become just holidays.

If we were serious about general education, courses in the major would support this integrity work by making room for interdisciplinary conversation and personal reflection. However, even a philosophy course on epistemology or ethics is unlikely to welcome the kind of messy, ad hoc questions about knowledge and value that students are really asking themselves:

> Why do the business students and the art students sneer at each other? What does it mean that my engineering professor and lit professor cannot understand each other at all? Why does my religion class seem so totally unrelated to my campus faith group? Does my education professor really think that I was brainwashed by my schooling? Why do we never talk about politics in one class and only about politics in another? Why were all of the students in my seminar

acting like the point of college was to get into graduate school? Would my environmental studies professor look down on my parents? Why don't any of the
things I like to read show up on syllabi?

To process such active fissures in experience requires a kind of inefficient
conversation, full of leaps and loops, awkwardly combining the goofy and
the grave, the half-baked and the overwrought, the granular and the grandiose. It is the rare class indeed that can make room for this sort of clumsy,
intimate conversation. And this may be just as well. The formal curriculum
already has enough to accomplish, and such integrity work may find a more
natural home in informal education, in late-night discussions and long rides
to away games.

The problem is that, while classrooms are typically too task-oriented
and impersonal, social spaces are often infected with more or less virulent
strains of anti-intellectualism. What is needed is a kind of third space, one
free from both scholasticism and anti-intellectualism. Finding such conversational spaces can make all the difference in general education, between
merely stuffing some information into your mental backpack and truly
integrating insights into your character and outlook. And these spaces do
emerge in dorm-room dialogues, dining hall debates, and walks across the
quad—that is, except when they don't. Integrity work does not require (or
perhaps even favor) a formal setting, but it does require certain supporting
conditions such as interpersonal trust, a spirit of serious play, and an ethos
of intellectual friendship. It is easy to espouse a "living-learning" ideal and
much harder to enact it. It is not enough to build dorms, staff dining halls,
and fertilize the grass on the quad. One must seed and carefully cultivate a
culture of conversation.

By expanding our definition of curriculum, we have widened the search
for a genuine response to our human need for roots and branches. However,
as we have canvassed the sprawling, entrepreneurial multiversity—with its
specialized, technical knowledge, its negative conception of freedom, its
culture of distraction and disconnection—we have found only curricular
evasions of the twofold task of formation. Let us conclude this section with
a review of the argument for this claim.

Despite its ostensible commitment to well-roundedness, the multiversity
has marginalized and distorted this ideal. Consigned to a compulsory corner
of the curriculum, well-roundedness appears not as a desirable aim in its

own right but as a sort of tollbooth on the highway of specialized career preparation. The ideal is further distorted through a series of reductions. Gen Ed targets not the whole person, but the whole intellect, and further reduces this idea of intellectual breadth to that of academic interdisciplinarity. We then hollow out even this reduced version of well-roundedness by assigning it the poor proxy of mechanical distribution requirements. Meanwhile, for this slight imposition on the student's freedom of choice, we overcompensate with endless options, proliferated through our interdepartmental trade wars. And so, having reduced well-roundedness to a weak check on academic overspecialization, we retreat to the level of the transcript. Far from a robust curricular engagement with the task of educating the whole person, what we now call general education amounts to a formalization of a reduction of a distortion, sealed inside a bureaucratic black box.

If Gen Ed is poorly designed to ensure well-roundedness, it seems pretty well designed to frustrate integration. Indeed, some early observers candidly described the new rules of curricular distribution as "scattering requirements."[135] One would think that life is already scattered enough. In our culture of distraction and overwork, we jump from this to that, checking off the items on our things-to-do list. And, like all of us, undergraduates cope with the fragmentation of experience through the quick fix of compartmentalization. They put academic work in one compartment and "the real world" in another. They divide the personal and the intellectual, classrooms and dorm rooms, campus culture and hometown values, current and former selves. The university should be working to heal these deeper rifts, helping students connect their studies with their past experiences, future paths, and nonscholastic presents. But we don't even provide space and support to work through the disconnects in the formal curriculum. It is not only Gen Ed classes that feel scattered. Students often struggle to understand how the courses in their majors fit together. Indeed, they sometimes struggle to see how the different weeks of a single course, or even the different points in a single lecture, cohere. If nowhere else, Gen Ed should be the place where students find an alternative to the grind, an antidote to fragmentation, a space to collect themselves and check their bearings. Instead, we propel students to various corners of campus through curricular wormholes of forced election. Such a system is not well designed to support students to form even rough maps of the universe of knowledge, let alone to undertake deeper soulcraft. And to what higher calling could a university aspire?

What stands in our way of truly facing up to the task of formation? We have begun to see that this is not a simple matter of curricular reform. Structural features of the modern multiversity obscure and obstruct the project of forming whole persons for meaningful, flourishing lives. In the next section, we discuss what is perhaps the most surprising of these structural features, the fact that the faculty itself has largely lost sight of this core educational project. The hollowness runs deeper than the formalism of our distribution requirements. Disturbingly, it extends right into the plexus of those who would be entrusted to embody and animate a formative curriculum.

A SKELETON FACULTY

The function of the college is to present to the students' attention in concentrated form all the questions that the sophomore in man has raised for himself through the ages and which he has then spent the rest of his history trying to resolve, rephrase, or learn to live with.
—William Perry[136]

Let a man once acquire the habit of turning every experience into a purely intellectual affair . . . and it is amazing how quickly he will shrivel in the process until reduced to a rattling skeleton. We all know it, we all see it. How is it possible then for [students] not to shy away in terror from these skeleton men?
—Friedrich Nietzsche[137]

In the previous section, we searched in vain, from the classroom to the dorm room, for signs of life in contemporary general education. Courses scatter, and there is no reliable provision of space for the sort of dialogues in which such experiences could be integrated into a genuine expansion of outlook and deepening of character. However, we neglected one important setting where such integrative dialogues might occur: advisement. Let's return to the example from the previous section of the computer engineering major who took the five heterogeneous Gen Ed classes. Ideally, there would be an advisor who really knows this student, someone with the time, interest, and intellectual curiosity to explore, say, how the ethical dilemmas of business relate to the legacy of slavery, or how our modern, technologically saturated lives compare to those of the Vikings and the Incas. While such dialogues might occur somewhat more frequently in smaller, more learner-centered institutions, at most universities it is unclear who is positioned to engage students in this way.

Compared to faculty, professional academic advisors are more readily available, more informed about curricular requirements and resources on campus, and better prepared to counsel students through personal difficulties. However, they are not necessarily prepared to work the intersection of the personal and the intellectual, to explore with students how the curriculum informs (and perhaps glosses over) the questions of who one should be and how one should live. As one recent article put it, perhaps a bit harshly, "Most academic advising is a rote, bureaucratic exercise in checking off boxes."[138] Faculty mentors may be better prepared to deal with questions of intellectual substance, but they are less readily available.[139] Office hours fill up, or students assume that they shouldn't bother a professor unless they have a pressing issue or fairly focused question. In any case, it is not clear that faculty are any better prepared for this kind of clumsy conversation that crosses disciplines and fuses the personal with the intellectual.

Obviously, faculty members differ one from the next, but we can make some useful generalizations based on how we educate, recruit, and incentivize the professoriate. Note, first, that professors are themselves products of the modern multiversity and its hollow, disjointed approach to Gen Ed. There are certainly exceptions to this rule. There are institutions where humane learning has not yet been crowded out by hyperspecialization, technicism, and jobbification. And there are zealous students on every campus who blow right past the bureaucracy to find the substance. I am not claiming that it is the most cynical credentialers who choose to stay in academia. But neither should we imagine that the professoriate is drawn from the most well-rounded liberal learners. The epigraph from William Perry gives us a glimpse into the academic imagination circa 1968. This existentialist, formative ideal is still visible, but in order to affirm it, Perry has to clear a bit of rhetorical room. Jokes about sophomores are almost as perennial as existential questions. With the phrase "the sophomore in man," Perry tackles this discourse head on, rehabilitating the maligned figure as the wonderful, unjaded voice in all of us. Fifty years later, I do not know how many students find their college education organized around Perry's ideal (fewer than half think that "developing a meaningful philosophy of life" rises to the level of "very important").[140] In any case, these are not the students that typically find their way into graduate school. Most doctoral programs are looking for students who quickly outgrew this "sophomoric" tendency, and they offer, just in case, a multiyear curriculum to help you distance yourself from those awkward human questions that do not resolve into matters of fact or opinion, cannot be crammed into a disciplinary compartment, and will not sort neatly into the professional and the personal.

William Arrowsmith—a classicist, translator, and humane intellectual whose interests ranged from Aristophanes to Antonioni, brings this point home with brutal honesty:

> The most remarkable and agonizing feature of graduate education is, I think, the gulf between one's studies and one's life, between what we read and how we live. Our studies are alienated from our lives and—such is our professionalism— we are usually required to side with our studies against ourselves, against our lives.
>
> We begin as graduate students to live professionally, and there is almost always a severe and personal loss. We become a little less human, we lose our involvement in the present. Alternatively, we compartmentalize our lives and keep something like bankers' hours with the books; the rest of the day is our own. But for the first time, one feels a real gulf.[141]

Some may be dazzled by this ability of *Homo academicus* to divide and winnow the self. A close reader of Nietzsche, Arrowsmith is uncowed by such ascetic feats. He refuses to equate seriousness with "stultifying professionalism" and "wretched pedantry."[142] The main form of rigor he finds in academia is rigor mortis. Sharp shears and a steady hand are not intrinsic goods: it makes all the difference what parts of yourself you are lopping off. When *Homo academicus* looks in the mirror, he sees a great "hunger artist"; Arrowsmith sees in him only "a small scholar and a learned but shallow man."[143] When he wants to talk to someone truly serious, Arrowsmith seeks out Perry's sophomore. Unlike most graduate students, he explains,

> The undergraduate still acts as though he were a single human being, still integrated; he asks that what he learns should have some pertinence to his life; he acts as though the present really mattered. He can be touched by the urgency of experience, in a book or a man, even when that experience lies beyond his own.

It is therefore good to teach him, since his demands show us what is urgent, present, and serious in ourselves.[144]

I think that Arrowsmith is right about this. Doctoral education too often breeds compartmentalization, alienation, and desiccation. And for those who manage to stay in touch with "the possibility of the search" (Walker Percy), who escape with "a ripeness of self" (Arrowsmith again), two further cullings await.[145] First comes the job search. Here, aspiring and accomplished monomaniacs have a big advantage. Search committees are looking for proven and potential research productivity, not the dynamic wholeness we examined in the previous sections. Candidates whose interests appear too varied will be described as "all over the place." Only the narrowly specialized are likely to be able to squeeze through the search committee's fine sieve.

Second, for any oddball lifelong-liberal-learners who happen to land tenure-track jobs, there awaits the powerful informal curriculum of the tenure and promotion process.[146] Whether this extended ritual is successful at sorting the scholarly wheat from the unproductive chaff is open to doubt. It is, however, undoubtedly successful at socializing the faculty into a very particular way of understanding themselves and their work. It is not just that faculty are incentivized to prioritize research over teaching and service (and note that mentoring does not even have a firm foothold in either of these devalued categories). The most profound lesson of this informal curriculum is its erasure of the vital formative links between mind and body, knowing and doing, the personal and the social, understanding and self-cultivation. We could not prioritize research over teaching and service had we not already learned to think of them as separate, distorting each in the process. We learn to think of research as a kind of disinterested, disembodied, dislocated knowing, purified of personal bias, creaturely needs, and the messy particulars of time and place. The humane tradition of the essay—with its existential mode of address from one searching subject to others—has now all but given way to the voiceless research report, written for everyone and no one. Not that we have time to read each other's work anyway. We prefer proxies such as grant dollars, citation indices, and publication poundage. This closes the vicious circle, as the push to publish ever more eats up the time one might have had for reading.

There is an ethics, if an attenuated one, in the way we talk about academic labor. We rely on the problematic ethical shortcut of contrasting self-interested inclination with altruistic duty. We then imagine a spectrum stretching from research as inclination (if admittedly as a strange hybrid of rarified intellectual interest and careerism), through the mixed bag of teaching (we call it "a load," but also remark on its rewards), to the other largely dutiful obligations we call "service." This has to be considered a professional miseducation, since it erases a concept central to both ethics and education: self-cultivation.[147] It is true that all serious learning entails some form of unlearning, as we surrender mistaken beliefs and reconstruct experience. However, what the informal curriculum of tenure and promotion asks developing scholars to unlearn is the very integrity of the work. In research universities, professors are told to divide their time between three buckets: 40% research, 40% teaching, and 20% service. We forget that all of this might well be described as one complex educational engagement: seeking understanding in community, we also tend to the conditions that foster community and support learning. In hell, all it takes to forget is a quick drink from the river Lethe; in academia, the process takes an average of fourteen years.[148]

Given this process of scholarly formation, I think we have to consider it a matter of dumb luck when we do find well-rounded and integrated professors on campus. Common sense dictates that if we really cared about general education, we would actively cultivate a faculty who themselves received a first-rate general education and who bring an ongoing commitment to their own personal formation. As Maxine Greene puts it, "A teacher in search of his/her own freedom may be the only kind of teacher who can arouse young persons to go in search of their own."[149]

In this light, consider the recent candid self-assessment from Steven Pinker, the Johnstone Family Professor of Psychology at Harvard University and winner of the Humanist of the Year award in 2020. Pinker was responding to William Deresiewicz's claim, in *Excellent Sheep*, that elite higher education fails to provide a "real education," one that addresses students "as complete human beings rather than as future specialists" and helps them "to build a self or (following Keats) to become a soul."[150] Deresiewicz was surprised by the tenor of the responses he received, finding it dismaying "that so many individuals associated with [elite] institutions said not, 'Of course we provide our students with a real education,' but rather, 'What is this real education nonsense, anyway?'"[151] Here is Pinker's version of the "guilty-as-charged" comeback:

Perhaps I am emblematic of everything that is wrong with elite American education, but I have no idea how to get my students to build a self or become a soul. It isn't taught in graduate school, and in the hundreds of faculty appointments and promotions I have participated in, we've never evaluated a candidate on how well he or she could accomplish it.[152]

To Deresiewicz's claim that we have lost sight of the core task of higher education, Pinker's response seems to be, "Really, well, I don't see it anywhere." If we supply the hidden premise, the counterclaim becomes a little more logical but even less flattering, as Pinker seems to be mounting what we might call "the argument from one's own importance." Here is the syllogism: (1) I am important; (2) I don't know how to do this; (3) therefore, it isn't important.

Actually, Pinker's retort is quite instructive if we, as Richard Rorty once put it, "take away the sneer."[153] This sort of cynical functionalism— the university is whatever the university currently does—is like a temporary blindness that could be cured if only the afflicted could see the medicine right in front of them. In this case, hyperspecialization leaves us unable to grasp the antidote of cross-disciplinary conversation. There is actually an interesting question at the heart of Pinker's retort: How could it be that the leading examples of an institution fail to embody the purposes of that institution? What if Pinker, instead of firing off his riposte to Deresiewicz from his office, had taken his concern out onto the quad. Permit me to play out the scene as a Pinkeresque character bumps into colleagues from philosophy, East Asian studies, and classics all eager to take up the question.

PHILOSOPHER: I get what you're saying. Imagine someone who believes that libraries are failed institutions whose true purpose is to host rowdy parties. Instead of writing opinion pieces about how "the library has gone quiet," maybe it's time to revise your theory in light of actual practice.

PINKERESQUE PROF.: Exactly!

PHILOSOPHER: But it's also true that practices can drift away from their animating ideals.

PINKERESQUE PROF.: I think the DJs would have noticed had their club gone quiet and started filling up with books.

PHILOSOPHER.: Except you're speeding up the film. When the change is gradual enough, and the name of the original practice stays plastered on the building, even radical metamorphosis can go unnoticed. It was this possibility that kept Kierkegaard up at night. "In all of Christendom," he asks, "is there a Christian?"[154]

PINKERESQUE PROF.: You're not going to win me over with religious examples.

EAST ASIAN STUDIES PROFESSOR.: Why that's remarkable! Who knew that Kierkegaard was Confucian? Can I share a wonderful moment in the *Analects?*

PINKERESQUE PROF.: If you must.

EAST ASIAN STUDIES PROFESSOR.: It's in Book Thirteen. Zilu asks what a leader's top priority should be. When the Master replies that the obvious first step is "to rectify names," Zilu blurts out that the Master must be joking, as surely there are more pressing things to take care of. So, the Master gives his lovable but blundering associate a verbal rap on the knuckles, calling him a "bumpkin" and telling him that "a *Junzi*—an exemplary person—should keep his trap shut when he's out of his depth." Then he explains that, and I quote, "when speech does not accord with reality, actions misfire, rituals wither, laws and punishments miss their mark, and the people do not know where they stand."[155]

PINKERESQUE PROF.: That sounds like a form of linguistic determinism, which I reject.

CLASSICIST: If I can jump in here, I don't think we need to debate Sapir-Whorf to grasp this point. Consider how the word "student" has drifted from its etymological roots as "one with a zeal for learning." Now it just means one in good standing with the registrar.

EAST ASIAN STUDIES PROFESSOR.: You couldn't have picked a more Confucian example. During the period in which the *Analects* was compiled, the term *shi*—student, scholar, apprentice—was, as you say, adrift. And so the Master presses for rectification: are you interested in being perceived as refined, or in actually refining your perceptions? Are you "just keeping up an unflappable pretense," or have you set your heart on the Way. In the Confucian tradition, if you have refinement but no ethical substance, you're just a "vulgar pedant." In fact, at one point, the

Master suggests that it is pointless to teach the credential chasers. He is looking for learners who are truly "agitated" in their desire to know, "fervent" in their search for enlightenment.[156]

PINKERESQUE PROFESSOR: I resonate with that word "agitated."

PHILOSOPHER: Well I guess MacIntyre is Confucian too, because he has this same worry about moral language hollowing out. He talks about a process of bureaucratization, when institutions start to cannibalize the very practices they were built to serve.[157] Hospitals, for example. The aim of a hospital is to support nursing, doctoring, and other medical practices. When things are going well, institutional metrics—donations courted, lawsuits settled, awards received, doctors and nurses retained, etcetera— are subordinated to goods internal to the practices, in this case life, health, comfort, dignity, and so on. But we often start putting the cart before the horse and the institutional logic invades the practices themselves.

PINKERESQUE PROFESSOR: Like the logic of quiet reading that supposedly corrupted the DJs?

PHILOSOPHER: OK, let's try a new thought experiment: To do their work, doctors and nurses need a roof over their heads, and they are happy to pitch in whenever the roof needs repairs. Lately, though, it seems that there are always more repairs to be done. Doctors and nurses have started spending most of their time up on the roof. Now the community, even the doctors and nurses themselves, have starting confusing healing with roofing. But you wouldn't know from the way they talk about "the spine" (the ridge), "bones" (rafters), "wounds" (leaks), and "bandages" (shingles).

PINKERESQUE PROFESSOR: Sorry, but your metaphor has sprung a leak. I think I would notice if these so-called doctors tried to fix my broken arm with roofing nails.

CLASSICIST: Look around. Don't you see that we're on that roof right now. The word "research" now means grant-getting, "teaching" means generating IUs, and "learning" means collecting credits.

[With that the Pinkeresque Professor has had enough and departs]

Alas, in the real world, faculty are too busy cranking out articles or answering email to linger on the quad. But the ideas presented here are not fanciful.

They speak directly to the Deresiewicz-Pinker exchange. Deresiewicz is essentially asking the Kierkegaardian question: Among all of the diploma holders, is there an educated person? And Pinker's reply suggests the way in which institutional corruption covers its own tracks. We think that what it means to be a professor is to do research and also to transmit to students the knowledge and methods of one's discipline. And so we set up universities accordingly. And then, when pressed, we react with rhetorical flourish: What other role could the faculty in such an institution possibly have?

As my quad colloquium suggests, the untimely voice of the past is our great resource in escaping such self-reinforcing spirals. Thus, humane critics of the contemporary university seek out voices that fit neither the present nor its version of the past. For instance, Arrowsmith honed his critique of *Homo academicus* in dialogue with Nietzsche's "unmodern observations" about the new ethos of academic research taking shape around him in the 1870s.[158] The second epigraph to this section gives you a sense of what Nietzsche thought of this new scholarly type. And I think I know which of Nietzsche's observations Arrowsmith would have offered, had he joined our quad colloquium: "It is therefore a matter of professional self-interest . . . to prevent the appearance of any view of the teacher's mission higher than what [the faculty] are capable of satisfying."[159]

Andrew Delbanco similarly rejects the idea that one will find an adequate description of this mission in our current manual of standard operating procedures. He reaches a bit further into the prehistory of the modern research university, finding his untimely alternative in an entry in Emerson's journal of 1834:

> The whole secret of the teacher's force lies in the conviction that men are convertible. And they are. They want awakening. Get the soul out of bed, out of her deep habitual sleep.[160]

Delbanco is well aware of our self-reinforcing loops, noting how this idea of teaching as awakening and reorientation will seem utterly out of place in a university that conceives of itself as making and transmitting "a growing sum of discoveries no longer in need of rediscovery once they are recorded."[161] And yet, as Delbanco suggests, Emerson's words still resonate:

> None of us who has ever been a student can fail to read this passage without remembering some teacher by whom we were startled out of complacency

about our own ignorance. For this to take place, the student must be open to it, and the teacher must overcome the incremental fatigue of repetitive work and somehow remain a professor in the religious sense of that word—ardent, exemplary, even fanatic.[162]

If education means awakening someone to the possibilities of soul action, then students need teachers who are themselves existentially in motion, teachers who exemplify this process of trying to get the soul out of bed. Delbanco is not talking about professing faith in a literal sense but simply suggesting that professors stand behind what they teach. Instruction requires mere content; formative education demands that ideas are voiced, held, lived. Though the classroom is neither a church nor a courtroom, teachers must *testify*. As Goethe writes to Schiller, after reading some Kant, "I hate everything that merely instructs me, without quickening or directly igniting my own activity."[163] When we divide fact and value, method and substance, life and work, we lapse into mere instruction. And, as we saw, names stand in need of rectification. A professor who has grown cynical and detached, or simply numb through overwork, is not in this sense a *professor*. We cannot claim to care about the whole student if we allow the life of the mind to become a disembodied, "purely intellectual affair," a game played by "rattling skeletons." "Educators, educate!", Nietzsche declares, "But first educators must educate themselves."[164]

This is the driving theme of Bruce Wilshire's bold and I think underappreciated book, *The Moral Collapse of the University*. Arriving right on the heels of Allan Bloom's famous polemic, Wilshire's title likely misled readers to suspect another moralizing screed.[165] In fact, Wilshire's project stands in marked contrast to Bloom's. Where Bloom wags his finger at students' sophomoric ways and the "Nietzschean" relativistic culture that reared them, Wilshire enlists Nietzsche (along with James, Dewey, Mary Douglas, and others) to help us examine our own scholarly habitus, and especially our urge to dissociate from the "archaic energies of identity formation" in ourselves and our students.[166] What Wilshire calls "moral collapse" is the kind of corruption we examined with MacIntyre, Confucius, and Kierkegaard. The problem is ethical disorientation, not moral misconduct. Indeed, for Wilshire, it is our unacknowledged fear of moral pollution that drives the collapse. In our rites of professionalization and specialization, Wilshire sees a "veiled purification ritual" that alienates us from the telos of education.

So, Nietzsche may be right that, before we can educate, we need to educate ourselves; but before we can educate ourselves, we must understand ourselves. And this, self-knowledge, is just what the compartmentalization of *Homo academicus* debars. On this point, Wilshire draws inspiration from another of Nietzsche's observations, the opening line of *The Genealogy of Morals*, "We knowers are unknown to ourselves."[167] We must try to understand how it is that we scholars could have developed, along with our erudition, an allergy to education itself. We describe teaching as a "load"; we prioritize graduate teaching; we laugh embarrassedly when the personal intrudes into academic discussion. "Educators, educate," but first we must understand and overcome our aversion to the messy particularities of human becoming. In the meantime, scholarship and instruction continue apace.

For Wilshire, and for Dewey before him, the central fault line in the academic soul, the root dichotomy distorting education, is the divorce of mind from body. In a passage that ties together some of the themes of this section and anticipates the next, Wilshire offers this understated indictment of the modern university:

> The research university purports to be also an educational institution. Not to grasp the significance of self as body-self undermines every essential feature of the educating act. Self-reflexivity and self-knowledge become impaired, or impossible. Thus, one's ultimate responsibility as a free knower becomes impaired or impossible: to discover and accept the truth about oneself—and to exemplify this self-awareness wherever appropriate. But also knowledge of one's most intimate relations to others in the community becomes impossible, e.g., relations to the young, to students. . . . It is still another destructive dualism to divide in any wholesale way the personal growth of the professor from the education of the young placed in his or her care.[168]

What form of soulcraft could heal such a basic rift? What does self-knowledge look like in this corporeal key? How do we rattling skeletons search for a more resonant core? How can we reembody the life of the mind? As it turns out, a surprising episode in the life of John Dewey speaks to these exact questions, offering us an extended case study of the arduous nature and integrative possibilities of soul action. In the next section, we travel back to 1916, where we find Dewey having just completed his brilliant deconstruction of the liberal-vocational dichotomy on paper, and just beginning to confront this rift in himself.

CHEST KNOWLEDGE

Next, then, compare the effect of education and that of the lack of it on our nature to an experience like this. Imagine human beings living in an underground, cavelike dwelling, with an entrance a long way up that is open to the light and as wide as the cave itself. They have been there since childhood, with their necks and legs fettered, so that they are fixed in the same place, able to see only in front of them, because their fetter prevents them from turning their heads around.
—Plato[169]

Head tilted up perhaps, cramped, gritting teeth, holding back tears, the little child's tensions and fears still held in the muscles and the joints of the middle-aged man's jaw. Lacking a strong body and a secure position in the world, the child as head has tried to go it alone.

So in 1916 Dewey consulted the pioneering psychobiotherapist.
—Bruce Wilshire[170]

If every university provides a key for its particular campus map, John Dewey offers us a legend for the curricular architecture of higher education itself. If you are interested in English language and literature, you need to head to the main quad. However, if you want to use English to make sense of the events of the day, you should head over by the parking lots, where you will find the School of Journalism. Curiously, the Biology Department is right across the quad from English, while the School of Applied Life Sciences sits over by Journalism. And we find the same pattern with Economics and the Business School, Mathematics and the College of Engineering, Political Science and the School of Government. For some reason, each major domain of human experience is doubly represented, first as a liberal, disinterested study and then again as an applied, professional pursuit.[171] What is this principle that is so clear that it goes without saying, so powerful that it can divide every domain of human experience and split every campus?

This is arguably the driving question of *Democracy and Education*, the book that Dewey himself described as having "most fully expounded" not only his views on education but also his philosophy in general.[172] And his answer is a surprising one. There is no conceptual principle. What divides

liberal and vocational education is "only superstition."[173] And yet, there is
something strangely stubborn about this superstition. As Dewey observes,
"The separation of liberal education from professional and industrial education goes back to the time of the Greeks," making it "probably the most
deep-seated antithesis which has shown itself in educational history."[174]
How could mere superstition become so entrenched that it shapes educational thought and practice for two and half millennia? In Dewey's discussion of the liberal/vocational dichotomy we find three main factors.

First, and it will be worth exploring this point in some detail, there is
our basic tendency to either/or thinking. It takes time and effort to notice
nuance and perceive each phenomenon on its own terms. In many situations, the capacity for rapid recognition is extremely useful. Right now, for
instance, I am looking for my copy of Dewey's *Art as Experience* to look up
his distinction between "bare recognition" and "full perception."[175] I recall
green text on a white background. I scan the shelves. This is no time to
think about what I am seeing (e.g., Why did I used to think that book was
so important? Why do I buy books I never read?). To finish this paragraph,
I need the Dewey volume ASAP. So I become a high-speed sorter: green/
not green; if green, Dewey/not Dewey; if Dewey, *Art as Experience*/not *Art
as Experience*. This high-speed wiring was originally laid in to help us survive. Stick or snake, path or cliff, shadow or swooping crowned eagle, these
are the kind of distinctions where speed matters much more than nuance.
Thus, in matters of survival and moments of convenience, we have the ability to shrink the world down to a toggle switch. Friend or foe; green or red
light; Dewey or Descartes?

Here's the rub: when you have such a handy switch, it is hard not to
use it all of the time. And it works pretty well when it comes to simple
conceptual pairs whose opposition is definitional. What is big is not small;
what is hot is not cold, what is near is not far.[176] The key word here is
"not." Through negation, we can streamline thought, essentially cutting
in half the number of concepts that one must keep track of. "Short" is a
perfectly nice word but you don't strictly need it once you have "tall."
The problem is that we don't limit ourselves to definitional contrasts. We
reduce more complex conceptual relationships to either/ors, which risks
blinding us to important features of reality, namely the both/ands and the
neither/nors. The person who is too rigid about the distinction between
poetry and prose will fail to appreciate Claudia Rankine's both/and book,

Citizen. The person who is too attached to the binary "healthy/sick," will fail to appreciate the fact that, though he is not sick per se, he is definitely not healthy.[177]

At least in such cases there is still some logical basis for the contrast. Dewey shows that the opposition between the liberal and the vocational falls into the further category of fully specious dichotomies. His method is simple: fill in each concept a bit, without resorting to the usual contrasts between them. What emerges is that, far from antithetical, the two concepts are deeply congruous. While he devotes an entire chapter to his reconstruction of vocation, his remarks on liberal education are more indirect and scattered. An education is liberal if it is "liberative of imagination" and "perfecting of judgment," cultivates "the disposition to penetrate to deeper levels of meaning," nurtures "self-directive thought and aesthetic appreciation," frees us "from the dominion of routine habits and blind impulse," and contributes to the "cultivation of the self."[178] Nothing in this list of aims is incompatible with vocation, which Dewey defines broadly as any continuous, purposive activity that "balances the distinctive capacity of an individual with his social service" (308). It is this "balance" that many previous accounts of vocation overlook. The etymology of the word itself suggests that we are *called* away from our personal concerns to service. By contrast, Dewey stresses the role of vocation in the practitioner's own formative quest. Each of our "diverse and variegated vocational activities" is an expression of what constitutes the "dominant vocation of all human beings at all times," namely "intellectual and moral growth" (310).

For Dewey, then, to find a true vocation is to find an educative medium. One way to recognize this is in the felt rightness of the work: "A right occupation means simply that the aptitudes of a person are in adequate play, working with the minimum of friction and the maximum of satisfaction" (308). However, the full worth of a vocation is found only over time. Vocations catalyze our growth by shaping experience in two ways. First, vocations contribute to the continuity of experience. Their purposive frames help us link our past, present, and future in meaningful ways. Without them, experience would deaden into repetition or fray into happenstance. With them, we experience events as meaningful consequences and harbingers. Life becomes episodic. Second, vocations contribute to the richness of experience helping us draw forth from our surroundings a rich, informal, lifelong curriculum. Dewey explains:

A calling is also of necessity an organizing principle for information and ideas; for knowledge and intellectual growth. It provides an axis which runs through an immense diversity of detail; it causes different experiences, facts, items of information to fall into order with one another. The lawyer, the physician, the laboratory investigator in some branch of chemistry, the parent, the citizen interested in his own locality, has a constant working stimulus to note and relate whatever has to do with his concern. He unconsciously, from the motivation of his occupation, reaches out for all relevant information, and holds to it. The vocation acts as both magnet to attract and as glue to hold. Such organization of knowledge is vital, because it has reference to needs; it is so expressed and readjusted in action that it never becomes stagnant. No classification, no selection and arrangement of facts, which is consciously worked out for purely abstract ends, can ever compare in solidity or effectiveness with that knit under the stress of an occupation; in comparison the former sort is formal, superficial, and cold.[179]

Far from viewing vocation as self-sacrifice, Dewey sees it as a way of pursuing our growth and flourishing. Instead of depicting vocational experience as dull and disconnected, Dewey envisions it as stimulating and integrating. Vocations offer mediums for soul action!

Indeed, if we follow Dewey in liberating the concept of the aesthetic from the artworld (where it means "related to art and beauty"), we can see both liberal learning and vocational experience as modes of *aesthetic appreciation*. When Dewey describes the non-aesthetic, he sprinkles in the term "anesthetic" to signal that the aesthetic is best understood through contrast not with the ugly or utilitarian, but with the routine, the numb, the somnolent.[180] Aesthetic experience, to recall the earlier quote from Emerson, is what gets the soul out of bed. Aesthetic appreciation does not mean prescribed praise for approved works of art but vital, dynamic responses to the world aided by art, nature, work, or whatever vivifies. For Dewey, appreciation "denotes an enlarged, an intensified prizing" (237). It suggests "a depth and range of meaning in experiences which otherwise might be mediocre and trivial," a "concentration and consummation," where experience too often remains "scattered and incomplete" (238). Thus, it is precisely in vocational experience that we find the hallmarks of aesthetic education and liberal learning: a richness and vitality of experience; a stimulus to thought, imagination, and meaning-making; a vehicle of self-cultivation.

There is, then, no logical reason why liberal learning and vocational education should have become antonyms. Rather, contingencies of culture and history conspired with our tendency to either/or thinking to press a pair of mutually supporting concepts into a false opposition. Still, if we are to explain the millennial stubbornness of this false dichotomy, we need to look both broader and deeper, and that is where Dewey's second and third layers of explanation come in. The liberal/vocational binary, Dewey suggests, is just one part of a thick network of mutually supporting dichotomies: leisure and labor, culture and utility, freedom and necessity, knowing and doing, mind and nature, individual and society, interest and duty.[181] We identify liberal learning with leisure, culture, and freedom, with personal refinement and the life of the mind; we identify vocational education with necessary preparation for socially useful, manual trades. The tight linkages among these conceptual cousins makes it difficult to interrupt one dichotomy without interrupting them all. And this compounds the problem of negative definition, as one misleading contrast devolves into full shadow play, absurd were it not for its real grip on our thinking and educational arrangements. Here is one of our familiar if faulty syllogisms:

1. Whatever vocational education is, it is not liberal education.
2. Liberal education relates to freedom and culture.
3. Therefore, vocational education must be mechanical and crude.

Or, starting from the other side of the dichotomy, we grab liberal education by its most convenient handle, reasoning that

1. Whatever liberal education is, it is not vocational education.
2. Vocational education is practical and concerns our contribution to society.
3. Therefore, liberal education must be useless and selfish.

We could think of these dualisms as weeds appearing separate above-ground but entangled in their roots. Digging up just one won't get the job done: it will simply spring up in a new spot. Indeed, Dewey's third layer of explanation concerns two taproots, as it were, of this conceptual network, one planted deeply in society, the other buried deep in ourselves. The social taproot is class:

Behind the intellectual and abstract distinction as it figures in pedagogical discussion, there looms a social distinction between those whose pursuits involve a minimum of self-directive thought and aesthetic appreciation, and those who are concerned more directly with things of the intelligence and with the control of the activities of others. (255)

In a surprisingly Marxian move, Dewey reads our deep assumptions about education, work, and the self as but superstructure to the basic fact of a classed society. To make this point, Dewey first revisits Aristotle, who appears ready-made to serve as an inegalitarian foil to our democratic virtue. We can cluck our disapproval when we learn that, in Aristotle's day, "slaves, artisans, and women [were] employed in furnishing the means of subsistence in order that others, those adequately equipped with intelligence, [could] live the life of leisurely concern with things intrinsically worth while."[182] But then Dewey begins to disabuse us of this modern conceit, noting that "there remains . . . a cleavage of society into a learned and an unlearned class, a leisure and a laboring class" (255). Certainly the landscape has shifted. Now "the manufacturer, banker, and captain of industry have practically displaced a hereditary landed gentry as the immediate directors of social affairs" (313). The fact remains, though, that "the great majority of workers have no insight into the social aims of their pursuits and no direct personal interest in them" (260). Then Dewey twists the knife, praising Aristotle for at least describing "the life that was before him" without "insincerity" and "mental confusion" (255). We pride ourselves on our egalitarianism, on the idea that what determines your life prospects is not your wealth or family name but how hard you pull on your bootstraps. And yet, judging from our actions rather than our rhetoric, we still seem firmly to believe that only some members of society are suited for lives of purpose, meaning, and leadership while others are best prepared for subservient roles of alienated labor. In the end, it turns out that there is an important difference between Aristotle and us: Aristotle was not a hypocrite!

If Dewey, in 1916, could be humble about the progress made in the 2,300 years since Aristotle, we should certainly be sober about the stubborn persistence of social sorting over the last century. Indeed, as Richard Rorty observes, Dewey did not "foresee that an increasingly greedy and heartless American middle class would let the quality of education a child receives become proportional to the assessed value of the parents' real estate."[183] We have private schools for the superrich, lavish quasi-public schools for the plenty rich, and bleak public schools for the poor and working classes. By quasi-public, I mean government-run schools with ample physical, emotional, and intellectual resources, located in wealthy enclaves where parents pay the equivalent of private school tuition in the inflated housing prices and taxes of these exclusive neighborhoods. In contrast, children living in

poor neighborhoods will typically encounter behaviorist pedagogy, a curriculum narrowed to transmission of skills needed for low-wage jobs, and
physical environments that range from the deeply anesthetic to the outright unsafe.[184] Meanwhile, since race and class remain closely coupled in
the United States, this so-called voluntary residential segregation has all but
undone any gains accomplished by de jure desegregation—five decades after
Brown, there were 2.3 million African American students attending what
the Civil Rights Project calls "apartheid schools," in which 99%–100% of
the students are non-White.[185] Merit, not family background, is supposed to
determine access to higher education, but SAT results read like a fine-grained
demographic map. There is 162-point gap between the median scores of
African American and White students and a 247-point gap between the bottom and top quintiles in median family income, with smooth progressions in
between.[186]

Such facts lead David Labaree to ask why, given the evidence that schools
are largely unsuccessful at solving the social problems we have laid at their
doorstep, we continue to educationalize more and more such problems.
His answer is that schools enable us to "formalize substance," giving us a
"mechanism for expressing serious concern about social problems without
actually doing anything effective to solve those problems."[187] Thus, while
we lack the will to tackle the problems of inequality, we also no longer quite
have the stomach for a bald-facedly two-tiered educational system: one set
of institutions for elites and another that doles out menial skills for menial
jobs for "menial" people. And so we create a formal solution: the common
school as a stage on which both cultural and utilitarian values can each take
a bow. This results not in a real synthesis, only an "inorganic composite."[188]
Thus, Dewey reads the modern curriculum as confusion of concessions: subjects such as literature are included because of their cultural cachet, but only
if "taught with the chief emphasis upon forming technical modes of skill"; a
subject such as "science is recommended on the ground of its practical utility,"
but only if taught "in removal of application."[189] We appease our class anxieties by titrating the useless and the unimaginative.

As I indicated, the second taproot is located in the soil of the self. To find
it, let us return to our campus map, stealing a page out of Plato's book. I
am thinking of the moment in the *Republic* when Socrates proposes that the
group first examine justice at political scale before inspecting the harmonies
and disharmonies of the soul:

The investigation we are undertaking is not an easy one, in my view, but requires keen eyesight. So, since we are not clever people, I think we should adopt the method of investigation that we would use if, lacking keen eyesight, we were told to identify small letters from a distance, and then noticed that the same letters existed elsewhere in a larger size and on a larger surface. We would consider it a godsend, I think, to be allowed to identify the larger ones first, and then to examine the smaller ones to see whether they are really the same.[190]

Similarly, the cordoning of campus has helped us to magnify the fissures in the soul. We have already read the divorce of head and hands, knowing and doing, in the large font of higher education's rigorous separation of pure and applied subjects. But let us examine this curricular architecture further.

In particular, the arts provide an interesting test case for our theory that each mode of human experience is doubly represented. At first, aesthetic experience seems to fit the model: on the quad, we find liberal arts majors and Gen Ed students studying poems, plays, paintings, and performances; over by the parking lots, we find studio majors learning how to dance and design, paint and sculpt, perform soliloquies and sonatas. Here, though, there is an interesting kink in the usual logic that divides inquiry from application. The word "art" in the phrases "liberal arts" and "arts and sciences" does not refer to aesthetic practices of creation and performance. It is used in the older, broader sense of principled practices that rely on teachable modes of inquiry and bodies of knowledge.[191] And this is just how we should understand the arts, as rich traditions of sense-making, as modes of embodied understanding. However, it is precisely this aspect of art that is suppressed in the curricular architecture. The arts appear on the quad not as modes of inquiry in their own right but as objects of discursive knowledge. The seminar on the history of ballet is not teaching you how to move/ think/feel like a dancer, but how to think historically. It is closer to a course on military history than it is to a ballet class.

Nor is it clear how often (fine, performing, industrial) art majors are being introduced to their specializations as disciplines of sense-making and as vehicles for self-formation. When this does happen, there is still the absurdity that some of the richest occasions for general education are being reserved for specialists. More worrisome is that this often does not happen at all. We study the arts as meaningful texts in one precinct and as crafts in another, and this maims both. Studio programs often become narrowly focused on technique, with a sprinkling of career preparation. The aspiring actor or cellist or architect may never be introduced to the arts as humane disciplines through which we seek to understand self and world. Thus, to the student qua future practitioner we offer know-how in the arts. To the learner seeking a general education we offer discursive knowledge (historical and philosophical, anthropological and sociological, political-theoretic and literary-critical) about artworks. What drops out is knowledge *through* the arts. We are uncomfortable with the very idea of embodied knowing.

This becomes even clearer when we examine our differing relationships with the several arts. Academics are most comfortable when dealing with thin symbol systems that abstract away from the messiness and the fleshiness of reality. Thus, we seem to be most comfortable with verbal arts, but even here we find a spectrum. As the embodied aspects of these arts (voice and metaphor; rhythm and rhyme) rise, our scholarly comfort falls. We are completely at ease with expository prose, comfortable enough with prose fiction and drama, but already somewhat uncomfortable with poetry. However, it is when we move from literature to the plastic, musical, and performing arts that the sensuous aspects of art become truly undeniable.[192] Here we find another hierarchy, among the senses themselves. There is a long history in the West of associating knowledge with vision, a history that is evident from the visual metaphors embedded in our everyday vocabulary related to thinking and understanding: we *see* a point, we find a study *illuminating*, we offer theoretical over*views*, we take a fresh *look* at the evidence, we speak of in*sight* and *brilliance*.[193] Thus, the visual arts may be a touch safer for study. Then comes music, especially music that approaches us primarily through the ears, via pitch, rather than through the gut via rhythm and vibration. Finally, dance could be said to have the hardest row to hoe in the academy. The academy is not very comfortable with the idea that there is a mode of knowing centered on the pelvis. Kinesiology is quite acceptable, maybe even dance criticism: but dance as criticism knocks the cogitator off-balance.

Why do we elevate telling over showing? Why do the sensuous arts need a discursive escort to appear on the main quad? Why do we separate knowing from doing, feeling, and moving? In the zoning of the campus map, we read the legend of our own dividedness. In the large font of the curriculum, we perceive our ambivalent relationship with our fleshy nature. Thus, the second taproot of our educational dichotomies is the dis-integration of mind and body within the modern soul.

Dewey was acutely aware of these psychic fissures, and healing them was central to his calling as a philosopher. In his late intellectual-autobiographical sketch, "From Absolutism to Experimentalism," he describes his younger self as riddled with "divisions and separations."[194] Struggling to recapture this "early mood," at one point even declaring the task "impossible," Dewey reaches for phrases with sufficient charge (153). He experiences the "isolation of self from the world, of soul from body, of nature from God" as an "inward laceration" (153). He feels a "hunger," "an intense emotional craving," "a demand for unification" (153). His failure to join the formal and abstract with the material and concrete reveals itself in the "stigmata" of the false facility and "specious lucidity" that marked his early writings (151).[195] As for the next three decades of Dewey's life, there are two different ways of telling the story, as a rapid rise to success and as a slow climb up the "rough, steep, upward path" that leads out of Plato's cave.[196]

The first story goes like this. In his PhD studies at Johns Hopkins (1882–1884), Dewey finally found the resources to heal these lacerations. In Professor George Morris he found a model of integrity, a remarkably "single-hearted and whole-souled man—a man of a single piece all the way through" (152). In "Hegel's synthesis of subject and object, matter and spirit, the divine and the human," Dewey discovered "no mere intellectual formula" but "an immense release, a liberation" (153). Dewey's career then takes off like a rocket: PhD, Johns Hopkins, 1884; chair, University of Michigan Philosophy Department, 1889; president, American Psychological Association, 1898; director, School of Education, University of Chicago, 1902; president, American Philosophical Association, 1905; founding president, American Association of University Professors, 1915. His scholarly output during this period was unreal. He published two books in the first four years after graduate school. In the 1890s and 1900s, he published key essays such as "The Reflex Arc Concept in Psychology" (1896), "My Pedagogic Creed" (1897), "Emerson—The Philosopher of Democracy" (1903), "The Relation of Theory to Practice in Education" (1904), and those eventually collected in *The Influence of Darwin on Philosophy* (1910). These decades also yielded a slew of significant books: *Outlines of a Critical Theory of Ethics* (1891), *Interest in Relation to Training of the Will* (1896), *The*

School and Society (1899), *Studies in Logical Theory* (1903), *Ethics* (1908), *Moral Principles in Education* (1909), *How We Think* (1910).

Such output bespeaks a unity of purpose, and the work itself was offered to help us reunify ourselves. Dewey pointed to an interactive psychology that transcended both the reductive materialism of the new observational psychology and the otherworldly idealism of the old intuitionism. He helped move us from the reflex arc (stimulus, response) to the hermeneutic circle (acting, we encounter a meaningful situation, and this elicits further meaningful actions and propels us into new situations). He never minimized the importance of the inner life. He just showed that it was not that "inner." Mind was right there in the supposedly brute sense data. Knowing was visible in doing. The soul was immanent in the body. As early as 1887, Dewey would write,

> Sensation is the meeting-place, the point of coincidence of self and nature. It is in sensation that nature touches the soul in such a way that it becomes itself psychical, and that the soul touches nature so as to become itself natural. A sensation is, indeed, the transition of the physical into the psychical.[197]

And throughout this period, we find Dewey developing his critique of the dualisms between the liberal and the vocational, culture and utility, leisure and labor, interest and duty, humanism and naturalism, the abstract and the concrete.[198] Thus, as Dewey headed into the war years, no one would be blamed for thinking that he had long since found his medium. According to this triumphalist narrative, Wilshire observes, Dewey "achieved influence fairly early," and "at fifty-seven he had pretty well summed up his views in the magisterial, tightly organized *Democracy and Education*."[199] By 1916, Dewey had not only achieved his own reeducation, but had also laid the groundwork for all of us to reintegrate head and hands.

There is another story to tell about Dewey's development as the philosopher seeking to heal the rift between body and soul. In this story, 1916 marks not a happy ending, but a difficult turning point, launching a new, deeper phase in Dewey's ongoing process of "discovery and reawakening."[200] The war years were difficult for Dewey. There was the deeply unsettling nature of the cataclysm itself, but also a series of painful personal attacks on Dewey because of his support of US entry into the war. This came on top of family worries: his daughter Evelyn began to struggle with depression even as the depression of his wife, Alice, grew more severe in the decade following a second death of a child (in 1904, the Deweys' son, Gordon, had died of typhoid fever at the age of eight, echoing the loss of their two-year-old son Morris from diphtheria a decade earlier). During these years, Dewey found himself "exhausted emotionally and physically," in the midst of what he himself appears to have described as a "breakdown."[201]

From his poems (written almost entirely during this period), his letters, and secondhand reports, Dewey's biographers have pieced together a portrait of a profound midlife crisis.[202] Dewey had worked himself up into a "state of tension" so severe that it was making him ill.[203] His physical symptoms included "neck aches, headaches, and blurred vision."[204] And his emotional experience seems to match Freud's account of the process of mourning: a painful withdrawal of prior emotional investments in the service of eventual fresh attachments.[205] Dewey all but lost his usual appetite for work, with even a few hours causing "him great fatigue and . . . painful depression."[206] His poems paint a picture of a man who feels trapped and emotionally frozen ("And shut me in this barren field / Docks and thistle its only yield").[207] One of his narrators begs God for just "a little space in which to move"; another describes himself as "joyless, griefless."[208] The poems are littered with images of cold ("the freezing years did harden"),[209] desiccation ("thistles, cockleburs, and a few grains"),[210] drudgery ("an unadventurous trudge"),[211] and suffocation ("They have choked and stifled him").[212] In the midst of this cold and barren landscape, Dewey was also discovering new sparks of interest, "springing like flowers from unfrozen sod"; this is clear from his poetic efforts themselves and more dramatically from his now well-documented affair (passionate, if platonic) with Anzia Yezierska.[213]

It was in the midst of this crisis, this period of "distraction and depression," that Dewey met F. M. Alexander and began what would prove to be a quarter-century-long engagement with the form of bodywork that now bears Alexander's name.[214] (The Alexander Technique involves a reeducation of deep psychophysical habits through postural manipulation and coaching). I see this as a crucial turning point in Dewey's biography. It is only recently, though, that the importance of Dewey's work with Alexander has come into focus. The entire first generation of commentators on Dewey's life and work either ignored it altogether or laughed it off as an instance of an overly forbearing Dewey being taken in by a quack.

It is worth quoting in full Frank Jones's recounting of this conspiracy of misprision:

> In the face of Dewey's positive statements about the moral and intellectual value of the technique, I have always found it difficult to understand the insistence by his disciples that its application was purely physical—as if the technique were a kind of Australian folk remedy which Dewey in the kindness of his heart had endorsed in order to help Alexander sell books. I ran into this attitude long before I met Dewey. Sidney Hook had given a lecture at Brown on some aspects of Dewey's philosophy. I had just discovered Alexander's books and had been impressed by Dewey's introductions to them. At the end of the lecture I went up to the platform to ask Hook about Alexander's influence on Dewey. He looked at me uncomprehendingly at first and then said with obvious embarrassment: "Oh yes! Alexander was an Australian doctor who helped Dewey once when he had a stiff neck." A little later in an article on Dewey in the *Atlantic Monthly* Max Eastman described Alexander as "A very unconventional physician . . . an Australian of original but uncultivated mind." "Dewey was smiled at in some circles," Eastman wrote, "for his adherence to this amateur art of healing but it undoubtedly worked in his case." In Corliss Lamont's *Dialogue on John Dewey*, Alexander again appears as a quaint character who was "concerned with your posture and that sort of thing." The speakers agreed that "Dewey thought Alexander had done him a lot of good," but none of them gave Dewey credit for intelligent judgment, and Ernest Nagel (according to Horace Kallen) attributed the whole episode to superstition. This picture of Dewey as the naive supporter of an ignorant Australian doctor has unfortunately been given increased currency in a recent biography, *The Life and Mind of John Dewey*, by George Dykhuizen (1973).[215]

For decades, all that was available was Dykhuizen's biography and the tributes by Eastman and Hook, cementing this picture of a minor episode with a faith healer. With the renaissance in Dewey studies in the 1990s and 2000s, matters have improved. While Jay Martin (in the biography that supplanted Dykhuizen's early effort) devotes only two paragraphs to Dewey's relationship to Alexander, he does acknowledge not only that Alexander helped Dewey feel better physically, but also that the technique provided Dewey with "a practical confirmation" of his own theories of the relation of body and mind.[216] Still, there is much to be desired in this account, as if Dewey found in the Alexander Technique simply one nice illustration of something he had already worked out.[217] I would argue that only his work in the lab school and his dialogues with Albert Barnes (in front of his famous collection of modern art) are comparable in importance as practical engagements that generated and deepened theoretical insights. Steven Rockefeller counts Dewey's work with Alexander as one of four main resources during this decade helping Dewey turn his crisis into an occasion for growth, adding a nature retreat (the Deweys' new farm in Huntington, Long Island), new emotional outlets (Dewey's poetry and a turn toward more self-disclosure in his correspondence), and important new relationships (Yezierska and Barnes). The work with Alexander, Rockefeller concludes, brought Dewey "relief and healing and a fresh sense of life and growth."[218] Rockefeller also better captures the importance of Alexander to Dewey's work, describing it as "deepen[ing] his insights into the relation of the body and mind" and as "crystallizing" a line of thought that had been developing for two decades.[219]

Even Rockefeller's more appreciative account hardly runs ahead of the evidence.[220] Dewey stressed the importance of Alexander's method and discoveries from the moment he began his lessons to his last days. From the start, he would recommend the Alexander Technique to others, including members of his own family. And already by August of 1918, Dewey appeared physically to be "a radically changed person" to someone who had not seen him for a while.[221] Dewey reported to Frank Jones that his lessons with Alexander first cleared up his vision problems and later led to improvements in his breathing. Where his ribcage had been "rigid" (leading presumably to shallow breathing), his ribs acquired a "marked elasticity," a fact still remarked on by doctors in his final years.[222] At the age of eighty-seven, Dewey declared, "My confidence in Alexander's work remains unabated. . . . If it hadn't been for [the] treatment, I'd hardly be here today."[223]

The evidence for impact on Dewey's work is just as clear. This shows up right away in *Human Nature and Conduct* (published in 1922 but building on lectures given in 1918), wherein Alexander plays a starring role in the key second chapter, establishing habits as "active means" and not mere tools at the disposal of the will.[224] Alexander's influence continues, McCormack shows, as late as the *Theory of Valuation* (1939).[225] It shows up most significantly in what is arguably Dewey's greatest work, *Experience and Nature*.[226] It is here that Dewey finally fully works through the mind-body dualism that had occupied him throughout his career, and when he reaches the "heart of the mind-body problem," it is Alexander he cites.[227] Dewey himself puts his previous knowledge of the mind-body relation in scare quotes, writing of his experience with Alexander that "the things which I had 'known'— in the sense of theoretical belief— . . . changed into vital experiences."[228] How could influence this plain have been so widely and persistently discounted? The answer seems clear. Dewey's readers have tended to read his work, even his critique of mind-body dualism, through a dualist screen. What could bodywork with Alexander, the thought goes, have to do with the development of Dewey's *theory* of psychophysical unity? As we have seen, even those who acknowledge the importance of Alexander to Dewey tend to parse this into remediation of physical symptoms, on the one hand, and a confirmation of theoretical insights, on the other.

It is the virtue of Wilshire's account that he reads Dewey's work with Alexander as an existential, psychophysical encounter that "drove him into his deepest critique of psycho-physical dualism."[229] The Dewey of *Democracy and Education* had discovered a vicious circle. A society that cleaves itself into a ruling class of knowers and a subservient class of doers will find itself dividing education into two tiers: one intellectual and cultural, another physical and utilitarian (whether this shows up in different institutions, divergent curricular tracks, or the conflicting "why" and "how" of individual subjects). At the same time, this sort of schizophrenic educational system will tend to reproduce class divisions. To escape the dichotomy, Dewey proposed a "travail of thought," a thorough process of reconceptualization enabling us to "construct a course of study which [was] useful and liberal at the same time."[230] However, even as Dewey was writing these words, he was discovering another vicious cycle, closer to home. Wilshire resorts to both Dante and Descartes to capture Dewey's ordeal of disorientation and dissociation:

> Like Dante's "Midway upon the journey of our life I found myself in a dark wood, where the right way was lost," life for Dewey was stale, flat, pointless— something was missing. All his efforts to achieve a theory that integrated body, self, and experience were blocked by the painful experience of his own life. He detected a rude discontinuity between his powers of inquiry and perception, and the very conditions of these powers in his functioning organism. It was a kind of waking nightmare in which Descartes' psycho/physical dualism could be expelled from Dewey's critical consciousness, but only to have it reappear in Dewey's own everyday behavior and carnal reality.[231]

One cannot *think* one's way out of the divorce of thinking and doing, mind and body. The prisoners in Plato's cave (see the epigraph to this section) are able to form all sorts of sophisticated thoughts about the shadows projected before them. It takes literal movement, and indeed the hand of another to "[drag] him into the light," before the prisoner may begin to glean the unreality of his cave-world.[232] As Dewey himself asserts, in *Art as Experience*,

> No thinker can ply his occupation save as he is lured and rewarded by total, integral experiences that are intrinsically worth while. Without them he would be completely at a loss in distinguishing real thought from the spurious article.[233]

It was in his work with Alexander, Wilshire asserts, that Dewey "learned the real meaning of the phrase 'mind cut off from the body.'"[234] This is not to denigrate the achievement of a work such as *Democracy and Education*, but one can gain only so much traction on the mind-body problem through disembodied prose. At some point, one needs literal traction! Wilshire again: "Dewey's case is particularly ironical. His asserting of general truths about the conditions of consciousness in the body prevented him from dilating his own consciousness and allowing his own body to take the lead in disclosing itself."[235] It was time to tackle the problem in a unified, embodied way.

Alexander's first impression of Dewey was telling, describing Dewey as "drugged with thinking" and prone to "fall asleep during lessons."[236] "Judging from the way Dewey talked and held his head and neck," Wilshire offers, it "was indeed as if his mind were disassociated from his body."[237] Dewey found himself to be "an inept, awkward, and slow pupil."[238] Attempting to compensate for his "practical backwardness" with his "powers of discipline in mental application" was no use.[239] Finding that he was unable to execute even simple directions to move in new ways, Dewey had what he described as "the most humiliating experience of my life, intellectually speaking."[240] Alexander, whose technique centered on the relation of the head, neck, and torso, slowly helped Dewey learn to act, for the first time, with both greater awareness and increased spontaneity. As Dewey declared, a decade into his work with Alexander,

> We need to distinguish between action that is routine and action that is alive with purpose and desire; between that which is cold, and that which is warm and sympathetic; between that which marks a withdrawal from the conditions of the present and that which faces actualities; between that which is expansive

and developing (because including what is new and varying) and that which applies only to the uniform and repetitious.[241]

Far from being "just a speculative question," Dewey declares, the "integration of mind-body in action is the most practical of all questions we can ask of our civilization" (12). And Dewey credits Alexander with the insight that the solution must involve "a procedure in actual practice," for to try to think our way out of the problem will only "increase the disease in the means to cure it" (13). "Until this integration is effected," Dewey writes, "we shall continue to live in a society in which a soulless materialism is compensated for by soulful, but futile, idealism and spiritualism" (12).

Thus, we should resist the narrative that 1916 represented the high point in Dewey's educational theorizing, at which point he went on to tackle other questions. I think Wilshire is right to read Dewey's later, more embodied works—*Experience and Nature* and *Art as Experience*—as sequels to *Democracy and Education*:

> The archaic background of experience is painfully difficult to reveal. But if it is not revealed all the talk about the unexamined life being not worth living is mere twaddle, and what passes for education a sham. Dewey contributes to what the Greeks meant by chest-knowledge, humane and ethical knowledge, the union of intellectual freedom and ethical responsibility, and he points to regenerative possibilities of experience.
>
> But it would be a mistake to infer from this that all of Dewey's thought about education prior to 1916 was a mistake. Indeed, it is because it is so brilliant that what it still leaves out—courageous self-engagement—is so evident. The culminating element in Dewey's epistemology is raw courage: chest and guts.[242]

Dewey himself was quite clear about the educational importance of the hands-on search for embodied self-knowledge:

> Education is the only sure method which mankind possesses for directing its own course. But we have been involved in a vicious circle. Without knowledge of what constitutes a truly normal and healthy psycho-physical life, our professed education is likely to be mis-education. . . . The technique of Mr. Alexander gives to the educator a standard of psycho-physical health . . . in which what we call morality is included. It supplies also the "means whereby" this standard may be progressively and endlessly achieved, becoming a conscious possession of the one educated. It provides therefore the conditions for the central direction of all special educational processes. It bears the same relation to education that education itself bears to all other human activities.[243]

This is not to suggest that we should replace books with bodywork. But this episode does reveal the limits of intellectualized integration and the irony of the phrase "*liberal* arts." Far from being freeing, as long as they remain a province of thin statements over fleshy expressions—estranged from embodied knowing and our experience as active, sensual, emotional creatures—the so-called liberal arts usher us to a front-row seat in Plato's cave. With Alexander's help, Dewey worked out an embodied solution to the problem of dualism. With the help of Dewey—not only the prolific theorist of integration at his desk but also the man who painfully retaught himself to stand and move and breathe—we have worked our way to a conclusion. If general education is to be the occasion of personal integration, and not itself a dis-integrative force, we must heal the rift between liberal and aesthetic education. We must rediscover a form of humane learning that is the stuff of chest and guts.

CODA

But what puts the soul in this active state?
—Charles Sanders Peirce[244]

In describing our efforts to live up to the task of formation, I have adopted the phrase "soul action." I wanted a phrase that captured the drama of inwardness, of discovering and developing one's subjectivity, but nonetheless staged that drama in the social and physical world. By itself, the word "soul" may suggest something intangible, accessed in the stillness and privacy of contemplative withdrawal. We do have phrases, such as "soul-searching" and "spiritual exercises," that connote activity, even physicality; but the searching is seen as inward, the exercises as meditative. Just as "journeying on foot, and running are bodily exercises," Ignatius of Loyola explains, spiritual exercises are ways of "preparing . . . the soul."[245] For this work, Ignatius recommends "solitude and seclusion," explaining that,

Ordinarily, the progress made in the Exercises will be greater, the more the exercitant withdraws from all friends and acquaintances, and from all worldly cares. For example, he can leave the house in which he dwelt and choose another house or room in order to live there in as great privacy as possible.[246]

By contrast, we have seen how a crucial chapter in Dewey's own soul action proved to be precisely interpersonal, tactile, and kinesthetic. Dewey needed Alexander to help him find his way out of his cerebellum and into fuller contact with his estranged bodymind. In his frozen, constricted state, what Dewey required was not inward reflection but outward movement; what he needed was greater psychophysical *range of motion*.

There is nothing wrong with associating soul with either spirituality or individuality as long as we do not thereby disassociate it from the physical or the social. I like the open-endedness of Peirce's four-word definition of soul as "that which can move."[247] Soul is vital, embodied form. Soul *moves* in two senses: as inspirited and inspiriting, as animating principle and enlivening effect. The vitality of dynamic form circulates through the intrapersonal, the interpersonal, and the sociocultural. However, the dissociation of mind and body cuts off that circulation. We have been tracking this circulatory disorder at both the level of the individual (Dewey's midlife crisis) and the social (the campus map), and from this we derived a specific curricular conclusion, that general education must be reunited with aesthetic education. If we are to face up to the formidable task of formation, we must reembody liberal learning.[248]

As it stands, formative education leads a kind of ghostly existence in the contemporary university. You can still catch a glimpse of it in campus architecture. A hilltop location; buildings with some history, solidity, and grandeur; communal quads and articulated pathways: all of this points to the idea that something important, something higher, is to be attempted here. And you can still read about it in all of the mission statements that include the compulsory reference to "educating the whole person." But it vanishes as soon as we try to grab hold of it. Our actual priorities are clear from the way we direct attention and resources: the contemporary university is concerned with research and development, instruction and training, sorting and credentialing, not to mention "beer and circus."[249] With an agenda this full, something had to be tabled: it just happens to be what is arguably the core project of higher education. If formative education had been decisively killed off, we could mourn, conduct an autopsy, attempt a resurrection. Instead, it has been consigned to a living death, filed away in the impersonal bureaucracy we call Gen Ed. I suppose that makes this essay—if I can give this already twisty metaphor a final, legal spin—a kind of *writ of habeas corpus*.

As we have seen, there is nothing impersonal about true general education, which involves stirring individuals to soul action, recalling each of us
to the task of figuring out who we are and what we stand for. Nor is there
anything formulaic or facile about educating the whole person. Idiosyncratic and unscripted, the quest for variegated, dynamic wholeness is as harrowing as it is enlivening. By contrast, the modern machinery of Gen Ed
evokes neither the passion nor the pathos of self-formation. The uniform
gray of bureaucratic compliance is accented only by occasional flecks of
curiosity and blotches of annoyance. Admittedly, this is a strange form of
compliance, since what is compelled is choice. However, Gen Ed represents
not a rich medium for positive freedom but an empty ritual of consumer
preference. Whereas the work of self-cultivation is simultaneously individualizing and deeply communal, the experience of Gen Ed somehow manages to be both generic and isolating. And if our "scattering requirements"
do not reliably widen, they certainly do not help students to integrate.

Indeed, what we have discovered is that this is not an accident but an
expression of the deep fault lines on which the multiversity is built. If disciplinary departments began as a division of common labor (e.g., to understand
and to educate; to enrich our individual and collective self-understandings; to
extend, reanimate, and critique our culture and politics), they have devolved
into competing firms, fighting for market share, each pushing an intellectual
product recast as an end in itself. And this splintering of knowledge makes it
difficult to maintain the connection between knowing and becoming, learning and living. Academics become estranged not only from each other but
also from their inner sophomore. Consider that the etymological meaning of
the word "philosophy" is "love of wisdom," and that the phrase "doctor of
philosophy" was meant to signal that one added to one's mastery of a specialized field the crucial ability to situate that field in the larger constellation of
human inquiry and understanding. To mention wisdom now is to become
the butt of jokes.[250] Or we could put the matter another way, saying that
what has been severed is the unity of teaching and learning. Professors begin
to lose touch with themselves as learners; students remain unaware that, as
liberal learners, they must direct and shape their own learning. Following
Dewey, we traced the further fractures that branch off from mind-body dualism into rifts between culture and utility, the liberal and the vocational, verbal
abstraction and sensuous form.

With the very foundations of the university riven by these curricular, cultural, epistemological, and existential fault lines, it should not surprise us when our holistic initiatives founder, backfire (scattering us further), or degenerate into empty rituals and rhetoric. To rescue holistic education from platitudes will require more than a rejiggering of requirements or a rebranding of Gen Ed. To face up to the twofold task of formation, to summon a community devoted to soul action, demands a thoroughgoing project of reimagination.

NEW STUDENT ORIENTATION

The undergraduate . . . is neither a child nor an adult, but stands in a strange middle moment of life when he knows only enough of himself and of the world which passes before him to wish to know more. He has not yet found what he loves, but neither is he jealous of time, of accidents, or of rivals. Perhaps the phrase from the fairy tale suits him best—he has come to seek his intellectual fortune.
—Michael Oakeshott[1]

Welcome to Orientation! Any minute, the students should be arriving in Academic Affairs to learn about registration and degree requirements. Then they will head off on a get-to-know-your-campus scavenger hunt organized by Student Life. However, they must have lost their way. The students have ended up in Humanities Hall, seated around the campus's eccentric professor of political philosophy. And he is way off script . . .

We might think this purely fanciful, if not for a manuscript discovered in the archives of the London School of Economics, revealing a surprising fact about their 1961 new-student orientation: it concluded with a talk from the great theorist of experience, education, and political life, Michael Oakeshott.[2] Did they not realize that Oakeshott was a double agent? In my scenario, the students were literally lost; here Oakeshott made it his mission to lead them astray. Welcome to Reorientation![3]

Oakeshott begins by acknowledging the inevitable orientation fatigue:

This I fear may be the last straw.

You have been talked to by the Director, by the Registrar, by the Librarian, by your Tutors; you have been prematurely advised about your careers; you have been told where the lavatories are . . . ; you have been received, paraded, welcomed, registered, and given a free tea. . . . I am left with nothing to say but what you have probably heard three times over.[4]

But of course Oakeshott does have something to say, something "not quite in line with what you've already been told."[5] While he wants to evoke what college can be, he knows that the students won't be able to hear him unless he can first poke some holes in their received ideas. "The distinctive feature" of a place of liberal learning, Oakeshott later argues, is that "those who occupy it are recognized and recognize themselves preeminently as learners, although they may be much else besides."[6] At first glance, this seems pretty intuitive. You emphasize different aspects of yourself in different contexts; college foregrounds your student identity. As it turns out, Oakeshott is making a stranger and more interesting claim: it is precisely the identity of student that most threatens to derail our self-recognition as learners. Thus, begins Oakeshott's anti-orientation:

> Almost everything that has happened to you since you arrived here, and much of what was told you beforehand, has tended to turn you into self-conscious "Students." . . . Indeed, some people seem to think that being a "student" is a sort of profession.[7]

At this point, we can imagine Oakeshott's audience feeling more than a little confused. Did the chair of the Department of Government really just tell us to stop thinking of ourselves as students?![8] It might have helped if Oakeshott had explained that there is nothing wrong with the word "student" and nothing sacred about the term "learner." Perhaps Oakeshott could not have foreseen just how adaptable the terms "learner" and "learning" would prove, gigging as press agents for late, flexi-capitalism; but he would have known that the Latin roots of "student" (*studere, studium*) suggest care, desire, zeal.[9] In any case, the distinction Oakeshott is making is axiological, not verbal. He is pointing to what David Blacker, following Michael Walzer, calls "spherical capture," the process by which one value sphere commandeers the vocabulary and practices of another.[10] Like an ant invaded by the zombie-fungus, the concept of the student in late capitalism only looks educational on the outside. It is now piloted by the same logic that reduces everything to what Oakeshott calls the "enterprise of extracting from the world satisfactions for our wants."[11]

So, having gotten the kids to himself for a moment, Oakeshott wastes no time in staging an intervention. You have been bombarded with "propaganda," he tells them,

> designed to make you believe that you are here to learn how to be a more efficient cog in a social machine. Forget it. You are here for nothing of the sort.

You are here to educate yourselves, and education is not learning how to perform a social function. "Society," no doubt, will make demands upon you soon enough, and you may find yourself (like the rest of us) a wretched cog in some vast machine which asks only that you perform what is called your function. But that is not what you have come here to learn; you have come here to get acquainted with truth and error, not with merely what is and what is not serviceable to a lunatic productivist society.[12] (333–334)

I wonder if the LSE director knew that Oakeshott, typically caricatured as an apologist for the Tories, would begin his orientation speech with a critique of capitalism![13]

Throughout his remarks, Oakeshott is driving home the point that stance matters. To illustrate, let's imagine a diverse group of people at a museum. The group includes an eager first-time visitor, a young artist sketching a favorite painting, an art-world connoisseur making the rounds, a graduate student applying critical theory, a donor cutting the ribbon for the new wing, a rival museum director sizing up the competition, and a security expert inspecting the alarm system.

While the GPS shows all of them at the same location, they are not truly occupying the same space. The connoisseur stands in a hall of mirrors, ringed by reflections of his own cultural capital. The grad student finds herself behind enemy lines, surrounded by hegemony. For the donor, the gallery is a big trophy case; for the rival director, a portfolio; for the security expert, a vault. It is likely only the artist and the first-timer who have begun to travel with the paintings into the variety of worlds they open. For the others, even while they stand in its midst, the museum remains closed.[14]

Similarly, you can be dropped off at college, move into the dorm, attend classes, ace exams, complete requirements, and toss your mortarboard . . . without ever arriving at the university as a *place of learning*. Oakeshott titled his remarks "On Arriving at a University," and the gerund is important. While these students have already arrived on campus, arriving at a university will require an intentional process. Though they are new at LSE, these are inveterate students; without an intervention, they are likely to assimilate learning to studenting.[15] Oakeshott reserves the term "learning" for the active and reflective pursuit of our formation. To be a learner is to accept the "responsibility of self-definition" and embark on "adventures in human self-understanding."[16] By contrast, what I am calling "studenting" is the familiar business of navigating the bureaucratic structures set up to make sure that you are progressing through degree requirements.

Admittedly, this contrast seems both romantic and reductive. Of course universities need to have some way of organizing and tracking student progress. Why assume that this credentialing function warps or supersedes learning? And why should we accept this monolithic picture of student life? Standing on the quad, we see students heading every which way, taking different classes, pursuing a range of majors, working on a variety of projects. The Oakeshottian response to this is that we must gain some distance before this scatterplot reveals its underlying linearity. To help us defamiliarize contemporary higher education, Oakeshott develops three untimely ideas: a distinction between instrumental and liberal learning, a recovery of the ancient notion of *skholê*, and a reversal of our received ideas about insularity. Let's explore each in turn.

★   ★   ★

Oakeshott is the first to acknowledge the value of instrumental learning, appreciating both its diversity and its depth. He applauds the way we proliferate practices from contract law to contract bridge, pipefitting to periodontics, midwifery to mortuary science. He finds it wonderful that we have "schools where one may learn to cook, to drive an automobile or to run a bassoon factory."[17] In the "vast variety of instrumental . . . practices," Oakeshott sees both constant innovation ("A human art is never fixed and finished") and genuine understanding ("To learn an instrumental art is not merely being trained to perform a trick").[18] Even so called "physical education"— Oakeshott gives the example of gymnastics—involves apprenticing oneself to "an intellectual art."[19] Refusing to reduce instrumental practices to generic skill sets, Oakeshott insists that the "arts and practices we share with one another are nowhere to be found save in the understandings of living, individual adepts who have learned them."[20] In communities of practice, we learn not only procedures and skills, but languages of description, modes of relation, and even ideals of conduct.[21] Thus, Oakeshott credits his "Sergeant gymnastics instructor" as the first person to show him the meaning of "patience, accuracy, economy, elegance and style."[22]

Oakeshott has only one concern about instrumental learning, but it is a big one. It stems from his reading of the human condition as one of inevitable parochialism. Recall the passage we considered in the prologue: "Each of us is born in a corner of the earth and at a particular moment of historic time, lapped round with locality."[23] Thus, we pursue our formation "not in some abstract, ideal world, but in the local world we inhabit."[24] By the time we are self-aware, what we are aware of is a self that is already defined by "its place in . . . an identifiable mode of imagining," by its ability to "move about in an appropriate way among images of a certain kind."[25] We inherit local dialects, as it were, of "sensing, perceiving, feeling, desiring, thinking, believing, contemplating, supposing, knowing, preferring, approving, laughing, crying, dancing, loving, singing, making hay, devising mathematical demonstrations, and so on."[26] Whether we are from the twelfth century or the twenty-first century, whether we hail from Paris or Provincetown, we are all provincial.

Parochial though it may be, each corner of the earth comes richly appointed. One finds nuance in its language of appreciation, depth in its inventory of desirables, complexity in its arts of production. There are always new models to get and new ways of getting them. In every local world, life can become, as it were, all consuming. And so we might never even notice that the persistent instrumental question, "How do we get what we (happen to have already learned to) want?," begs the more fundamental question of what is worth wanting. What is truly worth wanting to have, to participate in, to achieve, to become? This is liberal learning's defining question, but it is an inevitably fugitive one. It can be discovered, and it can be rediscovered, but it cannot be left running, as it were, like a fountain. "It has taken many shocks of awareness," Maxine Greene writes, "for me to realize how I existed within a tradition . . . as within a container."[27] Liberal learning begins again each time we confront the fact that we have shrunk reality to the circumference of our horizons, that there are other ways of world-making, that our worlds may be reworked.

The question is how to get this project off the ground. For we are apt to approach the scene of learning instrumentally. If someone asks you to give them a huge sum of money—not to mention four years of your life—it is understandable that you would expect an answer to the question, What is this good for? The problem is that any ordinary response will be self-defeating. The educator is being asked to demonstrate the value of liberal learning in terms the student already recognizes. In effect, the student is asking, How does liberal education help me get what I have already learned to want? This is impossible to answer, since the value of liberal learning lies precisely in its ability to interrupt this question-begging, instrumental posture, to reopen the question, What is worth wanting? At the end of the process, Greene is grateful to have learned that what she thought was the world was but one container within it. But that doesn't make it an easy sell. Here is the kind of extensive and illuminating dialogue we can expect at the threshold of liberal learning:

> EARNEST LIBERAL EDUCATOR: It is valuable and interesting to crack open containers and build passages between them. I can't wait to share this experience with you.
>
> CITIZEN OF CONTAINERLAND: Huh?

We seem to be stuck in a vicious circle: since the educational imagination is itself cramped, we need liberal learning in order to become aware of the possibility of liberal learning.

Given that liberal education does occur in various places, sometimes even in universities, its logical impossibility must be overstated. So what's the solution? Basically, you need to dodge the question while keeping the conversation going. The trick is to bring students along to the point where they shift from looking at liberal learning from their old vantage point to looking at everything, including their old vantage point, from new angles.[28] But let us not minimize the difficulties of unlearning, as if scales just suddenly fall from our eyes.[29] As Plato was the first to point out, if we do manage to turn the soul toward undiscovered aspects of reality, we initially see less, not more.[30] And no one likes to be partially blinded. We should not be surprised, Socrates says, if the person we have reoriented is "pained and angry at being treated this way."[31]

A classic psychology experiment illustrates just how uncomfortable we feel when stuck between gestalts.[32] A set of playing cards was doctored so that some of the hearts were black, some of the clubs red, and so on. Participants were asked to identify a random sequence of cards, some normal and some color-reversed (or "incongruous"). Each card was displayed repeatedly until recognized, at durations stepping up from 10 to 1000 milliseconds. The findings illustrate just how hard it is for us to sit with ambiguity, and how crafty we can be at preempting it. The most common response was obliviousness. Participants simply failed to perceive the incongruities, often repeatedly so. One participant perceived the black three of hearts as a three of spades through twenty-four consecutive exposures, another through forty-four straight viewings.[33] Participants also hallucinated compromises. Red spades and clubs were described variously as brown, purple, rusty, "olive drab," blurred, reddish but blackening, black on a reddish card, black with red edges, black but cast in a red or yellow light, and so on.[34] Finally, some participants experienced a breakdown of their ability to perceive the card in any coherent way. The experimenters noted not only gross perceptual failures (e.g., an inability to count the number of pips on the card) but strong affective responses. One participant blurted out, "I don't know what the hell it is now, not even sure whether it is a playing card."[35] Another, when shown a red spade card for a full 300 milliseconds, began to unravel before the experimenters' eyes: "I can't make the suit out, whatever it is. It didn't even look like a card that time. I don't know what color it is now or whether it's a spade or a heart. I'm not even sure what a spade looks like! My God!"[36]

There are ways to mitigate these risks, including hospitality, humility, and a sense of humor. You can ask your students what they need to be comfortable in this new place and try to provide it. You can explain that people who dig tunnels between containers are themselves a strange tribe. You can tell stories of your own container navigation, sharing how you have managed to cut out some windows and why you enjoy the view. And you can fess up that, just like everyone else, you still like to spend most of your time cozying up with warm cup of familiarity. Transformative educators can also take comfort in the fact that their students will arrive already feeling some dissatisfaction with their corner of the earth, since every container language simplifies, distorts, or simply redacts crucial dimensions of experience. Even as we take our world to be *the* world, we sometimes manage to tune into wavelengths that fall between the local stations. And we find ourselves looking for some way to boost the signal. John Donne understood this search for expanded articulation, understood that a container can be both a comfort and a coffin. For now, let's give him the last word on why liberal learning matters:

> To know and feele all this, and not to have
> Words to expresse it, makes a man a grave
> Of his owne thoughts . . . [37]

* ★ *

So Oakeshott is trying to help his audience begin to stretch their imaginations about what a university education might be so that they can go on to stretch their imaginations about everything else.[38] If we wanted to be fancy, we could call it meta-liberal-learning. I prefer "deprogramming." Three times in the first four pages, Oakeshott pleads with his audience to "forget" something they have been told (333, 334, 336). To the idea that their task is to fulfill the requirements of a major, Oakeshott counters:

> You are not here to get a degree—that is a by-product. Nor are you here to "follow a course." A university is a place where you educate yourselves and one another, and that is what you are here to do. (336–337)

In response to the idea that students are like a professional guild, Oakeshott counters that

> you are members of something much more like a confraternity of strolling players—to which I am, also, glad to belong. The police sometimes move us on; but we are tolerated, and to live in an area of toleration is much pleasanter than having a niche in society. (334)

In passages such as these, we find Oakeshott working to interrupt that familiar stance, the grind. When it is time to name the alternative, he reaches for an ancient Greek term, *skholê*. As Oakeshott points out, the typical rendering of *skholê* in English is "leisure," "but it is a lame translation" (335). For us, leisure is just the inversion of modern, alienated labor, "a holiday designed to make us work better when it is over, or merely . . . 'work' of another sort."[39] Leisure suggests dissipation of focus and relaxation of effort, all in the service of readying us for our impending return to the grind. By contrast, *skholê* "is at once a discipline and a release," involving a "continuous and exacting redirection of attention."[40] One experiences *skholê* not as empty but as "fully occupied."[41]

The untranslatability of this untimely concept thus exposes a blind spot in our understanding of effort and activity. We have a tendency to assume that we are "doing nothing," Oakeshott explains, unless we are "contributing to that blessed 4% per annum increase in productivity."[42] In moments like this, Oakeshott is working to trouble the image of ourselves as *Homo laborans*, "a creature composed entirely of wants, who understands the world merely as the means of satisfying those wants."[43] For Oakeshott, "there is something lacking in this happiness and something unsatisfying to human beings in this satisfaction."[44] Oakeshott explains:

> It is not only that everything that is produced in satisfaction of a want rapidly perishes, or that many wants demand recurrent satisfactions, but that the satisfaction

of every want generates a new want that in turn calls for satisfaction. Doing, and the attitude to the world it entails, is (as the hymn says) "a deadly thing." It is an activity of getting and spending, of making and consuming, endlessly.[45]

Caught in this endless cycle, Oakeshott concludes, *Homo laborans* "is a creature of unavoidable anxieties."[46]

No one denies the need to unwind, nor the pleasures of goofing off. However, in reaching for the concept of *skholê*, Oakeshott suggests that college represents the greater gift of being "freed for a moment from the curse of Adam, the burdensome distinction between work and play."[47] Labor is a burden demanding rest and recovery. It is, however, also a burden to move through life under the weight of thinking that we might be nothing more than what we see of ourselves when spending or spent. It is the lifting of this second burden, Oakeshott suggests, that makes college such a gift.

"The characteristic gift of the university," Oakeshott declares, "is the gift of an *interval*."[48] With this awkward word, Oakeshott is gesturing toward the idea of an episode with its own temporal-educational logic. Clearly, undergraduate education is neither a beginning nor an end: "No man begins his education at the university, he begins it in the nursery; and a man's formative years are not at an end when he takes his degree."[49] But neither is it well described as the middle of some continuous process of schooling, socialization, or career preparation. "Whenever an ulterior purpose of this sort makes its appearance," Oakeshott insists, "education (which is concerned with persons, not functions) steals out of the back door with noiseless steps."[50] College education is concerned with personhood, with individuals working out the direction of their formation, the terms of their self-understanding, the compass of their freedom. It is this existential frame that helps us understand Oakeshott's cryptic term, "interval." It is an "interim"[51] inserted between two main chapters of our lives, when one has simultaneously been emancipated from the "the frustrations of childhood" and granted a "merciful postponement of having to take up the often dreary responsibilities of an adult."[52]

Conventional wisdom has it that adolescence represents a transition from the carefree days of childhood to the responsibilities of adulthood. Oakeshott rejects this view, observing a deep continuity between our school days and our working lives. College represents not a transition between but an alternative to two different forms of what is ultimately a single existential mode, the grind. Experiences of self-direction and "flow" are the exception. Schoolchildren and adult workers alike usually find themselves driven by necessity, performing for others, and laboring in an alienated, timeclock mode.[53] By contrast, college represents a "reprieve from the 'rat race.'"[54] It allows a "release from old commitments entered into in the semi-conscious years of childhood, and the absence of haste to contract new ones."[55] It offers a glimpse of life as something other than an endless cycle of "getting and spending," a glimpse of yourself as something other than a hamster in a wheel.[56]

Thus, Oakeshott imagines college as a wedge between two periods of our lives ruled by necessity, prying open a temporary experience of *skholê*:

> Here is a break in the tyrannical course of irreparable events; a period in which to look round upon the world and upon oneself without the sense of an enemy at one's back or the insistent pressure to make up one's mind; a moment in which to taste the mystery without the necessity of at once seeking a solution.[57]

★   ★   ★

If you told readers unfamiliar with Oakeshott that his writings on education appeared in the "fifties and sixties," they might well think that you meant the 1850s.[58] He seems closer to Newman's *The Idea of the University* (1854) than to the Open University (founded in 1969). Oakeshott's contemporaries were calling for an expanded university, one that enrolled more diverse students, included new sources of knowledge, engaged contemporary social issues, and provided a wider variety of more practical majors (needed by a more economically diverse student body). By contrast, Oakeshott warned of the dangers of expansion, extolled the virtues of a centuries-old tradition of humane letters, railed against presentism, and stressed the tensions between liberal and instrumental learning. Then there is his disconcerting claim that "there is something properly and unavoidably 'cloistered' about a university."[59] The scare quotes suggest that Oakeshott is not ready to fully embrace a monastic conception of undergraduate education. Still, the imagery of detachment, seclusion, and shelter runs throughout his educational writings.[60] To celebrate universities in this way, as "places apart," flies in the face of what are now well-accepted ideas: campuses inevitably reflect surrounding cultures, academic inquiry is shaped by the prejudices of the day, and institutions of higher education in every era have served economic and political functions.[61] Even if isolation were possible, it would be undesirable, since contemporary social issues can enlarge and reinvigorate fusty disciplines. If we grant these points, as we should, must we then dismiss Oakeshott as a kind of academic survivalist, holing himself up with his rhetorical weapons in what remains of the ivory tower? While there is a grain of truth in this image, it is important to get clear on what Oakeshottian detachment is all about.

It is hard not to read Oakeshott's talk of detachment and shelter as nostalgia for college gates and pristine quads, as a reactionary wish for an enclave in which the privileged might enjoy undisturbed the addition of a few final coats of polish to groom them for polite society and the halls of power. While I am convinced that this is not what he had in mind, Oakeshott was undeniably ambivalent about the rapid democratization of higher education occurring during his lifetime.[62] I speak of ambivalence rather than pure aversion because, even in his earliest writings on education, we find him anticipating the charge of classism and taking pains to qualify his claims that liberal learning is a "luxury," a "privilege," a "gift," and a form of "leisure." It is a luxury, "but not in the sense that it is superfluous to all but the very sophisticated."[63] It is not a tithe but an unexpected gift that "inspires . . . gratitude" and "is understood as a repeated summons rather than a possession, an engagement rather than an heirloom."[64] It is a privilege, "but it does not depend on any definable pre-existing privilege or upon the absence of the necessity of earning one's living in the end."[65] It is not "something suitable only to a 'leisured class.'"[66] Indeed, logic dictates that it is not suitable to such a class at all, since liberal learning represents the gift of an interval, the offer of an unexpected period of *release* from the grind.

Though his progress is hampered by his own class anxieties, Oakeshott eventually arrives at an unqualifiedly universal argument for liberal learning.[67] "So valuable is this experience," Oakeshott declares in his 1967 Calgary lecture, "that I would not know how to deny it to anybody."[68] The syntax here is certainly suggestive, as if Oakeshott would like to justify exclusive admissions but simply cannot find a defensible principle. However, by the late essays, Oakeshott has graduated from a weak rejection of exclusivity to a strong defense of universality. Liberal learning is rooted not in the prerogatives of a particular class but in the predicament in which all human beings find themselves. All of us must respond "gaily or reluctantly, reflectively or not so reflectively, to the ordeal of consciousness."[69] We must make sense of ourselves through the hermeneutic resources (languages and locations, practices and traditions, histories and exemplars) that we find in and seek from our corner of the earth. But neither the meanings of these formative resources nor the relationships among them is simply given. These must be discerned through particular (and peculiar) efforts at understanding. As Oakeshott puts it, "A human being is condemned to be a learner," because "everything is *known* to him in terms of what it *means* to him," and "meanings have to be learned."[70]

Thus, liberal learning is a birthright, but not of a gentlemanly class. Indeed, even as they prepare another round of ringers, the Eton's and Andover's may breed a certain numbness to the need for liberal learning. Oakeshott suggests that, if anything, this need may be more keenly felt "upon the banks of the Wabash, in the hills of Cumberland, in a Dresden suburb or a Neapolitan slum."[71] While Oakeshott's geography of marginalization needs updating, there is sense in his claim that life on the margins "nurture[s] a disposition to recognize" the value of liberal learning whose

> reward is an emancipation from the mere 'fact of living', from the immediate contingencies of place and time of birth, from the tyranny of the moment and from the servitude of a merely current condition; it is the reward of a human identity and of a character capable in some measure of the moral and intellectual adventure which constitutes a specifically human life.[72]

This is the egalitarian implication of Oakeshott's reading of the human condition: liberal learning is not a special privilege; it is a human requirement.

Why then does Oakeshott balk at opening up the university? In Oakeshott's judgment, the expansion of the university is primarily an excuse for its ever further transformation into a credential distribution machine. Oakeshott is pointing out what amounts to a societal sleight of hand: we leap from the unquestionable premise that college is a good too valuable to hoard to the unrelated conclusion that everyone deserves a chance to queue up for a valuable ticket into the labor market. What Oakeshott wants for the kid from Naples or Indiana is the chance to experience the gift of an interval. Far from granting wider access to the experience of *skholê*, this bait-and-switch makes it increasingly difficult for anyone to attain the existential goods of college.

Worse, it turns out that there was a second bait-and-switch hidden within the first. First, credentialing replaces the quest for self-understanding. However, the credential is not the BA itself but a branded diploma, and it is precisely selectivity that secures this college-name-brand-recognition.

Thus, precisely to the degree to which higher education becomes enmeshed with credentialing it becomes a "positional good," one that is "valuable to some people only on condition that others do not have it."[73] In a positional market, increased access leads to increased stratification, which is precisely what we see in higher education.[74] While much is made of the financial rewards of various majors, institutional selectivity proves to be a much clearer predictor of future earnings.[75] There is nothing egalitarian about widening access if the newly admitted are accommodated by adding dilapidated cars to the back of the train, creating undergraduate "Tailies" as in the vivid class allegory, *Snowpiercer*.[76] Indeed, it is likely that expanded, stratified access increases inequality, since higher enrollments further cement the social norm that college is the proper way to establish one's merit on the job market, devaluing noncollege routes.[77]

In my view, while Oakeshott should have been much more worried about expanding the community of existential learners, he was not wrong to be skeptical of the idea that egalitarianism lay behind the version of expansion we underwent. Some have gotten rich through the massification of higher education, but not the masses.[78] Perhaps Oakeshott was writing for neither 1950 nor 1850, but for 2050. Consider David Blacker's recent observation that there may be an educational silver lining in the storm cloud of late capitalism.[79] Blacker certainly does not minimize the damage from the whirlwind, from social upheaval and existential disorientation to economic precarity and ecological peril. As an increasingly automated capital ransacks the planet for a last carbon fix, it turns out that "planned obsolescence awaits not just our consumer goods but we ourselves as well" (13). On this point, Blacker quotes the dark prediction of Yuval Noah Harari: "By 2050 a new class of people might emerge—the useless class. People who are not just unemployed but unemployable" (17). There is no sugarcoating this experience of being consigned to an "outcast humanity," of having to confront a "vertiginous uselessness whose implications threaten everything to which we have become accustomed" (35). For one thing, it means cutting loose the vocational anchors of our identity. For another, Blacker writes, it means letting go of the mythos of education-fueled, meritocratic social mobility:

> Stay in school, study hard and get ahead. "Maybe you will get ahead, maybe you won't" is now the only honest response to this zombie mantra. A few

will, to be sure, a few are still needed and will be for some time. But fewer and fewer. In the American experience this tectonic change in education's relation to the economy is all the more worrisome because it threatens to sever the long-cherished presumed linkage between educational effort and social position. This has long been a core legitimating ideal of our quasi-meritocracy: positions in society are deserved because of an individual's virtue, talent and hard work, etc. rather than merely guaranteed to them in the feudal sense via heredity. (11)

For some two centuries, formal education has profited by defining itself as an economic investment. However, live by the sword (of economic utility), die by the sword. As the economic argument crumbles, education enters an ever deeper legitimation crisis. Strange as it may seem, this is where the silver lining comes in. For the apotheosis of the "economy-education nexus" reveals its true nature (16). Guided by "no regulative image of the type of person it wishes to foster," our schools and colleges are "axiologically directionless" (24). As "this twilight of our institutional idols deepens," what stands revealed is their abiding nihilism (16). Though unpleasant, this insight is liberating. "With the yoke of economic utility shucked off," Blacker suggests, "our schools and colleges may now be freer to remake themselves in a different image" (10). "Without economic utility preempting every conversation and restricting every horizon," he explains, "there could be a mini-philosophical renaissance where alternative aims and purposes are considered" (13). Education could become "aesthetic or discovery oriented" or "humanistic in the classical sense of promoting a specific vision of the human good, a paideia" (13). Thus, if the planet will still support us, we may find something surprising at the end of the treacherous road to the post-work economy: education rededicated to questions of meaning and purpose.

Thus, it is quite far from obvious that Oakeshott's call for *skholê* and his critique of instrumentalism is the inegalitarian option here. It is true, Oakeshott was not particularly interested in social mobility. But neither is the jobbified university. Increased access is a powerful slogan, but the question is what we are accessing. Expanding the "sorting machine" serves capital, not the *demos*. What the people need, in important part, are spaces in which to make sense of their liquified identities and articulate inhabitable social imaginaries.

This is the reading of Oakeshott and his reorientation that I prefer, as an invitation to rethink the economy-education nexus in our "lunatic productivist society."[80] What first appears as a call for insular universities, for privilege preserving enclaves, turns out to be a call for universities still capable of interrupting our insularity. Such an untimely university would serve as a conservatory of practices and resources for raising and reraising that annoying and indispensable question, what is worth wanting?[81] Unless this question is to be preempted by the instrumentalist's hasty question—what is this good for?—there must be some buffer between the place of learning and the marketplace. There is no drive-through version of *skholê*. All Oakeshott asks for is a speed bump on the way to the quad.

You don't need me to tell you what education is. Everybody really knows that education . . . is the process of waking up to life. . . . It takes a heap of resolve to keep from going to sleep in the middle of the show. It's not that we want to sleep our lives away. It's that it requires certain kinds of energy, certain capacities for taking the world into our consciousness, certain real powers of body and soul to be a match for reality.

—MC Richards[1]

WIDE AWAKE: AESTHETIC EDUCATION
AT BLACK MOUNTAIN COLLEGE

It was the early hours of the morning west of the little sleeping town of
Black Mountain ("altitude 2,400 feet" read the road marker) nestled in the
Swannanoa Valley, when we spotted the hand-painted BLACK MOUN-
TAIN COLLEGE sign with its directional arrow along a country road.
—Michael Rumaker[2]

THE ROAD TO BLACK MOUNTAIN

Let's try a thought experiment. Imagine a place where general education
is more than a slogan, a college built from the ground up to foster the
development of the whole person. Here, faculty are recruited not to fill
departmental slots but to exemplify the quest for dynamic, integrated personhood. Students are greeted with the expectation that this is a place to
confront and cultivate oneself. The faculty and students do not see themselves as the employees and clients of a going concern: they are the college,
a self-governing community of experienced and novice learners. The ethos
here is experimental. The community has come together to learn from,
rather than act out, the stubborn educational antinomies between work and
play, compulsion and license, the social and the individual, the academic
and the existential. To clear space for this new venture, these poets of the
pedagogical overturn many of the basic constraints built into the grammar
of higher education, asking, for example, What if interdisciplinarity were
a starting point rather than a later bridging? How can we reunite the arts
and the liberal arts? How would the culture shift if faculty attended each
other's classes? What if requirements and grades were replaced with careful
individual advisement and culminating exams? What happens when you
reject the distinction between the curricular and the extracurricular? The
result is an (extra)curriculum that nurtures the connections between head

and hands, thinking and feeling, reflection and action, facts and values, knowledge and self-knowledge.[3] This community of learners prizes *soul action* in all of its forms and pursues it in every setting. Debating claims and declaiming poems, planting crops and sharing meals, constructing buildings and performing plays, interpreting texts and balancing budgets, faculty and students together encounter, educate, and enact their many-sided natures.

In the shadow of the contemporary university, it is hard to conjure even a blurry picture of such an integrated and integrating institution. And yet, as I will show, just such a place once existed. From 1933 to 1957, in the Blue Ridge Mountains near Asheville, North Carolina, there flourished a brilliant (and flawed and fragile) experiment, a community wholeheartedly devoted to the rigors and rewards of formative higher education.[4] In Black Mountain College (BMC) we have a concrete, historical example to sharpen our imaginations, a living reminder of a road not taken.

As the epigraph from Rumaker suggests, even during its time the road to Black Mountain was hard to find. Now the turnoff is further obscured by an overgrowth of nostalgia. And who wouldn't be starstruck by a college whose advisory council included John Dewey, Albert Einstein, Carl Jung, and William Carlos Williams and whose alumni and faculty formed a twentieth-century who's who in education (John Andrew Rice, Albert William Levi, and Paul Goodman), architecture and design (Walter Gropius, Josef Albers, and Buckminster Fuller), textile work (Anni Albers and Ruth Asawa), pottery (Karen Karnes and Shoji Hamada), photography (Hazel Larsen Archer, Harry Callahan, and Barbara Morgan), letters/criticism (Anaïs Nin, Eric Bentley, and Clement Greenberg), poetry (Robert Creeley, Edward Dorn, Robert Duncan, and Charles Olson), music (Heinrich Jalowetz, David Tudor, Stefan Wolpe, and Lou Harrison), dance (Merce Cunningham, Viola Farber, and Paul Taylor), theater (Arthur Penn and Xanti Schawinsky), neo-Dadaism (John Cage, Ray Johnson, and Robert Rauschenberg), and painting (Lionel Feininger, Helen Frankenthaler, Franz Kline, Elaine de Kooning, Willem de Kooning, Jacob Lawrence, Robert Motherwell, Kenneth Noland, and Cy Twombly).[5] Everything written about BMC risks becoming the next issue of the fan-club newsletter.

Tempting or not, such hagiography obscures our vision of the not-insignificant difficulties and dysfunctions of BMC.[6] Worse, it directs our gaze in the wrong direction. Even if we want to praise BMC for the quality of the people it attracted and nurtured, we do not want to equate that quality with gallery sales. At Black Mountain, aesthetic education was understood as general education. The goal was not to groom professional artists, Josef Albers quips, but to foster "living human beings, or in other words, professionals of life."[7] Occasionally, it is good to remind ourselves that there is no correlation between well-lived lives and Google hits.

Consider three central BMC figures I left off my who's who list. The soul of BMC's middle years was faculty member MC Richards. While Richards is probably famous enough to make the list, I wouldn't know in which category to place her. She was respected as a translator, poet, and potter, beloved as a teacher of literature and writing, and influential as a holistic educator and countercultural icon. However, what makes her truly exemplary is the way that her pursuit of personal integrity and a decent life led her to traverse and combine these different pursuits.[8] Or consider two of the liveliest students from BMC's later years: the poet, photographer, and publisher, Jonathan Williams; and the writer, visual artist, and prison educator, Fielding Dawson. Neither of these polymaths quite makes the who's who list. Williams is not anthologized like Olson, Creeley, and Duncan; and Dawson was recently described as the "best St. Louis writer you've never read."[9] Dawson himself is reported to have commented on the fame of certain BMC grads, "We were all famous, you just have never heard of us."[10] But, as with Richards, the soul action of each resonates in the intensity, diversity, and dignity of their attachments.[11] And, relatively speaking, these are still very public lives. Many BMC graduates left no such records.[12] Hagiography, then, not only edits out the vices but also distorts the virtues.

The trick is to remove Black Mountain College from its pedestal without lowering it all of the way into the dustheap of history. Those of us who want to argue that the example of BMC can help us revive and reorient contemporary higher education are likely to be met with disbelief: How could a college this small and short-lived possibly provide a model for contemporary higher education?[13] After all, the college existed for less than a quarter century, was never accredited, and served in total about 1,200 students.[14] How could such a model ever be scaled up, the skeptic asks, and why bother, since it proved unsustainable? While it is not usually recommended to begin on the defensive, I think it is best to address these objections up front. Not only will this help me make the case that BMC is worthy of our attention, but it will serve as a good introduction—for, as it turns out, issues of scale and longevity go right to the heart of what the Black Mountain was about.

⋆   ⋆   ⋆

Can you believe that something that would be so fluorescent could be so small?
—Charles Olson[15]

Let us begin with scale. Was BMC just a curiosity, a hothouse flower, too
small to be relevant to higher education today? Anticipating this dismissive
reaction, college leadership often tackled it head-on.[16] For example, address-
ing the BMC community in 1941, after a semester visiting at Harvard,
Albers acknowledged the striking contrast. Harvard could boast of a library
with six million volumes; BMC's makeshift library held only eight thousand. Harvard had a faculty in the hundreds and students in the thousands;
BMC was a community of only "seventy students and twenty teachers."
Harvard was "a place proud of a three centuries' tradition"; BMC was a
fledgling venture. And yet, Albers concludes in his typically understated
manner, "it was not discouraging for me to compare [Harvard's] status after
three hundred years with the status of another educational place which has
existed for only 8 years, an institution in which I believe."[17]

Bill Levi would return to this theme in his 1947 welcoming address.
Where Albers tells a David and Goliath story, Levi's tale is closer to *Gargantua
and Pantagruel*.[18] The giants of higher education, Levi suggests, are suffering
from what Louis Brandeis called "the curse of bigness." Their large size is
not so much programmatic as symptomatic, a sign of our "obsessive urge to
expand," the valuing of quantity over quality, and a "spiral of educational
inflation."[19] As Levi explains, whereas BMC continues to experiment to
discover what conditions actually best foster growth, Gargantua U "cannot
afford to ask the question, how large ought an educational community to
be?"[20] To wit: "Their gigantic plants, their enormous overhead costs, their
top-heavy administrative machinery automatically answer the question
for them."[21] To drive this point home, Levi turns, in Rabelaisian fashion,
to the topic of toilets. Imagine that a large university—he uses Yale as an
example—did treat the issue of scale as an open question and came to the
conclusion that the ideal size for an educational community was 250 souls.
Given how rapidly unused plumbing deteriorates, Levi calculates that Yale
would have to hire three full-time employees "just to flush the toilets in the
empty buildings between Yale Station and Chapel Street."[22]

I think that Levi is right to read the reflexive dismissal of small educational experiments as symptomatic, as an evasion of a genuine question

about the relative affordances of smaller and larger institutions. It is striking that those who object that an intentional community such as BMC cannot be scaled up to serve the multitudes are not more bothered by the fact that our current, large-scale institutions are so deeply unintentional and uncommunal. Black Mountain did not fail to achieve bigness. Small size was an intentional feature of this intentional community, flowing directly from its ambition to integrate living and learning and its credo that education is an interaction between persons in process. Historian Martin Duberman, expanding on a remark by Rice, captures the principle well:

> A central aim was to keep the community small enough so that members could constantly interact in a wide variety of settings—not only at meals, but on walks, in classes, at community meetings, work programs, dances, performances, whatever. Individual lifestyles, in all their peculiar detail, could thereby be observed, challenged, imitated, rejected—which is, after all, how most learning proceeds, rather than through formal instruction. "You're seeing people under all circumstances daily," as Rice put it, "and after a while you get to a point where you don't mind being seen yourself, and that's a fine moment."[23]

One hopes that within our massive multiversities and conventional colleges there exist at least some such pockets of genuine community, some spaces of self-disclosure and mutual recognition. The founders of Black Mountain were not willing to leave this to chance.

Let us gather the testimony of two more BMC luminaries who spent their careers thinking about issues of scale: Charles Olson and Buckminster Fuller.[24] In a talk about BMC a dozen years after it closed, Olson found himself returning repeatedly to the question of scale. Like Levi, Olson questioned the "bigger is better" logic, suggesting to his auditors that their perception of scale might be warped by inhabiting a system of higher education that had (circa 1970) "bombed out" over the past two decades to an enrollment of six million.[25] How could they even comprehend, he wondered, a college that "never had in one moment of time more than 150 people, and at the time I got there it was running just above seventy-five." "What does it do to your minds," he asked, "I mean that kind of unit of size"? He muses that it will "bend their idea" if they try to fathom "the amount of water" in that tiny "spoon." Fuller was also struck by how much was packed into so little, describing Black Mountain as a "'dwarf star' college during its most brilliant world-around sighted 'nova' period."[26]

*   *   *

A quiet harbor is a pleasant place. But the moment we think we have arrived,
we will be dead. Can we be sure that we will be treated as the dead should be?
By no means. The deader an institution is, the more tenacious it is of existence.
—John Andrew Rice[27]

Longevity is another issue that cuts both ways. Does the fact that Black Mountain folded after twenty-four years prove the unworkability of its model? The
college certainly had its flaws. It struggled financially from its first days until
its last. Another factor was BMC's governance model and intense culture. Its
penchant for charismatic leadership combined with a commitment to collective decision-making (through gatherings that were part seminar, part town
hall, part Quaker meeting, and part encounter group) led to burnout, not to
mention repeated schisms and excommunications. For two decades, the college showed a remarkable ability to rebound with a fresh wave of fundraising
and recruitment after each exodus, dip in enrollment, and financial crisis. In
the fifties, this elasticity finally gave out. As Black Mountain began to retract
into something closer to a writer's colony, it could no longer outrun its debt.[28]

However, it is one thing to admit that the college's flaws contributed to
its relatively short life and another to conclude that it was therefore a failure. This assumes that longevity is an unalloyed good in higher education,
an assumption that BMC contested from the start. It was not precarity its
founders feared but that "Black Mountain [would] go the way of most institutions, achieving codification at the sense of aliveness."[29] All institutions die,
Rice suggests in the epigraph; the question is whether they are "treated as the
dead should be." A decade and a half later, Levi would strike the same chord:

> It seems almost contradictory to speak of the *life of an institution*. New ventures
> live only *until* they become institutions. It is at that point that hardening of the
> arteries sets in, that primitive adventure has become mere routine, that former
> energy has turned into living death.[30]

Levi overstates his point for emphasis. As Alasdair MacIntyre rightly points
out, even healthy practices depend on institutional support. But MacIntyre
would agree with Rice and Levi that this potentially symbiotic relationship
often turns parasitic. What ensues is a confusion of means and ends.[31] Though
the practice withers, its purposive language is retained to disguise the inflation of means into ends, like the Latin college motto inscribed on a shot glass

for sale in the bookstore. Like Rice and Levi, I tend to fear the zombification of institutions more than I do the mortality of practices. For BMC, renouncing the bid for permanence was a small price to pay for twenty-four years of genuine aliveness. One hopes to sustain the vitality of our educational ventures. But when it comes down to it, it is better to be dead than undead.

Indeed, it was not just a matter of accepting precarity as a necessary evil. There was a positive ethos of impermanence at Black Mountain. From its founding to its final days, this was an educational community keenly attuned to what Hannah Arendt calls "natality," the human capacity to initiate, to begin anew, to surprise ourselves and others through words and deeds that scratch across the grooves of convention and repetition.[32] Academia is not unaware of this existential principle. Convocation, commencement, and sabbatical are all intended as rituals of renewal, and even summer and winter breaks serve to signal the possibility of a fresh start. But rituals themselves demand renewal lest they become rote. Sabbatical, for example, has become just another gear to the grind, rather than a reminder of the scholar's need for *skholē*.[33] And commencement, as you have no doubt heard, has become the first day of the rest of your cliché. Perversely, rituals meant to remind us that we are beings in process can themselves easily become inert structures, dead conventions.

Rice knew that fixity, natality's foe, had entrenched itself in the very grammar of educational thought, leading him (as narrated by Duberman) to an interesting architectural conclusion:

> the "educated man." What a term!, Rice scoffed: "educated" is "a perfect passive participle," perfect because it's over with, passive because you had nothing to do with it. . . . "Colleges should be in tents, and when they fold, they fold."[34]

A college that makes room for the natality of faculty and students, Rice suggests, must itself embody the provisional spirit that continually asks itself, What next? What are you going to do? Who are you going to be? And while BMC never quite resorted to tents, it did both preach and practice the idea that the college itself had each year to be reborn. Here is how Bob Wunsch welcomed students in the fall of 1943:

> I want to say now, at the beginning, that while we declare we are beginning the eleventh year of Black Mountain College, we are really beginning a new college. I think we must say this to ourselves each year, lest we begin to let the past become the dominant force in our lives, and already there are too many institutions throttled by the dead and the departed.[35]

Two years earlier, the college had moved across the valley to its new campus on Lake Eden. For its first eight years, BMC had rented the conference center of the YMCA Blue Ridge Assembly. Ideal in many respects, there was one major catch to this lease: the college had to fold up shop completely every spring and set up again each fall. By agreement, BMC had to clear everything from the buildings, storing all of its furniture and paraphernalia in the attic over the summer. This led to an annual fall ritual of unpacking and setting up anew. As Duberman describes, while this work was "arduous" it was also "psychologically valuable":

> The yearly reconstruction necessitated cooperation between the old and the new members, and also gave the new ones a tangible demonstration of the claim that each year the college started from scratch—and that all participated directly in providing its particular shape.[36]

In fact, the move to Lake Eden spelled more of a change than an end to this ritual. BMC now owned its 674-acre campus and could remain through the summer. But the existing buildings needed to be winterized and a new central building completed.[37] Writer May Sarton, who was a lecturer at BMC in 1940, vividly recalls this period of transition and construction as educative in its own right:

> The thing that holds Black Mountain together and keeps it from the phoniness I had feared is that they are building their new building with their own hands. . . . It is a great sight to see the trucks go down the mountains every afternoon filled with teachers and students, boys and girls. It is something hard to describe to watch Straus, the ex-German psychiatrist with a wonderful head of white hair throwing rocks to a young girl who throws them to a boy who sets them in the wall which others have prepared with a bed of cement. I helped on the wall one afternoon and felt happier at the end, more whole and ready for *thought* than I have in years. And how much better than putting all that into a football team! I don't know how colleges could be re-built . . . every . . . year but somehow or other that's what should happen. We simply cannot afford the intellectual slovenliness, immaturity, lack of reality, and sentimentality which the average college produces.[38]

Within a year or two, this beautiful new Studies Building (designed by Lawrence Kocher) had been completed, but there was to be no "quiet harbor" for Black Mountain College. With the stresses of the war years, intense debates over integration, mounting financial pressures, and further faculty schisms and departures, precarity remained a way of life at BMC throughout the forties.[39] And its final half-decade was even more precarious. However, for BMC's last rector, the poet Charles Olson, these final years do not tell a simple story of decline. In a pair of interviews just before his death in 1970, we find Olson still wrestling with the question of what it was exactly that he presided over in the college's final years.[40] In observing that "the ending of Black Mountain is as interesting as its founding," Olson is not making the banal point that both beginnings and endings are important for understanding a story.[41] He is saying that BMC's final days echoed its first, and that you cannot understand one without the other. Olson recalls this final period as days of "grits and hominy."[42] As the community dwindled and money ran out, the remaining few subsisted on what they could grow. Recalling Rice's camping metaphor, he concludes, "we were in that sense a tent."[43] Thus, Olson is inclined to view his selling off of the land as a return to BMC's itinerant beginnings as a renter, a reaffirmation of its ethos of impermanence.[44]

This interpretation is undeniably convenient. Coming from someone else, we might simply chalk it up to the rationalization of a guilty conscience. But this was Olson, the teacher whose mantra was Ezra Pound's "Make it new," the poet who became spokesman for the "open field" of "projective verse."[45] Olson did not adopt the rhetoric of impermanence because he was forced to shutter the campus: it was BMC's commitment to natality that drew him there in the first place.[46] In an autobiographical essay, written during a teaching leave in 1952, Olson produced this memorable calling card: "That is my profession. I am an archaeologist of morning."[47] Echoing the spirit of Arendt's philosophy of action, the projective-verse-like opening of Olson's essay reads:

> My shift is that I take the present as prologue, not the past. The instant, therefore. Is its own interpretation, as a dream is, and any action—a poem, for example. Down with causation (except, see below). And yrself: you, as the only reader and mover of the instant. You, the cause. No drag allowed, on either. Get on with it.[48]

Behavior has causes. If all you want to do is react and fall back on routines, you might as well delegate the task to the demographers (midcentury, positivistic sociology was a bugbear for Arendt and Olson alike), who can plot your course for you on their x-y axis.[49] But you also have it within yourself to act, to initiate. What are you waiting for? This is the question that Olson was always asking himself, his readers, and his students.

Indeed, like Rice, he posed this "what's next?" question to the college itself. Before closure appeared inevitable, Olson was already playing with the idea that Black Mountain might be evolving beyond its traditional campus model.[50] In one of his signature diagrammatic prose poems, Olson imagined a centrifugal Black Mountain College whose "federated operations" would include not only its traditional studios and institutes, but also a press, a journal, a theater, and an academy.[51] And indeed, many of these ventures came to fruition, with BMC's reach felt from San Francisco (Robert Duncan's theater group) to Mallorca (Robert Creeley's *Black Mountain Review*). In the late interviews, Olson is still talking excitedly about what Black Mountain became *after 1957* and about what it is still becoming. He rehearses how BMC emigres shaped other colleges and how BMC alums populated the painting scene in New York City.[52] He recalls how there was talk of new homes, for example occupying a floor of a skyscraper in New York City or setting up a beach campus in Venice, California.[53] He enthuses over new educational modalities such as a traveling seminar and a university of the airwaves.[54] He describes excitedly a plan drawn up by weaving instructor Tony Landreau, for a fully mobile Black Mountain College.[55] "There's three Black Mountains," Olson explains, "the Rice Black Mountain, the Albers Black Mountain, and this ragged-arse place that I and others were a part of."[56] But if campus life grew raggedy in those final years, Olson reads this not as disintegration of something solid but as the expression of a spirit that, while it had been truly nurtured by its "thought-earth" was now "reaching" beyond its home in the mountains.[57] The "tendency" of this "third Black Mountain," Olson hypothesizes, "was to find the world."[58]

On the question of longevity, then, we have discovered two possible readings. If we follow Olson's line of thinking, then BMC was not as short-lived as we thought. It is true that Black Mountain College settled its books in 1957 and the Lake Eden campus became Camp Rockmont for Boys. But there are more interesting ways to endure in history than as an unbroken charter. On Olson's reading, 1957 marks not an ending but a kind of transubstantiation, a dispersal of the soul action of BMC into new places and projects. Even if we accept 1957 as an ending date, we should still reject the notion that this represents a failure of longevity. Asked one too many times about the demise of the college, Richards rebuts the premise:

"Why did Black Mountain fail?", I am asked. It didn't fail! It lived its life passionately and earnestly; and because it was alive and not artificially preserved, it ceased in due course to exist as a body. How vividly it is living now in the imagination of persons![59]

BMC lived for twenty-four years, about two dozen years longer than most places attempt truly and fully to commit to an experimental ethos, to self-governance, to fusing living and learning, to robust interdisciplinarity, let alone to all of these things. Two years of such an object lesson would be quite valuable; two dozen is an embarrassment of riches.

★ ★ ★

By the term "wide-awakeness" we want to denote a plane of consciousness of highest tension originating in an attitude of full attention to life and its requirements.
—Alfred Schutz[60]

I have never yet met a man who was quite awake. How could I have looked him in the face?
—Henry David Thoreau[61]

As we have developed this sympathetic reading of the college's small scale and short life, we have also begun to peel back familiar labels to uncover something of BMC's distinctive ethos. To call BMC a utopia is to overlook its many warts. To call it an art school is to ignore the fact that the college explicitly disavowed such pre-professionalism.[62] Even the labels "intentional community" and "experimental college" tend to obscure more than they reveal.

While Black Mountain certainly stood for the proposition that community requires intentionality, it was not created for the purpose of exploring the nature of community. When asked whether Black Mountain was essentially a commune, Olson is emphatic: "When you come right down to the bottom of it, the *bindu* of it, she was a college. She wasn't some goddamned intentional community."[63] Certainly, BMC sought to keep open the question of what community is; but this was simply an outgrowth of its educational mission. After all, what college would foreclose such a deep and abiding question? Thus, calling Black Mountain an "intentional community" is not so much wrong as it is uninteresting. You can neither create nor sustain community unless you are intentional about it; and communities of learning must remain open-minded about what community entails. What is interesting is the particular form of community attempted at BMC. The goal was to create a community in which one feels neither forgotten nor typecast, but held in mind precisely as a person-in-process. And by all accounts, Black Mountain did manage to become that rare thing, a genuine space of mutual recognition, a place where one feels *seen*.

We ought to be equally careful when applying the label "experimental college." Certainly, Black Mountain takes its place in a long tradition of experimentation in US higher education.[64] Rice says as much in the first sentence of his "Foreword" to the first BMC catalogue, that along with "tested and approved methods of education," there would be "new methods tried out in a purely experimental spirit."[65] There is also no denying that Black Mountain was born out of a desire to create an alternative to a system perceived as lacking. At the center of the small group that founded the college was Rice, a man whose keen awareness of the gap between education and its institutional trappings, not to mention his extremely confrontational style, led to "stormy exits" from three professorial positions.[66] Picking up the story with Rice's dismissal from Rollins College in 1933, BMC alumnus Mervin Lane offers this efficient summary of Black Mountain's founding occasion and impulse:

> Conflicts between Rice, a divided faculty, and the administration at Rollins reached a peak of irreconcilability. He and a small group of sympathetic colleagues and students left. These were seekers sensitive to the constrictions of entrenched, hierarchical, bureaucratic inflexibility. They felt the need for a more cooperative, co-evolving, independent, experiential approach to learning, liberated from external pressures and the preoccupation with the apparatus of credentialing. They rallied in support of Rice's plan to found a small college where the curriculum would be oriented towards the uniqueness of individuals; where no unwieldy administrative, trustee-controlled system would hamper the free interchange between instructor and student; where open and honest dialogue would be pivotal not only to pedagogy but to living and working together in community; and where faculty and student representatives would make the decisions.[67]

So reaction and innovation were certainly part of the equation: reaction against a university ruled by "the managerial mind" with "dead roots in a dead past"; innovation of an egalitarian, experiential alternative.[68]

In the end, though, neither iconoclasm nor the desire to innovate take us very far in explaining what the "experimental spirit" truly meant at Black

Mountain.[69] First, the aim was renewal, not novelty. In the first bulletin, Rice goes on to explain that experimental practices were to be combined with "experiences which have already shown their value in educational institutions . . . but which are often isolated and prevented from giving their full value because of their existence side by side with thoughtless tradition."[70] The point was not to pilot new programs but to break through, as John Dewey would put it, "the crust of conventionalized and routine consciousness," to rediscover living versions of extant but zombified practices.[71]

Second, while the founders of Black Mountain did pride themselves on offering an alternative to existing institutions, they had something more ambitious in mind than iconoclasm. After all, those busy patting themselves on the back for exposing what is rote and lifeless in the conduct of others usually fail to notice that they themselves have begun to run in a groove.[72] Rice and the others set themselves the more serious challenge of breaking through the crust *of their own* conventions. To this end, BMC meetings featured a running debate over what the college was trying to achieve. In the thirties, for example, we find the community wrestling with the question of the pedagogical value of the teacher's personality, noting that some teachers lack the necessary force of personality to "infect" students with a desire to know, see, and be more, while others fall into a kind of pedagogical "imperialism," creating disciples.[73] In the forties, there was an "explosive meeting" over whether the college should devote the last of its meager annual budget to constructing fences or acquiring pianos.[74] In the fifties, we find a spirited debate (at one point, the anthropologist, John Adams, accuses Olson of talking nonsense) over whether the curriculum should be organized around the logic of inquiry or the psychology of learners.[75]

Ultimately, then, what makes Black Mountain innovative is not that it advanced a new definition of an educated person (though indeed it was organized around some rare ideals of personhood), but that it was a community committed to keeping open the questions of how we foster human growth and to what ends.[76] On the default view, an experimental program or institution is about beta-testing remedies to the problems at Big Standard U. By contrast, BMC was devoted to an ongoing effort to maintain a freshness of pedagogical vision.

However, even this fails to capture fully the spirit of experimentalism at Black Mountain. First and foremost, what the college offered was not an experimental curriculum but a curriculum of experimentation.[77] A consistent animating principle of the evolving curriculum was the creation of spaces where students (including faculty as lead learners) could pursue learning at the growing edge of experience. Maintaining a freshness of pedagogical vision was part of the larger effort, evoked in the epigraphs from Richards, Thoreau, and Schutz, to shake off somnolence and wake up to life. Rice captures this Thoreauvian educational ideal in his own memorable epigram. Critiquing the neo-scholastic "fundamentalism" of his contemporary, Robert Maynard Hutchins, Rice concludes, "When every day offers the adventure of seeking the word for the meaning rather than the meaning for the word, when action and word merge and become one, then shall we have the higher learning in America, and not before."[78] And this experiential or, perhaps better, existential ethos ran through the college's history from its early years ("I want to open eyes," Albers declared upon arriving at Black Mountain) to its final period ("Find out for yourself," was Olson's refrain).[79]

We can bring home the distinction between experimenting on education and education as experimentation by contrasting two cases, each involving only one of these forms of experimentation. First, consider the recent wave of enthusiasm around Massively Open Online Courses (MOOCs) as a form of "disruptive innovation."[80] Though MOOCs are experimental in the default sense—testing out a large-enrollment, virtual alternative to the selective, residential model—there is nothing particularly experimental about the experience they offer to students.[81] The second case is hypothetical. Imagine that, by agreement, all universities decided to adopt a formative, experiential model, not unlike the one at Black Mountain. Over time, college would come to be understood as a process driven by students trying to make sense of themselves and their world, as, in the words of Michael Oakeshott, "adventures in human self-understanding."[82] Lecture halls would be refitted into flexible spaces for meetings, discussion, and exhibitions. Standing courses and assigned readings would be phased out, replaced by reading groups tailored to support student inquiries. Tests would be scrapped in favor of genuinely searching essays, inspired by Ezra Pound's injunction to "[make] your own survey."[83] The professoriate would have to climb down from the bell curve onto the unpredictable terrain of Socratic dialogue, shifting from the roles of instructor and examiner to those of gadfly, matchmaker, midwife, and intellectual companion.[84] Before I get further carried away by the details, let me state the moral of the story. In this counterfactual world, all universities offer education as experimentation but, since this is the new normal, none count as experimental in the default sense. Or, we could draw the contrast between the two cases like this: in the first, it is the educators who are conducting the experiment and educational methods on which they are experimenting; in the second, the experimenters are the learners themselves (including those lead learners we call faculty) and the subject of the experiment is life itself, the worlds within and around us.

★　★　★

The danger of a history obviously is it appears to be in past time. And as I've said to you, Black Mountain to my mind is not only in past time but is a flag hanging out in the future which hasn't yet been, hasn't been redrawn.
—Charles Olson[85]

Utopias are often only premature truths.
—Alphonse de Lamartine[86]

We call it "higher education" for a reason. The term is not "higher training" or "further schooling." We are signaling a new phase of the formative process when socialization and instruction must yield more fully to individuation and investigation, when learners are charged with and supported to take more responsibility in determining the direction and shape of their own education. I take this as axiomatic, that higher education is not worthy of the name unless it amounts to formative education, which I understand as the attempt to discover, understand, do justice to, and integrate the diverse dimensions of oneself in light of the realities—the offerings and demands—of the world.[87] This is a formidable existential task. How does the contemporary university live up to it?

While educating the whole person remains a priority of the *official* curriculum, the *enacted* curriculum tells a different story. Walled off from living, learning is then conflated with "studenting," the navigation of the bureaucratic system that regulates the distribution of the external goods that have come to be attached to formal higher education. Rather than invite learners to confront their complex natures, the modern multiversity offers them a reductive picture of themselves as repositories of specialized knowledge and as pre-professional trainees. Meanwhile, the not-so-*hidden* curriculum of college life teaches students that they are consumers of information, credentials, and edutainment. Then there is our *null* curriculum of disintegrity. Through Gen Ed we impose what some candidly used to call "scattering requirements," but there is a noticeable void where we might expect to see some corresponding set of integration requirements. We teach students to debunk, largely leaving them on their own to rebuild a livable system of beliefs.[88]

This is not to say that we are unconcerned with general education. To the contrary, we are quite wrapped up in the idea. Who can blame us, when the images are so lifelike? We see a leafy quad. A student is heading to class. With a volume of poetry under her arm, she ducks under a Frisbee and navigates around two classmates arguing over string theory. The education of the whole person is alive and well . . . in the matrix. I do not claim to offer a red pill; but I think there are enough glitches to reveal that formative education is very far from the real business of the contemporary university.[89] What I am suggesting is that holistic rhetoric and Gen Ed requirements fit perfectly Louis Althusser's famous definition of ideology as the discursive structures and material practices that mediate "the imaginary relationship of individuals to their real conditions of existence."[90]

In search of a genuinely formative alternative, we looked for the road to Black Mountain. Navigating between nostalgia and dismissiveness, we discovered a college whose small size and short life represented not failures of marketing and management but a commitment to the rare ideals of self-cultivation and mutual recognition, natality and wide-awakeness. Now that we have found our way there, let's take our time and look around. How did the culture and community of BMC support students and faculty to encounter, understand, cultivate, and enact themselves? What familiar pedagogical forms had to be reanimated and transformed in this formative quest? We will begin on the porch of Lee Hall, looking in on an unusual form of student orientation.

AN ALLEGORY OF ARRIVAL

Of this very thing, then, there would be a craft—namely of this turning around.
—Plato[91]

At the center of Black Mountain's first, Blue Ridge, campus stands Lee Hall, whose broad front façade faces north, offering an exquisite view of the Craggy Mountains.[92] With a nod to the Parthenon, the building is fronted by a grand porch, with steps leading up to an "octastyle portico rising the full three-story height of the building and carried by massive, smooth-surfaced columns with simplified Doric capitals."[93] It was here that early BMC student Doughten Cramer first met with his faculty advisor, John Rice. Duberman's restaging is worth quoting in full:

> On a lovely, warm fall morning he and Rice sat in green rocking chairs on the porch of Lee Hall, Rice basking in the sun and the beauty of the view, Cramer nervously wondering what was expected of him. Rice's opening remark startled him: "You are now entering college for the first time. You have a whole new world before you. What are you interested in studying?" Cramer didn't know what to answer: "Interest had never decided my choice," he later recalled, "but I remembered that I had enjoyed history in school so I stuttered out, 'W-well, history is sort of fun.'"
>
> "What phase of history do you like?", Rice asked.
>
> Cramer was again at a loss; he'd never given the matter much thought before. Suddenly he had an inspiration: the Depression then at its height had considerably affected his own life, so he answered, "I want to know what caused the Depression and how future depressions can be prevented."
>
> Rice laughed—perhaps because it pleased him to see again how easy it was to start the process of self-propulsion in education, but perhaps, too, out of amusement at the contrast between the grand designs of the young and the limited resources of the community; "You've given the college a large order!" was all he said.
>
> After some discussion, they decided that Cramer should take Lounsbury's course on American history and study economics with Helen Boyden, whose Vassar and Radcliffe training had also included history.[94]

I appreciate that Duberman takes time to set the scene. The porch, the rocking chairs, the warm fall morning, the beautiful view: these are far from extraneous details. Cramer is looking out upon the mountains that would become central to his experience at BMC. In another reminiscence describing a single long hike, Cramer begins:

> The College's setting was extraordinarily important to me. The mountains of western North Carolina are beautiful beyond description, and it is as if the atmosphere of the College was consciously a part of the living beauty. It made one sensitive to everything.[95]

Obviously, Cramer is not there yet. This is an anxious first meeting, colored by uncertainty about Rice, the college, his studies, and himself; but the invitation is on offer. He is given a glimpse of *skholê*, of college as, in Michael Oakeshott's phrase, "the gift of an interval."[96]

I cannot help but recall the very different scene of my first advisement meeting as a freshman at Yale College in the mid-eighties. Having been assigned at random to an astronomy professor, I hiked up Science Hill and sat down in what I remember as an office so crowded that its occupant had to shove books and papers aside to clear a little room on his desk to sign the form approving my selection of classes. I hope I am misremembering, but I don't recall him looking up even once while asking me a couple of quick questions and signing off. The point of advisement is not only to meet with a mentor but thereby to arrange a meeting with yourself. But which version of yourself will you encounter: *Homo sapiens* or *Homo bureaucraticus*, treating life as a things-to-do list and oneself as a checker of boxes? Here is a meeting to shape your curriculum and thereby, not to put too fine a point on it, to shape yourself. It is bad enough if your advisor is not really present; it is absurd if you are not. To modern ears, this sounds like an exaggeration. To the ancients, it was an obvious first principle of education. It is only under conditions of *skholê*, temporarily unhitching yourself from the yoke of necessity, that you can get a look at what you are working with.

The scene on the porch at Black Mountain couldn't be further from my experience on Science Hill. Cramer does not have to interrupt Rice, who joins him on the porch for this very purpose. Far from being harried and distracted, Rice is "basking in the sun." He is relaxed and attentive, ready to be occupied by a conversation with its own logic, but not at all preoccupied. I am sure that the historical resonances of this setting were not lost on the classicist, Rice. It is thought that porticoes surrounded the central courtyard of Aristotle's Lyceum, and Stoic philosophy is named for the Stoa Poikile, the "Painted Porch" where Zeno of Citium taught.[97] The BMC porch faced the Craggies, not the agora, but this idea of a space simultaneously open and sheltered has roots dating back to the third century BCE, if not earlier. Indeed, the movement of the rocking chairs evokes the famous pacing at the Lyceum. To our ears, it sounds strange to speak of a Peripatetic School of philosophy. The fixed seating of the modern school bespeaks a deeper fixity, as passive pupils are fed predigested ideas.[98] In a tour de force of branding, this strange new institution associated itself with the idea of *skholê* while twisting its meaning a full 180 degrees.[99] Finding themselves in an institution premised on compulsion, schoolchildren would find it darkly ironic to learn that the root of the word "school" meant the chance to encounter and cultivate your own freedom.

In his *Reveries of a Solitary Walker*, the modern peripatetic, Jean-Jacques Rousseau, highlights just this distinctive rhythm of attentive openness, this mode of being richly occupied once we are no longer pre-occupied. As if describing Cramer and Rice in their rocking chairs, Rousseau writes that "the heart must be at peace . . . the person in question . . . suitably disposed. . . . There must be neither a total calm nor too much movement, but a steady and moderate motion, with no jolts or breaks."[100] Rousseau's phenomenology of reverie and its rhythm of attentiveness adds depth to our understanding of *skholê*. When we are driven by necessity, harassed by memories, distracted by plans, irritated by wants (that are inflamed by insecurity, envy, and fantasy, not to mention an entire political-economic system predicated on perpetual dissatisfaction), we are not truly or at least not fully ourselves. *Skholê* offers not only the abstract reminder that we are capable of freedom, but a reconnection with the elemental experience Rousseau called "*le sentiment de l'existence*." Though our instinct for self-preservation often shows up as reactive desperation or greedy acquisition, at its core is an unmediated form of self-affirmation, a pleasurable recognition of "the plenitude of life" within and around us.[101] In these happy moments, we rediscover our equilibrium: the work is done, my flaws will wait, the day is perfect, listen to my dog who has known all along what is important. It is in such a state, Rousseau suggests, that "the soul can find a resting-place secure enough to establish itself and concentrate its entire being there, with no need to remember the past or reach into the future."[102]

On this "lovely, warm fall morning," in "his green rocking chair," Cramer is invited to re-collect himself, but note that "concentrated" does not mean closed in. The dialogue with Rice is meant precisely to draw him out, the vista serving as a resonant reminder of open possibilities. "What interests you?" The question is so simple and so fundamental that it is embarrassing how often we forget to ask it. Apparently, Rice was the first educator ever to ask Cramer this basic question. At first Cramer is shy. He draws a blank. But before long he identifies a source of pleasure in his past studies (history) and one nexus of concern in his present life (how to avert the next great depression).

To call this an experimental form of advisement misses the point. This is not a pilot program in "open-air office hours" but a way of breaking through the crust of convention around advisement; not an alternative to choosing a major, but a reminder of what that should mean. We see the beginning of the process of Rice getting to know Cramer, inviting him to articulate how he conceives of himself in relation to the world, and starting to suggest resources for complicating and enriching that understanding. What this vignette reveals is that the phrase "new student orientation" conceals a crucial distinction. While instruction may be propelled by carrots and sticks, liberal learning must begin with an invitation, with an address to the learner's freedom. Formative education cannot get under way without at least a glimpse of *skholê*, without a reminder that we are more than, other than, a hamster in a wheel. Of course, students moving to a new scene of instruction need welcoming events introducing campus places and policies. However, it is precisely the inveterate student in us that needs a redirection of attention, from seeing ourselves as acquirers of information, earners of credits, and competitors for credentials to recognizing ourselves as searchers, as learners. As we pursue the higher learning, it is not orientation we need so much as reorientation, and this requires not a single event but an ongoing effort. Indeed, in the epigraph from the *Republic*, Plato's famously asserts that teaching itself is this *technê tes periagogês*, an art (craft, discipline) of reorientation. However, in the same passage in which he allows for the possibility of *metastrephein* (soul-turning, conversion) (518D5), he stresses the inevitability of *apostrephein* (reversion) (515e2). The idea that you may be looking in the wrong direction or missing the big picture ought to be woven, as Cramer remarks, into the very "atmosphere" of the college, turning the Craggies for him into a constant reminder that there are always unexplored trails and surprising vantage points.

★ ★ ★

In general, the effort of Black Mountain College is to produce individuals rather than individualists. . . . The first step in the process is to make the student aware of himself and his capacities; in other words "to know himself."
—John Andrew Rice[103]

How can man know himself? He is a dark and veiled thing; and whereas the hare has seven skins, man could skin himself seventy-times-seven times and still not say, "This now is you yourself, this is no longer skin." Besides, it is an agonizing, dangerous enterprise to dig down into yourself.
—Friedrich Nietzsche[104]

The view from the porch nicely evokes the promise, preserved in the etymology of the word, that *education* might mean something other than being
instructed, equipped, sorted, and credentialed, that our lives may testify
to a deeper process of *being led out*.[105] However, it is now high time to hit
the trails, trading the grand mountain vista for the actual twists and turns
of the formative hike. To leave the story here would be to add yet another
installment of that popular genre, educational kitsch.[106] Here is the ending
of that screenplay:

EXT. LEE HALL—DAY

MUSIC CUE: Copland's *Appalachian Spring*

As the music begins to swell, the camera pulls back from the porch to
reveal the morning mist rising from the blue ridge mountains . . .

Roll CREDITS.

I do not mean to impugn Duberman's recounting of Cramer's meeting with
Rice. On the whole, Duberman is an admirably sober and circumspect narrator. If anything, he is drawn to difficulty, alternately highlighting the
struggles of the college and his own struggles in coming to grips with its
history. He is no friend of kitsch, with its simplified and sweetened version
of reality. However, I do detect one misty-eyed moment in Duberman's
recounting of this open-air orientation, namely when he speculates that
Rice was pleased "to see again how easy it was to start the process of self-
propulsion in education."[107] True, he is talking only about the ease of *starting*
the process, but even this rings false for the simple reason that Rice himself
describes the early stages of formative education as particularly challenging
for student and teacher alike.[108]

　　Self-knowledge, described by Rice in the epigraph above as the "first
step in the process," is difficult enough. And clearly this is a priority in
a self-driven process of holistic formation. How can you root learning
in your concerns if you don't yet know what moves you? How can you
cultivate and integrate the varied parts of yourself if you don't yet know
what you are made of? Interestingly, though, it is Rice himself who gives
us reason to question whether this is truly the first step, suggesting that
self-knowledge depends on a prior process. Before the self can be known,
Rice posits, it must be surfaced. On Cramer's recollection, Rice's opening
words were, "You are now entering college for the first time." If this is

how it went, then Rice must have been relishing the paradox, since he held
the view that students typically enter college for the first time . . . twice.
Checking in at fall registration is what Rice calls the student's "superficial
self"; the student's "real self" typically lags behind.[109]

At first glance this sounds like a view—contrasting the true self and the
masked player of social roles—that was debunked a philosophical generation ago.[110] However, Rice is not saying that we have a true self prior to
all socialization, or that authenticity is to be defined in opposition to social
roles. In fact, Rice stresses how at Black Mountain "the whole community
becomes [the] teacher," because "the individual, to be complete, must be
aware of his relation to others."[111] Even if we reject the idea of an asocial,
atomistic self, there is intuitive appeal to Rice's rough and ready distinction between a true and false self. That we form and understand ourselves
through "webs of interlocution," to adopt Charles Taylor's formulation,
does nothing to gainsay the facts that communal life can be damaging—Rice
offers the example of the "intrusions of the desiccated schoolteacher"—
that traveling across social borders can be confusing, and that we all hide
and posture to various degrees and in various ways.[112]

It is from such elemental experiences that Rice crafts his believable if
simplified allegory of the doubled self:

> The immigrant into the world outside the home, in spite of the foretaste
> through public schooling, finds himself among strangers. . . . He then carries
> forward what he may have begun as a protective device . . . a superficial self to
> present to the world in lieu of reality.[113]

This means that the student arrives on campus in a heightened state of
ambivalence about whether this superficial self should and even could be
dismantled. On the one hand, the student has invested considerable time
and effort into this façade, which has been "elaborately decorated" and
given the "most tender care" (632). In a twisted form of self-esteem, one
takes pride not in who one is but in one's handiwork in fashioning a disguise.
It may well be that a student's "best thoughts and abilities have gone into
its making" (630). "By the time he gets to college," Rice quips, "this superficial self is often a work of art" (630). The student has reached the point
where it is difficult to say where the superficial self ends and the real one
begins. On the other hand, behind this "carefully designed mask . . . lives

the real [person], growing increasingly chaotic, miserable, and unhappy" (632). From this, Rice draws an obvious but untimely conclusion: the ambivalence about the affordances of this protective shell will bleed into an ambivalence toward the formative opportunities of college itself. The undergraduate arrives at once "longing for his deliverer [and] . . . ready to receive him as an enemy" (632).

If the word "enemy" sounds jarring, this may stem from our unfortunate tendency to try to match the tone of educational writing to its subject matter as if, because we often write about the young (who are assumed to be sweet and innocent), we must write about education as if it were an entirely pleasant and wholesome process. In discussing a theory such as Rice's, one feels the need to add a content warning: *this essay acknowledges the existence of intrapersonal and interpersonal conflict.* While we love to brand programs and institutions with the term "transformative," we hate to admit that there are no transformations without conflict, struggle, and pain. Perhaps it is because education has been conscripted into the role of sustaining social hope that we tend to prefer Kodachrome images of teaching and learning, since, as one of our contemporary bards has observed,

> They give us those nice bright colors
> They give us the greens of summers
> Makes you think all the world's a sunny day, oh yeah.[114]

In formative education, alas, storms are all too common. As Nietzsche remarks in the epigraph, "it is an agonizing, dangerous enterprise to dig down into yourself." This is why I suggested that isolating the interaction on the porch makes it into kitsch. Rocking chairs and friendly words notwithstanding, Rice himself held the view that college inevitably begins with a crucible, an active and uncertain struggle to disarm defenses and surface the self.[115] For Rice, the student's disunity entails a double task for the teacher, to serve as both ally and antagonist:

> The task of the college is to be [the student's] enemy-friend: the bitter enemy of the superficial self, the friend of the real self. But the real one is starved, emaciated. It must be fed back to life, while the superficial one must be attacked without mercy.[116]

But is this a wise approach? Don't learners need scaffolding, support, safety, care? And even if it were pedagogically sound, is such mercilessness morally justifiable?

In only its third year, faculty and students confronted these questions, and each other, in a discussion that Duberman calls "enormously impressive."[117] In the fall of 1935, at the end of his two-and-a-half month stay at BMC, Louis Adamic read a full draft of the Harper's article that would soon put the college on the map. This sparked a heated debate "that went on late into the night and continued for weeks—over meals, in studies, in the privacy of letters and diaries." (119). Part of what rankled the community was Adamic's portrayal of Rice as "top dog and Savior" (116). Some thought Rice's role had been overstated; others thought it all too accurate, with Rice preaching "the danger of a one-man college" while refusing to "see his power diluted" (117). There was also a feeling that Adamic had cast the college and its confrontational methods in too rosy a light. Here is Adamic on what Rice and others had come to call "group influence": "The BMC community . . . psychologically strips the individual, and there he stands revealed to everyone, including himself—and finally likes it."[118] Part of what impressed Duberman is how thoughtful and outspoken the students were in response. John Evarts challenged the idea that these public decortications were truly pedagogically motivated and done without malice. George Hendrickson pointed out that direct confrontation "sometimes only stiffened [a person's] defenses."[119] Then a student named George Barber really started laying into Rice, accusing him of not being able to "sense the delicate moment of when to stop," leaving a student feeling "hammered down" (117). In a comment that would become a commonplace, Rice's junior colleague, Robert Goldenson, simultaneously managed to back the students, acknowledge Rice's dialectical prowess, and reinforce Rice as "top dog and Savior": "We have a rough Socrates here . . . perhaps we need a little Jesus" (118).

To Rice's credit, he stayed in a non-defensive, listening posture throughout the meeting. When he finally spoke, he readily acknowledged his failings, praised Barber for speaking up, and urged more members of the community to share that burden: "You should make yourself into little anti-Rices," "stand up and fight," "sit on my shortcomings," and "deflate my power."[120] It is also true that many of Rice's former students, including some who felt very stung by him, credit him as "an inspiration," as teaching them "to question everything," as "an understanding and empathetic human being with genuine respect for students," as "the first person who started me really using my mind," as an internal dialogue partner for "many years," as "'the most profound influence' on their lives."[121] It seems that Rice truly had a gift for Socratic dialogue and formative conversation. It seems equally clear that he was a man with a mean streak whose dialectics could devolve into simple put downs.

To my mind, none of this invalidates Rice's agonistic account of transformative learning. Adamic returned to Black Mountain several times over the next two years, finding the college "already much changed."[122] In particular, Adamic found that the debate sparked by his article had helped the college more carefully draw the line between being a ruthless friend of someone's best self and being careless, tone deaf, or just plain cruel.[123] If agonistic pedagogy forces one to be especially attuned to the potential of educational harms, this is a good thing. Cruelties still occur in the pedagogy of sweetness and light, including the violence of aiding and abetting our tendency to disavow the unhandsome aspects of our condition. In my view, Rice's account—if not always his personal practice—is realistic, balanced, and humane.

Notice, first, the dual nature of Rice's approach: even as one whittles away at the superficial self, one is feeding the dormant one. In his time at BMC, Adamic observed five main ingredients in this diet for the real self: freedom, candor, good will, interpellation, and humor. Let us consider each in turn:

Freedom. When Adamic describes "the freedom of the place," I take him to refer to that found in any residential college, amplified by the unconventionality and experimental ethos of Black Mountain.[124] Arriving in a new community offers a freedom to be more than, other than you were. Instead of the expectation to fill an accustomed role, you are greeted by an open-ended interest in who you are and will be. This is an elixir for the dormant parts of yourself.

Candor. Adamic muses that there is probably more candor "on that mountainside than anywhere else in the United States." There was an imperative to speak your mind and walk the talk. This led to candid feedback that exposed and deflated the superficial self. Here, Adamic is pointing out that, while "discomfiting at times," BMC also offered you glimpses of authenticity that nourished the real self.

Good Will. This is a crucial counterpart to candor. While discourse at Black
Mountain was direct, even confrontational, Adamic found "most of the
talk . . . free of malice or pettiness." Though everyone's views are subject to challenge, "no one ever goes completely without a champion."
Encountering in others this "desire to help," Adamic concluded, convinces
BMC students that "a great mass of literature notwithstanding, humanity is basically a decent breed."

Positive Interpellation. Interpellation is my term, not Adamic's. It refers to the
structures of expectation built into modes of address. Every hail from an
interlocutor contains a text (what is said) and a subtext (the picture of
you implied by how that text is framed in order to reach you). It is just
such a structure of expectation that Adamic identifies as a catalyst that
can help surface the self, observing how BMC students are "constantly
invited verbally and by implication, to be intelligent, to mature, which is
slightly annoying but also rather flattering and pleasant."

Humor. Important as each of these elements is, Adamic considers humor
"the most important part of the diet for the 'real self.'" Neither positive
interpellations nor the atmosphere of good will eliminate the embarrassment of awkwardly climbing out of your chrysalis in full view. This, I
take it, is the reason why Adamic stresses how "young students learn to
laugh at themselves" at Black Mountain, adding that "Rice's own talent
for laughter helps them in this."

In the Kodachrome picture of education, this nourishing of the real self
is all that is needed. Just add soil, water, and sunlight, and the student will
blossom. But even a quick look at these elements reveals their shadow sides.
We really do care about authenticity . . . and we feel the need to hide. We do
want the freedom to renegotiate the terms of our identity . . . and we suffer
from Frommian "fear of freedom" and Sartrean "bad faith," acting as if our
nature or past (our "facticity") definitively answered the question of who
we are.[125] Yes, we have good will and a desire to help . . . and we are prone
to envy and schadenfreude. Truly, it is wonderful when we are able to own
our limitations and trust others, turning what could be a laughing at into a
laughing with . . . and we can struggle to find that trust and that distance
from ourselves, experiencing the laughter of others as humiliating.[126] When
we acknowledge such shadows, formative education becomes more fraught.

Thus, while Rice does seem to have sometimes lapsed into actual cruelty, we can read his violent language (confronting in the superficial self a

"bitter enemy" which must be "starved, emaciated," and "attacked without mercy") as an attempt to jolt us out of our tendency to romanticize the scene of instruction. On the romantic view, learners want only to find and actualize their true selves. In reality, Rice suggests, we encounter surprising cross-currents in the soul—active forces clouding self-awareness and subverting self-cultivation and self-enactment—whose sediments accrete over time into this stubborn shell-self.

We have considered the ingredients of the diet for the real self. What at BMC contributed to this chipping away of the shell-self? Though it may sound too vague to be satisfying, the most accurate answer is everything. The curriculum was just this: daily life in a close-knit community that prizes authenticity and errs on the side of the blunt and confrontational. We touched on this idea earlier in our discussion of scale, noting Duberman's observation that BMC's small size created an environment in which "individual lifestyles, in all their peculiar detail, could thereby be observed, challenged, imitated, rejected—which is, after all, how most learning proceeds, rather than through formal instruction."[127] I was then stressing the positive aspects of this experience, how it speaks to our basic need for recognition. But I never meant to suggest that self-confrontation was a walk in the park. To his credit, Rice readily acknowledges the intense demands of this life-wide curriculum of candor. When one student complained that "it's like living in a goldfish bowl," Rice replied, "Hell . . . a goldfish bowl is a monastery compared to this place!" I think Rice would approve of my pairing (as epigraphs) his claim that education entails searching for self-knowledge with Nietzsche's that the search is "agonizing."

On Adamic's retelling, the idea of "group influence" arose out of necessity:

> The original Black Mountain group . . . abruptly found themselves in extremely tight quarters and had to get along *on a basis of freedom*, not only as students and teachers, but as persons. . . . They had to rub the individualistic corners off one another's characters.[128]

What began as a communal necessity grew into an intentional educational ideal, giving the idea of well-roundedness a literal inflection. And it appears that "group influence" is a bit of a euphemism, given that what they had in mind was sanding the self. Life at Black Mountain was arranged as a steady siege on the fortifications of the false self.

That such a process should be life-wide should not surprise us. What would be strange is scheduling such personal change on Tuesdays and Thursdays from

1:30 to 2:45: *in this 3-credit course you will outgrow pretense and defensiveness to achieve self-knowledge.* It is only when we misunderstand ignorance as simple lack that we imagine that it can be dealt with in spurts: open up the tap here for a couple of hours; then head down to the next filling station. Once we acknowledge that ignorance is an active process—do we protect anything more fiercely than our illusions?—it is clear that transformative learning must be constantly reinforced from all angles.

To fully grasp this point, we need to get past familiar slogans about living and learning and overly tidy distinctions between formal and informal education. The formal/informal distinction itself blurs together several distinctions, each a bit fuzzy in its own right: Does the learning occur in or beyond the classroom? Is there a person in the situation understood to be the teacher? Is it intentional or accidental? Are we learning through direct contact with the phenomena or through representations (e.g., lectures and textbooks)? Sometimes these distinctions line up, as when a middle school social studies teacher delivers a lecture to teach students about the three branches of government. Or we can imagine a related "lesson" that is nonetheless teacherless, non-classroom-based, unintended, and directly experiential, as when an adult lives through a series of disastrous Supreme Court decisions leading to a political awakening and deep skepticism toward the ideas of legal reasoning, judicial independence, and the separation of powers. At the same time, it is not hard to see how these distinctions can get messy, individually and collectively:

- A resolves to hike every day to form a deeper connection to nature. (Here intentionality pairs with out-of-class, teacherless, direct learning.)
- B hears a poem about Stonewall read aloud and is moved. (Is this direct or mediated?)
- Going to the library to pull a book for class, C finds a different book, inspiring a change in major and career plans. (Here we find learning in a classroom-adjacent but still scholastic space, one in which the student was put in the way of an accidental, self-directed discovery by a teacher's intentional curriculum.)

Thus, we must be careful not to misunderstand this idea of "group influence," as if it were a matter of complementing intentional, teacher-led, academic learning with chance interactions among peers. At Black Mountain, students engaged with teachers in a wide range of settings beyond the classroom. And classes at BMC were themselves often set up to focus and intensify this group process.

Take theater, for example. As theater director Bob Wunsch explained to Adamic, "Our dramatics is tied up with 'group influence.'"[129] Wunsch elaborates, echoing Rice's emphasis on self-knowledge and the superficial self:

> We believe it is vitally important that a student knows what sort of person he actually is, what kind of fictitious self he has built up around that actual self, and what the social group in which he moves thinks of those actual and fictitious selves.[130]

Rice imagines life at BMC as a steady invitation to compare lifestyle and character. But this sort of personal comparison can be both too diffuse and too close to home. Drama simultaneously sharpens the outlines of character and offers some distance from the existential stakes of such comparisons. Thus drama becomes the formative art of recasting. While Wunsch would sometimes cast students against type to help them "identify with the aspirations, problems, and experience of people unlike themselves," he also employed the daring strategy of casting according to type.[131] "Our method," Wunsch explains,

> is to cast, for instance, an arrogant person in an arrogant rôle, in which his own arrogance stands out even more clearly than otherwise, so that not only the audience, which is the community, sees it, but he himself. We try to find rôles for boors, for the autocratically and over-egoistically inclined, for rich boys and girls whose main prop is their wealth . . . so that the place sees them, and they see themselves, in all the glory of their outstanding characteristics: which almost invariably leads to corrective processes within persons.[132]

If crossing the wires, as it were, may generate a current of empathy, plugging them right into their matching sockets can really throw off sparks.

Within this fishbowl of a college, the stage served to structure and intensify the dynamics of recognition. Drama distills, out of the confusing flow of life, distillates of character, intention, and action. At the same time, it finds the play in the joints of the structures of our stuckness. Candor, recognition, community: in theater, each of these plays its double role as support for the nascent self and siege on the superficial self. Thus, we have begun to get a feel for Rice's theory of our layered nature and for the two-pronged pedagogy needed to surface the self. We turn now to an extended example to flesh out this allegory of arrival.

★   ★   ★

Because they are *initium*, newcomers and beginners by virtue of birth, men
take initiative, are prompted into action. . . . This beginning is not the . . .
beginning of something but of somebody, who is a beginner himself.
—Hannah Arendt[133]

Quotes about the lasting influence of teachers are stock and trade. Less
often observed is that influence is negotiated. Only a dialectical formulation captures its complexity: even while it is true that (1) what reads as
exemplary and works as an influence is shaped by who we are and what we
care about; it is also the case that (2) who we are and what we care about is
shaped by our influences.[134] This helps to explain the curious sensation that
certain books were written just for us or that one day we will find our true
teacher. For Michael Rumaker, a student during BMC's final years, this
was not John Rice but Charles Olson. Nonetheless, Rumaker's memoir,
Black Mountain Days, offers a rich illustration of how the quest to surface
the self was catalyzed and supported by the college's atmosphere of candor and confrontation, its fusion of the aesthetic and the existential, its
refusal of the distinction between the formal and the informal, its belief
that both professors and fellow students play crucial educational roles, and
its embrace of an agonistic, transformative pedagogy.

We pick up his story with an experience that illustrates BMC's culture
of candor. Rumaker recalls how "outside the kitchen back door one day
after lunch," one of his classmates who was interested in photography,
Virginia, took a picture of him.[135] Though the photograph was unexcep-
tional, Rumaker launched into one of his trademark riffs of appreciative
exegesis. Virginia's response pulled him up short:

> I went burbling on about something or another, as I usually did, full of beans
> and nervous energy. Virginia, visibly unimpressed, as she calmly peered through
> her baby-blue rimmed glasses winding her film forward, said, in her slow, baby-
> talk voice, "You exaggerate everything."
>
> That shut me up. It offended me at first but then when I thought about it
> later in my study, it made sense.[136]

The lesson Rumaker took away from this was not the simple one that it is
good to be measured and bad to exaggerate. This casual, everyday intervention from a classmate tapped into a root concern of Rumaker's, one
that would later blossom in his dialogues with Charles Olson. As it turned

out, Rumaker's problem was not his conversational effusiveness but rather his writerly abstemiousness. Yes, truth was the key concern but, as Olson would later help him to see, "The lie of the imagination creates the truth of reality."[137]

The relationship Rumaker forged with Olson (and, through Olson, with himself) illustrates well Rice's allegory of the struggle to surface. Rumaker was drawn to visit Black Mountain by reports of the college's radical ways, but it was his encounter with Olson that led him to stay. This was not the ordinary prospective student visit with a student tour guide. Received by Olson himself, Rumaker was struck by his attentiveness and his "curiosity and enthusiasms sprawling and darting over enormously wide fields."[138] "He was," Rumaker ventured, "the first *total* person I had ever glimpsed" (20). Olson asked Rumaker, who was an aspiring writer, to share some of his work, and then proceeded to review it on the spot. Paging quickly through some weak poems (Rumaker describes them as "moonstruck adolescent yearnings," dull in rhyme and meter, amounting to "watered-down Keats or Shelly"), Olson then zeroed in on a promising short story. While Rumaker suspects that the story was also "badly written," Olson "detected the earnestness beneath the clumsy attempt, a hint, anyway, of a possible ability" (31). (This is what we called above a positive interpellation.) When Olson encouraged Rumaker to apply, Rumaker jumped at the chance, sensing that "maybe here I could finally learn to write; equally as important, maybe here I could find a place to be" (25).

Thus began a four-year mentorship, at once writerly and existential, one that included the agonistic dimension predicted by Rice. The feedback on his work, from Olson and other students in the writing workshop, was "unsparingly and brutally direct" (127). And, for a while, it appeared that Rumaker was making no progress. Growing increasingly frustrated with his student, Olson confronted Rumaker one afternoon during his sophomore year (151–152). Like a Zen master seizing the moment to deliver a well-timed verbal blow to an adept's preconceptions, Olson suddenly accused Rumaker of a "fearful solipsism," of writing in a cocoon of his own ego, of failing to "move out" and connect with others. The irony was that even as Rumaker was too self-referential (this is a polite translation of the shockingly graphic phrase Olson himself used), he was also prone to ignore his own experience and write forced prose delivering "social messages" (420). Rumaker was failing to make contact either with his own experience or with others. Finally, when Rumaker shared an "amusing" story about a devious landlady, Olson had had enough. "He tore the story to shreds," Rumaker remembers, seeing it as "a rehash of a rehash, about the about, experience two or three times removed from my own" (167).

I do not know whether Olson's practice of lambasting students in public is defensible, even with young adults. At the same time, it seems incumbent on us to take seriously Rumaker's own testimony. To be sure, it was a painful experience. As Rumaker recalls:

> I squirmed in my seat under his tongue-lashing, my head drooping lower, my spirit along with it. I had no words to defend myself; I was without protection, exposed, without skin. The heart went out of me, and with it the lovely airiness of the afternoon, up there in the pines outside the spacious windows, the broad expanse of valley and mountains in the distance—I felt myself shrinking, felt I could barely breathe. (169)

But even as Rumaker was struck by "the vehemence of Charles' anger," he was also struck by the precision of his diagnoses. Olson called him out for always wanting to be on the side of the angels, leading Rumaker to an epiphany about how much he feared losing his mother's love of him as her "boy-angel" (168). What Olson had been telling him about writing started to click:

> "Like Pausanius," the ancient Greek traveler and geographer, he'd instruct us, "go out and see for yourself and come back and tell us what you saw and heard, first hand." And this I found was the hardest thing to do for a variety of reasons: fear of exposure, of plunging into the imagination, the main ones; fear of facing not only the world but myself, another. The gist of it was to get the cataracts out of my eyes, unplug my ears, and speak direct with a singular voice—"the many in one"—rather than mouthing the stolen, second- and third-hand banalities of others, including my mother's. (167)

Insightful or not, it is hard to endorse such rough treatment. Later, at dinner, Rumaker was still feeling raw and exposed. Noticing several students from class staring at him, he felt publicly "humiliated" (170). At the same time, it is this very experience that Rumaker describes as the turning point in his education:

> Hard as Charles' fury was, his verbal slaps that afternoon awakened me into a second birth, for they marked the beginning of my writing life. That lacerating day commenced my leaving the coma of the amniotic sac of an unborn self I—not my mother alone, not my father alone—had up until that moment

encased myself in. It was Charles who broke through that self-imposed protective fluidity of unconsciousness I had tried to drown myself in out of fear and timidity. . . . It was his—I can put it no other way—beneficent fury that freed me into the world. (170–171)

With this Rumaker began to find his voice. The breakthrough was a story called "The Truck." After Rumaker read it to the workshop, Olson declared it a breakthrough, and his friend Tom's cheeks were "grinning red with pleasure" (420). An "additional wonder" was the reaction of Jorge Fick, an advanced student who had played the role of "prime tormentor," hazing the green Rumaker over the years (526). What struck Rumaker was "the agog look on Fick's face, like he'd seen a miracle (which I expect to everyone else, after so long a time, including me, it truly was)" (420).

If we think of this moment only as arriving at competence in a craft after a shaky start, then the word "miracle" is humorous hyperbole, as in "it took you long enough." I prefer an Arendtian reading, recalling the concept of natality evoked in the epigraph. "It is in the nature of a beginning," Arendt writes, "that something new is started which cannot be expected from whatever may have happened before." Arendt reads this capacity to initiate, this "fact of natality" as a kind of everyday miracle, a "miracle that saves the world, the realm of human affairs, from its normal, 'natural' ruin."[139] So we could say that Rumaker has been improving his writing and that it has now attained a certain level of quality. Bravo. But this is to misunderstand the revelatory nature of action, as if what natality primarily disclosed was "'what' somebody is—his qualities, gifts, talents, and shortcomings."[140] On our Arendtian reading, the "The Truck" marks a turning point not because it shows *what* Rumaker can do as a writer, but because it has sprung from *who* he is in a way that his earlier work did not. Rather than see Rumaker as moving from novice to advanced writer, we can read this literary education as an allegory of arrival in the spirit of Rice and Arendt. Where we leave off the story, Rumaker has arrived . . . as a beginner.

WHO IS THE FORMATIVE EDUCATOR?

The adolescent striving that makes itself felt over the whole world today needs to be met, needs to be given reality by an act of confrontation. Confrontation must be personal. Adults are needed if adolescents are to have life and liveliness. Confrontation belongs to containment that is non-retaliatory,

without vindictiveness, but having its own strength. . . . Let the young alter
society and teach grown-ups how to see the world afresh; but, where there
is the challenge of the growing boy or girl, there let an adult meet the challenge. And it will not necessarily be nice.
—D. W. Winnicott[141]

We are exploring Black Mountain College with the aim of expanding our imagination of higher education. To be clear, imagination does
not mean puffy white clouds on a sunny day. That is fantasy. I understand
imagination precisely as the ability to get past our wishes and clichés to
take in more of the real.[142] Imagination therefore requires concreteness
and specificity. Think of George Orwell in the *Road to Wigan Pier*, walking deeper and deeper into a mineshaft so that with the increasing strain on
his back and tax on his lungs he might begin to imagine a miner's day.[143]
Imagination is not make-believe but belief-testing. We seek to notice the
overlooked and learn to think the untimely because we are searching for a
more adequate basis for our beliefs.

In the contemporary, corporatized multiversity, what tends to get overlooked are questions of meaning, purpose, and personhood. By contrast, I
have pursued a formative conception of education as self-cultivation. With
Rice as our chief guide, we have explored the layered nature of the self, the
priority and difficulty of self-knowledge, the importance of pedagogical
beginnings, and the agonistic dimensions of teaching. Rather than rush to
the task of cultivation, we dilated the initial phases of the formative quest,
looking at how learners—on the porch and the dining hall, in the theater
class and the writing workshop—surface their selves, find their agency,
and explore their natures. Rather than dive right into the advanced class
in formative education, as it were, we followed Rice's advice to enroll in a
pair of prerequisites, since the self must be known before being shaped and
surfaced before being known. Finding yourself as a beginner, we concluded
with Rumaker, is itself a worthy educational result.

I have called this story of delayed arrival an "allegory" to signal that
what Rice offers is more evocation than systematic argumentation. Since
Rice wrote no formal treatise on higher education, we must reconstruct
his views from his autobiography and his conversations with Louis Adamic.
However, what we have found in these broad strokes is that you can get to
an interesting, untimely conclusion in just three short steps:

1. *Higher education is necessarily formative.* Below, I show how Rice substantiates this idea. Here, let me simply clarify one possible misunderstanding. To say that higher education is necessarily formative is not to idealize higher education. It is to reject the idea that we are simply transmitting discrete knowledge and information. It is to insist that personhood is always in play, that we are inevitably forming vision and values. That said, we may well be forming consumers, or people afraid to be alone with their own thoughts, or "rickety constructions of impulses ready to fall apart in what is called an 'identity crisis.'"[144] It would not even be a contradiction to speak of forming amoral, hyperspecialized technicists. Since the various aspects of us are interconnected, our hyperspecialized curricula do not avoid shaping the whole person; they simply roll the dice about how this will work out.[145] To ignore the ethical question, What is it admirable to become?, is not to avoid educating character, but simply to do so indirectly and, in all likelihood, poorly. Educators, as I demonstrate below with Rice, cannot do without some working answer to this question of what it is worth growing into.[146]

2. *Formative education is inescapably transformative.* This adds a crucial corrective since "formative" alone suggests giving shape to something shapeless, like molding a ball of clay. Certainly by adolescence, if not well before, all significant learning entails processes of *un*learning. We grow out of preferences, break old habits, let go of commitments, unravel comforting narratives, acknowledge blind spots, dispel illusions. To form is to transform. In saying this, we have to be careful not to gloss over the inevitably disorienting and painful aspects of unlearning. Letting go of commitments means mourning. Unraveling comforting narratives promises anxiety. Figuring out that the crucial fact has been parked in your blind spot is to be buffeted by waves of regret. You wouldn't know this from "transformative learning," a phrase that "gives us those nice bright colors." Frisbee on the quad; an inspirational lecture; only moving upward on the new rec center's rock climbing wall: this is transformative education, trademarked. The proper response to the trademarked variety is a vapid thumbs up. The natural response to actual transformation, we have been suggesting, is deep ambivalence.[147]

3. *Transformative education is inevitably agonistic.* As we have seen, this is especially true at the beginning of the process, when the formative educator must step into this charged field of ambivalence. Even as the educator

begins to befriend the green and growing self, he declares himself the opponent of those elements in the student that work to stall, trivialize, or sabotage
the formative process. Transformative education is doubly conflictual, since
it both triggers conflicts within the student and requires confrontation on
the part of the educator. Because the self is a layered and protected thing, it
must first be surfaced. And as Winnicott sums it up in the epigraph, "it will
not necessarily be nice."

Earlier, we followed Duberman in reading the scene on the porch as an
expression of Rice's commitment to "self-propulsion in learning." And it
is not wrong to see Rice as holding the progressive view that the student's
interest and agency are necessary conditions of formative, higher education. However, in order fully to understand Rice's view, we need to distinguish between two species of progressive education. Rice embraced a
version of what we could call the paradox of progressive education, namely
that while it is true that (p) significant learning must be self-propelled, it is
also true that (p') self-propulsion must often be kick-started by another.[148]
The tired debate between progressives and traditionalists turns on the first
part of this equation. The traditionalist denies the progressive lemma (p),
arguing that the process of learning should be driven not by the interest
of the learner but by the will and judgment of the more knowledgeable
teacher, who guides, instructs, and shapes. While progressives are right to
insist on (p), their reluctance to consider the second part of the equation
lends mainstream progressivism its untenably Romantic cast. Learners just
happen to know what they need to learn and naturally desire to head in that
direction. Teachers happily stand by to assist, serving as beneficent "guides
on the side." Motives are pure; collaborations are harmonious.

When we instead embrace the paradox, simultaneously affirming both
p and p', we forge a third way, one which I have elsewhere called "agonistic progressivism."[149] If progressivism proper is a self-conscious, modern,
European tradition, Rice (along with Richards, Olson, and others at Black
Mountain) finds his place in a looser confederation that crisscrosses cultures
and traditions, from the Zen koan to Oakeshott's theory of liberal learning.
Plato's Socrates is an agonistic progressive and so is Nietzsche's Schopenhauer, who serves as the model of the "true educator," who reveals

> to you the true original meaning and basic stuff of your nature, something
> absolutely incapable of being educated and molded, but in any case something
> fettered and paralyzed and difficult of access. Your teachers can be nobody but

your liberators. And that is the secret of all education; it does not provide artificial limbs, wax noses, or corrective lenses—on the contrary, what might provide such things is a parody of education. Education is rather liberation, the clearing away of all weeds, rubble, and vermin that might harm the delicate shoots.[150]

Agonistic progressives accept but then complicate the progressive mantra that we ought to follow the interest and lead of the student, adding that (1) pedagogy is often about creating the conditions in which this interest can emerge; and (2) following the lead of students often takes the form of directively leading them to the point where they can lead you.

★ ★ ★

What is the nature of the search? you ask. Really it is very simple, at least for a fellow like me; so simple that it is easily overlooked. The search is what anyone would undertake if he were not sunk in the everydayness of his own life. This morning, for example, I felt as if I had come to myself on a strange island. And what does such a castaway do? Why, he pokes around the neighborhood and he doesn't miss a trick.

To become aware of the possibility of the search is to be onto something. Not to be onto something is to be in despair.

—Walker Percy[151]

Now let's circle back and consider this initial premise. What does it mean to say that higher education is necessarily formative? Rice's starting point is to reject as "mere head-stuffing" what usually passes for higher education, proposing instead an ambitious, holistic aim: "The job of a college is to bring young people to intellectual *and emotional* maturity."[152] It is important to add that Rice is not proposing an emotional supplement to intellectual development, as with the contemporary prescriptions of "social-emotional learning." As Adamic explains, Rice thought that the educated person was one in "whom intellectuality and emotions will be blended or synchronized into all-round, balanced intelligence," an "all-around human maturity."[153]

For some, this sort of formative mission statement may set off alarm bells. Who is Rice to say what it means to be mature? Does he claim to have an exact blueprint of the educated person? Rhetorical questions such as these immediately put us on the defensive. They are basically arguments *ad populam*, threatening you with the derision of the crowd if you dare to ask for a more explicit argument. We can accede or expose and challenge hidden premises. Another possible response is simply to see what happens if we treat them as real questions. In this case, taken at face value and considered together, these two rhetorical questions actually prove quite manageable, even productive. I imagine the exchange along the lines of a Zen koan:

QUESTION: Who is Rice to say what it means to be mature?

ANSWER: He is a teacher. Those with no ideas on the subject had better choose a different line of work!

QUESTION: Does Rice claim to have an exact blueprint of the educated person?

ANSWER: I already said he was a teacher! Those with exact ideas on the subject had better choose a different line of work![154]

A formative educator, I am suggesting, must find a middle course between abdication and dogmatism. To deny any knowledge of maturity and immaturity is to abdicate the role. To claim specific knowledge of the end-state is to lapse into dogmatism.

We can develop this idea further with a thought experiment. If we were seeking to hire a formative educator, what would we list as the key qualifications? If I had to boil it down to three, they would be (1) awareness of one's students as distinctive persons; (2) an understanding of what formative resources (traditions, practices, ideas, texts, artworks, etc.) are likely to spark and enrich their ongoing conversations with themselves and others; and (3), skill in bringing these materials to life. Clearly, this is not the usual resumé; and it may well be that our usual hiring practices are ill-suited to fathoming intersubjective and intrasubjective qualities such as dialogicality and soul. But that is precisely the point. We are not usually searching for formative educators but for instructors (or for scholars who happen to be decent instructors). Though we sometimes wax poetic about college teaching, we operate according to the prosaic grammar of instruction: teaching is transmission to students (en masse); the curriculum is content to be "covered"; learning is acquisition. By contrast, formative education demands a dialogical stance (orienting to the concrete person who is your interlocutor), a hermeneutic sensibility (understanding persons and traditions as formed in interaction), and existential imagination (seeing how the subject matter illuminates what sorts of lives there are to be lived and what makes them worthwhile).[155]

Let's push this contrast even further. While instructors can be overheard talking about what they will "cover," formative educators are more likely to be wondering how they can create the kind of experience described by Kafka:

> I think we ought to read only the kind of books that wound and stab us. If the book we're reading doesn't wake us up with a blow on the head, what are we reading it for? So that it will make us happy, as you write? Good Lord, we would be happy precisely if we had no books, and the kind of books that make us happy are the kind we could write ourselves if we had to. But we need the books that affect us like a disaster, that grieve us deeply, like the death of someone we loved more than ourselves, like being banished into forests far from everyone, like a suicide. A book must be the axe for the frozen sea inside us. That is my belief.[156]

I like to imagine this quote emblazoned over an image of an axe driven into a block of ice, hung next to the compulsory library poster showing a young reader sunk into a beanbag chair as fuzzy and lethargic as the imperative this is meant to illustrate: "Find yourself in a book." Indeed, we could read Kafka here as searching for an axe for the frozen sea inside this cliché. As if his own belief about reading lay trapped and hidden under the ice, Kafka searches frantically, lurching from metaphor to metaphor. A book is a knife, then a hammer. Reading is disaster, banishment, suicide. OK, so maybe this isn't the right passage for our college brochures. But many of us will resonate with Kafka's gratitude for those books (and this surely also applies to nonverbal works of art) that *open us up*, that break through the hastily erected drywall pocketing our fears, shames, wounds, sorrows. Once we regain contact with ourselves, opening up flows of affective traffic (in this open-plan architecture of the inner life), we also find ourselves more open to the world around us.

If you find Kafka's hermeneutics of calamity a step too far, I ask you only to accept this more modest point: formative education founders unless one knows one's students and how to arrange a live encounter with what might move them. So, I posit these three necessary conditions: the ability to perceive in turn the student as person, personhood as quest, and culture as conversation. But are they sufficient? Indeed not, as this resume omits what might very well be the first principle of formative education. It is so basic that it often escapes notice; or perhaps we omit it because it sounds too personal. What I have in mind is this: formative educators must themselves exemplify this quest to understand, cultivate, and enact oneself.[157] This is to say that what catalyzes the educational process is simultaneously the achieved personhood of the teacher and the fact that they continue, as Jonathan Lear puts it, to strive "to live non-defensively with the question of how one should live."[158] To some extent, they must embody the "all around human maturity" of which Rice speaks. Just as crucial: they must be tuned in to what Walker Percy describes as simply "the search." In what might count as his version of the formative educator want ad, Rice describes someone who exemplifies both achieved and ongoing self-cultivation:

> A good teacher is always more a learner than a teacher, making the demand of everyone to be taught something. . . . A man who never asks himself any questions had better not try asking others. . . . A teacher must have something of humor, a deeply laid irony, and not be a cynic. In the center of his being he should be calm, quiet, tough. He must have in him the principle of growth; like a student, a sense of justice and a capacity for dejection.[159]

In sounding this idea, Rice joins a minor tradition stretching from Plato's Socrates through Nietzsche and Emerson to more recent critics of scholarly formation.[160] I think of Alfred North Whitehead's declaration that he had written *The Aims of Education* as "a protest against dead knowledge, that is to say, against inert ideas," explaining,

> The students are alive, and the purpose of education is to stimulate and guide their self-development. It follows as a corollary from this premiss, that the teachers also should be alive with living thoughts.[161]

Rorty is another member of this loyal opposition against the depersonalization of teaching, writing that "the only point in having live professors around instead of just computer [simulations] is that students need to have freedom enacted before their eyes by actual human beings."[162] To this I would add: not only freedom but also the work of integrating one's diverse dimensions into a livable unity of character and outlook. In genuine higher education, Rorty argues, we find charged interactions between persons-in-process: "the sparks that leap back and forth between teacher and students . . . [connect] them in a relationship that has little to do with socialization and much to do with self-creation."[163]

As I have suggested, the formative educator cannot operate without some ideas about what it means to be educated, about what it is worth growing into. But we now add that these must be lived ideas. The educator must embody the ideas of maturity that she espouses. This brings me to my second koanic response to the skeptic. On my view, maturity involves a growing awareness of the limits of your knowledge. This is why I suggest that we gently counsel out of the profession those who claim to have the final word on what it is admirable to become. The true formative educator works not from a template, a definition of the mature and complete human being, but from specific intimations of disavowal and disunity. From particular vantage points, we assay our gaps and deformations; from there, we essay revisable visions of our fuller integrity.

This is a tall order, maturity without fixity, knowledge without knowingness. However, as Rice explains in his autobiography, he found just such an educator in his high school Greek teacher, John Webb. Rice attended (and after college returned to briefly teach at) the independent Webb School in Bell Buckle, Tennessee, founded by brothers Sawney and John. While they were ostensibly co-principals, Sawney ran the show, asserting ever greater control over the years. Rice describes Sawney as a man who "once had an active mind, and an intuitive knowledge of boys" but "grew to be a tyrant, filled with his own glory."[164] Whereas Sawney inspired mainly fear, Rice reports that it was difficult to name the feeling he felt for John since "love is too narrow" and "worship too wide" (217). Rice develops his portrait of John through a running contrast with Sawney:

"Sawney was an actor; John Webb was a dramatist. The persons of his plays were ideas" (212).

Prone to "droning along," Sawney turned even his own ideas into tired quotations; John "was incapable of acting, that is, repeating, and peculiarly unable to act the parts that he himself had created, for he knew that language could die and meaning with it, and a thing said three times is no longer true" (212).

"John Webb never thought he knew enough; Sawney read the daily paper and became a prophet" (218).

"Sawney accepted without question the dominant beliefs of the South in his time, and of America" (220); John would take an idea, "if serious . . . and begin working on it, to reject or remake it for himself" (212).

"Sawney was a disciplinarian of outward order, and frightened or shamed the young into a similitude of goodness; John Webb's was an inner discipline, of the mind and spirit, grounded in freedom" (211).

A line of Sawney's, "often repeated, was, 'We would like to develop both character and scholarship here'"; John Webb responded, "I don't understand. To me they are the same" (220).

To be sure, Rice has positive things to say about pedagogy at Webb. Decades later, when he was touring progressive schools and listening to "breathless accounts of the latest thing," he found that the Webb of his student days—which had fused the traditional curriculum with a progressive emphasis on play and student-led activities—could match their innovations "point by point" and "go them . . . two better, for the school had both order and intellectual backbone" (205). For Rice, though, the impact of pedagogical methods pales in comparison to the importance of the example of robust personhood that he found in his teacher. What moved Rice was John Webb's integration of intellect and character; his independent-mindedness; his ability to bring out the felt importance, the drama, of ideas; his irritation at deadness and cliché; his combination of freedom and discipline. Webb evinced "soul action," the ongoing effort to meet the world in its complexity by developing one's diverse dimensions into a dynamic whole.

This portrait of Webb helps us put flesh on Rice's idea of "intellectual and emotional maturity." As Rice explains, it is all too easy for teachers, for any of us, "to grow old in harness" (215). The trick is really growing up, which Rice defines as holding on to genuine youth while adding in genuine maturity. Fearful of losing youth, we may cling to it; or we may forget to bring it along as we rush out the door. For Rice, this accounts for two common types of teacher: the "gray-haired youth" (215) who "just wants to be "one of the boys" (215); and the "top sergeant" (216) who equates maturity with the disposing of all "childish things." If the former is mired in "sentimentality," the latter is prone to "sadism" (215). "Untroubled by doubt or even thought," the top sergeant holds that "It doesn't matter what a boy studies, just so he hates it" (216). John Webb was living proof that one could navigate this dilemma without impaling oneself on either horn. In Webb, Rice found neither a cynic who had lost hope nor a sentimentalist who had traded it for fantasy, but someone still animated by the genuine article. His belief that "youth is the seed of a secret future" (216) made him immune to the cynic's nonchalant despair; his awareness of "tragedy" (217) and "the limits of his knowledge" (217) made him unwilling to sugarcoat reality.

Thus, we return to the idea that a formative educator must find a middle course between abdication and dogmatism. To deny any knowledge of maturity and immaturity is to abdicate the role. To claim specific knowledge of the end-state is to lapse into dogmatism, giving way to the immature

need for fixed templates just when students are looking for models of the
mature attempt to combine commitment and open-mindedness, to make
judgments, as Arendt puts it, "without a bannister."[165] Thus, as difficult as
it may be to define or attain, maturity is a concept that educators cannot do
without.

And yet it was just this concept, this ethical-existential ideal, that Rice
found missing as he made his way through college and grad school and into
academia. Formal education, he concluded, tended on the whole to mise-
ducate the emotions. There he found "ailing children" whose "heads are
crammed with facts."[166] He found that the imagination, "the chief distinction of man" receives at best "meager training."[167] Instead of a vital, poetic
curriculum in Rainer Maria Rilke's sense, a "high inducement to the individual to ripen, to become something in himself," Rice found mainly "a
boneyard."[168] He found that "while university students were older in years,
they were in no other way, only more hardened."[169] In graduate school, he
found not a formative education to ripen the scholarly imagination—to feel
one's way into the human dimensions of the topic, to perceive with freshness and clarity, to pose profound questions, to judge acutely and justly—
but rather a narrow training for "technicians."[170] And in his several forays
into academia, Rice found that this training had been all too successful.
Instead of grasping the world with Deweyan "chest knowledge"[171]—where
knowledge is intertwined with conduct, where thinking is illuminated by
imagination and enlivened by feeling, where knowledge of self and other
are intertwined—academics learn to distance and desiccate:

> Research is the report of what one has found out rather than of what one
> knows. The area of exploration is outside oneself, and, if not already dead, must
> be deadened . . . just as the herbalist cannot recognize a living specimen but
> must have it first pressed and dried.[172]

This points toward an important specification of Rice's claim that higher
education is necessarily formative, namely that a process of humane, holistic formation must reckon with the dead spots in experience. Rice puts it
eloquently:

> There is a technique to be learned, a grammar of the art of living and working
> in the world. Logic, as severe as it can be, must be learned; if for no other rea-
> son, to know its limitations. Dialectic must be learned: and no feelings spared,
> for you can't afford to be nice when truth is at stake. The hard, intractable facts

of science must be learned, for truth has a habit of hiding in queer places. These are the pencil, the brush, the chisel. . . . But they are not all. There are subtle means of communication that have been lost by mankind, as our nerve ends have been cauterized by schooling. The arts, especially the performing arts, are more and more valuable in such restorations. For these nerves must be renewed, in both ourselves as faculty and in the students who come to us.[173]

This winding, hortatory passage draws together several of the themes we have been tracing. We ought to understand higher education as an existential project, Rice suggests, as a contribution to the "art of living." But for this very reason, the arts must be central: formative education must be aesthetic education. But not only this. In the final line, Rice returns to the idea that formative educators must themselves exemplify the quest to understand, cultivate, and enact oneself. They must be seekers. When we combine these ideas, we derive a profound demand on the formative educator. Educators must tend to their own cauterizations, grapple with the dead spots in their experience, work to break through their own calloused layers.

★   ★   ★

And this freedom, this ripeness of self, is the indispensable element in all true teaching, simply because it speaks so compellingly to those who hunger to be free—that is presumably to all.
—William Arrowsmith[174]

Here, as in so many areas of educational discourse, we are beset by platitudes: lifelong learning; teachers as learners; cutting-edge research; sabbatical as a space for renewal. Grains of truth notwithstanding, such quarter-thoughts beg the interesting questions: In what ways does the very concept of lifelong learning actually obscure the central concept of ethical formation, that of one's life as a whole?[175] How exactly is the learning of teachers intertwined with the learning of students? What does it mean to set up an educational institution as a place of learning for the teacher? How might teaching be seen as an expression not merely of an active research program but of a formative quest? Are our slogans about the teacher as learner compatible with our practices of recruitment and promotion, our processes of faculty formation?

At Black Mountain College, faculty were not recruited according to the (now) common criteria of institutional pedigree, citation indices, grant dollars, and the like. To be sure, the Black Mountain faculty included its share of pathbreaking thinkers (e.g., John Cage and Buckminster Fuller), sought-after humanities scholars (theater critic Eric Bentley would go on to teach at Columbia and Harvard after BMC; the philosopher Bill Levi taught at Dartmouth and Chicago before coming to BMC; art critic Clement Greenberg would go on to lecture at Princeton, Yale, and Bennington), and accomplished scientists (the physicist Natasha Goldowski joined the faculty after working on the Manhattan Project and teaching at Princeton; Max Dehn was the first mathematician to solve a Hilbert problem). But this was largely unintentional. Obviously, they wanted people who knew their stuff, but what they were really after were faculty who exemplified what Rice called "the principle of growth." BMC sought scholar-teachers who saw living and learning as inseparable and came to BMC to be part of a community in which all were seeking self-knowledge and greater "intellectual and emotional maturity." And it succeeded in attracting much more than its share of scholars who remained liberal learners, of unhardened souls who had managed to acquire disciplinary rigor and intellectual sophistication without abandoning their inner sophomores.[176]

However, since faculty formation does not end with graduate school, recruitment is not enough. Whether or not it ultimately proves educative or miseducative, there is no doubt that the informal curriculum of academic life—the culture of your department and university, the promotion and tenure process, the types of conversations of which you find yourself a part—is formative. The most striking feature of the academic culture at BMC may have been its robust interdisciplinarity. This was a small faculty, undivided by departments, jointly sharing the task of governance. As mentioned earlier, college meetings amounted in part to a running interdisciplinary seminar on the aims of higher education. Interdisciplinarity was also built into the formal curriculum. In the college's first year, there were three

interdisciplinary seminars, each involving four instructors, all of whom attended every session. The intention was "to let students see the way in which an idea, a movement, a period of history, an art form, appear to a group of specialists, and also to get the student away from the habit of trying to please the teacher."[177]

The seminars started at 8 p.m. and ran long as necessary "to follow an idea."[178] One night in the creative writing seminar, a heated discussion "lasted until after midnight—and then broke out again the next morning at breakfast."[179] We should not underestimate how rare and demanding this sort of arrangement is. The four professors in one of these seminars were signing on to have their expertise (and worldviews) relativized weekly in front of their students and colleagues.

To the skeptic who sees this as not unlike sitting on a conference panel, we may respond that in fact the great majority of conferences insulate scholars in narrow, subdisciplinary cliques. If still not convinced, we might point the skeptic to another Black Mountain tradition: BMC faculty routinely attended each other's courses.[180] They were not attending to conduct teaching observations; they went as students.[181] Nor was this just a matter of professors refreshing their liberal education by attending an interesting lecture or two. In the contemporary university, the idea of the growth of the teacher is fixed by the image of the promotion and tenure ladder. At BMC, faculty were not climbing a ladder but walking a path: growth was not scripted but adventitious; not technical and professional but whole-personal and existential. The literature offers multiple stories of this teacher-as-learner ethos leading to true transformations. The most dramatic is probably that of MC Richards who arrived at Black Mountain a literature professor only to emerge as a translator, poet, and potter. She discovered pottery at Black Mountain, apprenticing herself to her colleagues, Karen Karnes and David Weinrib.

Formative education, we have said, requires a harrowing process of pecking away at the shell-self and risking exposure (recall that Rumaker described his emergence as feeling "without skin"). It requires an honest inventory of one's dead spots and a seeking out of experiences that can renew a sense of aliveness. And, we said, formative education cannot retreat to a convenient division of labor, with teachers providing and students receiving. Even as formative educators seek to assist in the self-formation of students, they must be actively devoted to their own formation, working through their own rigidities and narrow-mindedness. It is all for the good if formative educators evince admirable qualities, but key among these is the processual quality that Arrowsmith calls "a ripeness of self." What moves the student is not some finished thing in the teacher called character but the ongoing struggle to live fully and well. Recall this essay's epigraph. Richards (emphasis added) extols not perfect wide-awakeness but the *"resolve* to keep from going to sleep in the middle of the show." What catalyzes is the effort to restore feeling where we have grown numb, the struggle to reclaim freedoms given over to habit, deference, and convention. Thus, we can now add a fourth step to our syllogism: (1) higher education is formative; (2) formative education is transformative; (3) transformative education is conflictual; and (4) educators must take their own medicine! educators must take their own medicine.

It is hard to find the language to describe this stance. Professional development is impersonal and suggests an easy, additive model; by contrast, "personal growth" misses its intellectual substance and professional import, taking us from the HR office to the self-help section of the bookstore. We could call it the humanism of the teacher, as long as we follow Victor Kestenbaum in distinguishing a humanism of vigilance from the ordinary "creedal humanism" that defines humanism as a commitment to some pre-specified set of values anchored in "'models' and 'images' of the human . . . taken to be distinctly or essentially human."[182] For Kestenbaum, humanism is not a doctrine but a lived practice relying on the virtue of vigilance; "Humanism is vigilance become habitual."[183] Vigilance in turn is the excellence that aids our efforts to "do justice to the phenomena" by enabling us to stay in the "play between presence and absence."[184] Humanism as vigilance embodies a Jamesian commitment to a pluralistic universe, and therefore a stubborn resistance to "all the great single-word answers to the world's riddle, such as God, the One, Reason, Law, Spirit, Matter, Nature, Polarity, the Dialectic Process, the Idea, the Self, the Oversoul."[185] As Kestenbaum notes, this idea of vigilance goes beyond open-mindedness, at least as it is ordinarily construed as something focused on beliefs and reasons.[186] If the phenomena to which we are seeking to do justice are "a sunset, a recurring anxiety, a melody from a Haydn quartet, a two year-old's hands," then we cannot turn simply to overlooked "objections and counter-arguments" to save ourselves from myopic foreclosure.[187] Vigilance is not narrowly cognitive but holistically human, seeking "to presence these phenomena . . . through absent images, moods, feelings, attitudes, memories, reveries, musings, sensibilities, impressions, etc."[188] This helps us correct what might be a cognitivist bias in our stress on interdisciplinarity, in which we entertain rival disciplinary framings of a question or claim. And it brings us back to the aesthetic dimension of the quest to stay in contact with our growing edge.

At BMC, then, faculty embraced the idea that they themselves had to join this "agonizing, dangerous enterprise to dig down into yourself." The story that best captures this ethos is that of Buckminster Fuller's acting debut. Fuller was a core faculty member in the BMC summer institutes of 1948 and 1949, where he worked with students in constructing the first self-supporting version of his geodesic dome.[189] In the classroom and the dining hall, Fuller was known as a brilliant talker, dazzling students with his "passion and pace" as he espoused, in marathon sessions, a novel, integrated theory of everything.[190] His colleagues (Elaine and Willem DeKooning, John Cage, Merce Cunningham) found his conversation equally stimulating. The director Arthur Penn—a student who would later join the faculty—found Fuller's talking "about building to be 'one of the most exciting theatrical events' he'd ever known."[191]

But this was Bucky in his comfort zone, among students and friends. In his Black Mountain years, Fuller had yet to find the confidence that would lead to his being celebrated for his dynamic, unscripted public lectures. The turning point occurred in a quintessentially Black Mountain moment. Faculty not only attended each other's classes but also collaborated on artistic productions. In the summer of 1948, a production of Satie's *Ruse of the Medusa* (translated by MC Richards) was in the works, with Fuller recruited to play the Baron Medusa. Only things were not going so well. In rehearsal, the normally magnetic Fuller had become "gravely muted."[192] Penn was called in to work with Fuller, and before long they discovered the root of the problem: Fuller revealed that he was stricken by the fear of "making a damn fool of myself."[193] "He was just totally inhibited," Penn recalls, "he was paralyzed."[194]

Penn decided that the best therapy was to confront the fear head-on, designing a series of exercises to deliberately court embarrassment. Penn explains:

> I thought, the only thing that I can do with him, that I know to do, is be more absurd about it than he could possibly be, so I just got down on the floor and started rolling around and laughing and, you know. I said, "Come on Bucky, come on!" and, before you know it, the two of us were rolling and laughing and yelling and screaming and jumping.[195]

As Penn recalls it, the ensuing transformation was remarkable to see: "It was like somebody was just throwing chains off."[196] Fuller not only "blossomed" in the role of the Baron (John Cage called his performance "magnificent"); he turned some sort of corner in himself, later crediting Penn with helping him find his true voice, catalyzing his later success in his "thinking-out-loud" sessions.[197] Fuller the futurist had already dazzled with his dome. His animated hands-on explorations of the tetrahedron were spellbinding. "Bucky Fuller and his magic show," Elaine DeKooning called it. "He looked like the Wizard of Oz to me," Cunningham recalls, "just an extraordinary human being."[198] At BMC, however, Fuller went further, letting students and colleagues behind the curtain, showing all the awkwardness and beauty of a person struggling to turn a corner in himself.[199]

Thus, we arrive at an answer, or set of answers, to the question, Who is the formative educator?[200] First, we must recall the crucial point that, in an important sense, students themselves must be the drivers and lead architects of their own formative education. As Albers puts it, "Individual nourishment is the task of the individual himself."[201] So our first answer is: the student. But this does not mean that formative education can be entirely autodidactic. We need teachers to help us arrange a meeting with ourselves, to point us toward and help us make use of valuable formative resources, and to model for us the soul action that we are seeking to undertake. Learners need to see the fruits of formative labors, the achievement of character. This includes exemplary qualities such as emotional depth, imaginative range, intellectual precision, moral sensitivity, and political clarity. It also includes the distinctiveness of each character. It is moving to see how individuals cobble together a self with disparate materials and hold themselves together amid internal conflicts and external buffeting. And, as we have been stressing, learners also need to see the labor itself. They need examples of persons-in-process, models of how to engage the harrowing work of self-cultivation with courage, energy, grace, seriousness, humor, and perseverance. So, who is the formative educator? The formative educator is someone who can serve as a catalyst, midwife, and model. And we can now read the question as a statement: *who* is a formative educator. It is centrally the distinctive who-ness of the teacher that catalyzes and inspires.

THEATER AND WINGS

Because of its inherent tendency to disclose the agent together with the act, action needs for its full appearance the shining brightness we once called glory, and which is possible only in the public realm.
—Hannah Arendt, *The Human Condition*[202]

Everything that lives, not vegetative life alone, emerges from darkness and, however strong its natural tendency to thrust itself into the light, it nevertheless needs the security of darkness to grow at all.
—Hannah Arendt, "The Crisis in Education"[203]

Earlier we noted our tendency to dichotomize formal and informal education, imagining that beyond the intended lesson there is only the happenstance of experience. This distorts our understanding of formative education
in at least three ways. First, it blinds us to the crucial role of the relational
and the adventitious in the scene of classroom learning. The enactment of
curriculum depends, as it were, on the local weather; and this depends in
turn on the surrounding atmosphere, the ethos in which classroom learning
is embedded. Second, this dichotomy obscures all of those educational experiences that develop precisely *across* classroom and non-classroom spaces. It
was only by tracing Rumaker's zigzag route—from his chance exchange with
Virginia outside the dining hall to having his story torn to shreds in front
of his peers in Olson's writing workshop and back to the dining hall, where
Rumaker stewed over and digested the challenge Olson had laid at his feet—
that we could hope to understand his transformative experience. Finally, it
renders invisible the formative intentionality built into the spaces, practices,
and rhythms that structure everyday life in a place such as Black Mountain.

In our discussion of the college so far, one such experiential structure
has stood out: the stage. And this is a formative element that confounds the
distinctions between formal/informal, academic/experiential, curricular/
extracurricular, and intended/incidental. At BMC, we have found all of
the following: the stage in the classroom (Wunsch's theater pedagogy); the
stage as classroom (Bucky's debut); the classroom as stage (Olson's writing
workshop); and the community as ongoing theater-in-the-round (Rice's
"goldfish bowl"). In this section, I want to explore not only the extent, but
also the limits, of this dramaturgical conception of formative education. At
Black Mountain, it turns out, not all the world's a stage. Crucially, the college knew to temper its theatrical ethos with a complementary formative
principle, providing space for solitude and structuring time for recollection.

It is not only the literal stage that is of interest as we explore the aesthetic-
existential model of formative education that flourished at Black Mountain.
That said, we also should not minimize the centrality of the performing arts
to the life of the college. The BMC dining hall doubled as a performance
space, and many evenings were given over to plays, readings, dance recitals,
and concerts. In the early years of the college, for example, there was a concert every Saturday night. However, quantity doesn't tell the whole story.
Whether as company or audience, the BMC community was constantly
tackling difficult new material and forms. Black Mountain is legendary

for its early championing of avant-garde modernism, but this should not be confused with the search for a new canon. It is rather a restless search for forms that renew and extend our modes of perception and thought. In 1948, that challenge was the surrealism of Satie's *Ruse of the Medusa*. Only a couple of years later, we find MC Richards, David Tudor, and John Cage again challenging their received ideas about the theater by together working through the ideas of Antonin Artaud, then virtually unknown outside of France. (Richards would go on to publish the first English translation of *The Theater and Its Double*, in 1958, offering a key inspiration for a generation of experimental theater in New York and beyond.[204]) Or consider dance: while the larger world was still digesting the modernity of Martha Graham, Black Mountain was helping launch the important departure from Graham represented by the Merce Cunningham Dance Company, which held its inaugural performances at the college in August 1953.

The phrase avant-garde likely conjures up the detached, knowing stance of the aesthete. I am suggesting that the passion for aesthetic novelty and difficulty at BMC stemmed from what is essentially the opposite source: a commitment to wide-awakeness and a willingness to risk one's settled conclusions. Consider, for example, David Tudor's piano recital in August 1951, which included pieces by Schönberg, Webern, Boulez, Cage, Feldman, and Wolff.[205] It was not enough to embrace the difficult chromaticism, atonality, and serialism of the Second Viennese School: here Tudor is already trying to break through the crust of Schönbergian convention by opening himself to the "affective athleticism" of Boulez's "Piano Sonata No. 2" and the aleatory play of the New York School.[206] It is said that *de gustibus non-disputandum est* (in matters of taste, there can be no dispute). Black Mountain never got the memo. When Cage suggested that he devote his 1948 summer performances to working through the entire (if then small) oeuvre of Erik Satie—giving three half-hour evening concerts per week over the eight-week term—Albers insisted that Cage preface each concert with a ten-minute talk that could make these ultra-minimal compositions "seem reasonable."[207] Good idea until, in one of these explainers, Cage happened to decry the "deadening effect" of Beethoven's emphasis on harmony, setting off a war with BMC's Germanophiles.[208] Erwin Bodky promptly launched a series of counter concerts, featuring Beethoven's later quartets, prefaced by his own mini-lectures refuting those "who would disparage Beethoven's reputation."[209] The mounting tensions were only finally defused when a raucous food fight broke out in the dining hall—an informed and passionate public indeed.

It is not only the ideal of wide-awakeness that drove this interest in novel and difficult aesthetic forms, but also BMC's holistic educational impulse. Mirroring the interdisciplinarity of its curriculum, the BMC stage was itself partial to *Gesamtkunstwerk*. In the next section, I describe in detail the 1952 aleatory, mixed-media, theater-in-the-round piece (Cage's *Theater Piece No. 1*) now considered to be the first "happening." But already in the late thirties, under the direction of Xanti Schawinsky, Black Mountain was staging "total theater," proto-performance-art pieces such as *Spectodrama: Play, Life, Illusion* (1936–1937) and *Dans Macabre: A Sociological Study* (1938).[210] Indeed, Schawinsky's work was meant not only to draw from a range of art forms—theater, music, dance, painting, poetry—but also to be integrated into the "academic" curriculum. For Schawinsky, "the stage was to be a laboratory for synthesizing through non-analytical, non-literary means ideas being explored in all disciplines of the curriculum."[211] Schawinsky himself describes *Spectodrama* as "an educational method," in which a working group, bridging the arts and the sciences, creates staged representations to express the fruits of their inquiries, as they search for a "a new alphabet that might provide more complex means of . . . communication."[212] Though Schawinsky had already begun to develop a theater of "total experience" during his time at the Bauhaus, a holistic institution in its own right, at Black Mountain he found that he had more "professional and artistic scope" so that "an educational crack at the whole man seemed to be in order."[213]

To reiterate, this was no conservatory for aspiring actors. Black Mountain was equally committed to both sides of the equation clearly stated by Albers when he writes, "any education separated from art is no general education. Also, any art training unrelated to general human development is no education."[214] Given the college's small size, Emil Willimetz (student from 1937–1940) recalls,

> to have a play at BMC almost every available body needed to be impressed. As shy as I was in public performances, Wunsch managed to get me into Irwin Shaw's *Bury the Dead*, Clifford Odets' *Waiting for Lefty*, and Shakespeare's *Macbeth*.[215]

So the literal stage was a central feature of the Black Mountain (extra)curriculum, whether you were "impressed" to play a part, worked backstage, or participated as an audience member. However, as Albers indicates, the goal was not a theater program as such. Everything turns on whether the literal stage can become an existential one. Literal theater, we must admit, can fail as formative experience for performers and audience alike. Conversely, you don't need to be in drama class to experience the "theater of display and witness."[216] Indeed, as we have seen, all aspects of life in this fishbowl of a college—teaching and learning, working and playing, making and conversing—were shot through with a heightened awareness of the dynamics of self-disclosure and interpersonal recognition.

To frame this idea, we have been drawing on Arendt's concepts of natality and action, her distinction between generic, predictable behavior and the kind of self-enactment that can never "be expected from whatever may have happened before."[217] Behavior begets more behavior, and so we each trudge along in our usual mode—no less strange for its ubiquity—of being simultaneously wrapped up in personal concerns and out of touch with our distinctive personhood. But every so often a different sort of space opens up, what Arendt calls a "space of appearance."[218] As we are drawn together by a common concern, the distinctive vectors of our approaches are thrown into relief. The *res publica*, the public thing, occasions self-enacting "deeds" (Arendt's term of art for actions that speak volumes and words that make waves), which in turn stimulate the deeds of others, the meanings of which are found in yet further self-enacting responses.[219]

Formative educators of all stripes work to occasion such moments and rejoice when they occur, moments when an individual student suddenly steps forward from the ensemble to take a solo. It is not simply that people have been hiding, trying to blend in, and finally risk more authenticity. Rather, the dynamics of the group, and of the material itself, occasion the discovery of a new aspect of oneself, allow one to come into oneself in a new way. A student, let's call him Dan, suddenly reveals his Dan-ness not only to the group but also to himself. I have seen a good seminar group, without skipping a beat in their seriousness about the task at hand, laugh with delight at the grace of these serendipitous moments of, to coin a term, *personation*.

But disclosure is one thing and exposure is another. In the epigraphs to this section, we see that Arendt offers a both-and logic when it comes to this key aspect of human flourishing.[220] Arendt is clear that we need spaces of recognition and occasions for self-disclosure. For example, she prefaces her account of action with this passage from Dante:

In every act, what is primarily intended by the doer . . . is the disclosure of his
own image. Hence it comes about that every doer takes delight in doing . . .
since in action the being of the doer is somehow intensified. . . . Thus nothing
acts unless [by acting] it makes patent its latent self.[221]

However, she is just as clear that we need spaces of retreat from "the glare
of the public," from the demand to discover and enact our who-ness in
concert with others. This capacious, dialectical philosophical anthropology
suggests an important principle for formative higher education: human
growth requires a rhythm of engagement and withdrawal. And that is just
what BMC offered. To illustrate this rhythm, let's next peek in on Albers's
studio pedagogy, gathering another example of how a classroom space
can serve as a theater of display and witness. Later, we will see how Black
Mountain provided space to withdraw from the pressures of the interpersonal and modulated the tempo of discovery.

★   ★   ★

The more I think of it . . . the greatest thing a human soul ever does in this
world is to *see* something, and tell what it *saw* in a plain way. Hundreds of people
can talk for one who can think, but thousands can think for one who can see.
—John Ruskin[222]

As soon as the college was up and running, Rice's top priority was to find
someone to teach art. "Don't ask me how or why I know it," he was often
heard to say, "but if I can't get the right man for art, then the thing won't
work."[223] But finding the right person would not be easy. For Rice rejected
the traditional way of incorporating the arts into general education, as a series
of great works authored by others to be admired by the student. "The country is swamped with appreciators," he quipped.[224] At Black Mountain, the
goal was to foster persons "in whom there is a nice balance of forethought,
action, and reflection," and this meant engaging the students themselves
in practices of production and performance.[225] It is this active component,
Rice explains, that makes art "the best medium" for general education:

In history, sociology, psychology, economics, and the rest, there is plenty of
action to be reflected upon; but it is *not the action of the student himself*. . . . They
do not and cannot begin with the individual student as . . . the one who is
doing the doing. This is why we at Black Mountain begin with art. The artist
thinks about what he himself is going to do, does it himself, and then reflects
back upon the thing that he himself has done.[226]

As we saw earlier, Rice has a complicated relationship to learner-centered education. While he is happy to embrace learning-by-doing, he wants nothing to do with that strain of progressivism that elevates relevance over rigor. Rice was seeking an art professor devoted to the rigors of perception and production, not someone offering structureless sandboxes of self-expression. The trick is to steer away from freedom-as-license without colliding back into learning-as-compulsion. The arts steer us toward this truly progressive middle ground because artmaking is not about rule-following but neither is it a matter of making up the rules as you go along. As Rice puts it, "the arts are least subject to direction from without and yet have within them a severe discipline of their own."[227] But what exactly is this "severe discipline"? Here I read Rice as referring to the fact that an artist works in a medium, or a complex of materials and cultural givens that function as enabling constraints.

If that last phrase sounds paradoxical, it is because we tend to suffer from a case of myopia regarding freedom, mistaking freedom from constraint ("negative freedom") for the whole of freedom (which includes a "positive" aspect). To cure ourselves, let's try a thought experiment.

Imagine a baseball game in progress. There is a runner on first who has been given the green light to steal second base. As he takes his lead, it does seem correct to say that his freedom to steal is curtailed on all sides: the shortstop is covering second; the catcher stands ready to throw him out; the first baseman is holding him on; the pitcher, who has a solid pickoff move, is looking him back to first; if the play is close, the umpire will decide his fate.

But now notice what happens when we remove these constraints. First, let's delete the umpire and opposing team. While the runner is still free to run to second (in fact, he could crawl to the bag!), it is no longer clear in what meaningful sense he is still free to steal the base. Now let's remove his team as well. Is he still a baserunner? In any case, let's go ahead and remove the bases, and erase the boundary lines. In fact, let's uninvent baseball altogether, so that its rules and history never existed. What do we find?

A man stands alone in a field. There is nothing stopping him from sprinting 90 feet in any direction he chooses. At the same time, indeed as a result, he is utterly unfree to steal second base, or even to conceive of the project.

This is not to deny that some constraints prevent us from carrying out our projects. The recent roadwork near my house has most certainly reduced my freedom to pick up my daughters from school! It is to remind ourselves that action is not only vulnerable to being blocked: it can also be hollowed out. The freedom to conceive and carry out projects requires a thick medium of action, one that enables even as it constrains.

It is precisely because they push back in distinctive ways that artistic media enable distinctive forms of expression. The structure of granite determines how it chips. Paint drips, dries, and appears according to the laws of gravity, viscosity, and optics. Dancers too deal with gravity, along with the facts of anatomy. The alternating stresses of iambs locks the poet into a particular rhythm. And as a result, happily, one can say quite different things in a granite sculpture, a painted canvas, a choreographed dance, or a poem in iambic tetrameter. Conversely, the surefire way to tell that you have walked into a stinker of an art exhibition is when there is a pamphlet waiting for you at the end, explaining what the pieces were getting at. It turns out that what you saw were merely visual analogues of ideas already worked out in ordinary prose, not thinking in a medium. Contrast this with, say, Francis Alÿs's *Paradox of Practice 1* (1997) or Doris Salcedo's *Shibboleth* (2007). In the former we find someone pondering how "sometimes making something leads to nothing" (the piece's subtitle) and doing this thinking through the enabling constraints of movement, video, and a giant block of ice on a warm day.[228] In the latter, we encounter ideas—about the exclusion of immigrants and outsiders, about the barriers we erect and the passwords we expect—formed in concrete and steel mesh. MC Richards, offers this nice description of her encounter with medium at the potter's wheel:

> There was, first of all, something in the nature of the clay itself. You can do very many things with it, push this way and pull that, squeeze and roll and attach and pinch and hollow and pile. But you can't do everything with it. You can only go so far, and then the clay resists.[229]

Thus, even while art fosters independence, it teaches us that, in life, wishing doesn't make it so.

The problem for Rice was finding someone steeped in craft discipline who also saw artmaking as part of general education. When colleagues asked Rice if he wanted BMC to be an art school, they received a sharp reply: "'God no!' he'd thunder, 'that's the last thing I want.' They're the most awful places in the world.'"[230] Where the art schools were turning out "little tin pot artists," Rice wanted explorers of the very "grammar of the art of living."[231] Where professional artists tended to be "spiritual porcupines" "hiding in their lonely places," Rice wanted civic poets who would "go into the center of life *and belong there*."[232] Where the arts were full of brand-name individualists ("peddlers, each crying his own wares, and crying down his fellow peddlers"), Rice wanted genuine individuals, artists whose investigations of form were also a search for an "integrity of relationship," demonstrating how one devotes oneself to the polis while "giving up . . . nothing of" oneself.[233]

Let's review Rice's seemingly impossible wish list. He wanted someone to teach art experientially, as a firsthand process of discovery, not as a series of finished (if not fully embalmed) works completed by others. At the same time, Rice wanted someone who knew that the rigor mortis of scholasticism was not the only possible form of rigor in aesthetic education. He sought a commitment to craft that would counter the tendency in learner-centered education to treat freedom as license and creativity as vacuous self-expression. But that was not all. He also wanted someone who could untether such craft knowledge from art-school pre-professionalism, someone who taught art as general education, not as specialized training aiming to "turn out a professional dauber, designer, fiddler, or actor who will become 'famous,' [so that the faculty can] . . . bask in his glory."[234] Could there really be a teacher of art who simultaneously satisfied all three of these ideals? Indeed, almost miraculously, before the first term was up, Rice found just such a person in Josef Albers, the Bauhaus "crafts master" exiled by Hitler's rise to power.[235]

On Albers's first day at BMC, at a reception welcoming him and his wife Anni, he was asked what he hoped to accomplish. The epigrammatic Albers wasted no words: "I want to open eyes."[236] A year later, in the *Black Mountain College Bulletin*, he elaborated on his pedagogical approach:

> From his own experiences the student should first become aware of form problems in general, and thereby become clear as to his own real inclinations and abilities. In short, our art instruction attempts first to teach the student to see in the widest sense: to open his eyes to the phenomena about him and, most important of all, to open to his own living, being, and doing. In this connection we consider class work in art studies necessary because of the common tasks and mutual criticism.[237]

Albers wastes no time before signaling his commitment to experiential education. Throughout his career, he questioned the educational value of passing on the "deadwood" of a knowledge disconnected from conduct, a process he described (five years before Freire would famously expose education's "narration sickness") as "auditory discipleship."[238] As a critic of schooling, Albers was ahead of his time. Two decades before the publication of *A Nation at Risk*—the alarmist, Reaganite report that many use to date the turn toward high-stakes, standardized testing—Albers was decrying that we have confused the educated person with someone skilled in "memory acrobatics," and that we always place "retrospection before creation, and thus re-search before search."[239]

At the same time, Albers the crafts master was not about to let experiential education devolve into a free-for-all. He rejected what he described as the "poor heritage given to us by so-called progressive education."[240] Throughout his career, he consistently distinguished his aims—"disciplined seeing and sensitive reading of form. . . . [the] syntax and synopsis of visual articulation"—from what he called "the present fashion of self-expression and over-individualization."[241] On his reading, art education suffered alternately between the disease of discipleship—which comes in various strains, he mused, including "Picassobia," "Matisseitis," "Kleeptomania"—and an "epidemic . . . of self-expression."[242] Between imitation and premature bids to originality (he was known to scold students who signed their practice compositions), art students were missing out on the arduous but worthwhile task of developing their vision. In another formulation, Albers suggests that the art world seesaws between an objectivist version of realism and a subjectivist version of expressionism.[243] Art, he counters, is neither "a report on nature [nor] . . . an intimate disclosure of inner secrets."[244] The former reduces seeing to what Albers calls "outer sight" or "ocular seeing."[245] The latter just replaces seeing with saying. Albers champions the neglected third option, which he calls "inner seeing" or "inner perception conditioned by imagination."[246] Unlike self-expression, which is thought to be spontaneous, this "double-faced insight into our means and ourselves," insists the crafts master, requires sustained effort and remains "ninety-nine percent perspiration."[247]

Just as strong as Albers commitments to craft and experiential education was his belief in general education. He shared Rice's disdain for pre-professionalism.[248] "First, we seek contact with material," Albers wrote. "It is not our ambition to fill museums: we are gathering experience."[249] To understand Albers's approach, however, we need to distinguish several different ways of thinking about general education. Typically, we see Gen

Ed as something piecemeal, as a set of distribution requirements meant to hedge against specialization. The idea is that, since knowledge is divided, students ought to learn at least a little in each division. Albers falls into a second camp, one that seeks to provide students with foundational experiences, where knowledge remains undivided. Albers captures this idea in a topographical metaphor:

> Education is somewhat like a mountain (sometimes maybe like a hill). . . . The broader the base, the higher and firmer the top. The higher the top, the broader the view. Therefore, in school, in college, in university, first and second and third comes general education as a necessary foundation for all specialized studies which come later.[250]

Notice that, even as one progresses from basic exercises to more advanced work, the goal for Albers remains breadth of vision. Even within the foundational approach, Albers stakes out his own position. One familiar version of the foundational model sets out a list of books whose greatness transcends disciplinary splintering; another identifies core intellectual skills to be acquired before one proceeds into specialized study. Albers and Rice wanted Black Mountain to go a step further, aiming not only for intellectually synthetic courses but for experiences that integrate mind and body, knowing and doing, personal conviction and impersonal findings.

Again, art is no curricular cure-all. Indeed, we may find our experience in museums and concert halls deadening or distracting, an irony Dewey savors by coining the term "anesthetic."[251] Whether it is set "upon a pedestal" as the work of genius or stowed in side cubbies as a series of technical specializations, art is too often detached from ordinary experience. For Albers, then, it was not only a matter to turning to art as a foundation; one must also seek the foundational in art. At Black Mountain, he taught not only the foundations of drawing and painting, but searched for even more fundamental building blocks. He taught an entire course on color. The centerpiece of his curriculum was his introduction to design sequence, or *Werklehre* (literally learning how to work), engaging students in a hands-on investigation of the properties of materials. One part of the sequence, *matière*, concerned our haptic relation to materials, investigating their textural possibilities. In "materials," proper, students investigated capacities "such as compression, elasticity, and firmness, tested through folding and bending."[252] Anni Albers, who taught weaving at the college, speaks to the foundational role and formative potential of this approach:

> We are overgrown with information, decorative maybe, but useless in any con-
> structive sense. We have developed our receptivity and have neglected our own
> formative impulse. . . . And this fact leads to a suggestion: we must come down
> to earth from the clouds where we live in vagueness and experience the most
> real thing there is: material.[253]

While this advice certainly applies to aspiring artists, it was aspiring humans that the Alberses had in mind. Encounters with materials can nurture universal sensitivities of soul, Josef Albers suggests, helping "to discover and unfold ability, to discover and cultivate human relatedness."[254] For Albers, craft does have vocational implications, but not as training for a specific practice. In his classes, Albers worked to foster precision, economy of effort, and care for materials, dispositions needed in all forms of work.[255] And it is not only visual artists who need to learn how to see. More than three decades after attending Albers's classes, Rice offered this testimonial: "[He] gave you a pair of eyes—you saw things. . . . I've never forgotten him. . . . Hardly a day passes but my eyes say 'Albers.'"[256] The arts for Albers were not a specialized domain but a ground in which we found the roots of all of the capacities—civic, aesthetic, moral, spiritual—needed to lead a good and meaningful life. He targeted civic virtues such as the awareness that "life has greater forces than economic interests" and the quality of not waiting "to lead others or to be led" because one is "occupied in leading [one]self."[257] He sought to educate the imagination by expanding perception, writing that "the many-fold seeing, the many-fold reading of the world makes us broader, wider, richer."[258] He stressed ethical formation, speaking of how the arts constitute a "school of intentions," and how they cultivate the situational responsiveness central to practical wisdom.[259] And he speaks of the forming of a "spiritual constitution."[260] As Albers puts it at one point, "the fundamental art problems are always the same—the discovery and revelation of the human soul."[261]

But how does this cohere with Albers' disdain for self-expression and his aforementioned aim to open students' vision to the "phenomena about them?" Doesn't soul discovery and revelation amount to navel gazing? Here we need to further explore Albers' escape route from the dilemma between "objectivistic realism" and "subjectivistic expressionism," his idea that aesthetic education can yield a "double-faced insight into our means and our-selves." In this regard, Albers pedagogy resonates with Arendt's philosophy of action. Both point to a type of self-revelation that challenges the ordinary logic of self-expression.[262] Arendt makes this point in a memorable passage:

> This disclosure of "who" in contradistinction to "what" somebody is—his qual-ities, gifts, talents, and shortcomings, which he may display or hide—is implicit in everything somebody says and does. It can be hidden only in complete silence and perfect passivity, but its disclosure can almost never be achieved as a wilful purpose, as though one possessed and could dispose of this "who" in the same manner he has and can dispose of his qualities. On the contrary, it is more than likely that the "who," which appears so clearly and unmistakably to others, remains hidden from the person himself, like the *daimōn* in Greek religion which accompanies each man throughout his life, always looking over his shoulder from behind and thus visible only to those he encounters.[263]

Arendt contests the basic premises of self-expression, that one knows who one is and can decide when to share it. This presumes a level of self-transparency and autonomous control that we do not possess. It is not only that we disclose more than we intentionally express, but that our distinctive who-ness eludes willful self-expression. For Arendt and Albers alike, while self-knowledge remains both possible and worthwhile, it nec-essarily becomes heteronomous and indirect.

Here is where we return to the idea of the space of appearance. Earlier we considered the passage from Dante about the delight in actions that intensify our being and disclose who we are, "making patent the latent self." Albers was no Dante, but he did write poems, and in one he sounds this very theme:

> There is no world without a stage
> and no one lives for not-appearing.
> Seeing of ears invites to speak,
> knowing of eyes invites to show.[264]

Even as Albers was discouraging the usual competition of the atelier—Who is the most sophisticated or accomplished? Who is the next big thing?—he was constantly inviting students into a theater of comparison, into a space of appearance. The typical photograph of Albers teaching at Black Moun-tain shows a group of students tightly gathered around an array of student works spread out on the floor.[265] Albers is crouching down, pointing to a feature of one of the works, talking through what he sees in and through the work, what he notices about what it notices. As if it were a physics diagram, we can see the interaction of the vectors of attention: with their eyes fixed on the work in question, the students' lines of sight are inflected by Albers's looking, and indeed by what is revealed about their own angles of vision.[266]

To be clear, comparison here does not mean competition, unless it is a contest with oneself in a struggle to see more. This was not math class, with students called to the board to demonstrate the correct solution. Consider, for example, Albers's "four worlds" exercise, which tasked students with using the same four colors and a common formal language "to create four compositions as different in 'climate' or feeling as possible."[267] The point of the exercise is to understand how colors work—colors react to each other in juxtaposition in ways that are largely beyond our control—but Albers expected and welcomed a diversity of genuine understandings. "We have to conclude," Albers says, "that every need is manifold and that in any task there never is only one solution"[268] It is true that Albers had a dictatorial side. It was his way or the highway, except that his way was for you to work assiduously in finding your way. A complex figure, Albers is said to have been "an authoritarian who demanded that students think for themselves" and a "control freak" who engaged in classroom antics and delighted in surprises.[269]

A chief inspiration for students was Albers's "total absorption in whatever was at hand."[270] One student remembers that "the excitement that he conveyed was electric," adding that Albers "would look at things and see them as though he'd never seen them before. . . . It was a feeling of first time, every time."[271] Another student describes how this motivated her:

> It was his excitement at seeing a matière that made the difference. He'd go crazy at seeing these pieces that people brought in. We'd see him dancing around and carrying on! Well then, we'd go out and look at things differently. I did one piece using pressed fern leaves and mica, and put a huge amount of work into it. What would make a young girl go out and do all that? It was the fact that he so totally gave himself to the pieces that we brought in.[272]

And in a sense, Albers and his students, were seeing these things for the first time. *Materialgerecht*, doing justice to the material, is achieved not by converging on its supposedly singular essence but by articulating its manifold nature. Thus, Albers distinguishes between "factual facts" (physical facts, abstracted from experience) and "actual facts" (the way in which the physical enters always variously into the flow of experience).[273] In a poem titled "On My Work," Albers writes "that form demands/multiple presentation/ manifold performance."[274]

For Albers, aesthetic education runs aground when either knowledge or self-knowledge is taken as its singular aim. What Albers is searching for in his pedagogy is precisely lines of "congeniality," leading to a mutual disclosure of self and world.[275] Consider Albers's famous leaf studies.[276] In selecting and arranging one or more leaves, students are cultivating what Albers calls "substantial lived insight."[277] They are not wrapped up in a bid for self-expression. It is about the leaves, about structure, form, and color. But neither are they neutral cataloguers of nature. Perhaps an awkward expression captures it best: they are attempting to see *with* the leaves. They are cultivating what Albers calls "visual empathy."[278] As the students articulate the relationships among the leaves, they also enact their relationship to the leaves—their "elective affinities," to use Goethe's famous phrase. Even as the students help the leaves perform their manifold nature, the leaves help the students declare and discover themselves.[279]

It is the opportunity to witness this dance of disclosure—this mutual revelation of the leaves' manifold nature and the who-ness of each student— that accounts for Albers's electric state. One BMC student describes him as "totally animated, always on fire, giving off little sparks all of the time."[280] And here is Albers himself getting excited by the plurality of perspective revealed through a comparison of studies:

> See how different the mentality is, how different the attitude is, how different the tempo and climate, and the temperature. . . . See the difference in palettes. See the difference in placement. See the difference of concentration or distribution. . . . They don't come from one school; when you look [at them] straight and unprejudiced, they come from twenty schools. It looks that way. No! They come from twenty students who are just true to themselves.[281]

In this way, the college classroom can become a metaphorical theater, a stage on which to explore and enact character, stance, and vision. The students are not asked to declare their opinions on world events. They are asked to walk the woods on the hunt for interesting mica and ferns. And, in sharing their vision of and insight through these ferny friends, enrollment in the studio begins to increase. The number of bodies remains the same but now here and now there, a *daimōn* appears, a distinctive "who" that supervenes upon, but cannot be reduced to, the wheres, whens, and whats of the person. In the play of perspective, Albers and his students may witness the profound event that is coming into one's own, that is revelation of soul action. Emerson captures the magnitude of such moments when he writes,

> The power which resides in him is new in nature, and none but he knows what that is that he can do, nor does he know until he has tried. Not for nothing one face, one character, one fact, makes such an impression on him, and another none. . . . The eye was placed where one ray should fall, that it might testify of that particular ray.[282]
>
> ★ ★ ★
>
> Life is essentially periodic. . . . Lack of attention to the rhythm . . . of mental growth is a main source of wooden futility in education.
> —Alfred North Whitehead[283]

It is the rare social interaction that offers what we have been calling a theater of display and witness. At Black Mountain such spaces of interpersonal and intrapersonal encounter were especially prized. That said, even if we could maintain this charged state, we would not want to spend all of our time there. We do need to act before witnesses, but we also need a reprieve from this demand. A flourishing life involves a movement between appearance and withdrawal, a rhythm of engagement and release. And it is just these spatial and temporal structures we find at Black Mountain, embodying the intentionality built into so-called informal learning.

First, let's consider the architecture of appearance and withdrawal. As we have noted, students found many of the spaces at Black Mountain to have a fishbowl quality. In classes, at meals, during college meetings, in rehearsals and performances, on work shifts, in the communal dorm rooms, students found themselves repeatedly exposed to the intensity of the interpersonal, to the dynamics—at once delightful and disturbing, edifying and exhausting—of recognition and misrecognition, self-enactment and self-evasion. For this reason, there was one overriding residential principle at Black Mountain: each student must have a private studio or study (both terms were used).[284] To experience an Arendtian space of appearance, to meet others in their distinctiveness and bump into aspects of your own who-ness you hadn't anticipated, is indeed a gift. But then one needs a chance to *recollect* oneself, to *regroup*. The plural nature of these terms is fitting, as solitary space is not monologic. Consider the aphorism that was so important to Arendt: "Never is a man more active than when he does nothing, never is he less alone than when he is by himself."[285] To withdraw from the tumult is not to quit the work of self-discovery. Indeed, soul action may intensify as we sit with the discordant aspects of ourselves and work to understand why the example of others inspires, troubles, challenges, or resonates. We need a space where we can seek to understand and integrate those aspects of ourselves revealed in the tumult of interpersonal encounter. And just as it is with others that we find ourselves, so it is often when we are "alone" that we begin to take in the other with whom we have been interacting. In the "quiet" of the study, the voices of others may become loud indeed.

What the study does provide a pause in the "action," in the Arendtian sense. We experience a relaxation of the pressure of our accumulating record: this is what I prefer, what I do, what I stand for, what I laugh at, what I don't laugh at, whom I like, what I am interested in, and so on. The problem, Kierkegaard remarks, is that "life must be understood backwards. But then one forgets the other principle: that it must be lived forwards."[286] A moment of repose, a break in the action, provides at least some consolation amid this existential comedy. "What seems required," David Blacker writes (speaking of the importance of spaces for inwardness in a democratic society), "is some way to 'catch up' with ourselves, some method by which we might render the ends of our activities graspable, in both the sense of understanding them and also (potentially) manipulating or otherwise altering them."[287]

The literal space of the studio is crucial. It makes a difference to be able to close a door and sit at your own desk. It matters too that the college has set this space aside for you. The name on the door declares that one of the events at this college is your ongoing relationship with yourself. But the literal space is not enough. It is nothing more or less than a reminder of and home for a habit of inwardness. And, as I have already begun to indicate, the spatial and temporal dimensions of this practice are intertwined. When we speak of a contemplative "space," we mean something temporal as much as spatial. It is quiet, solitary space, furnished with various reminders of my ongoing conversation with myself; and it is a time to catch up with ourselves, a moment of repose, a break in the action.

That said, I do want to talk about a specifically temporal intervention, designed to facilitate this rhythm of appearance and withdrawal. In the scene on the porch, we considered how college students need a reorientation from the heteronomous, instrumentalist logic of studenting—dragging the highlighter across the page of the required reading; racking up credits en route to a credential—to a self-directed engagement following a logic of discovery. The former has a characteristic temporal structure: grind, grind, grind, release. In this mode, work loses its playful, world-discovering, self-engaged aspects; play loses its seriousness and becomes merely downtime. We called the alternative *skholé*, recalling the Greek term for seriousness unyoked from necessity, for freedom rising above license. *Skholé* is neither grinding through nor powering down, but tuning in. It is not an offbeat in the rhythm of production, but an alternative rhythm of engagement.

But *skholé* is not the kind of thing that can be permanently installed, like a statue of alma mater. Even at a place such as Black Mountain, attuned to wide-awakeness, the hum of engagement can start to flip over into a culture of busyness. We can start to turn our choices into a harness. We continue to plow a row merely because that is the continuation of the line. With *skholé* in mind, Michael Oakeshott called college "the gift of an interval."[288] Sometimes students need to be offered the gift of an interval within the college experience itself. BMC had a tradition to accomplish just this. Duberman explains:

> An invention of the second or third year was "the interlude"—a periodic announcement, without advanced warning, that all classes would cease for a week so that everyone could have a chance to try something they had to defer because of lack of time—whether reading Shaw, attempting to write poetry or sitting in the sun.[289]

To explain this tradition, all point to the intensity of the place. Interludes were called, Duberman explains: "when the schedule got too top-heavy with events, when the momentum of activity began to get manic." "It was by no means a sea of tranquility," Arthur Penn recalls, more like "a broiling ocean where everybody was at a kind of high pitch."[290] Charles Perrow concurs: "When tensions seemed to be near the breaking point, the Rector . . . might call an 'interlude.'"[291] Hannelore Hahn takes the story from there:

> Josef Albers would get up, and one evening, put his spoon against the glass—ding, ding, ding—and say, "As of this evening, until a week from tonight, all classes are suspended and this is a lesson in leisure time."[292]

The interludes were an interesting combination of an injunction and a release from obligation. Specifically, Perrow recalls, students were directed to branch out:

> All classes were cancelled, and students and faculty were enjoined to do a project that was completely different from what they had been studying or teaching. The wave of euphoria was instant, and trips to Asheville, hiking in the surrounding mountains, swimming in the little lake, building rafts, painting if you were in literature, intense reading if you were a painter, and cooking on your hot plate filled the days. One or two of these were necessary each semester, and they cooled the hothouse.[293]

Though it was "a time to ease off, to regroup," Duberman notes, the "interludes were not vacations."[294] In fact, as Sarton recalls, it would often be during the interludes when "the best work gets done."[295] Hahn emphasizes this same point, pointing not to a specific injunction but rather the desire to live up to expectation that you could organize your own time:

> The result of this trust that a human being will learn from that was phenomenal, because I don't remember seeing anybody getting drunk or going into town and wasting his time. No, double time, you worked harder at whatever was of interest to you. People really created during that time.[296]

Sarton tells a story that combines these themes of redoubling one's efforts and trying something new. In her English class, she gave a presentation on Yeats that so affected a classmate that when an interlude was declared the classmate spent the "the whole week studying . . . Yeats."[297]

Normally, we think of being freed *from* work. But if our work—as project, as search—has degenerated into busywork, then we need to be freed from that, freed to work. The interlude interrupts the "what is expected of me" mindset, returning students to the question of what interests them. Like a debt jubilee, it releases students from that particular state of unflourishing we might call "past due," that state in which we start experiencing each day as a back payment on promised work. Freed from the question, What am I most behind on?, students may ask something more interesting: What is in front of me? There is space to mull over events that flew by, to connect seemingly disparate experiences, to relocate one's agency as a learner.

Thus, even as Black Mountain arranged myriad encounters in which one found oneself stretched and refracted, it took care to ensure that there was time and space to recollect, to digest, to integrate. With its architectural insistence on personal space and its attunement to the rhythm of engagement, Black Mountain saw to it that students would have space for periodic retreat from the demand to enact oneself in the dance of interpersonal recognition.

LEARNING HERE AND NOW

I didn't understand what was going on but I knew something was happening.
—Fielding Dawson[298]

In his 1947 rectoral address, Bill Levi charted four dimensions of soul action: inwardness, outwardness, forward-looking, and backward-looking, explaining how the college sought to nurture each.[299] It is interesting to compare Levi's formative compass to the doubly dialectical theory of experience on offer in Dewey's *Democracy and Education*. Dewey sums up a crucial stretch of his argument as follows: "The idea of education advanced in these chapters is formally summed up in the idea of continuous reconstruction of experience, an idea which is marked off from education as preparation for a remote future, as unfolding, as external formation, and as recapitulation of the past."[300] I called this conception "doubly dialectical" because it seeks to interrupt educational hypostasizing on the twin axes of space and time.[301]

Let us look first at the spatial dimension. Is education best understood as an unfolding of what is already within the student or as a formative influence from outside? Such a question, Dewey suggests, has already gotten the whole thing wrong. It presumes that we already know what is internal and what is external when, as we saw above with Arendt and Albers, one of the elements of growth is precisely the ongoing dialectical disclosure of inner and outer worlds. My sense of what I am made of is occasioned and shaped by what I have encountered. There may be aspects of who I am lying dormant and hidden, having never encountered the environing conditions that would call them forth. Or life may lead me to significant reinterpretations of known aspects of my identity. For example, what we call our "needs," are made up both of what Jürgen Habermas calls "need dispositions" and the social "need interpretations" through which they come to be understood and expressed.[302] Thus, what I come to discover inside of myself is contingent on my life events and cultural-historical world. But the same is true in reverse. What I encounter "outside" of me is not my literal "surroundings" but rather my "environment" or, in Dewey's memorable phrase, "the things with which [one] varies."[303] To pinpoint a person's surroundings, all we need is a GPS device. To know a person's environment, we need to know a good deal more: their past trajectory and current intentions, their hopes and fears, their habits and practices. Otherwise, we cannot know what are the salient features, the active ingredients as it were, of one's surroundings. What we deem outside of us is simultaneously contingent on what is inside.

Now, let us look at the temporal axis, where Dewey again suggests a dialectical approach. For Dewey, calendars are overrated. They suggest a linear conception of time: here is a sequence of days, and here we are at this point in the sequence. But this is not where we live, in this calendar-day present. As Dewey rightly observes, we inhabit a "moving present" in a "constant reorganizing or reconstructing of experience."[304] We do not merely move along a timeline: our movement through life is marked by our continual redrawing of the line. Consider the simple example of aging. According to the calendar, our twentieth birthday came and went but once, and it sounds like science fiction to suggest otherwise. In fact, we will likely have multiple experiences of turning twenty, and the first of these may be far from the richest. When we first turn twenty, as it were, we have been sixteen and eighteen but never thirty or forty, and this shapes the moment. The fifty-year-old, revisiting that moment, has a very different sense of what it meant to turn twenty.

Consider a second, thicker example, featuring a character I will call Nathan. Nathan grew up in a small town. Later, he attended a big state university, and after graduating he moved to Los Angeles. The city in which he arrived was to him the quintessential big city, defined in large part in

contrast to the smaller places he had left behind. So far, the temporal structure seems linear: first there was his small-town past, then his college days,
and now his big-city present. But now let us play out the story, checking in
with Nathan some years later. Living in LA has changed Nathan's sense of
what makes a place big and what makes it small, and he now understands
very differently what it means to have come from his home town. Thus, we
can say that Nathan now, in the only way that matters, comes from a *different* hometown than the Nathan who first arrived in LA. And, since the past
frames the present, Nathan also now inhabits a very different "big-city"
present than the Nathan just out of college. In short, the calendar lies: life
is full of such spiraling temporal structures in which past and present shape
each other reciprocally.

Another name for this spiral structure is "the hermeneutic circle."[305] We
find ourselves in a present, framed by what we have brought from the past
but also containing novel, recalcitrant features. This inheritance (our store
of meanings, our diet of questions, our vectors of interest, our weights and
measures) simultaneously opens the present to us as a space of productive
encounter and limits this moment to *the* present of *this* past. However, the
assimilation of present possibilities—possible presents—to our past fund of
meanings is never absolute, and thus we always face the question, How well
has my past, as I have understood it, prepared me to meet the demands of
my present? As we work with the recalcitrant features of our present, we
may begin to rework our sense of the past.

The hermeneutic circle applies both to individual trajectories and to
the movement of tradition. The history of ideas—the "tattered maps"
left behind by alert spirits, and flawed human beings, who were trying to
take stock of where we had been and where we were heading—both funds
and limits our present.[306] But the same can be said in reverse: our present
enables us to perceive some aspects of these texts while making us oblivious
to others, and it leads us to construe those aspects of the text in particular
ways. What we call "the past," Dewey notes, should "be seen as the past *of*
the present."[307] We thus live within the spiral movement of tradition. (Here
I speak of genuine, living traditions, not traditionalism, or reverence toward
dead letters.) The constructions of past thinkers enable and constrain us in
meeting the demands of our present. At the same time, our present opens
up new ways of understanding traditionary texts. Take, for example, the
tradition of the self-portrait from Parmigianino and Van Gogh to Frida

Kahlo and Cindy Sherman. These artists are working within, reflecting on, an intervening in an unfolding set of ideas about the self. It is not implausible to say that one of the effects of this tradition—as it intersects with economic forces, technological developments, and so on—is the selfie. And now when we look back—peering over the crowds with their selfie sticks—at the *Self Portrait in a Convex Mirror* or *The Film Stills*, these works reveal new veins of meaning. And when we return from our fresh engagements with these renewed works, our selfie moment looks different in turn.

Thus, while Levi's and Dewey's compass roses look the same, there is an important difference in their approaches. Levi is suggesting that growth amounts to a leading out of the student's attention along these four lines. Dewey's dialectical or hermeneutic conception of experience complicates this, helping us to distinguish the hypostasized versions of inside and outside, past and future, from their living dialectical counterparts. The critical purpose of Dewey's heuristic is precisely to show how education has been deformed by allowing its attention to drift away from the flying present where past and present, inside and outside, are dialectically intertwined, toward one or another of these hypostasized impostors. In each of these four directions, argues Dewey, lie traps where we mistake education as "unfolding" from within or forming from without, as "preparation for a remote future" or "recapitulation of the past."

For Dewey, the important temporal question for education is not which way we lean on the linear timeline—toward conserving a calendar past or preparing for a calendar future—but how we become aware of the limits and possibilities of a given timeline. The calendar present is generic and shallow. It is a box to be checked, twenty-four hours to be used, as one recalls grand old worlds or ushers in brave new ones. The *pedagogical present* is singular and replete, containing within it both clues for understanding our current, dominant ways of understanding where we have been, where we are, and where we are going and pointers toward alternate timelines.[308] (I embrace the sci-fi ring of this last phrase, which I take to signal not that hermeneutics is far-fetched but that this beloved genre both engages in thought experiments about literal time travel and taps into the kind of time travel we engage in all of the time.)

Dewey's idea of reconstruction suggests a similar reorientation of attention regarding what we might call the "geography" of education. The important question is not whether education inclines toward what is taken to be inside the student (e.g., instincts, faculties, needs, meanings, commitments, an unfolding developmental logic, a true self, etc.) or outside the student (the logic of the subject matter, timeless truths, moral norms, social needs, etc.), as if we already possess a final charting of inner and outer worlds. But if the *innerwelt* and the *umwelt* are co-constructing, then the question is not where to locate the pedagogical capitol (and pedagogue's capital) on a ready-made map, but what resources we find in a *place* of learning for making sense of how we have understood and might better understand what lies within and around us.

The famous education rallying calls—to individualize or socialize, to conserve the past, or usher in a better future—are pleasant vistas to gaze on as one rides the conveyor belt, distractions from the pedagogical here and now where we might struggle for some genuine freedom of movement in our thinking and doing. And what do we call the practices that focus our attention on the pedagogical here and now: the arts. The arts do not need to be *applied* to education: they are some of our richest practices for dislodging us from the grooves of routine, opening up the spiral of experience. Education does not need to *employ* the arts: education is the communal pursuit of spaces that awaken us to the dialectics of experience, that attune us to the genius loci and the unrepeatable Now. Thus, at Black Mountain, what we find is not an already-worked-out-theory of formative, general education and a resort to one handy instrument, the arts, for achieving that desideratum. Rather, BMC was set up to be a home for aesthetic-educational happenings.[309]

★ ★ ★

One evening (though some say it was afternoon) in the summer of 1952 (memories differ as to the date), the BMC community gathered in the dining hall (on the location, all agree) for a mixed-media collaborative performance piece "composed" by John Cage and performed by Cage (lecturing), Merce Cunningham (dancing), David Tudor (playing the piano, and perhaps a radio), Robert Rauschenberg (exhibiting his white paintings and playing records), MC Richards and Charles Olson (reading poetry), and Nicholas Cernovich (projecting slides and film fragments).[310] Untitled at the time, it has come to be called *Theater Piece No. 1* and to be regarded as the first happening.[311]

The music program at BMC was far from conservative. Heinrich Jalowetz, a friend and student of Arnold Schönberg, had been its beloved, leading figure from 1939 until his death in 1946. And this mainstream, European avant-garde was still represented by his widow, voice instructor Johanna Jalowetz. Meanwhile, the summer of 1952 saw not only the return of Cage, but also the arrival of Stefan Wolpe. A student of Anton Webern, Wolpe would go on to direct the BMC program through its final years, further extending the influence of the Second Viennese School.[312] But as faculty member David Weinrib recalls, "These people, they come from your German radicalist tradition . . . but they could never make the next . . . leap."[313] Cage was upending more than tonal conventions. His new Zen-inspired, chance-driven compositions were meant to dissolve the foundational assumptions of even the most experimental strands of modernism: that composition flows from intention; that music is distinct from silence and from noise. Suffice to say that there were skeptics in the audience that night.

Skeptical or not, Jalowetz was the first to arrive. It was her custom to arrive early in order to get the best seat in the house. However, she was greeted by an unfamiliar setup. Cage had discarded the usual blueprint, noting that it embodies a highly consequential assumption:

> When you have the proscenium stage and the audience arranged in such a way that all look in the same direction—even though those on the extreme right and left are said to be in "bad seats" and those in the center are in "good seats"—the assumption is that people will see *it* if they all look in one direction.[314]

To upset this assumption, Cage arranged the space in a variation of theater-in-the-round that we might call "theater in, around, and through the square." As Cage describes it,

> The seating arrangement I had at Black Mountain in 1952 was a square composed of four triangles with the apexes of the triangles merging towards the center, but not meeting. The center was a larger space that could take movement, and the aisles between these four triangles also admitted of movement. The audience could see itself, which is of course the advantage of any theatre in the round. The larger part of the action took place *outside* of that square.[315] (See figure 1 for a sketch of this arrangement)

In a traditional theater—with its unidirectional tiered seating, dimmed house lights, and illuminated, raised stage—it is relatively easy to ignore the audience around you. Theater-in-the-round, as Cage rightly notes, disrupts this illusion by putting a portion of the audience in your field of vision. You are watching the show *and* you are watching others watching the show. Cage's arrangement

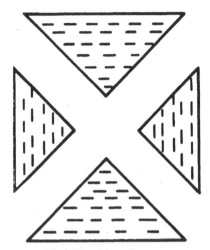

Black Mountain performance,
seats and stage-space, 1952

Figure 1
Adapted from John Cage, Michael Kirby, and Richard Schechner, "An Interview
with John Cage," *Tulane Drama Review* 10, no. 2 (1965): 52.

goes further by staging most of the action in a circle around the seating: with
Cage's lectern at six o'clock, the ladder atop which Richards and Olson would
read abutting the seating at seven or eight, Rauschenberg's phonograph at
twelve o'clock, paintings suspended from the ceiling at one o'clock, and the
piano at four o'clock.[316] Though recollections of the event vary widely, it
seems that Cunningham, whose dance crisscrossed the aisles, may have been
the only one to occupy the central area, and then only temporarily.

By emptying out this central space, Cage both intensifies and goes
beyond the alienation effects of theater-in-the-round. Cage's arrangement
intensifies the noticing of our noticing as the audience in the other three
triangular areas now becomes the primary object in our field of vision. But
it is not just a matter of making us more aware of how we perceive the
theatrical event, because the piece challenges the very idea, still operant in
theater-in-the-round, that there is a singular, theatrical event to perceive.
Rather than integrate the separate components onto a designed set, Cage
has invited them into a yet-to-be-defined space. Rather than knit them
together into one narrative matrix, he has organized them according to
randomly devised time compartments. For example, the one extant piece
of Cage's "score" instructs the projectionist as follows:

Begin at 16 min.
play freely until 23 min.
Begin again at 24:30
play freely until 35:45
Begin again at 38:20
play freely until 44:25

Thus, Cage creates a multifocal experience by emptying out the central focal area and ringing the seating area with multiple sites of performance, each making a distinct demand on our attention.

Before saying more about this centrifugal reading, it is worth noting a complementary, centripetal, Zen interpretation of this theater-in-around-and-through-an-empty square. After all, what Cage was reading that night was his Juilliard "lecture," a prosopoetic piece about Zen, music, and poetry foregrounding, in both form and content, silence, space, and emptiness. Focusing on the paintings and projections above them, the poets over their shoulder, the piano and phonograph beside them, and the winding path of Cunningham, the audience of *Theater Piece No. 1* may have found their attention drawn back to the emptiness before them by lines such as these: "our poetry now is the realization that we possess nothing"; "each something is a celebration of a nothing that supports it"; and "I have nothing to say and I am saying it."[317] On the Zen reading, Cage is not simply emptying the stage but staging emptiness. Here is a happening, *Theater Piece No. 1* announces, and *nothing* is what is happening.

Now let's return to the centrifugal reading, picking up the story with the arrival of Jalowetz. The veteran theater goer encountered not only a novel seating arrangement but an emcee reared on Zen koans. In his interview with Kirby and Schechner, Cage recalls his exchange with Jalowetz:

CAGE: She had made a point of coming early in order to get the best seat. And she asked me where the best seat was and I said they were all equally good.

SCHECHNER: Did she believe you?

CAGE: Well, she saw that she wasn't getting a reply in relation to her question so she simply sat down where she chose. She had no way, nor did I, of telling where the best seat was, since from every seat you would see something different.

I read Cage's response as synecdochical and pedagogical. The relativization of lines of sight stands in for a more general relativity of understanding. Like the teacher figure in the Zen koans, Cage is simply working with what the adept brings him, working to redirect her attention from the unproductive question she poses—where should I sit in order to take in the piece fully, not skewed by some peculiar angle of vision?—for the series of richer questions it begs: How should I sit with the anxious indeterminacy of meaning that any decent work of art presents? How do I, from my particular vantage, edit, direct, and unify the work? While I sit here trying not to miss anything, am I missing *nothing*?

Thanks to Cage's seating arrangement and Zen intervention, Jalowetz now has to choose her own seat and own the contingency of that choice. And the question of where one should sit opens onto the larger question of what one should be attending to. The simultaneous streams of performance throw into relief how we are always tuning in and tuning out, selecting and combining. *Theater Piece No. 1* not only juxtaposed the different modalities of painting, photography, poetry, music, and dance, but it featured layers within the visual, verbal, musical, and kinetic. According to some accounts, Cernovich's images (remembered variously as fragments of a black-and-white film, 35 mm photographs, and hand-painted glass slides) were projected onto Rauschenberg's white paintings.[318] Movement included Cunningham's dance and the mounting and dismounting of the ladder. Spoken word emanated both from the poet's ladder and from Cage's lectern. And there were overlapping aural streams from Rauschenberg's gramophone and Tudor's piano (which itself was more than piano, since it seems that one of the pieces he played was Cage's *Water Music*, which includes radio, a duck call, and water pouring). In such an environment, you cannot hide from the fact that your attention is selective. And as you inevitably integrate these selected fragments into a cohesive experience, you cannot escape the conclusion that it is you who have made this whole, you who has directed the performance.

Rauschenberg's *White Paintings* were very important to Cage, who cites them as the inspiration for his signature work, 4′33″.[319] When we see a painting in a gallery or museum, its multiple enframings—literal frame, proper names (of the artist and the work), institutional aura, curatorial comparisons, artworld discourse—heighten and direct our attention. We begin to look pointedly. We send out a search party, as it were, to find formal features, an artist's signature style, a commentary on social issues, and so on. What Cage admired about Rauschenberg's *White Paintings* was how their painterly poverty can help us to "unfocus our attention." Confronted by their blankness, our attention, while still heightened, becomes less teleological and more receptive. To draw a Deweyan distinction, the *White Paintings* both interrupt our "bare recognition" and invite our "full perception."[320] Or as Cage puts it, "Hallelujah! The blind can see again. . . . Blind to what he has seen so that seeing is as though first seeing." And when this happens, the emptiness of Rauschenberg's canvases transforms into a bustling presence. As Cage puts it, "the White Paintings [are] airports for the lights, shadows, and particles." Thus, Cage saw them not as meagerly finished, and sealed by the artist's signature, but as beautifully open to what lay around them. Once we let go of the distinctions between the work itself and the dust it gathers, between intention and accident, composition and noise, the *White Paintings* become collaborative performances, works not only of space but of time, with a duration equal to the time you behold them. The paintings become happenings.[321] Both Rauschenberg and Cage saw art as part of an existential ethic. "I try to keep wide-awake," Rauschenberg will later remark, echoing the idea we considered earlier with Alfred Schutz.[322] Or, as Cage puts it, art should be "an affirmation of life—not an attempt to bring order out of chaos nor to suggest improvements in creation, but simply a way of waking up to the very life we're living, which is so excellent once one gets one's mind and one's desires out of the way and lets it act of its own accord."[323]

This reading of the *White Paintings* suggests that our earlier observation about Cage's seating arrangement applies to the piece as a whole. *Theater Piece No. 1* is simultaneously a Zen garden and a Brechtian intervention, an experience for the wide-awake and some help in waking up, a space to encounter the replete and irreducible present and a confrontation with our habitual evasions of that encounter. It is, after all, very difficult to maintain this state of free-floating attention. For example, rather than let the *White Paintings* slowly accrue their atmospheric dynamics, we finish them off with a label ("art," "anti-art," "abstraction," "monochrome," "white," "Rauschenberg"). It is precisely this opening up and closing off of attention staged by *Theater Piece No. 1*, with its layering, movement, and arbitrary temporal matrix. The central area is empty, and then Cunningham appears and is gone again. The *White Paintings* confront us with their unsparing blankness, then they are filled with images of other times and places, until the projection time window closes, and the canvases empty out again. We hear silence, a poem, two overlapping poems, and silence again. Cage offers us a series of before-and-after shots of how we short-circuit perception with ready-made recognitions.

We see this same dialectic of empty and full on display in another interesting detail of the piece. "When people arrived," Cage reports, "they found an empty white cup on each seat":

> It wasn't explained to the audience what to do with this cup—some used it as an ashtray—but the performance was concluded by a kind of ritual of pouring coffee into each cup.[324]

The white cup echoes what we have just been saying about the Rauschenberg paintings, and attendee Francine du Plessix Gray recalls the additional detail that the "coffee was served by four boys dressed in white."[325] As each person took their seat, they wondered what the cup was for. Inside this practical question lurked a deeper question. The audience was greeted by an empty vessel, a nothing out of which a something might arise. Would they hold that space open throughout the event, or fill it with the habitual?

Cage was apparently partial to Huang Po, but perhaps he knew the *Mumonkan* as well, and in particular its wonderful koan 7:

> A monk said to Joshu, "I have just entered this monastery. Please teach me." "Have you eaten your rice porridge?" asked Joshu. "Yes I have," replied the monk. "Then you had better wash your bowl," said Joshu. With this the monk gained insight.[326]

At first glance, Joshu appears to be way off topic. In fact, he has hit the bullseye. The monk has arrived, full of assumptions. He assumes that he is ready to be enlightened, that enlightenment can be captured in words, and that this gift might come from the teacher. "Have you eaten your rice porridge?" The question serves to redirect the monk's attention back to the present moment and to everyday rituals. You are looking too far and too fast, Joshu implies; slow down and remember that the sacred may also be found in a bowl of rice porridge. After eating, comes washing up. Do not get ahead of yourself. Joshu's question also functions as more direct rebuke: why do you ask me to ladle something out when you are already stuffed full? You say you are seeking answers, but you don't seem to have prepared yourself to receive them. Maybe you had better wash your bowl.

Meanwhile, back in the Black Mountain dining hall, something surprising was happening. With his arbitrary divisions of time and invitations to his collaborators to "play freely," Cage had worked, as he put it, to get his intentions "out of the way," to let life speak "on its own accord." And sure enough, Cage and the others found themselves graced by an uninvited participant. A dog entered the space drawn by Cunningham's movement. "It didn't bark," Cunningham recalled, "it just started dancing up and down those aisles, and followed me around."[327]

It is no ordinary work which we are set to do, and it comes to us under no ordinary conditions. We are not here to reproduce, in this new locality, some old and well known style of college or university. . . . The hungry eyes of toiling millions are turned, with mingled hope and fear, upon us, to see what new and better solution we can possibly offer of the great problems on which their well-being and destiny depend.
—John M. Gregory[1]

Education is here placed among the articles of public care.
—Thomas Jefferson[2]

What are public universities and why do we need them? Here is an answer that gets right to the point: "If college opportunities are restricted to those in the higher income brackets, the way is open to the creation of and perpetuation of a class society which has no place in the American way of life."[3] This comes not from some leftist manifesto but from a report commissioned by Harry Truman, *Higher Education for American Democracy* (1947). Indeed, there should be nothing radical about rejecting a system that tracks family wealth into corresponding levels of educational and economic opportunity for the next generation. Recast as a positive claim, a democratic society must have educational institutions that offer both wide access and social mobility. However, it is exactly this combination that proves so difficult. As David Labaree has shown, our simultaneous pursuit of access and advantage "has not succeeded in shuffling the social deck"; rather, it has "lock[ed] us in a spiral of educational expansion and credential inflation."[4] "People who had an educational edge on the competition," Labaree explains, "were, by and large, able to maintain this edge by increasing their schooling at the same rate as those below them in the status order."[5] Each time we open the doors wider on the ground floor, we add levels to the structure. Thus, at the exact moment that access to the high school is widened beyond the middle class, we see the invention of curricular tracking. At Philadelphia's Central High School, for example, the new "commercial" track was put in place just in time (1898) for Central to drop its traditional entrance exam (1900).[6]

However, internal stratification was not enough to preserve advantage. With a tenfold increase in US high school attendance from 1890 to 1920, "middle-class students in the upper tracks were now heading to college, leaving [working class] children in the same relative position they occupied before—one step behind in the race for educational advantage."[7] The pattern then repeats itself in higher education. Sparked by the GI Bill and fueled by Labaree's spiral, US college enrollments increased eightfold between 1940 and 1980.[8] As before,

> the newcomers did not flood into the same institutions that had become home to the middle class students in the years between the wars. Instead, higher education created a series of new lower-level institutions to make room for the influx, leaving the college's core middle-class constituency safely protected in institutions that, instead of becoming more inclusive in the face of greater demand, chose to become more exclusive.[9]

For Labaree, Paul Simon was right all along: "One man's ceiling is another man's floor."[10]

Today we find a system of higher education finely calibrated to reproduce social-economic advantage. While the extreme contrasts are startling—the poor go to college at roughly the same rate (around 40%) as the ultrarich land a spot in an elite college[11]—more chilling may be the uncanny detail with which family income maps onto college access (see table 2).

Pick any part of the country and you will find a series of distinct class pathways. Table 3 shows one quartet from New Jersey. Passaic County is certainly affordable for students from all walks of life; but partly for that very reason its credential commands less respect in the labor market. For respect, one needs a degree from Rutgers or Princeton, but in both cases access narrows sharply. At Princeton, you are more likely to bump into an obscenely rich student (.1% signals an annual income of $3,881,715) than you are one whose family income falls in the bottom quintile.[14] Though not Princeton-pricey, even the in-state tuition at Rutgers remains steep. In the meantime, state flagships are increasingly "prioritizing affluent out-of-state

Table 2
Distribution of students by parental income in each college tier (2018)[12]

	Nonselective	Selective	Highly selective
Poorest quintile	14.3%	7.7%	6.0%
2nd quintile	18.2%	11.4%	8.5%
3rd quintile	21.5%	16.5%	11.7%
4th quintile	24.9%	24.5%	17.2%
Richest quintile	21.2%	40.0%	56.6%
Richest 10%	8.9%	22.2%	41.5%
Richest 5%	3.7%	11.4%	28.2%
Richest 1%	0.5%	2.1%	8.6%

Table 3
Class pathways in four New Jersey colleges (2014)[13]

	Passaic Co. Comm. Coll.	St. Peters College	Rutgers University	Princeton University
Net cost (in state)	$177/credit	$57,980	$29,991	$83,140
Net cost (out of state)	$310/credit	$57,980	$47,691	$83,140
Median family income	$35,900	$55,800	$103,500	$186,100
Poorest 20%	26%	12%	6.8%	2.2%
Richest 20%	9.6%	19%	47%	72%
Richest 10%	3.1%	9.5%	27%	58%
Richest 5%	1.2%	2.7%	12%	44%
Richest 1%	<1%	<1%	1.3%	17%
Richest .1%	<1%	<1%	<1%	3.1%
Grad median income (age 34)	$25,200	$45,500	$58,400	$90,700

students . . . over the moderate- and low-income state residents who they were created to serve."[15] According to James Angell, its third and longest-serving president, the University of Michigan sought to offer "an uncommon education for the common man."[16] Now only half of the seats in Ann Arbor are filled by students from Michigan. The in-state tuition ($34,500/year) is intimidating enough; with its out-of-state premium ($74,000/year), it seems that Michigan too has its sights set on the Ivy League.[17] By comparison, Rutgers has managed to maintain a large in-state enrollment (82%), but this goes to show that tuition is not the only barrier for less affluent students. A highly selective admissions process also selects for class. Thus, even the ostensibly public Rutgers enrolls seven times more students from the top quintile than from the bottom.

Anticipating the sticker shock faced by students and families, state universities resort to shameless spin. Here are examples from the costs pages at three Big Ten schools. At the University of Illinois at Urbana-Champaign (UIUC) ($37,842 in-state/$57,959 out-of-state) the word "Tuition" is tucked in a small font (yellow on light green) just above the extra-large, bolded phrase, "Invest with Confidence."[18] Indiana University Bloomington ($28,670/$56,620) adopts a similar strategy, heading their tuition and fees page with "IU Bloomington's costs are just one part of the equation," explaining that they "do a lot to manage costs and keep your return on investment high."[19] "Return on investment" is a hyperlink taking you to a page stating that "95% of IU seniors feel they've acquired job- or work-related knowledge and skills."[20] My favorite may be the University of Maryland, where an algebraic graffito shows how to solve $X^2 — 4X + 4 = 0$ in five steps.[21] The idea is that the tuition ($30,488/$59,290) is fair considering the skills you'll acquire. I prefer another reading: only with moderately advanced mathematics can one understand how such a large figure was ever derived.

Adjusting for inflation, the cost of attending a four-year public university has tripled since 1980 and risen 65% since 2000.[22] Even so, many publics charge premiums for professional majors. The University of Iowa charges you $26,883 ($48,846 out-of-state), unless you are a pharmacy major, in which case you will pay $34,683 ($50,225 out-of-state). If you major in classics at UIUC, you pay $35,210 ($54,046 out-of-state); if you major in civil engineering the bill rises to $40,474 ($61,872 out-of-state). At UVA, while education majors are given a slight break at $38,772 ($76,852 out-of-state), nursing majors pay a premium at $43,148 ($81,400 out-of-state). The argument for these variable rates is that some professions pay well, but, as we noted, this was precisely the promise of our state universities: that even people of humble means could aspire to such professions and improve their lot. The hope was that comprehensive public universities could serve as switching yards, rerouting class trajectories. With stratification across and within publics, we have all but settled on a two-track system, with blue-collar institutions delivering working-class outcomes and elite institutions perpetuating privilege.[23] What is driving our abandonment of the democratic ideal articulated by the Truman Commission Report?

No doubt many social and economic factors are at play. Here I simply want to explore one central ratcheting mechanism in the downward spiral of US public higher education. If we look at the interaction of economic forces and educational values, we discover a disturbing negative feedback loop:

1. Decreases in state funding of higher education drive up tuition, putting financial stress on students and families.
2. Financial stress fuels jobbification, a cycle-within-the cycle as credential-ization triggers program cuts that enfeeble general education, and this reinforces the credential mindset.
3. Jobbification cements the idea that higher education is a private not a public good.
4. Skepticism about the public role of universities saps taxpayer support for higher education, leading us back to where we began with decreasing state funding for public universities.[24]

Now let us look at each of these steps in greater detail.

Step 1. While there are multiple drivers of rising tuition, the main culprit appears to be the waning of state funding.[25] The dark humor of another former University of Michigan president, James Duderstadt, sums it up nicely: "We used to be state-supported, then state-assisted, and now we are state-located."[26] Between 2001 and 2019, average state higher-education per-student appropriations dropped 22.6%.[27] In 2012, tuition raced past state appropriations as a percentage of the operating budgets of public colleges and universities (the tipping point for four-year publics happened even sooner, in 2003).[28] At most state universities, state appropriations now constitute only a fraction of operating expenses. In many cases, the decline has been precipitous. At Berkeley, state support has declined from 50% to 14% over the past three decades.[29] At UVA, between 1987 and 2012, state funding fell from 37% to 14%.[30] That figure is now down to 8.6%.[31] Over the last two decades, state support plummeted at institutions from the University of Washington (66% to 34%) to the University of Kansas (34% to 18%).[32] A quick survey turns up no fewer than fourteen flagships at which the state funds a fifth or less of the budget: Rutgers (20%); Minnesota

(17%), UNC Chapel Hill (16%), UW Madison (15%), Arizona (13%), UT Austin (13%), Michigan (12.9%), Missouri (12%), South Carolina (11.6%), New Mexico (11%), New Hampshire (8.8%), Oregon (7.3%), UC Boulder (4.3%), and Penn State (3.9%).[33] One startling analysis, looking at the trend-lines from 1980 to 2011, discovered that thirteen states were on pace to *zero out* their funding by 2040, and another fifteen by 2070.[34]

As state support vanishes, tuition soars, putting tremendous financial stress on students and families. During the same period, 1973–2013, in which inflation-adjusted public college tuition rose 270%, median household income rose a mere 5%.[35] Unsurprisingly, student indebtedness has reached stratospheric levels, now totaling $1.75 trillion. As David Blacker points out, there is something especially insidious about this form of debt: since the bank cannot repossess your knowledge and skills, you are the collateral. Blacker thus sees student debt as a late capitalist form of indentured servitude.[36]

Step 2. Being caught in this vise-grip alters what students and families expect from higher education. It is, after all, perfectly rational to inquire into the terms of one's indenture. What is surprising is how readily universities themselves adopt the language of return on investment. A few years back, to find out what UC Berkeley cost (currently $46,008/$78,582), you had to click through a page informing you that "a Berkeley education earns our graduates an additional $26,333 each year in income over those who did not go to college."[37] This is textbook proofiness, but this statistical sleight of hand is just one feint in a larger shell game.[38]

It is good to ask about the value of college. Indeed, there is nothing wrong with construing this value in terms of use. For Marx, a use-value is anything that "through its qualities satisfies human needs."[39] It "makes no difference," he immediately adds, whether these needs "arise . . . from the stomach . . . or the imagination."[40] Use is as rich and variable as our needs and desires, our purposes and projects. Even for the supposedly use-less arts and humanities, practicality is not a problem. What could be more practical than figuring out how the world works, who you are, and what you stand for? When we fault someone for reducing value to utility, what we are really saying is that they have an impoverished imagination. Here precisely lies the (existential) use-value of liberal learning: it addresses our need to stop begging the fundamental question of what is worth want-ing. It saves us from the fate, as Emerson warned, of reducing life to "an affair to put somewhat between the upper and lower mandibles."[41] If you don't keep your eye on the ball, someone will swap out the capacious idea of use for this mandibular idea of utility. Actually, Berkeley's pitch pulls off an even more daring trick, vanishing use altogether. All that remains is "exchange-value," which, as Marx says, does "not contain an atom of use-value."[42] What is the value of a Berkeley education? Apparently the answer is, whatever you can trade it for.

Given this race to the bottom line, we should not be surprised that a majority of students now hold a completely transactional view of higher education. In their exhaustive recent study, Fishman and Gardner found that fully 54% of students (at the medium selectivity institutions in their sample) equate college with degree-getting.[43] Imagine someone who took a four-year journey, and when we asked him what he was seeking, he said receipts from all of the toll booths.

Once this credentialing mindset revs up, the jobbification cycle really begins to spin.[44] Students vote with their feet, heading toward programs that provide, or at least appear to provide, a clear path to a well-paid position. Universities respond by putting their most careerist foot forward, starving the arts and humanities and stifling the already muffled invitation to general education.[45] Between 2012 and 2020, enrollment in humanities majors declined alarmingly, at universities and liberal arts colleges alike: Boston University (down 42%), Ohio State (46%), Tufts (nearly 50%), Vassar (nearly 50%), Bates (nearly 50%), Notre Dame (50%), SUNY Albany (75%).[46] This is when professors in the arts and humanities start to look both expensive and expendable. Right on cue, we see program closures:

- An astonishing 651 foreign-language programs were cut between 2013 and 2016.[47]
- In 2018, the College Art Association was tracking threatened arts and humanities closures at fifteen public universities. including five flagships.[48]
- Just since 2021, philosophy majors, if not entire departments, have been eliminated at six institutions and targeted at another four.[49]
- At Emporia State University, the cuts are so widespread (anthropology, English, French, German, history, Latin American studies, philosophy) and the situation so fluid that a recent article in the student paper led with this request: "If you or your professor receive an email letting you know that your program has been suspended, please reach out to *The Bulletin*."[50]

What does general education mean if it excludes the study of language, literature, culture, and the meaning of life? And so the cycle spins: turning the curriculum into a job fair tightens the equation between college and credentialing; reducing college to an exchange-value undercuts the perceived value of humane learning.

Step 3. As the university becomes more jobbified, it becomes more and more difficult to perceive higher education as a public good. The discourse around "public goods" comes out of neoclassical economics, where it is assumed that most goods are private. Public goods are the exception to the rule that production and distribution can and should be driven by individual consumption and market mechanisms. Far from a lofty ideal, on this economistic view, "public good" is a synonym for "market failure." The idea is that market mechanisms are disrupted by the presence of "non-rivalrous" goods (e.g., looking at a painting in museum), for which "each individual's consumption . . . leads to no subtraction from any other individual's consumption of that good."[51] Market efficiency is further undermined by so-called free-riders who consume "non-excludable" goods (e.g., fish, in public waterways) without paying, who benefit from positive "spillover effects" or "externalities" generated by the consumption of others (e.g., when one house's renovations lifts real estate values for the whole block), or who pass on the costs of negative externalities (e.g., pollution). Externalities are easy to find in education. When we teach a kindergartener to care about others, this educational good will be enjoyed not only by that student, but also by all those with whom he or she later comes in contact. Conversely, when we fail to teach students the difference between sound arguments and rhetorical manipulation, we all suffer under the demagogues who come to power. As a result, it has seemed prudent to educate collectively, breaking with market logic to invest in educating each other's children.

Notice, though, that these paradigmatic examples of educational externalities involve young people engaged in civic and moral education. The argument weakens as we move into secondary and especially tertiary education, and as the coupling of education and credentialing grows tighter. It is easy to see why we all might benefit by teaching a young child to read. It is harder to see our collective interest in the teaching of AP Physics to a kid gunning for MIT. It is harder still to make the case that you stand to benefit by helping to fund your neighbor's kid's marketing degree at Michigan

State. The most common defense of public higher education is—recalling the agricultural roots of the land-grant universities—what we could call "the fertilizer argument."[52] If we send our farmers to Corvallis or Lincoln or West Lafayette, they will learn new techniques for increasing crop yield, and we will all reap the bounty with more food on our tables. In a testament to Montana State University, Sarah Vowell updates this argument. Vowell recounts the story of Maurice Hilleman, who grew up raising chickens on the outskirts of Bozeman and was headed after high school to a position at J.C. Penney before his older brother nudged him to try for a scholarship at MSU. Hilleman got the scholarship, finished first in his class, and went on to develop more than half of the "standard recommended vaccines—including those for measles, mumps, meningitis, pneumonia and both hepatitis A and B." "In a century soaked in genocide," Vowell writes, "his work saved millions of lives, including, potentially, yours and mine. J. C. Penney's loss was humanity's gain."[53] Today, for every Hilleman, there is a battalion of Big Ten business majors whose educational gains do not so much ripple outward as fall safely into their own wallets.[54]

Step 4. Thus, we arrive at the final step in the death spiral of contemporary public higher education. With the attenuation of the arts, humanities, and general education, and the predominance of a credential mindset, the goods of higher education appear entirely rivalrous and privative. It is one thing to say that we should collectively fund higher education as a space where intellectual, moral, aesthetic, and civic dispositions are formed. College as a party-punctuated professional pathway is a much harder sell. Given the strength of anti-tax rhetoric—protesting the funding of such luxuries as food inspection, roads, and courts—it is difficult for state politicians to make any argument for raising taxes, let alone one tied to higher education. And if they did make such an argument, who would blame overstretched families for rejecting it? When higher education is framed as a private investment in future earnings, how can you make the case for collective investment? In such a climate, state appropriations to higher education will continue to decline, and around the spiral we descend.

To be sure, feedback loops are hard to interrupt. At the same time, this analysis has revealed a weak link in the seemingly inexorable logic of privatization. The public argument that is failing is narrowly economistic, as if the common good were synonymous with GNP. Two decades after the

Truman Report, presidential hopeful Robert F. Kennedy launched his presidential campaign at the nation's first land grant, Kansas State University. He then traveled to Lawrence to speak at Kansas's flagship public university, where he had this to say about "the mere accumulation of material things":

> Gross National Product counts air pollution and cigarette advertising, and ambulances to clear our highways of carnage. It counts special locks for our doors and the jails for the people who break them. It counts the destruction of the redwood and the loss of our natural wonder in chaotic sprawl. It counts napalm and counts nuclear warheads and armored cars for the police to fight the riots in our cities. . . . Yet the gross national product does not allow for the health of our children, the quality of their education or the joy of their play. It does not include the beauty of our poetry or the strength of our marriages, the intelligence of our public debate or the integrity of our public officials. It measures neither our wit nor our courage, neither our wisdom nor our learning, neither our compassion nor our devotion to our country, it measures everything in short, except that which makes life worthwhile.[55]

It does matter whether universities contribute to our economic well-being, but RFK reveals the calamity of reducing well-being to a simplistic metric for one aspect of human flourishing. Indeed, the dominant, economistic conception of public goods is not only reductive: it's not really public. As Charles Taylor suggests, what economists call public goods are really just "convergent" private ones: this matters to me and it matters to you and we happen to pursue it collaboratively. Genuine public or "common" goods, Taylor says, matter to me *because* they matter to you.[56] This upsets the usual market logic in which goods are understood as commodities and the public as temporarily non-rivalrous consumers. In pursuing the goods described by Taylor, we are pursuing the public itself. Our relational prizing is always also a prizing of relation. On this view, the public is understood not as a standing body but an always fugitive formation, a way of coming together to dialogue about our shared fate. This brings into view a much deeper connection between higher education and public life. We do not gather to learn together in Bozeman, Lawrence, and East Lansing because of a market failure. This is not a fertilizer co-op. We are convening the public. Or at least this is what higher education could be if we reject the jobbification and naked transactionalism of the contemporary university. A degree-holder, even a degree-holder with some technical skills and information, is hardly a satisfactory vision of the educated person. Of this I believe we can convince anyone who will listen. If we rededicate ourselves to general education, the citizenry may start to see education as a public investment, as an investment in the public. But we cannot begin to realize a curriculum that cultivates the full humanity of our students when we are killing off the arts and humanities. This is not a call for an otherworldly, impractical education. As I explain in the essay that follows, "Job Prospects," humane learning and true vocational education go hand in hand.

Unhappily we cannot spend all of our time at the workbench. We are not only apprentice workers, we are apprentice men; and the apprenticeship in this latter trade is harder and longer than in the former one.

—Jean-Jacques Rousseau[1]

JOB PROSPECTS: VOCATIONAL FORMATION AS HUMANE LEARNING

Happy Hunger Games! And may the odds be *ever* in your favor.
—Effie Trinket

LIFE IN PANEM

Another year, another round of austerity measures for the humanities. While some institutions have boldly cut whole departments, eliminating disciplines as old as the university itself, most have adopted the trusty strategy of slow starvation punctuated by the annual hunger games in which departments send forth tributes to defend their "value propositions" and battle for resources. The games are rigged of course. To survive, you must choose from among the available WMDs (weapons of metric dominance): grant dollars, enrollment levels, employment stats for your graduates, and so on. The discursive battles that ensue are so familiar that we know the lines by heart.

ACT ONE, SCENE 1: A budget task force meeting

ADMINISTRATOR: "As you can see, times have changed and we are facing increasing fiscal pressures. In this new climate, it is more important than ever that each unit pull its own weight. That is why we are developing these new program evaluation metrics and have asked you to gather data on how your alumni are faring in the job market."

HUMANITIES PROFESSOR: "But don't you see how these metrics are biased toward technical and pre-professional programs! You are prioritizing vocational aims and devaluing liberal education. Isn't college more than job preparation?!"

ADMINISTRATOR: "Yes, of course, but if we can't demonstrate return on investment, students will take their tuition dollars elsewhere, and we will be having this debate down the street at the coffee shop since we will all be out of a job."

This strategy of defending the humanities by pointing to the extra-vocational aims of higher education had a good run. Typically, all it took was a reminder that the university prepares not only workers but future citizens for our democratic society and administrators would turn the heat back on in the English Building and put down the furniture they were carrying out of Philosophy Hall. But they say you have to learn to accept yourself. By the day, the contemporary corporate multiversity grows increasingly comfortable with the idea that it exists to advance R&D, sponsor semipro athletics, and provide workforce vetting, training, and credentialing. And so the rhetorical force leaks out of this first strategy. Nowadays, when we confront administrators with the question of whether college is more than job preparation, they hardly flinch.

For this reason, many humanists now adopt a second strategy. Turning back to our script, we find,

ACT ONE, SCENE 2: A strategic planning session

HUMANITIES CENTER DIRECTOR: ". . . that concludes my presentation. As you can see, we have some exciting new initiatives and the humanities remain vital despite the recent budget cuts. But faculty attrition is taking a toll, and we ask you to make it a priority to reinvest in the humanities in the coming years."

DIRECTOR OF STEM RESEARCH CENTER: "Forgive me for saying this, but it sounds like what you are mainly worried about is protecting your own jobs when you should be thinking about our students' job prospects. You mentioned philosophy, art history, and medieval studies. Sounds like good job training . . . for a barista!"

HUMANITIES CENTER DIRECTOR: "That's funny. I thought you all believed in evidence, not hearsay. So let's look at the data and clear up this myth once and for all. In an AAC&U survey, employers said that what really matters is not the student's major but broad skills that cut across majors.[2] And it is striking that what these employers found lacking in their new hires were precisely the skills you get from humanities courses:

- only 30% of employers found recent college graduates well prepared to make ethical judgments;
- only 28% felt fully comfortable with the communication skills of their new hires;

- only 26% were satisfied with their critical thinking skills;
- and fewer than one in five found their new hires well prepared to deal with people from different cultures.[3]

Meanwhile, data shows that any career earnings gap for humanities majors is insignificant compared to that between college grads and high school grads. Indeed, a recent Brookings study found that, while business majors outearn history majors in the first decade of their careers, this is reversed from year fifteen on.[4]

Here I have given the Humanities Center director the last word, along with plenty of room to make her case. An actual exchange of this sort would play out differently. For example, if the STEM director had seen these same statistics, he might retort that art history majors earn just sixty cents on the dollar compared to engineering majors across the course of their careers.[5]

Nonetheless, the Humanities Center director's basic point still stands: even if all we care about is our graduates' monetary return on investment, the humanities hold their own. Consider one final comparison: while architecture majors earn 13% more on average than philosophy majors across their careers, philosophy majors still double the earnings of those without a college degree.[6] Even when we restrict our focus to college graduates, it turns out that institutional selectivity is a more important factor than choice of major (see table 4).

So, humanists have two main strategies for parrying arguments about return on investment: we can remind our doubters and defunders that a college education is more than a vocational education, or we can assert our parity in readying students for the job market. Before pointing out their flaws, we should acknowledge the not-so-minor virtue shared by these counterclaims: they are true. There are indeed important extra-vocational

Table 4

Average annual salary, ten years post-degree, by major and institution type[6]

Major	Highly Selective	Very Selective	Selective	Nonselective
Math, Computer Science, and Engineering	$79,811	$61,581	$58,631	$52,740
Humanities/Social Sciences	$76,468	$58,344	$53,197	$44,852

dimensions of higher education; and it is a myth that humanities majors fare poorly on the market. Nonetheless, neither strategy gets us very far. We are not going to win the metrics game, and no one cares much anymore when we walk away from the table muttering mantras about educating the whole person.

These strategies are not only weak but dangerous. The purist rejection of vocational aims taps into an idea well worth leaving behind: namely, that liberal education is an education for leisure, a finishing school for the aristocracy. There is a discursive gravity in this area so that one tends to slide from the noncontroversial claim that life is about more than work to the objectionable idea that work and workers are somehow unworthy. While the second strategy sheds this tweedy, aristocratic baggage, it gives too much away. Short-term victories in the metrics game come at the cost of reinforcing the bottom-line mentality. And sooner or later, the humanities will be killed off as "insufficiently responsive to market trends."

Or maybe the humanities will persist, lumbering on in zombie form. Indeed, one group of scholars thinks that we have already entered a period of "living death in higher education."[8] It is a fantasy to think that the humanities can survive for long, with their integrity intact, in the university of the bottom line. As Megan Laverty explains:

> We now know that how individuals, objects, or activities are described affects our understanding of them. We only need to consider how "managerial new-speak" has shaped professors' and students' experiences of the university. Academics naïvely believed that they could enlist managerial redescriptions—the language of productivity, content-delivery, service-providers, and customers—while remaining invulnerable to their corrosive effects. Any ironic distance that they might have enjoyed is lost now that students "shop" for university degrees that will yield the highest return on the tuition they invest, market surveys determine the closure or introduction of programs and courses, and students' evaluations play a role in tenure and promotion decisions. Current students destined to become future scholars are likely to lack the words and concepts necessary to appreciate the full import of their education.[9]

For many activities, you need to have the right gear; for all activities you need to have the right concepts. You really shouldn't attempt winter mountaineering without an icepick and crampons. But you can't teach at all if you are not oriented toward learning. You might be lecturing and leading discussion, grading papers and holding office hours, but still not really teaching. What you are doing might be better described as satisfying the customer, fulfilling a teaching load, or getting good evaluations. We could make a similar point from the student's perspective. A sophomore sits in a humanities classroom. They might be asking themselves philosophical questions, learning to think historically, or truly listening to a poem. Or they might be preparing for an exam, satisfying a Gen Ed requirement, or building a strong application for law school. Framing matters.

Philip Jackson identifies two different species of teaching, framed by rival conceptual traditions.[10] In one, the teacher is seen as possessor of knowledge; in the other, the teacher is seen as exemplar, gadfly, and dialogue partner. In the one, the student is seen as receptacle-to-be-filled; in the other, as person-in-process. In one, teaching is seen as transmission of detachable knowledge and skills; in the other, as transformation of a whole person. As Jackson points out, while the idea of teaching as transformation has a longer history, the idea of teaching as transmission (what Jackson calls the "mimetic" outlook) has come to dominate over the last couple of centuries. While we still speak about the value of the humanities and indeed about transformative learning, Jackson (glossed by Laverty) warns that, "When attention is given to the transformative outcomes, they are described in a mimetic idiom, which effectively vitiates their intrinsic or formative (as opposed to merely informative) value."[11] What ensues is a kind of zombie liberal learning wherein only the husk of the humanities remains.

Talk about picking your poison: Shall we hold tight to our (wooly) principles as we head over to the unemployment office or gamely embrace this brave new spreadsheet? Somehow we must avoid both choices, but what other avenue do we have? That there is indeed another way becomes clear when we notice that these two strategies actually share a key assumption. While one stresses the bottom-line of job placement and the other points to humanistic values beyond the vocational, both accept the contemporary university's vertiginous reduction of vocational education to training and credentialing.[12] What would happen if we were to accept that vocation is central to college education while rejecting this reductive picture of vocational education?

To my mind, the answer is clear. Technical and careerist concerns would occupy a relatively minor place in a more capacious vision of vocational development. By my count, vocational enactment entails no fewer than six essential tasks:

1. Finding a worthy form of work to which you are suited.
2. (Acquiring technical proficiency in your chosen field.)
3. Cultivating the ethical understanding necessary to enact your vocation with integrity and public purpose.
4. (Determining how to land a position in your chosen field.)
5. Learning how to grow into and through your work.
6. Learning how to grow out of your work, if and when the time comes.

I have parenthesized tasks (2) and (4) since these are the bread and butter of the contemporary university. What I want to argue is that each of these four further tasks, while sorely neglected in undergraduate education, represents a necessary condition of full vocational enactment.[13] Thus, as soon as we widen our view beyond training and credentialing, a surprising fact comes into focus: the contemporary university is not really vocationalized at all, only *jobbified*. Indeed, a truly vocationalized university would be a site to behold! And when we reject the reduction of vocational education, the humanities are freed from the deadly dilemma of limping along in the metrics race or flying against the wind. For, as I hope to show, each of these neglected tasks of vocational development involves humane learning.

To be clear, this is not simply a call to do more. What the intensely myopic focus of the jobbified university produces is not an incomplete vocational education but rather a vocational miseducation. It is as if someone, after promising to build you a boat, delivered a hull and a stenciled name plate, reassuring you that later you can always add options such as a sail, compass, rudder, or life preserver. Indeed, one can argue that all college really delivers is the stenciled name plate. In moments of candor, most will admit that it is not until after college, in one's actual apprenticeship to a practice, that one acquires the majority of needed knowledge and skills. This suggests that in fact the credentialing function alone dominates, that colleges are basically deluxe head-hunting firms repackaging the sorting performed by the schools and the SATs in an elaborate four-year prescreening.[14] On this deeply cynical, but unfortunately more than plausible reading, what colleges provide is mainly exchange-value. They might offer some use-value, by weeding out some candidates and ranking the rest by GPA, but the most significant winnowing procedure has probably already occurred during the college admissions process. And recall the point above about the importance of institutional selectivity (see table 4). The best explanation for why the line is so long outside a club is usually just because the line is so long outside the club. True, some universities have bigger libraries or more state-of-the-art gyms. And maybe the faculty is stronger at some institutions than at others. But there is a strong case to be made that higher education operates on the crudely circular, exchange-value logic of the rope line: the highest-ranked universities attract the most applicants and thus can be the most selective, this selectivity being the chief factor in their high rankings.

But let us set aside for now this most cynical interpretation. We certainly hope that college is more than an elaborate shell game, more than queuing for a credential while "paying for the party."[15] In many fields it is not hard to see that there is much to learn in advance of on-the-job apprenticeships. For example, it hardly seems arbitrary to ask future engineers to work through calculus, matrix theory, and linear algebra in advance of their professional practice. Let us assume for the sake of the argument that, on the whole, contemporary higher education does a good job of imparting the knowledge and skills needed to land a position and perform its characteristic tasks. Would we then say that we are doing a good job at vocational education? The answer is clearly no, and for the same reasons that our proud new sailboat owner is not ready to set sail. Even if the boat were seaworthy, the sailor has no idea where he is going. Our myopic focus on skill sets and resumes puts students in the absurd position of preparing for a chosen line of work before choosing a line of work. The jobbified university begs the fundamental vocational question, what form of work expresses my hopes and engages my talents?[16] In the next section, we consider how the university might support students to live with this question more honestly and reflectively.

THE GREAT VOCATIONAL QUESTION

Nothing is more tragic than failure to discover one's true business in life, or to find that one has drifted or been forced by circumstance into an uncongenial calling.
—John Dewey[17]

If what I have said so far is right, then the common refrain that higher education has become narrow and vocationalized is exactly half true. The contemporary university is indeed narrow, but it is only jobbified. We are interested in only a small portion of the complex and expansive project of vocational formation. But, we have to start somewhere, one might reply. With this, I heartily agree, and the place to start is with the core vocational task of finding a genuine calling. As it stands now, I suggested, we find ourselves in the absurd business of training and credentialing students for their chosen line of work before they have had the opportunity to choose a line of work. Let me now qualify and defend this admittedly provocative claim.

Obviously, no one denies that career choice must precede training and networking. The assumption is that this is accomplished through selection of a major. But when do students select their majors and under what conditions? A university truly devoted to vocational formation would encourage students to proceed slowly and carefully to head off the tragedy identified by Dewey. We would support students to see major selection as an opportunity to wrestle with the great vocational question: What form of work expresses my talents and values and opens up the world in interesting ways? But of course that is not what we do. Many universities admit students directly into a school, settling the matter before the student even steps foot on campus. But can't an engineering student take class in arts and sciences? Can't an education student take a class in business? Certainly, but as these examples illustrate, an important psychological shift has already occurred. Students think of themselves as an "engineering student," an "education student," and so on. As William Deresiewicz notes,

> Although the notion of breadth is implicit in the very idea of a liberal arts education, the admissions process increasingly selects for kids who have already begun to think of themselves in specialized terms—the junior journalist, the budding astronomer, the language prodigy. We are slouching, even at elite schools, toward a glorified form of vocational training.[18]

Our defenses of early specialization vary. We say that we are simply acceding to parental demands for guaranteed employability after four years of expensive tuition.[19] Or we reason that we must defer to the autonomy of students. To interfere would be paternalistic. Most students seem pretty confident in their plans. Who are we to question their goals?

Rather than being cowed by this rhetorical question, why don't we simply answer it: we are educators. It is our job to pose questions. Indeed, the deferential posture exudes bad faith. Let us examine the ironies, one by one:

The decision has already been made.

Well, yes, because our admission process forces students—the vast majority of whom possess only the fledgling self-knowledge of a seventeen-year-old—to choose from among options with which they have likely never had any substantive contact.

We must avoid paternalism.

Then why are we deferring to decisions that, as we have already acknowledged, are typically made under the shadow of intense parental pressure?

We should defer to the autonomy of students.

The last two points make it clear that these early decisions are typically heteronomous. "Deferring" here is a weasel word. It conflates two different ideas: deferring to a preexisting, thin, negative version of freedom (for example, you have the right to choose your own classes), and honoring the potential for autonomy by creating conditions that will nurture its growth.

Students are confident in their choices.

Some are and some aren't. Let's consider how a university might nurture the autonomy of each. True, many students initially seem confident in their declared major. However, as they start to learn more about themselves and see what the field is actually like, many begin to doubt their choice. And in cases where parental pressure played a significant role, students often begin to chaff against this heteronomy. Some lucky students find a way to transmute it into autonomy, finding a genuine calling where they were told to find it. For many students, though, tensions between parental expectations and their personal interests and ambitions eventually come to a head. A university that truly valued autonomy would be prepared to support students through these disorienting episodes. Indeed, we would welcome them as the quintessentially teachable moments in autonomy-promoting education. And this makes it clear how we ought to respond to those students who are disinclined to doubt: we must occasion such moments. We have a responsibility to nudge them toward self-examination.

A period of exploration.

Hear, hear! And delaying the selection of a major is a good start. But this will not matter if there is no exploratory ethos. For example, how many universities still value what Oakeshott called "the gift of an interval," and how many instead have fallen in line with what Josef Pieper calls the culture of "total work"?[20] As Walker Percy's Binx Bolling explains, it is common to be "sunk in the everydayness of . . . life"; we need to be awakened to "the possibility of the search."[21] Instead we celebrate certitude, as we saw in the prologue, affixing to those without a major the negative label "undeclared." A university that truly took vocation and autonomy seriously would be organized to provoke the certain and support the searching to wrestle with the question, What kind of work speaks to my interests, is suited to my talents, and is worthy of my efforts? While some faculty and staff are available for such vocational dialogues, it must be acknowledged that higher education today is poorly set up to facilitate vocational discernment.[22]

The point is not merely to expose our confusion, hypocrisy, and wishful thinking. Our bad faith has real consequences. It is as if we were inviting the tragedy described by Dewey in the epigraph.

Vocational choice is not a tick box. The search for meaningful, worthwhile work is among a very small number of core existential tasks. Occupations are, as Maxine Greene puts it, our "diverse ways . . . of gearing into the world."[23] To find one's métier is to organize one's talents in the service of something worthwhile, to tap into the world's complexity and interest, to find a voice in the dialogue of social life. The search for vocation is nothing less than a quest to find a medium in which we can achieve a fluency and freedom. If the word "quest" sounds like adolescent melodrama, so be it. Given its uncertainty and high stakes, the search for a vocation is dramatic. And it is adolescent, wonderfully so, to think that joining the social order might constitute an event rather than a disappearance.[24] The trick is to find the middle path between disenchantment and romanticization. On the disenchanted view, you just have to pick a line of work and get on with it. On the romanticized view, you just need to look inside to see what you were always meant to do. One negates the genuine pathos and romance of the search for a medium; the other distills it into a sickly syrup. Both make short work of this necessarily protracted process by locating inside of us something that is only discovered by moving out into the world.

Consider the garden designer Piet Oudolf, famous for his dense, flowing, meadow-like plantings, layered with grasses and seldom-used perennials chosen not only for their color when flowering but for the structural features of their seed heads. In a documentary about his work, Oudolf searches in vain for the biographical source of his love of plants.[25] Maybe it was his childhood bike rides through the dunes, he muses, eventually rejecting this suggestion. In the end, he settles on this formulation: "It was something I needed and didn't know it." Oudolf at work is a picture of fluency. We watch as he thinks and draws in four dimensions, picturing the riotous blooming and sublime decay of each plant in his complex clusters. Imagine Jackson Pollock, painting with plants, and with no chip on his shoulder about the spontaneity of his gestures. Oudolf explicitly rejects the traditional genius narrative, according to which anyone who eventually finds a clear-throated and distinctive voice in a medium must have known all along that they had something to say in that medium. Instead, Oudolf, stresses how the plants seemed to find him, and not particularly early in his life. In his twenties, he worked as a bartender, a waiter, a fishmonger, and a steelworker. He did turn to nursery and landscape work in his late twenties and start his own design firm at the age of thirty-two. But it would be another six years before he bought the farm where he would begin building a nursery to grow and study the plants that would become the medium for his mature work.[26]

Even a story like this—of a somewhat late bloomer who went on to achieve international acclaim for his distinctive aesthetic vision—is likely to downplay the challenge of truly facing up to the great vocational question. If we have tended to trivialize this core existential task, it is probably because we have wished to leap over it. After all, knowing what sort of work might organize your talents in the service of something worth doing requires at least three types of understanding difficult to achieve. First, since we are all prone to parochialism and myopia, we need exposure to something of the range of human projects and prizings. Then, to know which of these projects are worthwhile requires some degree of ethical understanding, some maturing of judgment about what matters and why. Finally, there is that minor consideration, self-knowledge, without some measure of which one cannot know what sorts of work are suited to one's dispositions and talents. This sounds like a very tall order. If only we had a curriculum focused on exposing students to noteworthy attempts to understand what is worth striving for in a human life with the aim of cultivating self-knowledge and practical wisdom. Of course, we already have such a curriculum, and it is called the humanities.

However, we ought to distinguish between the humanities—disciplinary precincts of the modern research university, each characterized by distinct questions, bodies of literature, and modes of inquiry—and the project of humane learning. There are three reasons for not equating them. First, the tradition of humane education long precedes the modern disciplines.

Second, humane learning can and does occur outside the humanities, for example, in the natural sciences, the arts, and professional fields such as architecture, law, and medicine. Third, the humanities can and do sometimes fail to live up to their potential as vehicles of humane learning.[27]

Let's consider this third point in more detail. It is hard to imagine a humane education that failed to include the study of literature, history, and philosophy; but it is not hard to imagine courses in such subjects failing to inspire students to confront the great vocational question. No historical account or philosophical treatise, political tract or satirical essay, poem or play, symphony or novel has a magical power to inspire students to deepen their knowledge of self, broaden their understanding of nature and culture, or sharpen their intuitions about how they might best gear into the world. As we noted earlier with Laverty, it matters how the humanities are framed and how they are taught.

For many students, first contact with the humanities will come in the form of Gen Ed requirements. And this is a potentially productive frame. General education could be understood as an invitation to self-understanding, a call to develop all of the worthwhile dimensions of ourselves, a reminder that the world is too complicated to be understood from just a single angle. But this message is rarely received. Most students experience Gen Ed as a bureaucratic requirement, a pointless imposition.[28] Students can be forced to drag their bodies to a lecture hall and fill seats, but unless they bring themselves—some genuine interest in understanding who they are, what to make of the world they have found themselves in, and what to strive for—the relational, existential process of humane education cannot get off the ground. If students experience their Gen Ed classes as an inconvenience, as drudgery, or even as a surprisingly pleasant diversion, it doesn't matter whether the course falls in the category of humanities or not.

Of course, instructors can and should try to create their own counter frames. It is an important part of teaching to explain to students that the quality of learning is dependent not only on the quality of the material and how the course is taught, but also on their own stance. Indeed, one could make a whole study of pedagogical beginnings, looking at the means by which teachers interrupt, provoke, and redirect students in an effort to help students assume a genuine learning stance.[29] That said, the university must have its faculty's back. It must do what it can, at the institutional level, to frame college as the project of becoming an educated person, to issue the invitation to humane education, and to fend off forces that corrupt that enterprise. Institutional structures and cultures matter.

And here we must make a distinction between the walk and the talk. As we noted in the previous section, the phrase "transformative learning" is more popular than ever, featured liberally on college websites and brochures. But notice how this goes hand in hand with the rise on R1 campuses of online learning and the new centers of teaching and learning with their own more-revealing syntax and proposed division of labor. Professors will provide the "content"; "instructional designers" will build out the online interface to "deliver" that content. The only problem is that there is no such thing as educational "content." You might find the same "content" streaming over both Hulu and Netflix; if you order a book online, the contents of the package will be the same whether it is arrives via UPS or the USPS. In matters of teaching and learning, at least in the transformative tradition, form and content cannot be so easily disentangled. And when pedagogy collapses from transformation to transmission, it does not matter if the information transmitted is the names of philosophical schools, art historical periods, or literary movements. The medium is the message. Humane learning, through the humanities or other subjects, never gets off the ground.

Let's look more closely at this distinction between genuine humane education and mere transmission of humanities content, drawing on humane letters themselves for assistance. Philosopher Michael Oakeshott will help us frame the problem, and novelist J. D. Salinger will help bring the point home. In order to find a calling, we said, one needs exposure to something of the range of human cherishings, ambitions, and projects, exposure to a wider sense of what there is to be hoped for, sought after, and held dear. Humane education is central in this first step in vocational education because it is oriented to precisely this class of axiological questions: What is meaningful to do, worthy to achieve, and admirable to become? How should we live, individually and collectively? What practices have human beings devised for themselves to embody and pursue these goods?

Historically, one shorthand for this process has been to say that we are exposing students to "culture," but this term has been reduced to a kind of semantic Rorschach test. For some, it connotes the supposed elevation and refinement of certain approved forms of cultural production. For others, it connotes what everybody already possesses, what unites us with those in our group and differentiates us from those in others. The term becomes

mainly diagnostic: Are you a ranker or a leveler? Oakeshott rejects both of
these positions as alternate versions of the same, taxidermy theory of culture. If the levelers encase culture in a museum display box and the rankers
enclose it in a group identity, both construe culture as something settled,
homogeneous, and sealed off. Oakeshott's alternative view of culture as
dynamic, open-ended conversational encounter is worth quoting at length:

> Human self-understanding is, then, inseparable from learning to participate in
> what is called a "culture." It is useful to have a word which stands for the whole
> of what an associated set of human beings have created for themselves . . . ,
> but we must not be misled by it. A culture is not a doctrine or a set of con-
> sistent teachings [but] . . . a continuity of feelings, perceptions, ideas, engage-
> ments, attitudes and so forth, pulling in different directions, often critical of
> one another and contingently related to one another so as to compose . . . what
> I shall call a conversational encounter. Ours, for example, accommodates not
> only the lyre of Apollo but also the pipes of Pan, the call of the wild; not only
> the poet but also the physicist; not only the majestic metropolis of Augustin-
> ian theology but also the "greenwood" of Franciscan Christianity. A culture
> comprises unfinished intellectual and emotional journeyings, expeditions now
> abandoned but known to us in the tattered maps left behind by the explorers; it
> is composed of lighthearted adventures, of relationships invented and explored
> in exploit or in drama, of myths and stories and poems expressing fragments of
> human self-understanding, of gods worshipped, of responses to the mutabil-
> ity of the world and of encounters with death. And it reaches us, as it reached
> generations before ours, neither as long-ago terminated specimens of human
> adventure, nor as an accumulation of human achievements we are called upon
> to accept, but as a manifold of invitations to look, to listen and to reflect.[30]

Notice first that, despite his donnish, hortatory tone, Oakeshott does hold
a version of intercultural pluralism. This is not to deny his chauvinistic
tendencies: Oakeshott is clearly impressed by the Greco-Roman, Judeo-
Christian tradition, which he presumptuously refers to as "ours." Nor
would it be any great pluralistic achievement were Oakeshott to acknowledge the existence of multiple cultures only to assert that his own group
had alone discovered true Culture amid these sundry folkways. To the contrary, though, Oakeshott stresses that every culture is but the contingent
creation of some "associated set of human beings."

While this intercultural pluralism is laudable, what distinguishes Oakeshott's view is his intracultural pluralism, his rich evocation of the pluralism

within each culture. If the singular, indefinite pronoun in the phrase "a culture" helpfully highlights the first form of pluralism, it tends to hide the second. While it can be useful to have such an umbrella term, Oakeshott observes, it misleads us into thinking that we have some singular, uniform thing in our sights—say, "Western culture"—when in truth each culture is itself internally plural, and on multiple levels. A culture, for Oakeshott, is not a uniform doctrine but it is also not a great debate, as if we agreed on what to dispute and how to discuss it. The internal dynamics of cultures are too complicated to plot along one axis. Cultures are, if you will, both heteroglot and polydox, a layering of rival languages, modes of imagining and describing, within each of which we find conflicting positions. This is why Oakeshott's prose is so full of lists. He is constantly on guard lest our abstractions dull our perception of this internal variegation. Do we look to the ancient world or the Christian tradition when thinking about what it means to lead a good life? If we seek *eudaimonia*, then we must wrestle with the further tension between Apollo and Pan. If we seek piety, then we must weigh the merits of Augustine and St. Francis. There are tensions within tensions, and Oakeshott is just getting started. Shall we seek to know the world through the eyes of the poet or those of the physicist? Is the human condition captured best through myths about gods worshipped, dramas about impermanence, lighthearted tales, meditations on death? The point and counterpoint of the cultural conversation occurs in each of our characteristic modes, in our "feelings, perceptions, ideas, engagements, attitudes."[31] Even when Oakeshott seems ready to collect this multilevel multiplicity into one phrase, "a manifold of invitations," he quickly adds another list, noting that some of these invitations are to look, others to listen, and still others to reflect.

In this way, Oakeshott provides a corrective to the leveler's assumption that culture is a shared identity, which tends to erase the tensions and polyvocality found within cultures. Shall we, then, count Oakeshott among the rankers with their "great books"? This is the typical misreading of Oakeshott. No doubt, Oakeshott considered certain works great. Aristotle's *Ethics*, Hobbes *Leviathan*, and Hegel's *Phenomenology* are three that come to mind. But the whole project of canon formation clashes with Oakeshott's views on education, culture, and history. First, canonization presumes that works possess a value independent of the questions and concerns particular readers bring to them. Though Oakeshott was horrified by child-centered education and railed against the fashion for relevance, his constructivist epistemology does make him a kind of progressive educator, if an admittedly strange one.[32] Second, Oakeshott would object to the reverential tone that creeps into most discussions of "great books." As we saw in the passage above, Oakeshott describes cultural artefacts not as aesthetic wholes but as "tattered maps," not as "human achievements we are called upon to accept" but as invitations to go further. In another passage, Oakeshott suggests that in every cultural inheritance we find not only "the substantial" but also "the somewhat flimsy," not only "the refined" but also "the commonplace."[33]

Finally, canon formation invites a variety of historical misunderstandings. We find historicism (the great works as representatives of historical periods), whiggishness (the books arrayed on a great historical ladder with us sitting on the top rung), and presentism (the authors seated around a contemporary seminar table). Where the presentist finds "eternal verities," Oakeshott sees "fragments of human self-understanding"; where the historicist finds "terminated specimens," Oakeshott sees "unfinished journeyings"; where the Whig finds a unidirectional march, Oakeshott sees,

> a "contingent flow" of intellectual and emotional adventures, a mixture of old and new where the new is often a backward swerve to pick up what has been temporarily forgotten; a mixture of the emergent and the recessive.[34]

Oakeshott neither wrenches culture out of history like the presentist nor embalms each artifact in a historical period, whether horizontally like the historicist or vertically like the Whig. There is no uncrossable gulf between past and present. We find ourselves inside that contingent flow. What we call the "present" is just our current state of making sense of, and making use of, our past. Some aspects of the past emerge with a freshness and contemporaneity; others recess into dusty neglect.

It is not just that the present swerves backward to rediscover, but also that so-called past artifacts are themselves forward looking, calling to anyone who would listen, "hear me now!" The projects these works describe—to make something beautiful, to discover a hidden truth, to build something great, to feel something fully, to understand something completely, to see something accurately, to respond to something justly, and so on—are incomplete, as are the efforts to record, assess, and understand them. In this way, they are invitations; they call for a response. How do you understand and assess this "experiment in living," this "strategy of being"?[35] Once we have been hailed by our fellow explorers, by their "tattered maps," we must wrestle with how to make this project our own and take it further. At the least, we must ask ourselves, on what grounds will we refuse this call to think and feel, perceive and value, conceive and conduct ourselves in its characteristic way? It is in this sense, and only this sense, that culture forms the basis of humane education. Upon joining the conversations within and across cultures, students encounter rival "images of approval and disapproval," polyvocal provocations to weigh what is worthwhile, a manifold of invitations to understand and declare themselves.[36]

Oakeshott, then, is neither a ranker nor a leveler. He imagines us not outside of culture assessing its products, but inside its flow assessing ourselves with its rich, contingent, and conflicting resources. For Oakeshott, culture is neither a homogeneous worldview, nor even a grand debate, but a polyvocal conversation,

> being carried on between a variety of human activities, each speaking with its own voice, or in a language of its own; the activities (for example) represented in moral and practical endeavor, religious faith, philosophical reflection, artistic contemplation and historical or scientific inquiry and explanation.[37]

In a debate, a single discursive logic is unfolded into two poles, as claim and counterclaim. By contrast, conversation is guided not by a single (dia)logic but by an ethos, by virtues that enable participants to pursue with conviviality and endure with grace a continual upsetting of norms. Conversation includes not only rejoinders but also "disjoinders" that entirely reframe the issue at hand. It is like setting the table with two places, putting the napkin on your lap, saying grace, and picking up your fork, only to watch your companion pick up two spoons, turn the table on its side, and start drumming a rhythm.

Among the virtues needed to endure such gestalt shifts, Oakeshott identifies a disposition that integrates seriousness and playfulness:

> Without the seriousness the conversation would lack impetus. But in its participation in the conversation, each voice learns to be playful, learns to understand itself conversationally and to recognize itself as a voice among voices. As with children, who are great conversationalists, the playfulness is serious and the seriousness is only play.[38]

We must not misunderstand Oakeshott's reference to children. Where the conventional view contrasts childlike whimsy and adult gravity, Oakeshott sees children as role models precisely because they resist this false dichotomy. For Oakeshott (serious) playfulness is an excellence in the art of conversation. It is the virtue of "conversability," the disposition toward "acknowledgement and accommodation" of other voices.[39]

If the delicate dance of polyvocality is sustained by this special form of humility, it is undermined by a species of pride. "Each voice," Oakeshott writes, "is prone to *superbia*, that is, an exclusive concern with its own utterance, which may result in its identifying the conversation with itself." This vice is especially pernicious because it leads to a situation in which we mistake some form of monologue for a real conversation and don't even realize what we have lost. Consider, for example, the dominant voice in the contemporary scene, advertising. Within this single register, we find what appears to be a quite capacious conversation between rival modes of imagining. One ad extols sport and fitness; another draws on images of family life; and a third features meditative repose. It is not until we check out, as it were, that we come to realize that all the ads were selling the same life, a life of consumption. For the "conversation to be appropriated by one or two voices," Oakeshott suggests, is "insidious" because the "established monopoly" immediately covers its own tracks.[40] The excluded voices are "convicted in advance of irrelevance" and may only "gain entrance by imitating the voices of the monopolists."[41] Though this only affords "a hearing for a counterfeit utterance," it sustains the fiction that the conversation continues.[42]

It is this process of appropriation and counterfeiting that is involved when the humanities and humane education diverge. When it is hard to tell the difference between being on campus and being at a shopping mall, when the curriculum is framed as career training (with some annoying Gen Ed requirements tossed in), when teaching is understood as transmission of information, the humanities speak not in their own humane voices but in a counterfeit register. Culture becomes not the interplay of rival visions of character and conduct, seeking and satisfaction, but just a token in some other currency.

At this point, we can let Salinger pick up the story from Oakeshott, for it is just this sort of counterfeiting that precipitates the crisis at the center of his novella diptych, *Franny and Zooey*. It is the fall of Franny's senior year in college, and she has suddenly returned home in a bad state. As she explains to her older brother Zooey, she had come to suspect the motives of everyone around her at school, to doubt the integrity of the whole endeavor, and then to loathe herself for being judgmental. Unsurprisingly, carping at herself for carping at others was no solution, and neither was her attempt to withdraw into her studies. She had come to a conclusion that she simply could not shake:

> I got the idea in my head, and I could *not* get it out—that college was just one more *dopey, inane* place in the world dedicated to piling up treasure on earth and everything. I mean treasure is *treas*ure, for heaven's sake. What's the difference whether treasure is money, or property, or even *cul*ture, or even just plain knowledge? It all seemed like *exactly* the same thing to me, if you take off the wrapping—and it still does![43]

Let us be clear: Franny's problem is not an overspecialized and jobbified curriculum. She is a liberal arts student exposed to a rich and well-rounded curriculum. Though we are not told what college she attends, her midcentury, privileged, ivy/seven-sisters milieu is clear. In the opening novella, "Franny," she is at Princeton, visiting her boyfriend, who has been studying Rilke (6); admires Tolstoy, Dostoyevsky, and Shakespeare (13); and can't quite conceal his pride that his Flaubert paper won praise from the professor (13–14).[44] She arrived on a train where everyone "looked very Smith," except for one "Bennington/Sarah Lawrence type" and two "absolutely Vassar types" (9). As for her own education, we learn that she has elected the honors track (17), until recently was a theater major with a good part in the play (27–28), takes classes in political science (147) and French Lit (145), is writing a paper on Restoration comedy (145), and is surrounded by "pedants and conceited little teardowners" who like to make arch comments about Turgenev and Stendhal (17, 15). Franny is being exposed to "the best that has been thought and said," only the colleges seem to have forgotten the crucial beginning of Arnold's famous definition of culture: "Culture is the pursuit of our total perfection by means of getting to know, on all of the matters that most concern us. . . ."[45] Turgenev is just trivia if you are looking to score points. Poetry might as well be pork bellies, if you are trading in cultural cachet. Culture is not a thing to be possessed but a pursuit of understanding on matters of true concern, a pursuit of our formation as whole persons.

Like the proverbial sophomore, Franny had headed off to college in the hopes of finding others on "the search." She was sorely disappointed:

> I don't think it would have all got me quite so down if just once in a while—just *once* in a while—there was at least some polite little *perfunctory* implication that

knowledge *should* lead to *wisdom*, and that if it *doesn't*, it's just a disgusting waste of time! But there never is! You never even hear any *hints* dropped on a campus that wisdom is *supposed* to be the *goal* of knowledge. . . . In almost four years of college, the only time I can remember ever even hearing the expression "wise man" being used was in my freshman year, in Political Science! And you know how it was used? It was used in reference to some nice old poopy elder states-man who'd made a fortune in the stock market.[46]

Instead of being drawn into an adventure of self-understanding, animated by the multiplicity of images of what matters in a human life, Franny finds but one image reappearing in various guises: acquisition. In the competition to see who has the biggest pile, Franny observes, it doesn't really matter what sort of treasure it is. It may be a pile of money, of insidery knowledge about this or that, or even of great books. Look, there, in the pile, it's a copy of Wordsworth's poems. The owner of this pile must be very cultured and well read! But instead of speaking volumes—for example, I think of his sonnet of 1807 that begins, "The world is too much with us / Late and soon / Getting and spending / We lay waste our powers"—the volume speaks only one word, treasure.[47] Thus, while Franny had the finest humanities education on offer, this was not humane education.

When we meet her, Franny has dropped her theater major, and for the moment left school altogether. She is using this hiatus not to retreat from but to intensify her process of vocational discernment. Franny is unde-clared. As I noted in the prologue, it is ironically the undeclared students who often best fit Oakeshott's description of the "declared learner" who craves something more than mere studenting, who welcomes the question at the heart of both ethics and education, What is worth wanting (to have, to do, to become)? And it is this attempt to enrich one's vocabulary of aspi-ration that is required if one is to seriously engage with the primary task in vocational development. Even while humanists continue to gather their employability statistics, we should take note of the fact that any vocational education worthy of the name begins with humane learning.

WORKING WITH INTEGRITY

No one knows who will live in this cage in the future, or whether at the end of this tremendous development entirely new prophets will arise, or there will be a great rebirth of old ideas and ideals, or, if neither, mechanized

petrification, embellished with a sort of convulsive self-importance. For the "last man" of this cultural development, it might well be truly said: "Specialists without spirit, sensualists without heart; this nullity imagines that it has attained a level of humanity never before achieved."
—Max Weber[48]

Let us review the argument so far. In response to the charge of impracticality, the humanities have flip-flopped between two problematic strategies. For much of our history, we have staked our claim on our contribution to nonvocational dimensions of higher education; more recently, we have opted to play the game, touting the roughly equivalent "return on investment" enjoyed by humanities students. It turns out that these seemingly opposed strategies share a key premise, that vocational preparation is nothing more than job training and credentialing. What these twin strategies conceal is that the humanities are indeed central to any decently robust conception of vocational education. To this end, we noted four crucial, but frequently overlooked, humane dimensions of vocation: finding a worthy form of work to which you are suited, becoming aware of the ethical geography in and around your practice, finding in that work sources of your ongoing self-cultivation, and preparing yourself to leave that work if and when the time comes. In the previous section, we explored the first of these dimensions, considering what sort of education is required to support students to confront the great vocational question, "What kind of work expresses my hopes and engages my talents?" What is required, we concluded, are institutions that—far from pretending that this question can or should be answered once and for all by teenage college applicants—take as central to their mission exposure to something of the range of the ends and means that human beings have devised for themselves so that students may explore and expand their understandings of who they are, what projects are worthy of devotion, and what sort of lives are meaningful and admirable. We called such a curriculum "humane," stressing that it is neither limited to nor guaranteed by the disciplines called the humanities. What matters is sustaining the dynamism and pluralism of the conversation that is culture. When the moral imagination shrinks to "getting and spending," even the humanities become inhumane. And when we beg the great vocational question, when we fail to help students expand their ethical imagination and find their medium, vocational education becomes a sham, or worse. Pick a lane and lay on the gas, says the jobbified university. But there are far worse things than gaps in your resume. I fear we may be speeding students toward the everyday tragedy described by Dewey, an alienated life in which one never discovers the conditions of their full fluency and agency.

This, however, is not the only crucial, neglected dimension of humane vocational education. Imagine a group of students who, whether by luck or by means of the sort of humane, soul-searching educational process we have described, find lines of work they find congenial, interesting, meaningful, important. Imagine, further, that the university helps these students become well-versed and well-credentialed in their chosen fields. Would these graduates be poised for successful careers? Could they thank their university for delivering on the promise of vocational education? The answer is no and for a very important reason. If we arrest vocational education at this point we have produced only *technicists*, not true engineers, or nurses, or pharmacists, or teachers, or what have you. By a "technicist," I mean someone who mistakes the technical dimensions of their practice for the whole of the work. No one denies that we want practitioners who know how to solve the standard problems in their fields, practitioners skilled at finding and employing efficient means to given ends. Surely, though, such instrumental reasoning constitutes only one aspect of our working lives. To equate professional practice with this sort of tunnel vision is a recipe for disaster. A full enactment of vocation requires that one be able to think about ends themselves.

This may sound familiar, as if I were issuing just one more call to do a better job incorporating "professional ethics" in the college curriculum. However, there is an important difference between what I have in mind and the standard, instrumental-moral approach to professional ethics. Rather than challenge the assumption that professional practices are merely technical, this standard model simply supplies a set of external moral boundaries within which these instrumental, amoral activities may operate. Thus, we find the proliferation of codes of conduct, describing the lines that professionals, on moral grounds, should not cross. And, of course, there are such lines, and it is very bad when people cross them. But it is not enough to produce skilled technicians who are also decent human beings.[49] Such decent technicians, while knowing what to do in an instrumental sense and knowing what not to do in a moral sense, would still be clueless about the substantive ethics of their practice, about the purpose and value of what they are doing. I realize how this might sound. Admittedly, philosophers have a bad habit of prescribing that everyone ought to become a philosopher, an argument that we would certainly not accept from stockbrokers, speech therapists, or software engineers. To this charge, I reply that it depends what you mean by being a philosopher. I am not suggesting that every lawyer and dentist needs to know Kant and Hegel, any more than every philosopher needs to know habeas law or how to perform root canals. However, it is essential that all practitioners learn how to perceive and reflect on the ideals that animate their practices. I see three main arguments for this claim. The first is an argument from self-cultivation; the second (which has two variants) I will call the argument from integrity; the third is an argument from public responsibility.

Here I will offer only a brief statement of the first argument since the entire next section concerns the relationship between vocation and self-cultivation. The basic idea is that in order to grow in and through one's work, one must maintain contact with the goods of one's practice; and in order to stay in touch with those goods, one must have some understanding of what they are. Mere technicians, even those with conscience, who have never reflected on the deeper aims animating their practice, will have trouble making that work into a vehicle for their own ongoing growth. Sooner or later, they will stagnate.

Let us turn, then, to the argument from integrity. First, let us recall that the word "integrity" has both a broader and a narrower meaning, as does its complementary term "corruption." Broadly speaking, integrity and corruption refer to the presence or absence of wholeness, coherence, and authenticity. Consider these examples: if you overcook the pie, the berries will lose their integrity. The band has maintained its integrity despite its fame and changes in personnel. This computer code has become corrupted. This man has no integrity: he just says what he thinks others want to hear. Despite the fire, the building maintained its structural integrity. This is the overarching concept, but it is one particular, moral application of this general idea that has come to dominate usage of the terms "integrity" and "corruption." When we speak of "a corrupt CEO" or "the rare politician with integrity," we are asking about the coherence of a person's words and deeds. To be a person of integrity is to have your actions reflect your stated ideals. The opposite is a hypocrite, if not an outright liar, cheater, embezzler, and so on. It goes without saying that this species of integrity is vitally important: bad actors who hide behind the veil of professionalism and abuse the power of their position can wreak immense damage. Nonetheless, in focusing so exclusively on this species of individual moral corruption, the standard model of professional ethics turns a blind eye to the way in which whole practices drift and degrade until they are no longer what we think they are. An ethical calling requires us to understand and defend the integrity of practices themselves.

What forces threaten to corrupt vocations, and what forms of integrity work are needed in response? As I mentioned, I see two main variants here, associated with the pair of thinkers whose related interventions in the early 1980s helped usher in a new chapter in ethics and social theory. The publication of Alasdair MacIntyre's pathbreaking *After Virtue* was followed just two years later by Michael Walzer's important and underrated *Spheres of Justice*, twin challenges to what Michael Sandel has described as "the procedural republic and the unencumbered self."[50] This was a key moment in a larger renaissance in ethical theory, a modern rehabilitation of aretaic ethics, foregrounding notions of character, excellence, and flourishing.[51] It was also a turning point in social and political theory, the launch of the so-called liberalism-communitarianism debate.[52] While neither MacIntyre nor Walzer identified as communitarians, they did challenge key assumptions of the reigning version of liberal political theory, such as its atomistic philosophical anthropology and its knee-jerk contrast between tradition and reason. Because they sought to rehabilitate concepts of practice, community, and tradition, and to recover thicker notions of justice and the good, they were sometimes seen as advocating a return to oppressive ethical conformity and consensus. This is an almost perfect misreading: their key contribution was indeed to remind us that the good is multifarious. In different ways, each sought to challenge the false choice between a universalism of thin principles and a relativism of value preferences, outlining a version of substantive ethical pluralism.

Such axiological pluralism has deep significance for vocation and vocational education. Practices are not simply different strategies for securing some overarching good. The multiplicity of practices reflects the diversity of goods and indeed of rival comprehensive conceptions framing and ordering such diverse goods. Nor are these larger frameworks, as we saw in the prior section, themselves monolithic or fixed. Every tradition is itself composed of disagreements over, and an evolving sense of, what is valuable

to have, excellent to achieve, wondrous to behold, worthwhile to participate in, and admirable to become. The key point is that, for MacIntyre
and Walzer, such goods only become visible in particular contexts. Thus,
MacIntyre speaks of the "goods internal to practices"; and Michael Walzer
refers to "spheres of justice," diverse "moral and material worlds" where
we find not only distinct goods but rival logics of distribution.[53] When
such practices are corrupted or the boundaries between spheres dissolve,
we experience a deep, structural form of axiological corruption. An anal-
ogy from biology might be helpful. We are currently witnessing a rapid
rise in the species extinction rate and a drastic loss in biological diversity.
Similarly, we can and do experience a loss in diversity in the ethical realm.
Species of valuation—distinctive ways of prizing, of showing care, of
finding importance—disappear from the world just as have the passenger
pigeon, the Western black rhinoceros, and the Pyrenean ibex. One difference is that, unlike biological extinction, the decline in axiological diversity
often goes undetected. Certainly, some ethical worlds die a clear death, but
many take on zombie forms. The spirit departs but the rituals and the language associated with the given axiological sphere or practice live on.[54] The
practice is gradually corrupted until it loses its integrity, but by then ersatz
forms have come to function in their place and all appears well. It is as if a
group of hippos had been disguised to appear as Western black rhinos, fool-
ing the black rhino census.

What kind of corruption do I have in mind, and just what are these axiological imposters? Without overstating the differences in their accounts,
MacIntyre and Walzer each emphasize different threats to ethical pluralism.
MacIntyre helps us perceive a key internal threat to practices, which I will
call "bureaucratization," namely the tendency of practices to be swallowed
up by the institutional machinery built to sustain them. Walzer's main
worry involves inter-spherical relations, and specifically the tendency of
one sphere to become subordinated to another such that its goods are no
longer valued for their own sake but only as means for securing the goods
of the dominant sphere. Let's follow David Blacker in calling this second
process "spherical capture."[55]

First, let us consider "bureaucratization," the process by which institutions, built for the very purpose of protecting and advancing practices, nonetheless begin to subvert them. The basic distinction between
practices and institutions is intuitive enough. Journalism is a practice;

the newspaper is an institution. Doctoring and nursing are practices; the hospital and the insurance company are institutions. Painting, sculpting, curation, and preservation are practices; the museum is an institution. In distinguishing the two, MacIntyre is not at all suggesting that practices would be better off without institutions. He takes pains to point out that indeed "no practice would survive any length of time unsupported by institutions."[56] And MacIntyre further admits that it can sometimes be difficult, even in healthy practice-institution relationships, to find a clear boundary line between the two. After all, practices require community, a sense of their own history, and ways of welcoming initiates: three aspects of practical life in which institutions play a crucial role. Thus, practices and institutions can knit into "a single causal order."[57] Nonetheless, there remains an important difference between the two, namely that practices deal with internal goods and institutions with external goods. A good is anything found worthy to have, do, behold, or become. Each genuine practice has a distinctive ethos, and is organized around a distinctive set of goods. These goods are called "internal" because it is only through apprenticeship and participation that practitioners can learn to appreciate them. External goods such as money and power are generic, requiring no special cultivation of perception, judgment, or character. The other key difference is that internal goods are cooperative while external goods are competitive.[58]

Consider the example of chess. Now there is certainly nothing insidious about chess clubs. To the contrary, the practice is better off for there being a place where players can find an opponent, not to mention a nice quiet hall with tables, sets, and clocks. The club hosts classes, grandmaster visits, tournaments, and each year members gather to discuss the World Chess Championship finals, move by move. The practice of chess flourishes because of, not despite, the activities of the chess club. But of course, all of this costs money, and so dues must be collected, members recruited, ledgers kept, officers elected, disputes settled, and so on. In this example, in which institutional structures are relatively simple and closely modeled on the practice, it is easy to imagine the relationship as a symbiotic one. With a little imagination, though, we can picture a scenario in which this symbiosis breaks down. If MacIntyre were to submit an indie about chess to Sundance, this might be the logline:

Lately, the President of the Westside Chess Club has cared much less about the Latvian Gambit and much more about beating the Eastside Club. Now all of the Westsiders seem obsessed with external goods (membership numbers, financial reserves, seeding for the annual all-city championship), having lost track of the internal goods that drew them in the first place (the beauty of great games; the unique forms of intensity, resourcefulness, and analytic prowess it brings out in the players).[59] We close on an early summer evening: the officers are at the club arguing about Robert's Rules of Order, not even noticing that they are alone. Cut to: the city park, with its run-down chess tables. As the sun sets on the Westside Club, the core players have gathered to get back in touch with the game itself.[60]

It is relatively easy to script a happy ending in this case. While chess clubs are nice and useful, the game is clearly the thing, and all you really need is a set and a partner. If the cart gets in front of the horse, we can just cut tack. In many fields, though, the lines between practice and institution have grown deeply tangled. Consider the relationship of the practices of doctoring and nursing to the institutions of the hospital and insurance company. Again, the claim is not that healing practices need no institutional support, only that such support can devolve into domination, leading to a corruption of the practice, as external goods are mistaken for internal goods. Rather than view hospitals as that set of structures which best support the practices of doctoring and nursing, the fear is that doctors and nurses may start to see themselves as hospital employees. Consider this interview with a family doctor from Camden, New Jersey, who helped form a family medicine group that would insist on such radical innovations as taking time to talk with patients:

> In our system we have an asymmetry in price. So we pay a whole lot of money if you cut, scan, and hospitalize patients. If they have procedures, if they go through machines, we pay an enormous amount of money for those things. If you talk to a patient, you actually lose money in many instances. So when a cardiologist walks in the room and talks to your family member, that's actually a loss leader. That doctor is losing money every moment they stay in a room with your family member. The way they make money is by getting you out of that room back into the scanner that they're leasing in the back of the office. That's not their fault. That's the fault of how we've structured the incentives in the system.[61]

The word "bureaucratization" suggests long lines and a deluge of paperwork. As this example shows, though, the process I am describing is no minor annoyance. It is a deep and insidious form of corruption. The problem is not individual moral corruption, such as double billing by hospital administrators, but axiological corruption of the practice itself. We have come to mistake medicine for cutting and scanning! What makes it insidious is that the word "health" will continue to be used throughout this process by which, as Michael Sandel puts it, "market values crowd out non-market values."[62] If you know you have lost your compass, then at least you know what you are up against. This deeper form of corruption amounts to a more radical form of moral disorientation. In this example, though we are living through the decay of the practices that help us stay in touch with the meaning of health, the word "health" remains, like the reading on a broken compass. In health, education, and a wide range of modern professions, we may be lost without even knowing it. Or, to adapt Weber's famous imagery, while practices should wear their institutions like a light cloak, the concern with external goods often becomes a steel-hard shell.[63]

Let us turn now from MacIntyre's account to Walzer's, shifting our focus from this breakdown of boundaries within the "single causal order" of a practice-institution pair to the erosion of boundaries between spheres. Like MacIntyre, Walzer's aim is to counter bloodless talk of generic goods and rights with thick descriptions of the ethical worlds that serve as home to our distinctive modes of prizing, assessing, and distributing. Whereas MacIntyre drills down to the level of practices, of which there are hundreds (imagining, for example, a compendium from A to Z, here are just some of the candidates in the Ba–Bo range, as it were: Baking, Banjo Playing, Beekeeping, Bicycle Repair, Bocce Ball, Botany), Walzer enumerates eleven core social goods: (1) membership (in a political community), (2) security and welfare, (3) money and commodities, (4) (professional) office, (5) working conditions (not being stuck with more than one's share of dangerous, grueling, or dirty work), (6) free time, (7) education, (8) kinship and love, (9) divine grace, (10) recognition, and (11) political power. As Walzer shows, in seeking to understand and secure these goods we have drawn on and developed diverse traditions of ethical thinking. Each has become home to a "distinctive social and moral logic."[64] Walzer does not see these axiological spheres as fully autonomous. He readily admits that "what happens in one distributive sphere affects what happens in the others."[65] Nonetheless, Walzer insists, even the vague standard of "relative autonomy" proves its worth as a "critical principle," the force of which we feel every time this standard is "violated, the goods usurped, the spheres invaded, by powerful men and women."[66] In every sphere, we will find unequal distribution of the good in question. As problematic as these "simple" inequalities can be, when the relative autonomy of spheres is eroded and goods are made "convertible," such monopolies aggregate into full "tyranny." Walzer's core thesis is that the search for one-dimensional justice is self-defeating; we must pursue "complex equality" through the liberal "art of separation."[67]

Compared with MacIntyre's overstocked ethical emporium, we might well find Walzer's shelves somewhat bare, wanting a bit more plural in his pluralism. Indeed, whereas vocational and other practices are the very engine driving the diversification of goods in MacIntyre, Walzer lumps all vocations together under the concept of office.[68] And we might take issue with other exclusions and categorizations. For example, we might fault Walzer for making no place for friendship or for goods of aesthetic experience and expression.[69] We might also feel that the abstractness and breadth of some of Walzer's spheres work against his own aim of rerooting democratic politics in a theory of goods understood in their rich, evolving multifariousness. After all, it is Walzer himself who points out that even basic "physical necessities" are the bearers of rich and varied social meanings: "Bread is the staff of life, the body of Christ, the symbol of the Sabbath, the means of hospitality, and so on."[70] This is even more true, Walzer adds, when we move from necessities to "opportunities, powers, reputations, and so on."[71] Social theory tends to abstract goods "from every particular meaning," a process by which, Walzer says, they are "for all practical purposes, rendered meaningless."[72] Why then does Walzer hide such an important good as *health* in the abstract category of "security and welfare"? Similarly, while building and dwelling are among the most basic and phenomenologically rich human activities, it is hard to locate in Walzer's spheres the need for a *home* in the built environment.[73] Criticism along these lines appeared immediately, for example in the review by Ronald Dworkin, who accused Walzer of being "bewitched by the music of his own Platonic spheres," complaining that Walzer's typology is "fixed, preordained," assuming "only a limited number of spheres of justice."[74] To this, Walzer retorted that such essentialism was "contrary to the method and intention of [his] book."[75] Mapping the spheres is empirical and interpretive work, he explained, and our understanding of how to draw the boundaries around distinctive social goods "will change over time."[76]

Indeed, any alert reader of Walzer must be struck by the provisional, programmatic quality of the work. What matters is the concept of an axiological sphere—and the accounts of domination, tyranny, ethical pluralism, and complex equality based on this concept—not the exact roster of eleven spheres. Walzer's sketches of these spheres are clearly provisional and themselves point toward an expansion of the list. For example, in the chapter on education, Walzer finds not one but three distinct goods each with its own distributive logic (according to free exchange, desert, or need): (1) because of its close connection to membership, basic schooling should be subject to universal, collective provision according to need; (2) because of its close connection to office, specialized schooling should be distributed on the basis of desert; and we find yet a third axiology in (3) general (higher) education which is motivated by the ideal of attaining a "reasonable and humane conduct of life."[77] Or consider the discussion of free time. This seemingly unitary good immediately refracts into different spectra under Walzer's lens. "Holidays and vacations are two different ways of distributing free time," he concludes; "each has its own logic—or, more exactly, vacations have a single logic, while every holiday has a particular sub-logic, which we can read out of history and rituals."[78] Or, again, "Sabbath rest is more egalitarian than the vacation because it can't be purchased: it is one more thing that money can't buy."[79] Certainly, there is a centripetal force at work in *Spheres*. Walzer corrals the manifold of goods into eleven spheres, each of which is found to emphasize, combine, or inflect one of his three basic distributive principles.[80] But again and again, Walzer's muse pulls him outward, and it is this centrifugal tendency that makes the book a classic. What interests Walzer is the historical, cultural, and phenomenological variegation in our collective construction of the worthwhile. The discussion of money and markets is concretized in the rise of the department store. To then test the limits of commodification, we look with Malinowski at the gift logic at work in the Trobriand Islands, only to refract this further by investigating the gift in the Napoleonic Code. Walzer loves to zoom in and learn from the details: from Stalinist praising to Athenian shaming; from the sharing of grueling work on a kibbutz to the phenomenology of rest; from the concept of the date (as a form of courtship) to the history of the titles "Mr.," "Mrs.," "Miss," and "Ms." Den Hartogh is probably right in his assessment that the architecture of Walzer's theory is unstable, but his conclusion is also on point: "Walzer's true genius . . . [lies] in his mastery of the phenomenology of the moral life."[81]

Thus, while it remains an open question just how we should map social goods into distinct spheres, Walzer's basic model remains quite useful. Like MacIntyre, Walzer's aim is to unearth the multiplicity of moral sources and to remind us of the fragility of this pluralism. We must be on guard against convertibility and spherical capture. The integrity of the spheres must be defended. For example, one of Walzer's extended examples involves the town of Pullman, Illinois. In 1880, George Pullman, the specialized railroad car magnate, created a planned community just south of Chicago, centered around a new set of factories and populated by his employees. The town included "private homes, row houses, and tenements for some seven to eight thousand people, shops and offices (in an elaborate arcade), schools, stables, playgrounds, a market, a hotel, a library, a theater, even a church," all owned by Pullman.[82] As Walzer explains, though Pullman did not engage in the typical company-town abuses—rent gauging, scrip and inflated prices, and so on—there was something deeply troubling about the whole setup. In Pullman, Illinois, the boundaries between the spheres of membership, security, money, and political power were dissolved. Indeed, the logic of convertibility extended even to education and religion, as colorfully captured by one resident: "We are born in a Pullman house. We are fed from a Pullman shop, taught in a Pullman school, catechized in the Pullman church and when we die we shall be buried in a Pullman cemetery and go to a Pullman hell."[83] Most troubling for Walzer is the conflation of the logics of ownership and governance. That Pullman's employees retained their US citizenship was beside the point: by creating a 4,000-acre fiefdom around his factories, Walzer observes, Pullman turned his employees into "guest workers, and that is not a status compatible with democratic politics."[84] This is a fairly obvious case of tyranny. Let us consider another, more subtle, case of spherical capture.

What I have in mind is the relation of sports and politics (in light of the preceding discussion, I will take the liberty of hypothesizing that sports has become home to distinct notions of excellence, virtue, and worth and thus constitutes its own sphere). As Walzer would predict, there is no question of entirely disentangling the two spheres. Indeed, in many sports, the highest honor is to represent one's country in international competition. The Olympics is about nationalism as much as it is about athleticism. If Olympic sports are entwined with global politics, all sports run up against politics in the more general sense of negotiating the distribution, limitation, and organization of power in a community. The recent election for the presidency of the US Women's Soccer Federation is a case in point. Former star goalkeeper Hope Solo, having recently been cut from the team, ran for the presidency on a platform of combating corruption and fighting for equal pay for female athletes. In a case like this, it can be hard to separate the sport itself from the politics of the sporting community and indeed from national political questions, such as our continued failure to address gender discrimination. The reverse is also true, that sports can bleed into politics. Sports is a sphere with wide participation, first- and secondhand, and its vocabularies of praise and blame have wide currency in the culture at large. As the US presidential election was heating up in the fall of 2012, so did Mitt Romney's use of sports metaphors. Likening President Barack Obama to a coach with a losing record, Romney declared that "It's time to get a new coach. It's time for America to see a winning season again."[85] Politicians are said to *swing for the fences*, campaigns to need *a ground game*; debaters to deliver the *knockout punch*.

As we said, the boundaries between spheres are never impermeable. Nonetheless, as Walzer predicts, once the boundaries dissolve past a certain point, palpable corruption ensues. It is one thing to reach for the occasional sports metaphor as we all do, for example "drop the ball" or "three strikes," and another to begin to conceive of political processes as if they were sporting events. Thus, talk of "dark horses" and candidates running "neck and neck" are not just colorful and convenient metaphors but symptoms of a deeper conflation of sports and politics. We perceive politics as a game; elections as a horse race. Coverage of elections constantly veers away from the ideas espoused by candidates to the points scored or lost in so espousing them. Don't get me wrong, there is something genuinely, beautifully good about come-from-behind victories. Thank goodness we have sports to refresh our moral imaginations with examples of a certain kind of raw courage, heart, pluck, and perseverance. If you missed Michael Chang's defeat of Ivan Lendl in the 1989 French Open, drop what you are doing and watch the match now. But the goods of politics are distinct. Presumably, they involve struggling together, across our differences, with the question of how we ought to live together, finding in our very disagreements a continuing commitment to take collective, reflective responsibility for our shared fate. Of course, we will continue to pay lip service to "the importance of debate," "pressing social issues," and so on. However, as the spherical integrity of politics continues to weaken, political goods will dissipate until they are nothing but paper-thin tickets to some other sort of prize.

And we can run the analysis in reverse. The example that comes to mind is a recent ugly incident in men's freestyle wrestling. It was November 2017, during the quarterfinals of the Under 23 World Championships in Poland, when the Iranian wrestling federation's policy of forbidding their wrestlers to wrestle against Israeli opponents finally came into effect. Iran's outstanding 86 KG freestyle wrestler, Alireza Karimi-Machiani, was in the quarterfinals, facing a tough Russian opponent. In the other quarter on the same side of the bracket was an Israeli wrestler paired with a US opponent. The quarters run simultaneously, and so, even as the Iranian coaches were coaching Karimi, they were watching the other mat to see whether the Israeli wrestler would be advancing. When it became clear that he would, Karimi's coaches, in order to avoid having him wrestle against or forfeit to the Israeli in the semifinals, told Karimi to throw the match. Regardless of what you think about Iran's nonrecognition of Israel, or Israel's treatment of Palestinians, all of those who know the beauty of the sport of freestyle wrestling felt the intense wrongness of what happened in the next twenty seconds. With just over a minute left, the wrestlers went out of bounds. Karimi was leading 3–2, controlling the match. The Russian seemed to have no answer for Karimi's head-hands defense. As they headed back to the center, Karimi looked over at his coaches. At the restart, Karimi relaxed his stance, allowing the Russian in on a double leg without sprawling. Falling to the mat, Karimi then gave up five easy, consecutive leg-laces to lose 14–3, by technical superiority, with forty-five seconds still on the clock. Afterward, Karimi looked defeated. Even the Russian wrestler looked more confused than celebratory. It is not only that Karimi's hard work had been sacrificed to geopolitics: the whole 86 KG bracket had been invalidated. For twenty seconds we got a good look at an ethical zombie. It still looked like wrestling, but the practice had been perverted. The heart gone.

In this way, MacIntyre and Walzer draw our attention to forms of deep, structural, axiological corruption. As I mentioned earlier, this is not to minimize the damage done by individual moral corruption. The double-billing doctor, the plagiarizing professor, the confidentiality-betraying therapist: these are deeply troubling actions. At the same time, such transgressions ultimately reinforce the norms they violate. Such miscreants may cover their tracks for a time, but when their actions finally come to light, it reaffirms the

values of fairness, honesty, and trust. However, it is one thing to be betrayed
by individual bad actors, and another when a community of practice suffers widespread moral disorientation. What makes bureaucratization and
spherical capture so dangerous is that they distort rather than eliminate the
goods in question. It is, as we noted, like having a broken compass. We are
never more lost than when we don't know we have lost our way.

For this reason, we must insist that true vocation entails the kinds of
integrity work described by MacIntyre and Walzer. Given the threat of
bureaucratization, practitioners must work to ensure that internal goods
are not mistaken for external goods. Given the threat of spherical capture,
practitioners must work to ensure that the goods definitive of their sphere
are not made into a sub-currency of another sphere. And this brings us to
the conclusion of the second argument, the argument from integrity. In
order to recognize counterfeits and stand up for the goods under assault,
one must understand the ethical terrain in question. A full enactment of
vocation requires a degree of ethical acuity, responsiveness, and reflectiveness. Thus, any vocational education worthy of the name must help practitioners learn how to ask and keep open the question, How do the aims of
my local practice, as institutionalized and socially positioned, relate to the
genuine goods of my practice? In light of the dangers of bureaucratization,
I must ask, Am I a chess player or a ward heeler? Am I a doctor, or a cutter
and scanner? Given the dangers of spherical capture, I must ask, Am I politician or a jockey? Are we a wrestling team or a branch of the state department? Such questions arise in every practice: Is this a museum or a tourist
attraction? Is this a university or corporate R&D? Am I a lawyer or a biller
of hours, a journalist or an entertainer, a farmer or petrochemist, a teacher
or a warden, a psychotherapist or a psychopharmacologist? A practitioner
who has never given much thought to the *telos* of his or her practice, to that
for the sake of which we engage in the work, will find it difficult to detect
these deeper forms of corruption.

We turn now to a third argument for the claim that vocational education
must cultivate reflectiveness about the nature, aims, and social importance
of one's work. Earlier I called this the argument from public responsibility,
and it is really just the flip side of Walzer's warning about domination and
spherical capture. If the argument from integrity suggests that vocation
demands that one ask whether one's local practice has drifted away from
its animating ideals, the argument from public responsibility suggests that

one must also ask how one's practice fits into the broader pursuit of flourishing lives and just communities. In other words, ethical practice requires that one be aware that the goods one seeks in one's practice are not the only goods. In Walzerian spirit, we ought to avoid the logic of convertibility, even when we work within the dominant sphere. And even when the boundaries between spheres remain intact, there is the question of how we commensurate and prioritize rival goods in our pursuit of the common good. Our awareness of other social goods thus inflects how we think about our own practice and provides constraints on our work.

It may be misleading, however, to speak of this consideration in terms of constraint. After all, we want our work to be—we want ourselves to be—part of something larger. To have a vocation is to have a place to stand in public life, a place from which to seek the recognition of others. Since this suggests that we can and do join existing public dialogues through our work, it is important to add that our occupations constitute, to adopt Harry Boyte's phrase, "public work" not because all occupations are governmental or even because all professions contribute to the common good, but even more elementally because in occupying our social roles we are together "making public," working to make the polity not just an administrative apparatus but a space where the good in its several aspects may be sought, cherished, articulated, debated.[86] When we introduce students to professions as if they were isolated practices, we not only leave them unprepared to negotiate tensions between the aims of their practice and other social goods, but we condemn them to that sad fate of a purely private existence.

In the jobbified university, vocational preparation tends toward technicism. The problem is not that there are no skills to teach, no information to pass on. The problem is myopia. The narrow focus on how to get the job and handle its characteristic tasks leaves two cornerstones of vocational formation in the blurry background: the ethical sources on which the integrity of each practice depends and the social context within which the work assumes its public importance. True vocational education fosters ethical and social awareness, cultivating the ability to defend the value and integrity of the goods animating one's practice and to articulate how these goods relate to those of other spheres. Having established this second corrective to the reductive view of vocational education, we return to the question of the contribution of humane learning to vocational enactment. Here, though, no elaborate, new argument is required. For it was the point of the previous section to establish that humane education is about cultivating ethical perception and judgment by opening students to the variety of moral sources, qualitative vocabularies, and comprehensive conceptions. This is the province of art, literature, and philosophy. And the study of anthropology, education, history, and political-economy is also recommended if one wants to construct a map of social endeavor and human formation on which one can locate one's chosen practice. As we noted, it matters how these disciplines are conceived and taught. Their presence alone does not guarantee that students will achieve a humane understanding of their professions. However, their absence guarantees that vocational education will fail to rise above technical training, leaving students vulnerable to ethical disorientation and deprived of public work.

A NEW ORGAN

He not busy being born is busy dying.
—Bob Dylan

Another quick review of our progress is in order. We have now recovered two of the four dimensions of vocational enactment ignored by the jobbified university in its myopic pursuit of training and credentialing: finding a worthy form of work that engages one's talents and aspirations, and cultivating the ethical sensitivity and social awareness needed to enact that vocation with integrity and public purpose. These are no minor omissions. When we gloss over the question of calling, we invite the tragic alienation described by Dewey. When we treat value questions as an afterthought, a code of ethics stapled onto a technical pursuit, we invite dangerous forms of ethical corruption and disorientation. Though it will not be mentioned in any prospectus, this is all part of the "return on investment." In restoring the neglected dimensions of vocational education, we are not only helping the university make good on its promise to prepare students for their working lives, but we are also making a more powerful case for the humanities, one that does not need to rely on hackneyed distinctions between practicality and culture, between paychecks and public-mindedness. Humane learning provides resources for self-understanding, exposure to a wider range of ideas about what is worth prizing, and an instigation to begin to articulate what one stands for. Such learning increases the chance of finding a genuinely worthwhile and congenial form of work; and it mitigates the technicist tendency to mistake the clever manipulation of means for the achievement of worthwhile ends.

It is now time to lift a simplification in my account. Before rushing into training and credentialing, we said, one ought to give some serious thought to what kind of work suits one's dispositions and talents, one's ambitions and values. And one ought to learn about the ideals that distinguish and connect our various traditions and practices. Humane collegiate education creates a space to explore who one is and what one stands for, providing an introduction to the gamut of human projects and prizings. I stand by this basic claim. Young adults can and should confront the great vocational question as part of the process of choosing a major and career. However, we have left out a crucial fact: vocations themselves rank among the most powerful vehicles of self-knowledge and self-cultivation. We choose our projects not merely to express who we are, but also to understand who we are and to help us give shape to who we would like to become.

And central to this vocational formation is precisely our ability to perceive, to value, and to achieve a set of goods largely inaccessible to those uninitiated in the practice (that which we called, following MacIntyre, "internal goods"). As MacIntyre rightly points out, it cannot be simply that we choose practices in order to express our current values and ambitions, since what apprenticeship to a practice offers us is precisely a means for overcoming "inadequacies of desire, taste, habit, and judgment."[87] Thus, it was also a simplification to suggest that first one clarifies one's values and then one chooses work in line with those values. Practices are themselves deep axiological resources, sites where we encounter, as I have noted elsewhere, the poetry of the moral life.[88] Thus, having opened the great vocational question, we must learn to keep it open, since our understanding of ourselves and what matters to us will continue to evolve during the work itself. One must continue to search for one's calling even as one pursues it. And this brings us to what I earlier listed as the fifth necessary task of vocational development, learning to pursue one's calling in the spirit of self-cultivation, learning how to grow into and through one's work.

To grasp this idea, we must first let go of the stubborn assumption that vocational education means preparatory training for a particular line of work. This gets the whole thing wrong, as Dewey tirelessly pointed out. First, all of us have a variety of vocations, paid and unpaid, even if only one makes it onto our W-2 form.[89] Second, this puts the educational cart before the vocational horse. "Education *through* occupations," Dewey writes, "combines within itself more of the factors conducive to learning than any other method."[90] Third, what we learn through work is not only about that work: vocations open us to the interest and complexity of the world at large. For Dewey, the organizing principle of our "variegated vocational activities" is an existential one: "The dominant vocation of all human beings at all times is living—intellectual and moral growth."[91]

This existential framing does not imply that vocation is *selfish*, only "self-ful." To grow in and through one's work, one must avoid the twin extremes of self-abnegation and self-absorption.[92] Choosing a vocation means choosing a medium—a distinctive set of enabling constraints—in which to find both self and other and bring them into fruitful interaction. In this sense, all teachers are involved in vocational education, attending closely to the zone of contact between mind and material. Such "insight into soul-action," Dewey declares, "is the supreme mark and criterion of a teacher."[93] Activists, agronomists, archers, architects, air traffic controllers, and amateur historians of ska music all mind the world in particular ways. Or rather, vocations call forth particular worlds from the open-ended repleteness that is reality, by providing an "axis which runs through an immense diversity of detail," a vector of concern shaping what we, as the saying goes, *care to notice*.[94]

Here I think of the advice that the poet Rainer Maria Rilke gives to Franz Kappus in *Letters to a Young Poet*. When he first reached out to Rilke, Kappus was an aspiring poet, just finishing high school. By the time their correspondence ended, six years later, Kappus had graduated and become an officer in the Austro-Hungarian army. However, the "young poet" in the title refers every bit as much to the adult Kappus as to the adolescent one. As the correspondence progresses, it becomes clear that Rilke's advice is not about the literal craft of poetry but about the search for what we might call a poetic calling. Rilke urges Kappus to find the kind of work that offers a "high inducement for an individual to ripen, to become something in himself."[95] And he warns Kappus away from "professions petrified and no longer linked with living," from any calling so "burdened with . . . conventions" that it leaves no "room for a personal conception of its problems."[96] But Rilke does not apply this advice as we might expect, urging sonnets over bayonets. Indeed, he makes a point of telling Kappus that some occupations only "feign a greater freedom," specifically steering him away from "unreal half-artistic professions . . . [that] pretend proximity to some art."[97] Like others, poets must sort out what is living and what is lifeless in their calling. All professions, from the literary to the military, present their share of conventions, constrictions, and distractions.

While some professions foreground self-expression and others operate in the key of duty and service, both types pose problems for what I am calling a "poetic calling." The danger at one extreme is that you may end up serving nothing but yourself, isolated from "contact with the big things of which real living exists."[98] But there is another danger lurking in fields that stress duty and service, especially in the so-called helping professions, where poor working conditions and indignities of remuneration and recognition become part of the definition of what it means to serve. It is one thing to *shed our baggage.* We hope that our vocations puncture our solipsism and bleed our narcissism, that they teach us to outgrow our pettiness and fearfulness, and that they might even help us to take responsibility, as Cornel West recently put it, for our inner gangster.[99] It is another thing to *shelve ourselves,* distancing from desires, abandoning ambitions. To paraphrase Langston Hughes, what happens to institutions predicated on dreams deferred? Over time, such cultures of service can twist into something else, into dead zones animated only by convulsions of resentment. As Rilke puts it to Kappus, many lines of work are "full of enmity against the individual, saturated as it were with the hatred of those who have found themselves mute and sullen in a humdrum duty."[100] Or, returning to Salinger, Zooey puts the matter succinctly: "In my opinion, if you really want to know, half the nastiness in the world is stirred up by people who aren't using their true egos."[101]

This gives us a sense of what it means to find a poetic calling and to pursue one's work in a self-ful way. But let us return to this puzzle, glimpsed earlier, that it simultaneously takes self-knowledge to choose the right line of work and takes experience in practices to know oneself. If work is central to our formation, then perhaps we were wrong earlier to stress the importance of self-knowledge in facing up to the great vocational question. After all, how is it possible for me to choose the wrong line of work if that work will remake the "me" in question? Does this take the bite out of the epigraph with which we began this essay, Dewey's remark that "nothing is more tragic than failure to discover one's true business in life, or to find that one has drifted or been forced by circumstance into an uncongenial calling"? What does it mean to find congenial work?

Actually, this word "congenial" is quite interesting. Originally, the dominant meaning was "partaking of the same genius, disposition, or temperament; kindred, sympathetic" (OED #1).[102] The word described a feature of the world, a state of fit between two entities (persons, activities, things). Over time, "congenial" took on a subjective meaning: "to one's taste or liking" (OED #2); "producing a feeling of comfort or satisfaction" (Cambridge).[103] The word "genius" in the first definition has also become psychologized. Now we think of a person's intellectual capacity or creative originality, but the word originally referred to the spirit watching over each person and place (e.g., genius loci). The Greeks called this attendant spirit a *daimōn*, and it is built into their term for flourishing, *eudaimonia* ("eu" means "good" or "well"). Unlike modern happiness, we are not the only or even best judges of whether we are flourishing. In an important sense, the question is an objective one: Does this person have a good *daimōn*? Is this a life well-lived? We may be the arbiters of our subjective feelings, and, as Arendt explains, we have some control over whether we "display or hide" *what* we are, our "qualities, gifts, talents, and shortcomings."[104] By contrast, *who* we are "remains hidden from the person himself, like the *daimōn* in Greek religion which accompanies each man throughout his life, always looking over his shoulder from behind and thus visible only to those he encounters."[105] Self-knowledge is possible but necessarily indirect, as our *daimōn* reveals itself in our beings and doings through "flashes of the spirit."[106]

Calling is the finding of this kindred spirit, a conviction that in you something in the world can become what it needs to be, and that in this worldly practice you can become what you need to be. The dialectical revelation of this Janus-faced good, drawing self from world and world from self, is not a preparatory step but itself the life of practice. Thus, we can see the first and third vocational tasks—finding one's calling and understanding the ethical geography in and around one's work—as necessary but insufficient conditions for this fifth task. You must have some self-understanding and some sense of the range of human projects to see how a vocation might express your talents and ambitions. But this refers to your current self. You will hope to grow and change in light of the work. You need to have some sense of the goods that animate your practice to know why they matter in themselves and in relation to other social desiderata. But the ethical terrain of the work will open to you only over time. Work practices thus require a kind of bootstrapping: we must invest to gain entry, but it is only through deeper entry that you can understand what that investment entails. However, as Talbot Brewer points out, save for purely instrumental pursuits, all activities have this sort of dialectical structure.[107]

There is a beautiful illustration of this dialectical process of humane vocational growth in John Berger's *A Fortunate Man*. Berger's subject is the career of a country doctor, Dr. John Sassall. From where we sit now, this might seem like an awkward illustration of the humanistic dimensions of vocational development. After all, the humanities are now typically understood precisely as the non-sciences, medicine is a quintessential STEM field, and medical education is sometimes faulted for producing technicians unable to see the person behind the disease. Before turning to Berger, then, it might be useful to set this alienation of medicine and the humanities in historical context.[108] Before the humanities remade themselves as areas of research in a new kind of university, not only were the boundaries among academic disciplines less rigid, but humanistic education was not contrasted with the vocational. Indeed, earlier modes of humanistic education, while certainly part of the tradition of liberal learning, were aimed at "the active man of affairs who retains a solid and lasting interest in the literary studies of his youth."[109] Early humanist educators hoped to foster wisdom, eloquence, and a learned grasp of Latin, but all of this was framed as a practical education, whether the pupil went on to be an orator or a courtier, a diplomat or a general, a priest or a personal secretary, a lawyer or a court physician.[110]

In fact, the histories of humanism and medicine are closely intertwined from the trio of great medieval physician philosophers—Ibn Sina (Avicenna), Ibn Rushd (Averroes), and Moses ben Maimon (Maimonides)—through Renaissance medical humanists such as Linacre, Paracelsus, Vesalius, and Browne. Rabelais was a doctor. Both Schiller and Keats also had medical training and careers, if short-lived. Freud, of course, began as a neurologist. And the tradition of the writer-physician continues through such figures as William Carlos Williams and Walker Percy, whose contrasting views on their double calling are instructive. Williams recalls that medicine was the "very food and drink, the very thing which made it possible for [him] to write."[111] Percy also drew inspiration from his medical practice, noting that "the first intellectual discovery of [his] life was the beauty of the scientific method."[112] For Percy, though, a tension began to emerge: "an extraordinary paradox . . . that the more science progressed and even as it benefited man, the less it said about what it is like to be a man living in the world."[113]

By contrast, Williams continued to see a deep resonance between medicine and the humanities:

> Was I not interested in man? There the thing was right in front of me. I could touch it, smell it. It was myself, naked, just as it was, without a lie telling itself to me in its own terms.[114]

As a physician-humanist, Williams ponders the human condition from no lofty vantage. He is in it, knee-deep: no more willing or able to deny our animality, our frailty, and our dependence than he is our personhood and our striving to lead lives of meaning and purpose. Thus, a humane doctor rejects both airy idealism and cynical materialism. Nakedness here is contrasted not with being clothed but with being cloaked. What Williams expresses is the ability to extend our awareness and our sympathy to the human-all-too-human aspects of human existence, to perceive our nature and condition unobscured by wishes and fears. At the same time, Williams's metaphor of nakedness is potentially misleading, as if letting reality speak in its own terms were as simple as disrobing it or, worse, as if language, culture, and history were but coverings, disguising a more basic, physical truth about who we are.

It is, by contrast, one of the many virtues of Berger's account that it reveals precisely the arduous, dialectical nature of self-knowledge and vocational growth. *A Fortunate Man* retraces the career of physician-humanist Dr. John Sassall, an English country doctor who embraced in a new and remarkable way a role his own times were making obsolete. In Berger's spare, haiku-like prose ("and on the block of butter small grains of toast from the last impatient knife"), complemented by the equally quiet and observant photographs of Jean Mohr, we enter the Forest of Dean, meet its people, and observe Sassall at work, from house calls to receiving patients in his rural surgery.[115] If the book gives us access to Sassall's inner life, his practice, and the lives of his patients, its true subject is Sassall's own increasing access to a wider world, revealed through the interplay of these three registers.

The book begins with an accident and an amputation, a vivid demonstration of Sassall's competence in crisis. When Sassall began his work, having chosen a remote country practice after serving as a navy surgeon, he had "no patience for anything except emergencies and serious illness."[116] He had a heroic understanding of his vocation as the stoic, resourceful, master clinician who performs under pressure, a view his rural practice made it easy to live out:

> He was always overworked and proud of it. Most of the time he was out on calls—often having to make his way over fields, carrying his black boxes of instruments and drugs, along forest paths. In the winter he had to dig his way through the snow. Along with his instruments he carried a blow lamp for thawing out pipes.
>
> He was scarcely ever in his surgery. He imagined himself as a sort of one man hospital. He performed appendix and hernia operations on kitchen tables. He delivered babies in caravans. It would almost be true to say that he sought out accidents.[117]

However, Sassall began to realize that while "emergencies always present themselves as *faits accomplis*," it is mainly our ignorance of the lead-up that makes situations emergent. Over time, he was struck less by his skill in coping and more by his blindness in anticipation. As different emergencies called him back to the same cottage over a period of years, a kind of gestalt-switch occurred.[118] The emergencies receded and the connective tissue of those events—the lives being led in that cottage—snapped to the foreground. Taking a medical history was one thing; actually understanding the unfolding stories of his patients' lives another.

What is puzzling about this is that Sassall would already seem to be in the perfect position to achieve such understanding. Who better than a country doctor, living among his patients and trusted with intimate details, to understand their lives? But this is not how experience works, through an accumulation of details, as if proximity plus duration equals understanding. Sassall did decide to split his practice in half so that he could spend more time listening to his patients, but listening and hearing, looking and seeing, are not the same thing.[119] The richness of our commerce with the world is limited by our imagination, by what we know how to notice and the questions we know how to ask. But what shapes our imaginations? According to Dewey, it is precisely our practical-intellectual activities, our humane callings, that promise "to enlarge the imaginative vision of life."[120] This suggests a paradox for Sassall: to heal he must grow and to grow he must heal. If experience is full of such circles, not all of them are vicious. Sassall is caught in the same circle in which we all find ourselves, the hermeneutic circle.

"A picture holds us captive," Wittgenstein famously observed.[121] What appears to us as a feature of the world often proves upon reflection to be a part of our linguistic-conceptual structures for apprehending the world. This accords with the point stressed by both Dewey and Gadamer, that true experience takes the form of disconfirmation.[122] We have always already grasped the world with specific modes of apprehension and what registers is that which challenges these pre-judgments. True experience takes the form of insight, which always entails a double recognition: we register both the overlooked and the overlooking, both that a feature of the world had escaped us and that we have escaped our faulty former understanding.

Why, then, is insight difficult, even painful? After all, escape from a captor sounds simply like relief. Here is where Gadamer might help us extend and revise Wittgenstein's adage (lest we be held captive by Wittgenstein's picture of our picturing!), trading in its passive voice for an active construction. We are the captors. We cling to the pictures that enable us to hold the world captive, to subdue the blooming, buzzing confusion of an uninterpreted world. Letting go is not easy, a fact even Gadamer struggles to calibrate between his somewhat mild description "pulled-up short" and his Aeschylean evocation of insight as fundamentally tragic.[123] Perhaps we could simply say that real insight requires nothing more and nothing less than getting over ourselves.

Consider, in this light, Berger's description of the picture that held Sassall captive:

> He dealt only with crises in which he was the central character: or, to put it another way, in which the patient was simplified by the degree of his physical dependence on the doctor. He was also simplified himself, because the chosen pace of his life made it impossible and unnecessary for him to examine his own motives.[124]

For a time, this circle was vicious enough as each component found confirmation in the others. To the heroic doctor, medicine appears as crisis control; in such a practice, patients present as emergencies; in a life structured as a series of emergencies, Sassall strikes himself as heroic. But then something opened up in him and the circle of experience began to spiral outward. Sassall was pulled up short by the aspects of his patients' lives that thwarted his expectations:

> He began to notice how people developed. A girl whom three years before he had treated for measles got married and came to him for her first confinement. A man who had never been ill shot his brains out.[125]

Sassall came to feel that a doctor does not have the luxury to consign whole portions of the human drama to the lazy category of the unimaginable. He began to look at his own need to construe medicine as "only fights within the jaws of death."[126] He began to realize, Berger writes, "that imagination had to be lived with on every level: his own imagination first—because otherwise this could distort his observation—and then the imagination of his patients."[127]

A moment ago, I called this process "getting over oneself," noting the inevitable pain involved in letting go of one's crutches and vanities. And the process was painful for Sassall. But it was also soul-expanding. Berger captures both the price and reward of self-knowledge. Having set himself the task of situating his treatment in an understanding of the patient as a "total personality," Sassall was forced to confront how little he knew even about his own totality. As he started to make more time to listen to his patients, he also opened up space to listen to himself. This cost Sassall, as he began to suffer bouts of depression. The reward was progress in what Freud called *Nacherziehung* or "after education."[128] Though we have pegged liberal learning to the years from age eighteen to twenty-two, perhaps liberal learning only truly begins in an Augustinian moment. Sassall had reached the point, like Augustine before him, when he could declare, "I have become a question to myself."[129] Against the lazy contrast between the liberal and vocational, we see here vocational experience as itself a process of liberal learning. While Sassall continued to devour the medical journals as they appeared, he also began reading more widely, reflecting on existence and mortality, poverty and community, psychology and culture. New ideas opened new conversations with his patients, which in turn led him to new questions. As the circle of Sassall's experience grew, it became impossible to say whether he healed himself to heal others or healed others to heal himself.

To capture the dialectical nature of this vocational *Bildung*, this process at once painful and soul-expanding, Berger offers a perfect passage from Goethe:

> Man knows himself only inasmuch as he knows the world. He knows the world only within himself, and he is aware of himself only within the world. Each new object, truly recognized, opens up a new organ within ourselves.[130]

Figures like Sassall exemplify a rare form of humane understanding, hard won in the circuits between self and other. What Berger shows is not only that the full enactment of vocation depends on the humane quest for self-understanding, but that practice itself is fertile soil for one's ongoing humane education. And the example of Sassall lifts us clear of tired debates over whether to fund STEM or the humanities, whether higher education is about practicality or culture, whether we should prioritize career readiness or critical thinking and civic participation. The goal in Sassall's case was no more and no less than practicing medicine in its integrity by learning to see clearly the world inside and around him. To achieve this required an education encompassing both gall bladders and great books.

Thus, with the help of Goethe and Gadamer, Dewey and Berger, we see how life is lived in circles. Tragically, our orbits may be fixed or even grow narrower over time. But it is also possible for experience to spiral outward, opening onto greater contact with the world in its complexity. Some vocations are paid and some unpaid; some deemed "trades" and others "professions." But all vocations are structures of expectation that organize significant worlds. Whether such a world will be narrow or wide, self-reinforcing or full of Rilkean "incitements to ripen," depends on how one enacts one's vocation. The story of John Sassall is the story of two enactments of what is ostensibly one and the same calling. Sassall begins his career as a country doctor, only to discover that he did not yet know either how to live among his patients or how to truly heal. He was trained as a doctor. He set up shop in the country. But he still needed to learn how to become a *country doctor*. What enables one to enact vocation as an ongoing formative process? If vocations are modes of mindedness, how do we teach vocations as modes of open-mindedness?

"Open-mindedness," Jonathan Lear declares, "is the capacity to live nondefensively" with Socrates's famous query in the *Republic*, "the question of how one should live."[131] This connects with Dewey's concern that we pursue our various vocations without losing track of our dominant vocation of ongoing growth. These Socratic and Deweyan questions are closely interwoven: What am I achieving and becoming through this work? What is worthwhile to achieve and admirable to become? Is this practice worth putting at the center of my life? Am I leading a good life? How should one live? However, Lear adds an interesting wrinkle to this Socratic-Deweyan fabric. Notice that in his definition of open-mindedness, Lear stresses nondefensiveness. This is because keeping Socrates's question open is for us a source both of aliveness and of anxiety. Indeed, the anxiety can be profound enough that we may accept, and even surreptitiously seek out, various forms of deadness as an acceptable price of quieting that anxiety. Instead of keeping the question open, we fall into various forms of "know-ingness," implicit social agreements to act as if certain significant, open questions have already been answered, or never need arise, or are embarrass-ingly sophomoric, irrelevant, or quaint. This insight sets Lear up to make a surprising claim about professions. Professions are themselves institutional-ized forms of knowingness, "defensive structures" instilling deadness in the name of standards, methods, and other defining conventions.

   To see Lear's point, recall the conclusion of our discussion of MacIntyre and Walzer, that practicing with integrity requires that one keep alive the question, how do the goods animating my vocation relate to the aims of my local practice as institutionalized and socially situated? Or consider again the moral of Berger's narrative: having amazed all around him with his resourcefulness, skill, and heroism, Sassall then had to confront the ques-tion, what does it mean to be a doctor? Lear's point is that organizations like the American Medical Association were built for the express reason of ensuring that such questions do not arise. Their purpose is precisely to con-vince the public that a definitive answer to the question of what it means to be a doctor has already been found. In this way, Lear's hunch about pro-fessions squares with Andrew Abbott's classic sociological analysis of pro-fessionalization.[132] The discourse of professionalism exists to legitimize a certain approach to a field of practice, to grant exclusive jurisdiction to a certain community of practice, and to assure society at large that this com-munity has the expertise and integrity to be trusted both to regulate its own training and certification and to monitor its own conduct. Each profession vouches to society not only that it has answered the question of what it means to be an architect, doctor, engineer, lawyer, teacher, and the like, but also that it alone possesses such wisdom. To bring his point home, Lear riffs off of a famous remark by Freud, who referred to educating, governing, and healing as three "impossible professions."[133] Freud was not suggesting that we throw up our hands in despair, but simply recommending—in light of the dark undercurrents and self-defeating strategies he had discovered in his patients—that we adopt a deeply humble, even tragic, stance in such human-all-too-human practices. Such humility flies in the face of a certain kind of technocratic confidence characteristic of professions: we under-stand the problems and have the tools to fix them. Lear expands Freud's list, citing philosophy as paradigmatic example of an impossible profession. Inspired by Socrates's question, Lear suggests, philosophy is precisely an eclectic set of traditions and practices devoted to disarming our defensiveness about the examined life. If we understand professions, by contrast, as elaborate structures to keep certain questions from arising, it becomes clear that the idea of "professional philosophy" is an absurdity, like a wooden house built to contain termites.[134] The American Philosophical Association, Lear boldly concludes, is built on an illusion, a fantasy, a wish.

While Lear may be right that philosophy has an especially close connection with the ideal of the examined life, what we have seen is that all vocations require self-examination, as every vocation potentially represents both a corkscrew for opening up self and world and a professional workshop on complacent nominalism (a doctor is someone with a current and valid medical license, and so on). When dealing with the latter, Lear prescribes a dose of irony, especially the Socratic and Kierkegaardian strain distilled in questions of the form, "Among all doctors, is there a doctor?"[135] Complacency interrupted, one is again forced to face Socrates' persistent question, What is X? What is courage, beauty, health, justice, knowledge, learning, piety, and so on? What does it mean to try to respect and realize these goods in the world? What does it mean to be a soldier, artist, doctor, lawyer, scholar, teacher, or religious leader?

In order to stay in touch with his "dominant vocation," Sassall had to learn to live nondefensively with the questions, "What does it mean to be a doctor?" "How do I grow into and through this role?" At stake was not only the welfare of his patients but also his own aliveness. For humans are creatures for whom becoming is part of their being, and he not busy being born, is dying busily.

With this, we have established the necessity of the third neglected task of vocational formation. What is the role of humane learning in this dimension of vocational enactment? Here we want to avoid lapsing back into the preparation model. This spiraling movement of vocational experience is itself a profound classroom, itself a humane education. That said, it is worth asking how a humane collegiate education could help prepare students to enter and navigate these dialectics of vocational growth. Some of prior points about the humanities still apply. The humanities are rich in resources for ripening that Augustinian moment when one becomes a question to oneself, replete with models of self-encounter and narratives of self-overcoming (such as Berger's, *A Fortunate Man*). Meanwhile, the hermeneutic practices at the heart of the humanities—reading primary texts, explicating and debating those texts in communities of inquiry, writing essays in which neither the voice of the text nor your own voice drops out—are themselves dialectical practices teaching one how to move from vicious to productive circles, staging the dialectical unveiling of self and other.

The preparation model treats the practice as given and understood, equipping the novice with what it assumes are the needed skills and knowledge. But what if we want to teach our students precisely to eschew such knowingness? If we acknowledge that it is an open question what—and who—the work entails, that crucial features of the landscape will only emerge once the journey is underway, how can we help students prepare for the journey? While the humanities are not prime purveyors of technical tools, they do offer gear of a different sort, what Kenneth Burke calls "equipment for living."[136] Literature, broadly construed, is a trove of techniques for sizing up the sort of situations that don't come predefined, an archive of angles envisioned, a store of stances adopted. In humanities classes we are not loading in formulae; but we are equipping students with an expanded range of naming and noticing, offering students some practice in recognizing the contingency of current self-understandings, and some preparation for making sense of the unfamiliar landscapes likely to unfold in the dialectics of vocational experience.

THE LAST BUTLER

Constant revolutionising of production, uninterrupted disturbance of all social conditions, everlasting uncertainty and agitation distinguish the bourgeois epoch from all earlier ones. All fixed, fast-frozen relations, with their train of ancient and venerable prejudices and opinions, are swept away, all new-formed ones become antiquated before they can ossify. All that is solid melts into air, all that is holy is profaned, and man is at last compelled to face with sober senses his real conditions of life, and his relations with his kind.
—Karl Marx and Friedrich Engels[137]

Conversely, the absolute absence of a burden causes man to be lighter than air, to soar into the heights, take leave of the earth and his earthly being, and become only half real, his movements as free as they are insignificant.

What then shall we choose? Weight or lightness?
—Milan Kundera[138]

We have now identified three dangers in the contemporary reduction of vocational development to training and credentialing. First, we saw how short-circuiting the search for a calling courts the tragic failure to unfold one's potentialities in the fullness and freedom of fit. Then we considered how technicism, perpetually preempting the question of what matters by focusing on what works, invites axiological disorientation and degradation. And we have just seen how the reduction of vocational education to preparation sets our students up for stagnation. Vocational formation can and must mean more than readying oneself for a chosen line of work. For one thing, as we noted, no one has only one vocation. Specialization risks alienating us from our "dominant vocation," not to mention hollowing out the chosen calling itself (for only someone with "variegated vocational activities" will have the fullness of character to access the full dimensionality of the work; and the narrowness of the specialist breeds the myopia of the technicist). Even when we bracket off the issue of specialization, the preparation model remains problematic, for it mislocates the key juncture of education and vocation. Preparatory training is trivial compared to the education afforded by vocations themselves.

What we discovered is that each vocation represents a mode of educative experience with a spiral structure. Allowing the work to open new veins of meaning in oneself reveals in turn new layers of the work. Thus what seems like a superficial job may actually represent a failure to perceive or unwillingness to travel this self-expanding, work-deepening path. The dead-end job turns out to be a cul-de-sac in yourself. On the other hand, is it always wise to double down in this way? Maybe we chose the wrong line in the first place, or perhaps the world has changed making it impossible to pursue this work in its integrity. What advertises itself as adventure, communication, and service may really be drudgery, manipulation, and servility. The work may contain rich layers of meaning and value . . . or we may be suffering from a kind of occupational Stockholm syndrome. Even if F. H. Bradley is right that we cannot specify our duties in advance of knowing our station, might we not come to feel bound by an opposing obligation, the duty to leave one's station?[139] Thus, I propose as the sixth necessary task of vocational development learning how to recognize and seize the moment to grow out of one's work, if and when that time comes. To perceive the puzzle and pathos of this final and perhaps most delicate dimension of vocational growth, I will offer a reading of Kazuo Ishiguro's *Remains of the Day*. First, though, we need a quick review of the laws of gravity.

A human being, Iris Murdoch observes, is "the kind of creature who makes pictures of himself and then comes to resemble the picture."[140] This is why Charles Taylor calls us "self-interpreting animals," not for the trivial reason that we offer various interpretations of ourselves and our situation, but because we then, in significant ways, live out those interpretations.[141] Michael Oakeshott condenses this idea into a Hegelian epigram: a human being "is *in* himself what he is *for* himself," later offering this helpful gloss:

> A human being is a "history" and he makes this "history" for himself out of his responses to the vicissitudes he encounters. The world he inhabits is composed not of "things," but of occurrences, which he is aware of in terms of what he understands them to be.[142]

For Oakeshott, this insight into our condition leads to an optimistic conclusion: we possess a fundamental freedom that no one, not even the agent herself, can dispose of. Each person must seek out, select among, make sense of, and integrate various cultural resources into livable answers to the questions "Who am I?" "What is my situation?" and "What is worth wanting, doing, and becoming?" Our answers stake out a world of meaning and possibility, a world that both constrains and enables choices of various sorts. While this type of choice, this freedom of movement within worlds, is certainly important, what concerns Oakeshott here is, to put it baldly, the choice of our choices. The fact that we inhabit worlds shaped by a chosen relationship to formative resources means that, with effort and time, it is possible to rework the terms of our self-understanding and worldly engagement. This does not mean, of course, that believing you can fly makes it so. But we self-interpreting animals are subject to more than regular g-forces. In our lived worlds, we find a baroque assortment of gravitational anomalies:

- This one cannot get off the couch; that one cannot take a day off from running.
- This one must be the center of attention; that one must be the outsider.
- This one is always picking up strays; that one is always dropping balls.
- The hale fellow only feels comfortable with hand extended; the straight-A student with hand raised; the gardener with hands in the soil. And so on.

Now, when Oakeshott says that this is a kind of freedom of which "a human being cannot divest himself," he doesn't mean that we can't try.[143] And try we do. We shop for off-the-shelf personae. We are drawn to

doctrines that seem to require no interpretive work. We try to get a hold of
the teacher's edition, with the answer key in the back. But you can't blame
us for being frightened by this radical, unshakable form of freedom. After
all, part of what we want from a world-picture is a secure home. Sure, we
hope it has some picture windows, but Philip Johnson's glass house won't
cut it. Our need for shelter is at least as basic as our need for exposure. For
testimony on this point, we can call on any of number of witnesses. Consider first, Simone Weil, who, in her rich, dialectical account of the needs of
the soul, gives pride of place to our profound "need for roots."[144]

Similarly, Hannah Arendt includes in her list of six basic conditions
of our humanity both "natality" and "worldliness."[145] Natality is Arendt's
name for the human capacity to begin anew. We behave in various ways
and this behavior is both understandable through conventions and predictable by means of statistics. However, no matter how routinized and
conventionalized our behavior becomes, each of us always remains capable of enacting ourselves in word and deed in ways that echo our original
"an-archic" insertion into the grid of conventions, initiating the kind of
self- and other-surprising, self- and world-renewing actions that, because
they cannot be labeled and counted like behaviors, stimulate the natal reactions of others.[146] While Arendt considered natality to be not only central
to individual flourishing but also socially salvific—I am thinking of the
"glad tidings" passage in the *Human Condition* and especially how natality
appears as the sliver of hope at the end of *Origins of Totalitarianism*—she
also recognized its limits.[147] Children need a dependable world if they are
to mature into natal actors. And then we need a stable world in which to
stage our unpredictable, disruptive actions. Meanwhile, we are not only
natal beings but mortal ones, with a deep need for the durable and lasting.
Finally, Arendt points to the simple fact that none of us would last long trying to respond to all we encounter as if for the first time:

> Clichés, stock phrases, adherence to conventionalized, standardized codes of
> expression and conduct have the socially recognized function of protecting us
> against reality, that is, against the claim on our thinking attention events and
> facts make by virtue of their existence. If we were responsive to this claim all
> the time, we would soon be exhausted.[148]

Even the thinker who famously linked it with evil, acknowledges the
importance of banality. We are, then, both natal and worldly beings,

self-interpreting animals who do and to some extent must live in denial of the freedom this fact about us entails.

That said, abiding alienation from our natality must be considered a form of despair. This might show up as overt emotional distress, or only in the subtle signs of someone sagging under the gradual realization that they have become nothing but a digestive tract with a credit card. Or perhaps it reveals itself in the habitus of the humorless pedant. Laurence Sterne offers this helpful definition: "Gravity, a mysterious carriage of the body to conceal the defects of the mind."[149] It could be that the despair is never noticeable as such. At one point, Kierkegaard drops this bomb: "The greatest hazard of all, losing one's self, can occur very quietly in the world, as if it were nothing at all."[150]

If we sometimes sag under the weight of convention, the modern stress on voice and perspective has created new gravitional difficulties. To see things from multiple angles is one of life's pleasures. To be liberated from those ideas that back us into corners or teach us to hate ourselves is one of life's necessities. But for two centuries now, alert spirits have attested to the fact that the waning of grand narratives is far from an unalloyed good. As early as 1807, Wordsworth registered his buyer's remorse over our life of "getting and spending," crying out, "Great God! I'd rather be / A Pagan suckled in a creed outworn."[151] When our lived worlds start to strike us as flimsy, contingent "worldviews," we may well find existence to be, as Milan Kundera famously put it, *unbearably light*, an anguish of the arbitrary. Indeed, for the young narrator of Elizabeth Bishop's "In the Waiting Room," gravity seems to fail altogether, as a simple trip to the dentist with her aunt turns into a harrowing unravelling of the fabric of the ordinary.[152] She becomes aware of the contingency of her location: in a dentist's waiting room, in Worcester, Massachusetts, on "the fifth / of February, 1918" (5). She looks sidelong at "shadowy gray knees, / trousers and skirts and boots" (1). Suddenly, the questions begin to crash upon her like "a big, black wave / another, and another" (4):

"How had I come to be here"? (3)
Why do I react like my "foolish, timid" aunt? (1)
What does it mean to be "an *Elizabeth*"? (2)
"Why should I be my aunt, / or me, or anyone?" (3)
"Has anything "stranger / . . . ever happened?" (2)

As the contingency of her situation settles in, she experiences a profound vertigo, like "the sensation of falling off / the round, turning world. / Into cold, blue-black space" (2).

How do we navigate these twin forms of despair? How do we remain, like Virginia Woolf's Jinny, flowing but rooted?[153] How do we achieve Deweyan "continuity," ensuring that our experience neither grinds into mechanical repetition nor fragments into the haphazard and the arbitrary? Interestingly, Dewey's other name for this middle ground was "vocation." Vocations give us an axis of salience, orienting us in what would otherwise be a Jamesian "blooming, buzzing Confusion," giving us habits of noticing that call forth an environment from our surroundings.[154] As purposive frames, informed by traditions and communities of practice, vocations help make the current situation legible in terms of prior experience without reducing the present to the past. Except of course, when they don't. For Dewey, vocation is a regulative ideal, with continuity already built into its definition. In the life of practice, there is no such guarantee. We may well grind monotonously or flit about disjointedly. Our vocational pathways may open onto wider vistas or lead to existential dead-ends

Unlike sports stadiums, life offers no skybox from which we might survey and rank competing routes. We reflect on forks in the road, feel relief or misgivings, play with what-ifs; but we cannot know what would have been, what *we* would have been.[155] It is similarly unclear how one can tell, from the inside out, whether a vocational environment is educative or miseducative. As we noted earlier with MacIntyre, we join practices in part to learn new modes of perception and canons of value.[156] How then can we see limitations of a line of work with vision honed by that very practice? The puzzle is how to vouchsafe independence of judgment and freedom of self-determination without reverting to an impoverished, atomistic model of the self. After all, practices are the very medium in which we fashion our freedoms, hone our judgments, and cultivate our character. What if staying true to the ideals of one's calling ensures not a determinate mode of open-minding, but precisely the sclerotic habitus famously predicted by Weber.[157] What if, as Jonathan Lear asks, our virtues turn out to be "neurtues" (neuroses disguised as virtues)?[158] Professions can be a way of life. But so can disavowal.

Precisely this set of questions lies at the heart of Kazuo Ishiguro's rightly celebrated novel. *Remains of the Day* is no heart-warming tale. As it turns out, very little remains of the day. Salman Rushdie, for one, chose two adjectives to describe Ishiguro's novel: beautiful and cruel.[159] What makes it cruel is the precision with which Ishiguro shows us the limits of a person, the confines of a lived world. Where Kundera's Prague 68ers experienced an anxious lightness, Mr. Stevens suffers, if anything, from an excess of gravitas. Far from falling off the "round, turning world" like Bishop's narrator, Ishiguro's narrator is pinned to the map, a fixture of Darlington Hall, where he has served as butler for decades. Stevens is planted in this place and in this role. His identity is rooted in a vocation, his vocational identity is rooted in a tradition of practice, and that tradition is itself rooted in the dense network of social mores that constitutes the English class system with its ideal of the gentleman. In short, Stevens is not a man prone to vertiginous epiphanies of contingency.

However, by the time we meet Stevens, the year is 1956, some four decades into the rapid social and economic changes that have transformed Britain since World War I. It is not only Stevens's career that is near its end, but an entire era of domestic service. Looking at the statistics for female domestic servants, we find that, in 1901, fully one in three British women in paid employment worked as domestic servants; by 1951, that number had declined to 1 in 10.[160] Meanwhile, the bulldozing of the great country houses had reached a peak in 1955, with one house being demolished every five days.[161] Darlington Hall may still be standing, and Stevens is still employed, but everything has changed. Lord Darlington is dead and Stevens now works for an American businessman, Mr. Farraday. Where Darlington Hall once boasted a staff of twenty-eight, Stevens now manages a "skeleton team" of three (6). Where Lord Darlington rarely conversed with Stevens (occasionally staging a chance meeting at the one bookcase near the stairs when a topic could not be avoided), Farraday wants to banter with Stevens. Where Darlington had depended on Stevens to manage frequent, elaborate gatherings attended by leading figures in British society, Farraday thinks Stevens ought to take a vacation and "see this beautiful country of yours" (4).

While Stevens is aware that times are changing—for example that fewer people are going into domestic service (7), that even the nobility now often travel without servants (19)—he insulates himself from the realization that his very way of life is on the critically endangered species list.[162] He chalks up some of the changes to quirks of his new employer (4), others to the advent of "electricity and modern heating systems" (7), and still others to a "sharp decline in professional standards" (7). Among the figures we considered earlier, it is Wordsworth who seems to offer the best description of Stevens, as someone "suckled in a creed outworn." And yet, while Stevens is certainly not located where Wordsworth's narrator begins, neither is he quite in the place that narrator wishes to be transported to, namely a time before traditional creeds have worn thin, when one could inhabit wholeheartedly a still-enchanted world. Ishiguro locates us neither in a state of modern alienation nor in a prelapsarian fullness of meaning. It is the special province of *Remains of the Day* to explore what it is like to deeply inhabit a creed *just as it is wearing out*. Ishiguro places us within Stevens's interpreted world precisely at a time when internal contradictions and external forces have begun to put pressure on its coherence and adequacy. We do not sit outside, assuredly measuring its circumference, but we can see places where Stevens's life narrative is wearing thin, patches where his explanations barely paper over evidence of alternative understandings. Ishiguro artfully casts the light so that these existential possibilities, these other worlds, bleed through like the underlayers of a palimpsest. Indeed, we could say that *Remains of the Day* is fundamentally an account of existential openings and closures, moments when Stevens feels the limitations of, returning to Murdoch, the "picture" he has come to "resemble," only to double down and add a fresh coat of paint.

Ishiguro establishes this pattern right from the start, foregrounding moments when Stevens's worldview wobbles until he can reinforce the structure. Here are three examples from the first seven pages:

1. *"You fellows, you're always locked up in these big houses helping out" (4).*
When urging Stevens to travel, Farraday redescribes the life of a butler as a form of captivity. "I mean it, Stevens," Farraday declares, "It's wrong that a man can't get to see around his own country." Stevens counters that it has been his "privilege to see the best of England over the years, sir, within these very walls" (4). And Stevens has indeed met—or at least served— the leading figures of his day. Eden, Halifax, and Churchill have all come through Darlington Hall, as did George Bernard Shaw, whom Stevens once caught admiring his beautifully polished silver (135). But there is truth to Farraday's observation that Stevens's experience has been narrow and secondhand. Stevens fends off this truth.

2. "A series of small errors" (5).

When we meet him, Stevens is wrestling with a new development in his career: he is making mistakes. While he assures us that each of these errors is trivial in itself, the pattern is clearly troubling, as Stevens had begun to "entertain all sorts of alarmist theories as to their cause" (5). It could mean that he is over the hill. Maybe his mind is going. Whatever alarming explanations Stevens entertained consciously, there is a deeper truth announcing itself through his "mischievements," to adopt Walter Kaufmann's brilliant translation of *Felleistungen* (that is, Freud's term for statements spoken as slips, grudges grafted onto forgettings, actions appearing as inactions, concerns masquerading as mistakes). For a description of this truth, we won't do better than the searing prose of Marx and Engels, who observe how capitalism has

- "pitilessly torn asunder the motley feudal ties that bound man to his 'natural superiors,'"
- "left remaining no other nexus between man and man than . . . callous 'cash payment,'"
- "drowned . . . chivalrous enthusiasm . . . in the icy water of egotistical calculation,"
- "stripped of its halo every occupation hitherto honoured,"
- "converted the physician, the lawyer, the priest, the poet, the man of science, into its paid wage labourers."[163]

My point is that, at some level, Stevens must be feeling profoundly bereft (since it is after all his life being swept away along with these "ancient and venerable prejudices") and deeply disoriented (as all that was solid in the foundations of his vocational identity evaporates beneath him).[164] However, rather than look beyond the surface cracks, his trivial mistakes, into the tectonic shifts below, Stevens crams his crisis into a technicality, remarking, "I had become blind to the obvious, . . . that these small errors of recent months have derived from nothing more sinister than a faulty staff plan" (5).

3. "An unmistakable nostalgia" (9).

Stevens tells us that what finally cleared his vision was a letter he received from Miss Kenton (now Mrs. Benn, having married twenty years earlier and moved to Cornwall). In what he himself describes as "long, unrevealing passages," Stevens nonetheless detects "distinct hints of her desire to return" to Darlington Hall. If Stevens is right to see desire here, his hermeneutic is a funhouse mirror, a perfect illustration of Freud's mapping of the strange routes by which our desires enter the world.[165] As the novel slowly reveals, Mr. Stevens and Miss Kenton felt much more than mutual professional respect, but only Miss Kenton was able to perceive this fact. Stevens can feel, but not own, his longing and regret. First, he executes the maneuver Freud describes as "turning back on the self" so that "I want her" becomes "she wants me." The drive is then further transformed by the process Freud called "sublimation"—the elevation of an embodied desire into a more rarified, culturally approved aim—so that "she wants me" becomes "she wants to work for me." How can Stevens not see that it is neither Mr. Farraday's Ford nor staff planning, but love, that drives him from Oxfordshire all of the way to Cornwall? It is because his sense of professionalism precludes it. His love for Miss Kenton clashes with a key element in his vocational self-understanding, that a great butler utterly submerges his private self into his professional role (a point Ishiguro underlines by concealing Stevens's given name throughout the novel). When the world does not fit our worldview, it can be bent to do so. Detecting his loneliness and need for intimacy, his worldview wobbles, but he redresses his desire and once again sets the structure aright.

These three early episodes teach us the basic footwork in Stevens's dance of disavowal, one that only becomes more desperate and clumsy over the course of the novel. My aim has been to capture this dynamic accurately but sympathetically, avoiding condescension. After all, while Stevens's world may be narrow, so is that of each of us. We all inhabit, as Oakeshott puts it, "a corner of the earth, lapped round with locality."[166] Likewise, we all find ways to distance from desires that clash with our sense of who we are or should be. And you don't need me to tell you just how powerful are the forces, within us and around us, deferring the "sober" reckoning described by Marx and Engels, when we will finally face the "real conditions of life and our relations with our kind."[167] We all settle for realism, capitalist realism, in which "it is easier to imagine the end of the world than to imagine the end of capitalism."[168]

But it is not just a matter of checking our condescension toward Stevens. We also need to resist the urge to prejudge the practice of butlering. This problem that we are tracking in the phenomenology of vocation requires that we take seriously the way in which practices reveal aspects of the good. We must reject the idea that we can queue up directly at the Bureau of Ethical Guidance and then, checklist in hand, judge practices from the outside. Admittedly, this is harder with some practices than it is with others. I suppose the success of shows like *Downton Abbey* proves that we are not only repelled but fascinated by the chance to see class, the murky waters in which we daily swim, at arm's length and crystallized into caste. However, once we have finished the popcorn, the charming Mr. Carson and his staff resolve back into the oppressed, whom we view either as knowing if silent critics of the class system or as victims of false consciousness. Here I want us to be open to the possibility that even a practice as morally dubious as butlering contains real existential resources for its practitioners. To be clear, attempting such sympathetic entry into Stevens's world is not to deny its limitations. The novel is, as I have said, about these limitations, about the lies that one must tell oneself in order to smooth over contradictions and avoid inconvenient facts. But we need to resist the fantasy that, unlike Stevens, we can step outside traditions and practices to form our moral code. Like it or not, we find ourselves at sea with Stevens, aboard Neurath's boat. It may be possible to replace a great many planks without drowning, but such work must be done gradually and carefully. Thus, we want neither to celebrate nor to condemn Stevens's way of life, but to follow him in confronting its limitations, from the inside out, in his search for a new beginning.

Luckily the path we want to follow is well marked, for in the concept of dignity we find all of the following: (1) the key to a sympathetic reading of the richness of Stevens's practical world; (2) the site of some of its core contradictions; (3) a possible way to rebuild his vessel amid these epochal sea changes. That dignity is the central node in the network of beliefs and values that orients and sustains Stevens, what Taylor calls a "hypergood," requires no subtlety of interpretation.[169] *Remains of the Day* is a kind of travelogue of Stevens's motor trip from Oxfordshire to the West Country in the novel's present, 1956. Each night, Stevens makes a record of the day's journey, straying into reflections on his calling and detailed reminiscences of life in Darlington Hall between the wars. Dignity is the compass bearing by which Stevens navigates both present and past. The topic arises in his present-day conversations (with Harry Smith and Dr. Carlisle in Moscombe, and then again in his closing confessional with the stranger on the bench in Weymouth).[170] And it is the central organizing theme of his reminiscences.

On Stevens's recounting, to be an English butler, at least in the heyday of the 1920s and 1930s, is to be part of a community of practice, an ongoing conversation about the ideals that animate the pursuit. The servants' hall was the scene of running debates about who the best butlers were and in what their greatness consisted (28–44). The basic answer was well agreed upon: a great butler is "possessed of a dignity in keeping with his position" (33). But what is this special form of dignity? Stevens explains that it amounts to a highly austere professionalism demanding unwavering loyalty, perfect emotional restraint, and (as we already noted) a complete submersion of the private self. The book's central episode, Stevens's recounting of the night his father suffered a stroke, vividly illustrates all three aspects (70–110). While his father was dying upstairs, Stevens managed to pull off without a hitch the culminating dinner party of one of the most important events in Darlington Hall's history, a multiday conference on post-Versailles tensions attended by eighteen dignitaries (along with their entourages) from Britain, France, Germany, and the United States. Even grief this profound can and should be controlled in the name of loyalty to one's employer, fidelity to one's craft, and the honor of serving in a "great house." Stevens sums up this ideal with a vivid metaphor:

> The great butlers are great by virtue of their ability to inhabit their professional role and inhabit it to the utmost. They will not be shaken out by external events, however surprising, alarming, or vexing. They wear their professionalism the way a decent gentleman will wear his suit: he will not let ruffians or circumstance tear it off of him in the public gaze; he will discard it when, and only when, he wills to do so, and this will invariably be when he is entirely alone. It is, as I say, a matter of "dignity." (42–43)

As examples and images like these attest, there is nothing abstract about the ideal of the gentleman. It is an embodied habitus, a unique blend of stoic negations. The great butler is uncomplaining, understated, unflappable. People look for ethos in mission statements when it is right there in the muscles of the jaw.

Of course, I don't expect you, upon hearing this reconstruction of the goods internal to the practice of butlering, to want to sign up. I only want us to notice what Stevens stands to lose. "Orientation to the good," Taylor writes, "is not some optional extra . . . but a condition of our being selves with an identity."[171] By virtue of his calling, Stevens occupies a coherent moral geography with dignity as its capital, central precincts of honor and loyalty, professionalism and emotional restraint, and important if further-flung provinces such as propriety and a sense of discretion, meticulous foresight and keen attention to detail. Undeniably, this cluster of ideals is problematic in various ways. But we should acknowledge that (1) this is true of all livable ideals (alas, it is impossible to carry the perfect ones out of the seminar room), and (2) this particular ethos is more than capacious enough to orient a lived life, to frame an inhabitable world, to satisfy one's need for roots.

Why, then, is Stevens troubled as he enters this evening of his career? How has his ethos come to feel pinched or incoherent? I have already suggested one of the novel's two main answers to this question, that it cannot accommodate the stubborn reality of Stevens's love for Miss Kenton, which has survived even a twenty-year separation. While Stevens does make an emotional breakthrough when he meets with her in Cornwall, it is the novel's second major arc I want to pursue here: Stevens's relation to class and his identification with Lord Darlington. Butlers occupy a unique, ambiguous class position. Seamstresses and solicitors may not, on any given day, have cause to compare their differential social status. Those in "the service" enact that differential in all they do. And yet, as head of the down-stairs shadow family, the butler has pride of place among the underclass of domestic servants. As servant, he is a member of the working class. As head servant, closely identified with the head of the upstairs household, he has a borrowed nobility.

As long as Stevens stays in Darlington Hall, this ambiguity need not be resolved. (It is for this reason, not literal geographic range—as if today frequent flyer miles were a sign of depth of experience or breadth of vision!—that Farraday is right about Stevens' insularity.) It is only when Stevens embarks on his "expedition" to the West Country that he is forced to confront his class contradictions. Case in point is the scene when Stevens runs out of gas in Devon. Arriving as he does in Farraday's fancy vintage Ford and dressed in smart new clothes (Stevens almost decided to wear one of the fine suits handed down to him by Lord Darlington before deeming this impractical for a motor trip, deciding instead to spend a chunk of his savings on a "new costume" worthy of Darlington Hall [11]), it is no surprise when Stevens becomes an object of curiosity for the group of locals putting him up for the night. This borrowed finery extends to Stevens's habitus, which differs markedly from that of these working folks, as Stevens possesses much of the polish, speech, and cultural literacy of the upper class set whom it is his job to understand and serve. To the locals, Stevens is, as Dr. Carlisle will explain to Stevens the next day, a "pretty impressive specimen" (208). Where things get tricky for Stevens is when the conversation turns to the very topic of how to tell "a true gentleman from a false one that's just dressed in finery" (184). "It's not just the cut of your clothes," Mr. Tayler says to Stevens, "nor is it even the fine way you've got of speaking. There's something else that marks you out as a gentleman" (185). And as we've noted, Stevens does subscribe to gentlemanly ideals. We cannot fault him for wanting to accept the groups' verdict that he possesses something beyond the trappings of class, or to suggest that that something is dignity. But once the topic shifts to great men and international affairs, it is clear that Stevens is all but encouraging the group's mistaken impression that he is a member of the upper class. He lets drop, without explanation, that while Churchill had "come to the house on several occasions," Mr. Eden and Lord Halifax were actually the more important and thus "more frequent visitors." Though he will later dismiss this "regrettable . . . business" as an "unfortunate misunderstanding," Stevens has plenty of chances to set the record straight (193, 187–188).

Indeed, once the organic intellectual, Harry Smith, arrives and gets up on his soapbox, Stevens is forced to choose a side. "Dignity's not just something for gentlemen," Smith declares, but stems from being "born free" into a country where you can vote and "express your opinion freely" (186). Here Smith, in his exuberant, unpolished way, offers Stevens a potential life raft, an egalitarian view of dignity that might give Stevens a way to remain true to his hypergood without having to deny the reality of his position in the social hierarchy. But Stevens demurs, noting that while he and Smith were at "cross purposes," it was "far too complicated a task" to explain his view "clearly to these people" (186). Stevens chooses the identification with Darlington over solidarity with the "broad and agricultural" frames and "muddy Wellington boots" in the room (182). His greatness as a butler depends on the greatness of Darlington Hall, which depends in turn on the idea that Lord Darlington himself is a great man, a true patriot working behind the scenes to steer the ship of state to safety. However, as we come to find out, first through what Stevens reveals accidentally, and later as Stevens himself begins to admit the fact to himself and us, Darlington is at best a dupe of the Nazis—giving Ribbentrop a platform from which to spread his deception that Germany posed no threat to Britain—and possibly an outright sympathizer. In distancing himself from the likes of Smith and—as we then learn in a reminiscence—from the idea of democracy itself, Stevens borrows not Darlington's nobility but only his proto-fascism.[172]

Though Stevens motors out of Devon convinced that Smith is something of a comic figure (209), self-doubt is festering beneath the surface. By the time Stevens has been to Cornwall and is on his way back to Darlington Hall, something seems to be breaking open inside of him. In the novel's closing scene, Stevens is sitting on a bench on a pier in seaside Weymouth. Though "there is still plenty of daylight left," they have just switched on the colorful lights for which they are known, eliciting a hearty cheer from the boardwalk crowd. The sun is, not to put too fine a point on it, finally setting on the British Empire and, with it, on Stevens's way of life. But if his day as one of the great butlers in one of great houses is over, the question remains of what the evening entails. There is a second set of lights coming on. Striking up a conversation, a man sitting next to Stevens tells him that, in fact, "the evening's the best part of the day" (244). Stevens is not so sure. But something is shifting in him, and he is starting to separate the man from the idealized Lord Darlington. Even going this far leads him to a very dark conclusion about himself. If he felt his heart breaking in his conversation with Mrs. Benn, the paragon of emotional restraint now actually chokes up (he cannot admit this fact directly, of course, but narrates how his benchmate offers him a hankie) as he reflects that

> Lord Darlington wasn't a bad man. He wasn't a bad man at all. And at least he had the privilege of being able to say at the end of his life that he made his own mistakes. His lordship was a courageous man. He chose a certain path in life, it proved to be a misguided one, but there, he chose it, he can say that at least. As for myself, I cannot even claim that. You see, I trusted. I trusted his lordship's wisdom. All those years I served him, I trusted I was doing something worthwhile. I can't even say I made my own mistakes. Really—one has to ask oneself—what dignity is there in that? (243)

Stevens reels under the twin realization that he has never given any thought to two questions that should have been unavoidable: how well does titular nobility map onto the real article and is nobility even something that can be borrowed? When we leave Stevens, we don't know whether these questions and his newfound access to long-suppressed feelings will be enough to lead him to evolve his ideals without abandoning them, and to see whether they might not be better realized in new callings.

As the sun sets, Stevens resolves to learn to banter. We can read this as hopeful, as a sign that he will now learn to develop a voice and interests of his own. But even in the book's final pages, we find Stevens backsliding again, construing this banter as but a duty to please his new employer. He resolves to practice while Farraday is still away thinking that "perhaps . . . I will be in a position to pleasantly surprise him" (245). But who knows? Maybe Stevens will surprise himself and make contact with his natality, establishing new roots and branches. Whatever Stevens's fate, the moral for vocational formation is clear. One must not only find and learn to grow through one's vocation, one must learn when and how to leave it. I will end with the words of Jean-Jacques Rousseau, which serve as the perfect coda to Ishiguro's thick exploration of dark alleys and dead-ends in the life of vocation:

> You trust in the present order of society without thinking that this order is subject to inevitable revolutions, and it is impossible for you to foresee or prevent the one which may affect your children. The noble become commoners, the rich become poor, the monarch becomes subject. Are the blows of fate so rare that you can count on being exempted from them? . . . Happy is the man who knows how to leave the station which leaves him and to remain a man in spite of fate![173]

PREFACE

1. Michael Oakeshott, *On Human Conduct* (Oxford: Clarendon Press, [1975] 1990), vii.

2. Marion LeRoy Burton, *President's Report, University of Michigan* (1920-1921), quoted in Julie A. Reuben, *The Making of the Modern University: Intellectual Transformation and the Marginalization of Morality* (Chicago: University of Chicago Press, 1996), 231. For an example of the work it takes to craft a substantive and living core curriculum (in this case, at Boston College), see Mary Thomas Crane, David Quigley and Andy Boynton, eds., *Curriculum by Design: Innovation and the Liberal Arts Core* (New York: Fordham University Press, 2023).

3. As the reader will see from the extensive notes, this remains a scholarly book despite its essayistic approach.

4. I am thinking of figures such as Montaigne, Emerson, Nietzsche, Woolf, and Weil. And the tradition continues with essayists such as John Berger, David Foster Wallace, and Adam Phillips.

5. Ezra Pound, *A B C of Reading* (Reading, UK: Faber and Faber Limited, [1934] 1961), 40.

PROLOGUE

1. Alasdair MacIntyre, *After Virtue: A Study in Moral Theory*, 3rd ed. (South Bend, IN: University of Notre Dame Press, [1981] 2007), 219.

2. Michael Oakeshott, "A Place of Learning," in *The Voice of Liberal Learning: Michael Oakeshott on Education*, ed. Timothy Fuller (New Haven, CT: Yale University Press, 1989).

3. I don't mean to suggest that this miseducation begins in college, only to note with alarm that it continues there. As William Deresiewicz notes, our hurried college students "are winners in the race we have made of childhood." Deresiewicz takes aim not only at elite higher education institutions, but at:

> everything that leads up to and away from them—the private and affluent public high schools; the ever-growing industry of tutors and consultants and test-prep

courses; the admissions process itself, squatting like a dragon at the entrance to adulthood; the brand-name graduate schools and employment opportunities that come after the B.A.; and the parents and communities, largely upper-middle class, who push their children into the maw of this machine (William Deresiewicz, "Don't Send Your Kid to the Ivy League: The Nation's Top Colleges Are Turning Our Kids into Zombies," *New Republic*, July 21, 2014, https://newrepublic.com/article/118747/ivy-league-schools-are-overrated-send-your-kids-elsewhere).

Deresiewicz elaborates his critique of the college-industrial complex (my term) in William Deresiewicz, *Excellent Sheep: The Miseducation of the American Elite and the Way to a Meaningful Life* (New York: Free Press, 2014).

4. William Butler Yeats, "The Second Coming" (1920), https://www.poetryfoundation.org/poems/43290/the-second-coming.

5. I return to this issue in "Job Prospects," discussing the bad faith of defending premature major selection in the name of respecting student interests and avoiding paternalism (see pp. 208–210).

6. Oakeshott, "A Place of Learning," 24.

7. Oakeshott, "A Place of Learning," 23. In "New Student Orientation" and "Job Prospects," I explore further this ordeal of the self-interpreting animal (see pp. 103–104 and 251–253).

8. Interrupting this studenting mindset is the focus (and point) of "New Student Orientation," where I unpack and defend Oakeshott's account of liberal learning.

CAMPUS TOUR

1. Bill Readings, *The University in Ruins* (Cambridge, MA: Harvard University Press, 1996), 169.

2. The Cooperative Institutional Research Program (CIRP)'s "Freshman Survey" was launched by the American Council of Education in 1966 and has been administered by UCLA's Higher Education Research Institute (HERI) since 1973. All US higher educational institutions are invited to participate. HERI then selects and weights the results to reflect the population of all full-time first-year students (since 2000 this has been approximately 1.5 million students at 1,500 institutions). In 2010, for example, the survey was completed by 261,511 students representing 420 institutions. From these, 201,818 surveys from 279 institutions were selected to form the stratified, weighted sample. Its annual report, *The American Freshman: National Norms,* and longitudinal studies are available at https://heri.ucla.edu/publications-tfs/. I calculated these decade averages myself, drawing on the 2016, 2017, 2018, and 2019 installments of *The American Freshman* and on M. K. Eagan et al., *The American Freshman: Fifty-Year Trends, 1966–2015* (Los Angeles, CA:

Higher Education Research Institute, UCLA, 2016). Note that there is no data for the meaning question in 1966, for the financial question in 1973, or for either in 1988. The high point on the meaning question was the first year it was included, 1967 (85.8%); its low point was 2003 (39.3%). The low point for the financial question was 1970 (36.2%); its high point is the most recent year for which we have data, 2019 (84.3%). The two slopes crossed in 1979. By the end of Reagan's first term, the importance of the meaning of life had fallen to less than half of what it was in the late sixties, and the importance of being very well-off financially had increased by 77%.

The discussion that follows in the text is a survey of contemporary conditions in US higher education, though some of what I say surely points to broader trends. For instance, the shift I track here, from a thirst for meaning circa 1968 to an increasing desire for stock options over the subsequent decades, tells a broader story. Consider that the generation of 1968 made itself heard not only in Berkeley but in Berlin and Belgrade, Paris and Prague, Stockholm, Mexico City, and Tokyo.

3. See IPEDS Table 322.10, "Bachelor's degrees conferred by postsecondary institutions, by field of study: Selected years, 1970–71 through 2019–20" (https://nces.ed .gov/programs/digest/d21/tables/dt21_322.10.asp?current=yes) and Table 325.92, "Degrees in economics, history, political science and government, and sociology conferred by postsecondary institutions, by level of degree: Selected years, 1949– 50 through 2019–20" (https://nces.ed.gov/programs/digest/d21/tables/dt21_325 .92.asp). To derive an overall percentage for the humanities, I combined totals in Table 322.10 in five subcategories: "Area, ethnic, cultural, gender, and group studies," "English language and literature/letters," "Foreign languages, literatures, and linguistics," "Liberal arts and sciences, general studies, and humanities," and "Philosophy and religious studies." Since Table 322.10 combines history and the social sciences, I pulled the number of history majors from Table 325.92.

4. See IPEDS Table 322.10.

5. See Alan Finder, "Cornell's Worried Image Makers Wrap Themselves in Ivy," *New York Times*, April 22, 2006, http://www.nytimes.com/2006/04/22/nyregion /cornells-worried-image-makers-wrap-themselves-in-ivy.html.

6. Finders, "Cornell's Worried Image Makers."

7. Readings, *University in Ruins*, 10.

8. Readings, *University in Ruins*, 11.

9. Readings, *University in Ruins*, 10. As far as I can tell, the logo Readings describes is this one: https://www.sportslogos.net/logos/view/1gn6f1h3qe7xqmhgkgrj /Syracuse_Orange/1989/Primary_Logo. For the traditional seal, adopted in 1871, see https://www.syracuse.edu/150years/150-years-timeline/.

10. Readings, *University in Ruins*, 10.

11. Syracuse University Brand Guidelines (https://www.syracuse.edu/wp-content/uploads/syracuse-university-brand-guidelines-19.pdf), 9.

12. Syracuse University Brand Guidelines, 18.

13. Jefferson said that he wished "most to be remembered" for three things, specifying "the following inscription, & not a word more": "Here was buried/Thomas Jefferson/Author of the Declaration of American Independence/of the Statute of Virginia for religious freedom/& Father of the University of Virginia" (see https://www.loc.gov/exhibits/jefferson/207.html; I have updated Jefferson's archaic spelling of "independance").

14. For some nice maps and engravings, see http://juel.iath.virginia.edu/node/109. For Jefferson's thinking, a good place to start is the Monticello site (see https://www.monticello.org/research-education/thomas-jefferson-encyclopedia/jeffersons-plan-academical-village/). As I discuss in the text, the idea of separate pavilions connected by covered walkways was inspired by quite practical considerations (curbing the spread of disease, minimizing the effects of fire, staying dry between classes). Woods suggests a possible philosophical inspiration for the phrase, "academical village," noting that Jefferson—who was an admirer of the *Encyclopédie Méthodique* (seeking to become its US distributor)—owned volume 61 (1789), on architecture. This volume included an extract from a Monsieur Paw's research on the layout of Greek schools of philosophy. Students would build primitive huts around the teacher's house. "An accumulation of such habitations," Paw writes, "presented from afar the appearance of a village where one learned ethics like a trade" (quoted in Mary N. Woods, "Thomas Jefferson and the University of Virginia: Planning the Academic Village," *Journal of the Society of Architectural Historians* 44, no. 3 (1985): 272; Woods emphasizes this entire sentence).

15. What I call "humane letters" Jefferson lists as "Ideology, General Grammar, Ethics, Rhetoric, Belles Lettres, and the fine arts." Later, he glosses "ideology" as "the doctrine of thought," and says that "General Grammar explains the construction of language." See Thomas Jefferson, "Report of the Board of Commissioners for the University of Virginia to the Virginia General Assembly, [4 August] 1818," Founders Online, National Archives, http://founders.archives.gov/documents/Madison/04-01-02-0289.

16. Jefferson, "Report of the Board of Commissioners for the University of Virginia."

17. Sullivan's (forced) resignation was announced on June 10, 2012; she was reinstated on June 26.

18. Appointments to the seventeen-member board (then sixteen) are made by the governor of Virginia. The board arrayed against Sullivan "included lawyers, developers, a coal-mining executive and a beer distributor, but no voting member had an education background. Because of rapid turnover in the wake of the election of Gov. Bob

McDonnell, a Republican, it included only four members of the search committee that picked Sullivan two years before" (Andrew Rice, "Anatomy of a Campus Coup," *New York Times Magazine*, September 11, 2012, https://www.nytimes.com/2012/09/16/magazine/teresa-sullivan-uva-ouster.html). According to the *Washington Post*, "the campaign to remove Sullivan began around October [2011]" (Daniel de Vise, Jenna Johnson, and Anita Kumar, "University of Virginia president to step down," *Washington Post*, Education Section, June 10, 2012, https://www.washingtonpost.com/local/education/university-of-virginia-president-to-step-down/2012/06/10/gJQAKQDYSV_story.html?tid=a_inl&utm_term=.c9f3cf6b7fd8).

19. There is some uncertainty whether specific departments were targeted and, if so, which ones. Sullivan told the *Times* that the "elimination of the classics and German departments . . . [was not] ever discussed" (Rice, "Anatomy of a Campus Coup"). However, "based on conversations with more than a dozen current and former board members, state and university officials, faculty and others with direct knowledge of the events," the *Post* reported that "The Dragas group . . . felt Sullivan lacked the mettle to trim or shut down programs that couldn't sustain themselves financially, such as obscure academic departments in classics and German" (de Vise, Johnson and Kumar, "University of Virginia president to step down").

20. Rice, "Anatomy of a Campus Coup."

21. Responsibility Center Management (RCM) devolves budgeting to individual units as a means of promoting entrepreneurship and distributing responsibility for controlling costs. Though Harvard has practiced a form of decentralized budgeting since the early nineteenth century, RCM per se was introduced at The University of Pennsylvania in 1974. Use of the model has risen rapidly over the past fifteen years. In the span of just three years (2008–2011) the share of public research universities using RCM more than tripled (6.4% to 21.3%) (Kenneth C. Green, Scott Jaschik, and Doug Lederman, *The 2011 Inside Higher Ed Survey of College & University Business Officers*, 2011, https://www.insidehighered.com/sites/default/server_files/files/insidehigheredcfosurveyfinal7-5-11.pdf). From 2011 to 2015, the share of all universities using the model rose from 14.2% to 24% (Laura DeLancey and Susann deVries, "The Impact of Responsibility Center Management on Academic Libraries: An Exploratory Study," *portal: Libraries and the Academy* 23, no. 1 [2023]: 8). At that time, more than 50% of leading public universities used RCM (Darren Deering and Daniel W. Lang, "Responsibility Center Budgeting and Management 'Lite' in University Finance: Why Is Rcb/Rcm Never Fully Deployed?," *Planning for Higher Education Journal* 45, no. 3 [2017]: 94). Though RCM has likely spread further, *Inside HigherEd* stopped asking its budget-model question of university business officers in 2015.

22. Remarks of Rector Helen Dragas, Meeting with Vice Presidents and Deans, June 10, 2012. The transcript is posted under "Rector Dragas' Remarks to VPs and

Deans" on *UVA Today*, https://news.virginia.edu/content/rector-dragas-remarks
-vps-and-deans.

23. Disruptive innovation is the watchword of Clayton Christensen and his followers, first developed in *The Innovator's Dilemma* and later extended, in a series
of coauthored books, to schooling, health care, and higher education. See Clayton M. Christensen, *The Innovator's Dilemma: When New Technologies Cause Great
Firms to Fail* (Cambridge, MA: Harvard Business School Press, 1997); Clayton M.
Christensen, Michael B. Hill, and Curtis W. Johnson, *Disrupting Class: How Disruptive Innovation Will Change the Way the World Learns* (New York: McGrawHill,
2008); Clayton M. Christensen, Jerome H. Grossman, and Jason Hwang, *The Innovator's Prescription: A Disruptive Solution for Health Care* (New York: McGraw-Hill,
2008); and Clayton M. Christensen and Henry J. Eyring, *The Innovative University: Changing the DNA of Higher Education* (San Francisco: Jossey Bass, 2011). Not
only did this last title come out the year before the UVA fiasco, but the application of Christensen's brand to higher education (easy to predict in any case) had
also been previewed much earlier in shorter pieces. See, for example, Clayton M.
Christensen, Sally Aaron, and William Clark, "Disruption in Education," *Educause
Review* (January 10, 2003), https://er.educause.edu/~/media/files/articles/2007/1
/erm0313.pdf?la=en; and Clayton M. Christensen, Scott D. Anthony, and Erik A.
Roth, "Disrupting Diplomas: The Future of Education," in *Seeing What's Next:
Using the Theories of Innovation to Predict Industry Change* (Cambridge, MA: Harvard
Business School Press, 2004), 99–128.

For a nice critique of Christiansen's thesis and especially of the bankrupt
worldview for which his work has provided academic cover, see Jill Lepore,
"The Disruption Machine: What the Gospel of Innovation Gets Wrong," *New
Yorker*, June 23, 2014, http://www.newyorker.com/magazine/2014/06/23/the
-disruption-machine. Lepore exposes Christiansen's "hand-picked" and "murky"
cases, "dubious" sources, and "questionable" logic, showing how the proofiness
of the Christiansen school only increases as it seeks to spread its Hobbesian moral,
"disrupt or be disrupted," from the manufacture of "drygoods" to practices such
as medicine, education, and journalism devoted to complex social goods. For an
inside view of such disruption in progress, see Robinson's case study of a midwest-
ern state flagship "partnership" with Coursera (Rashid Robinson, "Learning On-
Demand: Massive Open Online Courses and the Privatization of the Educational
Experience," PhD diss., University of Illinois at Urbana-Champaign, 2021).

24. Karl Marx and Friedrich Engels, "Manifesto of the Communist Party" (1848),
trans. Samuel Moore in cooperation with Engels (1888), https://www.marxists
.org/archive/marx/works/1848/communist-manifesto/index.htm, chap. 1.

25. See "Rector Dragas' Remarks to VPs and Deans."

26. See David Brooks, "The Campus Tsunami," Op-Ed, *New York Times*, May 3,
2012, http://www.nytimes.com/2012/05/04/opinion/brooks-the-campus-tsunami

.html; and John E. Chubb and Terry M. Moe, "Chubb and Moe: Higher Education's Online Revolution," Commentary, *Wall Street Journal*, May 30, 2012 (updated), https://www.wsj.com/articles/SB100014240527023040194045774166312065832 86. The emails, available at http://www.readthehook.com/files/article-documents /kington-emails.pdf, were obtained by a FOIA request from the UVA student newspaper, the *Daily Cavalier*, which broke this aspect of the story with a series of tweets containing snippets of the emails.

27. In the email that would later lead to his resignation, Kiernan speaks of two "important Virginia alums" working with him and Dragas on "this project" (i.e., replacing Sullivan with someone more disruptively innovative). One of these is Paul Tudor Jones; as far as I know, the other was never identified. See "Full Text of Darden Foundation Board Chair's Email," *Daily Progress* (June 12, 2012), https:// dailyprogress.com/news/full-text-of-darden-foundation-board-chair-s-email/article _8abcfabc-a59c-5013-a190-a75408f22d8a.html.

28. Dragas asked Jones to serve as the board's unofficial disruption consultant. Too busy, Jones recommended his Greenwich neighbor, Kiernan, the Goldman Sachs partner turned hedge fund manager and self-appointed spokesman for the "radical center." On the relationships among Sullivan, Dragas, Jones, Kiernan, and others see Rice, "Anatomy of a Campus Coup." For Kiernan's foray into political theory, see Peter D. Kiernan, *Becoming China's Bitch: And Nine More Catastrophes We Must Avoid Right Now. A Manifesto for the Radical Center* (Nashville, TN: Turner Publishing Company, 2012).

29. "Full Text of Darden Foundation Board Chair's Email."

30. "Full Text of Darden Foundation Board Chair's Email."

31. Paul Tudor Jones II, "OP-ED: Aspiring to Achieve Greatness," *Daily Progress*, Sunday, June 17, https://dailyprogress.com/news/op-ed-aspiring-to-achieve -greatness/article_be382c81-3059-56a2-81c5-3eb85627c978.html.

32. As quoted in Nick DeSantis, "After Leadership Crisis Fueled by Distance-Ed Debate, UVa Will Put Free Classes Online," Technology Section, *Chronicle of Higher Education*, July 17, 2012, http://www.chronicle.com/article/After-Leadership -Crisis-Fueled/132917.

33. DeSantis, "After Leadership Crisis."

34. I say more about marketization and exchange-value in "Public Hearing" (see pp. 194–196) and "Job Prospects" (see pp. 206–207).

35. Louis Althusser, "Ideology and Ideological State Apparatuses (Notes toward an Investigation)," trans. Ben Brewster, in *Lenin and Philosophy and Other Essays* (New York: Monthly Review Press, 1971), 128. Here, Althusser is specifically pointing to the 'obvious' fact that production is the key to political-economy. He wants to interrupt that ideological commonsense so that we can come to see capital from

the "point of view of reproduction [of the means of production]" (128, emphasis removed).

36. This is a central theme in the writings of A. Bartlett Giamatti, the Renaissance scholar turned Yale president turned Major League Baseball commissioner. Giamatti sees both the university and the ballpark as instructive examples of the dialectic of freedom and order. See, for example, A. Bartlett Giamatti, *A Free and Ordered Space: The Real World of the University* (New York: Norton, 1988); and Kenneth S. Robson, ed., *A Great and Glorious Game: Baseball Writings of A. Bartlett Giamatti* (Chapel Hill, NC: Algonquin Books, 1998).

37. See https://www.coursera.org/uva. Not all of the ninety-one icons are clip art: ten are photographs (three shots of the US capitol, two unpotted plants, a close-up of the statue of Jefferson in front of the Rotunda, a detail from a painting, an overgrown landscape, a picture of JFK, and a bust of Patrick Henry).

38. "From Thomas Jefferson to Littleton W. Tazewell, 5 January 1805," Founders Online, National Archives, https://founders.archives.gov/documents/Jefferson/99-01-02-0958.

39. The first quote is from a letter from Jefferson dated May 6, 1810, quoted in Woods, "Planning the Academic Village," 269; the second comes from Jefferson's previously cited 1805 letter to Tazewell. As Woods demonstrates, developments in hospital design were an important inspiration for Jefferson.

40. Jefferson, Letter to Thornton (May 9, 1817), quoted in Patricia C. Sherwood and Joseph Michael Lasala, "Education and Architecture: The Evolution of the University of Virginia's Academical Village," in *Thomas Jefferson's Academical Village: The Creation of an Architectural Masterpiece*, ed. Richard Guy Wilson (Charlottesville: University Press of Virginia, 1993), 17.

41. Woods, "Planning the Academic Village," 273.

42. There is a nice photograph of the Pavilion III entry in Sherwood and Lasala, "Education and Architecture," p. 25, fig. 17.

43. Sherwood and Lasala, "Education and Architecture," 17.

44. Richard Guy Wilson, "A Classroom as Big as the Lawn: Jefferson Wanted Students to Learn All the Angles," *Virginia Magazine*, https://uvamagazine.org/articles/a_classroom_as_big_as_the_lawn.

45. For a thoughtful critique of ten faulty ideas leading us to assume that the "economies of attention" on traditional campuses are inherently superior to those possible in online spaces, see Richard A. Lanham, "The Audit of Virtuality: Universities in the Attention Economy," in *The Future of the City of Intellect*, ed. Steven Brint (Stanford, CA: Stanford University Press, 2002).

46. Craig Steven Wilder, *Ebony and Ivy: Race, Slavery, and the Troubled History of America's Universities* (New York: Bloomsbury, 2013).

47. See Jefferson, "Report of the Board of Commissioners for the University of Virginia," pars. 3–4. I have left the word "White" uncapitalized as it is in the original.

48. Wilder, *Ebony and Ivy*, 137–138.

49. There are a range of institutions that simulate a college experience for the underclass. For eye-opening tours, see Marc Bousquet, *How the University Works: Higher Education and the Low-Wage Nation* (New York: NYU Press, 2008), chap. 4; and Tressie McMillan Cottom, *Lower Ed: The Troubling Rise of For-Profit Colleges in the New Economy* (New York: The New Press, 2017). For two recent treatments of how higher education exacerbates class inequality, see Suzanne Mettler, *Degrees of Inequality: How the Politics of Higher Education Sabotaged the American Dream* (New York: Basic Books, 2014); and Anthony P. Carnevale, Peter Schmidt, and Jeff Strohl, *The Merit Myth: How Our Colleges Favor the Rich and Divide America* (New York: New Press, 2020).

50. Raj Chetty et al., "Income Segregation and Intergenerational Mobility across Colleges in the United States," *Quarterly Journal of Economics* (2020), 1569. The study includes all college students in the United States from 1999 to 2013. The "Ivy-Plus" category adds Duke, MIT, Stanford, and the University of Chicago to the eight Ivy League colleges.

51. Gregor Aisch et al., "Some Colleges Have More Students from the Top 1 Percent Than the Bottom 60. Find Yours," The Upshot, *New York Times*, January 18, 2017, https://nyti.ms/2jRcqJs. To qualify as the 1%, you must have an annual income of more than $630,000. This article and the *Times'* interactive tool (https://www.nytimes.com/interactive/projects/college-mobility/) are based on the Chetty data. I use this tool for the comparison between UVA and Piedmont Community College.

52. One of the fascinating findings in Robinson's study is that Coursera itself is ambivalent about that architecture, capriciously flip-flopping between a sequential rollout format (feels like college) and an on-demand format (feels like Netflix). See Robinson, "Learning On-Demand."

53. Oakeshott, "The Idea of a University," in *The Voice of Liberal Learning: Michael Oakeshott on Education*, ed. Timothy Fuller (New Haven, CT: Yale University Press, 1989), 103.

54. Herbert Spencer, "What Knowledge Is of Most Worth," in *Essays on Education and Kindred Subjects* (London: Dent, [1861] 1911), https://oll.libertyfund.org/title /eliot-essays-on-education-and-kindred-subjects-1861-1911, pars. 7–8. The full passage reads:

> In education, then, this is the question of questions, which it is high time we discussed in some methodic way. The first in importance, though the last to be considered, is the problem—how to decide among the conflicting claims

of various subjects on our attention. Before there can be a rational curriculum, we must settle which things it most concerns us to know; or, to use a word of Bacon's, now unfortunately obsolete—we must determine the relative values of knowledges.

55. Donna St. George, "U-Va.: A Donor in the Crisis," *Washington Post*, Education Section, August 4, 2012, http://www.washingtonpost.com/local/education /u-va-a-donor-in-the-crisis/2012/08/04/b9e0e146-ce86-11e1-aa14-708bac2c7ee9 _story.html.

56. Gerald Grant and David Riesman, *The Perpetual Dream: Reform and Experiment in the American College* (Chicago: University of Chicago Press, 1978), 377.

57. It is interesting to compare the staffing of the three units a decade later. Classics has faculty of eleven and a staff of two; Germanic Languages and Literatures has a faculty of fourteen and a staff of three. The new center (http://www .uvacontemplation.org/) has twelve directors (including associate directors), two research professors (one who is also a director), three managers, two coordinators, nine instructors, and nine interns.

58. David L. Kirp, *Shakespeare, Einstein, and the Bottom Line: The Marketing of Higher Education* (Cambridge, MA: Harvard University Press, 2003), 136.

59. "Franchise fee" is what Darden's associate dean called it, as quoted in Kirp, *Shakespeare, Einstein, and the Bottom Line*, 137.

60. Kirp, *Shakespeare, Einstein, and the Bottom Line*, 136. "Internal tax rate" is Snyder's term.

61. See University of Virgina, Darden School of Business, *Pillars, Issue 28 (Fall 2022)*, 17, https://issuu.com/dardenreport/docs/pillars_28_fall2022_online; and National Association of College and University Business Officers and TIAA (2023), "U.S. and Canadian Institutions Listed by Fiscal Year (FY) 2022 Endowment Market Value and Change in Endowment Market Value from FY21 to FY22," https://www.nacubo .org/Research/2022/NACUBO-TIAA-Study-of-Endowments. The Darden endowment is 11.6 times greater than that of Virginia State University as a whole.

62. John T. Bethell, Richard M. Hunt, and Robert Shenton, "Harvard A to Z: From Aab to Zeph Greek—and Everything Crimson in Between," *Harvard Magazine*, May–June, 2004, https://www.harvardmagazine.com/2004/05/harvard-a -to-z.html.

63. Zachary M. Seward, "For Sale by Owner: Historic Colonial: FAS Sells Massachusetts Hall to Central Administration for Planned Office Expansion," *Harvard Crimson*, January 22, 2006, http://www.thecrimson.com/article/2006/1/22/for -sale-by-owner-historic-colonial/.

64. See, for example, Benjamin Ginsberg, *The Fall of the Faculty: The Rise of the All Administrative Faculty and Why It Matters* (New York: Oxford University Press,

2011), chaps. 1–3. In "Public Hearing" (193–194), I document another key budget pressure, the historic decline of state support.

65. Michael Delucchi, Richard B. Dadzie, Erik Dean, and Xuan Pham, "What's that smell? Bullshit jobs in higher education," *Review of Social Economy* (2021), DOI: 10.1080/00346764.2021.1940255, table 1, p. 3. I have added together two categories, "Executive/Administrative" and "Other Professionals." Disaggregated, the rates of increase are 164% and 452% respectively. The authors base their calculations on data publicly available via the National Center for Educational Statistics.

66. Data from "Executive Compensation at Public and Private Colleges" (updated June 8, 2015), Facts and Figures, *Chronicle of Higher Education* (Chronicle.com) as analyzed by Andrew Irwin and Marjorie Wood for the Institute for Policy Studies (see http://www.ips-dc.org/one_percent_universities/) and reported in the *New York Times* (see http://www.nytimes.com/2014/05/24/opinion/fat-cat-administrators-at-the-top-25.html?ref=topics).

67. See http://news.harvard.edu/gazette/story/2011/10/the-newest-live-in-the-oldest/.

68. Mario Savio, December 2, 1964. Available on YouTube. See, for example, https://www.youtube.com/watch?v=tcx9BJRadfw.

SOUL ACTION

1. Ralph Waldo Emerson, "The American Scholar," in *Essays and Lectures*, ed. Joel Porte (New York: Library of America, 1983), 57. The title of my essay is also inspired by this line from Dewey: "The supreme mark and criterion of a teacher . . . [is] insight into soul-action" (John Dewey, "The Relation of Theory to Practice in Education," in *John Dewey on Education*, ed. Reginald D. Archambault [Chicago: University of Chicago Press, (1904) 1974], 319).

2. R. G. Collingwood, *The Principles of Art* (Oxford: Clarendon Press, 1938).

3. Søren Kierkegaard, *Concluding Unscientific Postscript*, trans. David F. Swenson and Walter Lowrie, ed. Walter Lowrie (Princeton, NJ: Princeton University Press, [1846] 1941), 166.

4. On the "whole child" as a floating signifier whose value can be presumed as self-evident, see Bronwen M. A. Jones, *Educating the Neo-Liberal Whole Child: A Genealogical Approach* (London: Routledge, 2022), 7–8. Jones offers a Foucauldian reading of the contemporary turn (in the UK) to well-being, emotion, self-regulation, and character as an expression of neoliberal governmentality and bio-power. Interestingly, she notes how these new policy initiatives/discourses simultaneously produce and negate the object on which they focus, creating "a kind of Schrödinger's whole child" (168; I have corrected the spelling of Schrödinger).

5. Roger Waters, "Another Brick in the Wall, Part II," from Pink Floyd, *The Wall* (Harvest/Columbia Records, 1979), https://genius.com/Pink-floyd-another-brick -in-the-wall-pt-2-lyrics.

6. Dead Kennedys (lyrics by Jello Biafra and John Greenway), "California Über Alles," *Fresh Fruit for Rotting Vegetables* (Cherry Red Tentacles, 1980). Adapted from https://genius.com/Dead-kennedys-california-uber-alles-lyrics.

7. "Repressive desublimation" is a term coined by Marcuse to name the process by which advanced capitalism controls not by thwarting but by infantilizing desire. See Herbert Marcuse, *One-Dimensional Man: Studies in the Ideology of Advanced Industrial Society* (Boston: Beacon Press, 1964). *Eros*, the force by which we are drawn to make contact with the real even while inevitably frustrated by its independence from our wishes, is traded for the frustration-free packaging of libido in commodity culture. Conscience disintegrates along with the decline of the reality principle; "naughty" impulses are liberated; dissent diverted.

8. For demonstrations of these theses, see, for example, Hannah Arendt, "The Crisis in Education," trans. Denver Lindley, in *Between Past and Future: Eight Exercises in Political Thought* (New York: Penguin, [1958] 1977); Chris Higgins, "Worlds of Practice: Macintyre's Challenge to Applied Ethics," in *The Good Life of Teaching: An Ethics of Professional Practice* (Oxford: Wiley-Blackwell, 2011); and Charles Taylor, *The Sources of the Self: The Making of the Modern Identity* (Cambridge, MA: Harvard University Press, 1989), 35–39.

9. Richard Rorty, "Education as Socialization and as Individualization," in *Philosophy and Social Hope* (New York: Penguin, 1999), 272.

10. Richard Rorty, *Philosophy and the Mirror of Nature* (Princeton, NJ: Princeton University Press, 1979), part III.

11. For Oakeshott, it is because we share the condition of learner that we cannot be said to share a nature. For example, "Each man is his own self-enacted 'history;'" and the expression 'human nature' stands only for our common and inescapable engagement: to become by learning" (Michael Oakeshott, "A Place of Learning," in *The Voice of Liberal Learning: Michael Oakeshott on Education*, ed. Timothy Fuller [New Haven, CT: Yale University Press, 1989], 21; cf. 28). The essential historicity and linguisticality of human experience, our embeddedness in tradition, is the central theme of Hans-Georg Gadamer, *Truth and Method*, trans. rev. by Joel Weinsheimer and Donald Marshall, 2nd rev., Continuum Impacts ed. (New York: Continuum, [1960] 2004); *Lebensformen* or "forms of life" is the related concept famously developed in Ludwig Wittgenstein, *Philosophical Investigations*, trans. G. E. M. Anscombe, Reissued German-English ed. (Oxford: Blackwell, [1953] 1997). Gadamer links his own view to Wittgenstein's only once in *Truth and Method*, but approvingly (561).

12. Hans-Georg Gadamer, "Education Is Self-Education," *Journal of Philosophy of Education* 35, no. 4 (2001). "These analogies of clay and wax," Oakeshott writes,

"of receptacles to be filled and empty rooms to be furnished, have nothing to do with learners and learning" (Oakeshott, "Learning and Teaching," in *The Voice of Liberal Learning*, 44). For Oakeshott's conception of our inalienable freedom as self-interpreting animals who actively shape our formative worlds, see Oakeshott, "A Place of Learning," 18–23. I unpack his argument in "New Student Orientation" and "Job Prospects" (see pp. 103–104 and 251–253).

13. The dialectic of influence and individuation has occasioned a discipline-defying, genre-expanding conversation among the independent-minded, including classic essays, such as Ralph Waldo Emerson, "Self-Reliance," in *Essays and Lectures*, and Friedrich Nietzsche, "Schopenhauer as Educator," trans. William Arrowsmith, in *Unmodern Observations: Unzeitgemässe Betrachtungen*, ed. William Arrowsmith (New Haven, CT: Yale University Press, [1874] 1990); an actor's reflections, such as Vasily Toporkov, *Stanislavski in Rehearsal*, trans. Jean Benedetti (New York: Routledge, [1949–1950] 2004); a literary critic's psychology of poetry—I refer to Bloom's series of "revisionist" works beginning with Harold Bloom, *The Anxiety of Influence: A Theory of Poetry* (London: Oxford University Press, 1973); intellectual history in an existentialist key, see Robbie McClintock, *Man and His Circumstances: Ortega as Educator* (New York: Teachers College Press, 1971); and belletrist ruminations on apprenticeship, such as George Steiner, *Lessons of the Masters*, The Charles Eliot Norton Lectures (Cambridge, MA: Harvard University Press, 2005). There is also a renewed interest in questions of imitation, initiation, and emulation within philosophy of education. The conversation staked out by R. S. Peters, in "Education as Initiation," in *Philosophical Analysis and Education*, ed. R. D. Archambault (London: Routledge and Kegan Paul, 1965), and by Philip W. Jackson, in "The Mimetic and the Transformative: Alternative Outlooks on Teaching," in *The Practice of Teaching* (New York: Teachers College Press, 1986), and extended by Bryan Warnick, in *Imitation and Education* (Albany: State University of New York Press, 2008), has been joined by some interesting more-recent work—for example, in Timothy McDonough, "Initiation, Not Indoctrination: Confronting the Grotesque in Cultural Education," *Educational Philosophy and Theory* 43, no. 7 (2011); Mark E. Jonas and Drew W. Chambers, "The Use and Abuses of Emulation as a Pedagogical Practice," *Educational Theory* 67, no. 3 (2017); and Douglas W. Yacek, *The Transformative Classroom: Philosophical Foundations and Practical Applications* (New York: Routledge, 2021).

14. McClintock, *Man and His Circumstances*. At once erudite and existentially charged, McClintock not only writes about Ortega (both his experience of and views on self-formation) but writes with Ortega to his generation about their own formative tasks.

15. McClintock, *Man and His Circumstances*, 37.

16. It is no stretch to add Ortega to Rorty's edifying duo. All three thinkers drew from Dilthey and saw history as reason's medium and not merely its object or captor. For Gadamer's appreciation of Ortega's development of Dilthey's thought,

see Hans-Georg Gadamer, "Dilthey and Ortega: The Philosophy of Life," (1985) in *Hermeneutics between History and Philosophy: The Selected Writings of Hans-Georg Gadamer*, vol. 1, eds. and trans. Pol Vandevelde and Arun Iyer (New York: Bloomsbury, 2016).

17. McClintock, *Man and His Circumstances*, 36.

18. McClintock, *Man and His Circumstances*, 36.

19. McClintock, *Man and His Circumstances*, 36.

20. John Dewey, *Democracy and Education: An Introduction to the Philosophy of Education* (New York: Macmillan Company, 1916), 8.

21. I return to this idea that, while students must drive the formative process, we must awaken their formative agency in "New Student Orientation," "Wide Awake" (see the sections An Allegory of Arrival and Who is the Formative Educator?), and "Job Prospects" (see pp. 208–209).

22. In thinking through the implications of this distinction, I benefited from discussions with Jeremy Alexander, Jeff Bloechl, Samantha Ha, Greg Kalscheur, Brian Robinette, and Stanton Wortham in a reading group at the Lynch School of Education and Human Development at Boston College.

23. Friedrich Nietzsche, "From On Truth and Lie in an Extra-Moral Sense," in *The Portable Nietzsche*, ed. and trans. Walter Kaufmann (New York: Penguin, 1976), 47.

24. Antonio Damasio, *Looking for Spinoza: Joy, Sorrow, and the Feeling Brain* (Orlando, FL: Harcourt, 2003), chap. 3.

25. George Lakoff and Mark Johnson, *Metaphors We Live By* (Chicago: University of Chicago Press, [1980] 2003).

26. For a genealogy of the idea of the self as interior space, see "Inwardness," part II in Taylor, *Sources of the Self*.

27. See "well-turned, adj," OED Online, June 2020, Oxford University Press, https://www.oed.com/view/Entry/227669?redirectedFrom=well-turned& (accessed July 22, 2020). I have expanded an abbreviation and adjusted to American spelling.

28. This is fragment (DK) B101: "ἐδιζησάμην ἐμεωυτόν" (attributed by Plutarch in *Against Colotes*), translated by Haxton. See Heraclitus, *Fragments*, trans. Brooks Haxton (New York: Penguin, [c. 500 BCE] 2003), §80, p. 51.

29. This is fragment (DK) B45: "ψυχῆς πείρατα ἰὼν οὐκ ἂν ἐξεύροιο πᾶσαν ἐπιπορευόμενος ὁδόν· οὕτω βαθὺν λόγον ἔχει" (attributed by Diogenes Laertius), translated by Wheelwright. See Philip Wheelwright, *Heraclitus* (Westport, CT: Greenwood Press, [1959] 1981), §42, p. 58.

30. Alasdair MacIntyre, *After Virtue: A Study in Moral Theory*, 3rd ed. (South Bend, IN: University of Notre Dame Press, [1981] 2007), chap. 15.

31. Iris Murdoch, "Metaphysics and Ethics" [1957], in *Existentialists and Mystics*, ed. Peter Conradi (New York: Penguin, 1998), 75. I unpack this idea with the help of Oakeshott in "Job Prospects" (see pp. 251–253).

32. This is fragment (DK) B115: "ψυχῆς ἐστι λόγος ἑαυτὸν αὔξων" (attributed to Socrates by Stobaeus). Its proximity to other Heraclitean fragments in the Stobaeus anthology and resonance with other Heraclitean observations about the soul have led to its tentative inclusion among the fragments. The editors of the Loeb edition suggest specifically that a "comparison with [B45] makes its attribution to Heraclitus plausible"; see André Laks and Glenn W. Most, eds., *Early Greek Philosophy*, vol. 3: *Early Ionian Thinkers, Part 2*, Loeb Classical Library (Cambridge, MA: Harvard University Press, 2016), 189n1.

I have combined elements of multiple translations. As an alternate translation, Laks and Most offer "Soul is an account that increases itself" (Laks and Most, *Early Greek Philosophy*, vol. 3, p. 189n1). McKirahan/Curd have "The soul has a self-increasing logos" (Patricia Curd, ed., *A Presocratics Reader* [Indianapolis: Hackett, 2011], 45). The translation "To the soul, belongs the self-multiplying Logos" appears in Hermann Diels, "Heraclitus," in *The Encyclopedia of Religion and Ethics*, vol. 6, *Fiction-Hyksos*, ed. James Hastings (New York: Charles Scribner's Sons, 1914), 593. (The source of Diels's translation is unclear. He cites only his own Greek/German *Fragments der Versokratiker* and the Bywater volume, which omits B115.) In rendering B115, I have also drawn on Albert Cook, "Heraclitus and the Conditions of Utterance," *Arion: A Journal of Humanities and the Classics* (New Series) 4, no. 2 (1975): 453–454. Cook reads B115 as an echo of B1's "when they make trial of words and deeds," offering this interpretive gloss: "human life is properly seen as an increment (*auxon*) of speech-acts" (454).

33. As Lear has argued, the divorce between philosophy and psychology has simultaneously crippled our ability to answer the central philosophical question, How should I live?, and to advance the core psychological project of "working out the logic of the soul" (see Jonathan Lear, "Preface: The King and I," in *Open Minded: Working Out the Logic of the Soul* [Cambridge, MA: Harvard University Press, 1998], 7–9). Throughout his work, Lear works to mend this gap, pursuing philosophical and psychological (specifically psychoanalytic) ideas together, "with a sense of liveliness and openness" (15). My colleague, David Goodman, has arranged fruitful marriage counseling for psychology and the humanities with the launch of the Center for Psychological Humanities and Ethics in the Lynch School of Education and Human Development at Boston College (https://www.bc.edu/content /bc-web/schools/lynch-school/sites/Psychological-Humanities-Ethics.html).

34. McClintock has developed the concept of formative justice across a number of works, culminating in Robbie McClintock, *Formative Justice* (New York: Collaboratory for Liberal Learning, 2019). For his earliest published formulation, see Robbie McClintock, *Homeless in the House of Intellect: Formative Justice and Education*

as an Academic Study (New York: Laboratory for Liberal Learning, 2005), 72-101. Here I am quoting from a definition of the concept McClintock posted on his former website (see, http://robbiemcclintock.com/shelving/C-12-Form-Just.html, accessed March 26, 2017). This is close to the formulation in the abstract of Robbie McClintock, "Formative Justice: The Regulative Principle of Education," *Teachers College Record* 118, no. 10 (2016), 1. The phrase I elided is "and groups" as here I am emphasizing the personal side of formative justice. Note though that the distinction between distributive and formative justice is not a distinction between justice at the collective and individual levels. As McClintock makes clear, formative questions are at once existential/ethical and social-political.

35. For an antidote to the fantasy that architects design in only three dimensions, and for a salutary metaphor of formative experience, see *Stewart Brand, How Buildings Learn: What Happens After They're Built* (New York: Penguin, 1994).

36. MacIntyre, *After Virtue*, 224.

37. See Plato, 246a–253e, for example, Plato, "Phaedrus," trans. R. Hackforth, in *The Collected Dialogues of Plato*, ed. Edith Hamilton and Huntington Cairns (Princeton, NJ: Princeton University Press, [c. 380 BCE] 1961), 493–500.

38. Plato, "Phaedrus," 500 (523e).

39. Giovanni Ferrari, *Love among the Cicadas: A Study of Plato's Phaedrus* (Cambridge, UK: Cambridge University Press, 1987), 192, 194.

40. Ferrari, *Love among the Cicadas*, 200.

41. This is Ferrari's translation of Plato, 253d3–d6. See Ferrari, *Love among the Cicadas*, 185.

42. This is not to suggest that Plato would want to put *thumos* in the driver's seat even when it is oriented to the esteem of the temperate. In the *Republic*, Plato clearly denigrates both the psychology and politics of timocracy where life is organized around "the love of victories and honors" (Plato, *Republic*, trans. C. D. C. Reeve [Indianapolis, IN: Hackett, (c. 380 BCE) 2004], 243 [548c5]).

43. Jean-Jacques Rousseau, *Emile, or on Education*, Introduction, Translation, and Notes by Allan Bloom, 2nd ed. (New York: Basic Books [1762] 1979).

44. To get in touch with this is to experience what Rousseau calls *"le sentiment de l'existence."* I explore this concept further in "Wide Awake" (see p. 127).

45. Cf. Frederick Neuhouser, *Rousseau's Theodicy of Self-Love: Evil, Rationality, and the Drive for Recognition* (Oxford: Oxford University Press, 2008), 13. I concur with Neuhouser that the traditional contrast between a healthy (*amour de soi*) and corrupt (*amour propre*) form of self-love captures neither the importance of nor internal divisions in the concept of *amour propre* as Rousseau develops it (see p. 15, and p. 15n24).

46. See G. W. F. Hegel, *Phenomenology of Spirit*, trans. A. V. Miller (Oxford: Oxford University Press, [1807] 1977), 111–118; Jessica Benjamin, *The Bonds of Love:*

Psychoanalysis, Feminism, and the Problem of Domination (New York: Pantheon Books, 1988), for example 12, 32–36, and passim.

47. "L'homme en tout et par tout, n'est que rapiessement et bigarrure." I take Cotton's "wholly and throughout" for "en tout et par tout" and Frame's "patchwork and motley" for "rapiessement et bigarrure." See Michel de Montaigne, "We Taste Nothing Pure," in *The Complete Works of Michel De Montaigne*, vol. 6 (Charlottesville, VA: Intelex Corp., 2017), 140 (Reprint of Michel de Montaigne, *The Works of Michel de Montaigne: 10 volumes with letters and notes on the life of Montaigne*, trans. Charles Cotton, ed. and rev. W. Carew Hazlitt, with an introductory essay by Ralph Waldo Emerson [New York: Edwin C. Hill, 1910]); and Michel de Montaigne, "We Taste Nothing Pure," trans. Donald M. Frame, in *The Complete Works: Essays, Travel Journals, Letters* (New York: Knopf, 2003), 621.

48. Michel de Montaigne, "On the Inconsistency of Our Actions," in *Complete Works (Cotton)*, vol. 3, 240, 246, 246.

49. Montaigne, "On the Inconsistency of Our Actions," in *Complete Works (Frame)*, *290*, 294.

50. Montaigne, "On the Inconsistency of Our Actions," in *Complete Works (Frame)*, 294.

51. Simone Weil, "The Needs of the Soul," trans. Arthur Wills, in *The Need for Roots: Prelude to a Declaration of Duties toward Mankind* (London: Routledge, [1949] 2002).

52. Sigmund Freud, *Civilization and Its Discontents*, trans. James Strachey (New York: W.W. Norton & Company, [1930]), 16–18.

53. Sigmund Freud, "Beyond the Pleasure Principle," trans. John Reddick, in *Beyond the Pleasure Principle and Other Writings* (New York: W.W. Norton & Company, [1930] 2003), chap. 6; and Freud, *Civilization and Its Discontents*, 77ff.

54. Montaigne, "On the Inconsistency of Our Actions," in *Complete Works* (Cotton), 241.

55. Nietzsche, "Schopenhauer as Educator," 167.

56. Quoted in Helen Molesworth, "Imaginary Landscape," in *Leap before You Look: Black Mountain College, 1933–1957*, ed. Helen Molesworth (Boston: Institute for Contemporary Art, 2015), 51.

57. Henry David Thoreau, "I Am a Parcel of Vain Strivings Tied," in *The Portable Thoreau*, ed. Carl Bode (New York: Penguin Books, [1841] 1977).

58. We could also read "once" to mean that, far from securing the narrator's diverse inclinations securely, the wisp of straw was only coiled around a single time.

59. The phrase "differentiated unity" comes from Jonathan Lear, "Restlessness, Phantasy, and the Concept of Mind," in *Open Minded*, 89. Compare the opening of Jonathan Lear, "Inside and Outside the Republic," in *Open Minded, 219.*

60. Dewey, *Democracy and Education*, 308.

61. Dewey writes, "Any one occupation loses its meaning and becomes a routine keeping busy at something to the degree in which it is isolated from other interests" (Dewey, *Democracy and Education*, 307).

62. On the limitations of the moral-dilemma approach, see Edmund L. Pincoffs, "Quandary Ethics," *Mind* 80 (1971).

63. Maxine Greene, "Wide-Awakeness and the Moral Life," in *Landscapes of Learning* (New York: Teachers College Press, 1978), 43. It was in Greene's classes where I encountered the concept of "wide-awakeness" which she developed in dialogue with writers such as Thoreau, Woolf, Dewey, Camus, Arendt, and Schutz, always sure to model how we might grapple with our own moral somnolence through encounters with the arts and attention to the everyday "plagues" around us. The term itself comes from Alfred Schutz, whose definition serves as an epigraph in "Wide Awake" (see p. 119), an essay that aims to build upon this tradition.

64. John Dewey, *Human Nature and Conduct: An Introduction to Social Psychology* (New York: Modern Library, [1922] 1930), 258.

65. This quote appears as an epigraph to Bernard Cooper, *My Avant-Garde Education: A Memoir* (New York: Norton, 2015). Thanks to Cristiano Casalini for pointing me to this book.

66. Various thinkers including Kant, Weber, and Habermas have spoken to the affordances and limitation of this disjoining. In *Worlds Apart* (Hanover, NH: Wesleyan University Press, 1963), Owen Barfield stages a reengagement across these divides. In *Cosmopolis: The Hidden Agenda of Modernity* (Chicago: University of Chicago Press, 1990), Stephen Toulmin sketches the road not traveled. By contrast, Bruno Latour asserts via his title that, in fact, *We Have Never Been Modern*, trans. Catherine Porter (Cambridge, MA: Harvard University Press).

67. See Gadamer, *Truth and Method*, 70–87.

68. Seamus Heaney, "Song" (1979), in *Opened Ground: Selected Poems, 1966–1996* (New York: Farrar, Straus & Giroux, 1998), 173.

69. Gadamer, *Truth and Method*, 77.

70. Gadamer, *Truth and Method*, 74. I have removed a parenthetical note from the translators that "experiencing" translates *erlebende*. Gadamer contrasts experience as psychological uploading (*Erlebnis*) and as intersubjective unfolding (*Erfahrung*).

71. J. R. Oppenheimer, "Atomic Weapons," *Proceedings of the American Philosophical Society* 90, no. 1 (1946): 7.

72. Quoted in *In the Matter of J. Robert Oppenheimer: The Security Clearance Hearing*, edited by Richard Polenberg (Ithaca, NY: Cornell University Press, 2002), 46.

73. See Max Weber, *Die Protestantische Ethik Und Der Geist Des Kapitalismus: Vollständige Ausgabe*, ed. Dirk Kaesler (Munich: Verlag C.H. Beck, 2004), 201; and Max

Weber, *The Protestant Ethic and the Spirit of Capitalism*, trans. Talcott Parsons, Routledge Classics ed. (London: Routledge, 2001), 128. Thanks to Anke Pinkert for discussing the connotations of "*Fachmenschen*." On Weber's ventriloquization of Nietzsche, see Stephen A. Kent, "Weber, Goethe, and the Nietzschean Allusion: Capturing the Source of the 'Iron Cage' Metaphor," *Sociological Analysis* 44, no. 4 (1983): 301–302.

74. Virginia Woolf, *The Waves*, Oxford World Classics (Oxford: Oxford University Press, [1931] 1998), 83.

75. Here I am mining the dance scene itself for evidence that Jinny's shifting responses are authentic and agentic. Woolf also makes this point by bookending the scene with glimpses into Bernard's and Rhoda's struggles with authenticity. Attempting to write a letter to "the girl with whom he is passionately in love," Bernard is strangled by self-consciousness (Woolf, *The Waves*, 62). He narrates the composition process as if he were his future biographer; he wonders how someone intimately careless would cross his t's. Rhoda draws an explicit contrast between Jinny's agency at the dance and her own struggle to find such genuine fluency, lamenting that "Jinny rides like a gull on the wave, dealing her looks adroitly here and there, saying this and saying that, with truth. But I lie; I prevaricate" (86).

76. On *metis* see, for example, Nicholas C. Burbules, "2001: A Philosophical Odyssey," in *Philosophy of Education 2001*, ed. Suzanne Rice (Urbana, IL: Philosophy of Education Society, 2002). For a pithy definition of *virtú* see Arendt, "What Is Authority?", in *Between Past and Future*, 137. In Woolf's portrait of Jinny, I see a counterpoint to the masculinist tradition in which integrity is viewed as a rigid and fragile thing threatened by relational responsiveness, which it reads as vicious changeability and codes as female. Strange as it may seem—after all, Machiavelli names this excellence of meeting the moment after the word for man—I am suggesting that we can see Homer and Machiavelli (and we could add Aristotle on *phronesis*) as precursors in this countertradition.

77. Woolf, *The Waves*, 84.

78. I take this to be one of the great lessons of psychoanalysis from Freud and Winnicott to Jonathan Lear and Adam Phillips.

79. Max Weber, "Science as a Vocation," in *From Max Weber: Essays in Sociology*, eds. and trans. H. H. Gerth and C. Wright Mills (New York: Oxford University Press, [1918] 1946), 147. I have removed the scare quotes around the phrase "moral achievement" and around the word "inconvenient" in the phrase "inconvenient facts."

80. *New York Times* and Serial Productions, *Nice White Parents* (reported by Chana Joffe-Walt; produced by Julie Snyder), Episode 5, "'We Know It When We See It,'" August 20, 2020 (https://www.nytimes.com/2020/08/20/podcasts/nice-white-parents-school.html?action=click&module=audio-series-bar&region=header&pgtype=Article), 10: 42–11:38.

81. Arlie Hochschild, *Strangers in Their Own Land: Anger and Mourning on the American Right* (New York: New Press, 2018), chap. 2.

82. Disavowal works not by denying facts but by erasing the connections between them, rendering them inert. Octave Mannoni captured this canny psychic strategy in a phrase (Octave Mannoni, "Je Sais Bien, Mais Quand Même" [1964], in *Jacques Lacan: Critical Evaluations in Cultural Theory*, ed. Slavoj Žižek, vol. 1: *Psychoanalytic Theory and Practice* [London: Routledge, 2003], 125–144). Combining elements of Morag's and Myer's translations best captures this pseudo-accommodating, can't-be-bothered shrug: "Yes, I know, but anyway . . ." (Talia Morag, *Emotion, Imagination, and the Limits of Reason* [London: Routledge, 2016], 236; and, Clive Myer, "An Interview with Noel Burch: Playing with Toys by the Wayside," in *Critical Cinema: Beyond the Theory of Practice*, ed. Clive Myer [New York: Columbia University Press, 2011], 285).

Wallace-Wells (building on Robinson Jeffers and Samuel Scheffler) makes the point that it is part of the broader pattern of "civilizational disavowal," our "day-to-day . . . denial of fragility . . . [and] our own mortality," to locate responsibility in the outright climate change denialists, who are only a force in one country, if a rich and powerful one. Reading this as a case of US "narcissism," Wells sees the complacent, soft denialism practiced by virtually all of us as the true culprit. See David Wallace-Wells, *The Uninhabitable Earth: Life after Warming* (New York: Tim Duggan Books, 2019), 209, 293, 149.

I offer an extended case study of disavowal in The Last Butler section of "Job Prospects."

83. Weber, "Science as a Vocation," 147.

84. From J. Robert Oppenheimer, "The Open Mind" (1948), quoted in Walker Gibson, ed., *The Limits of Language* (New York: Hill and Wang, 1962), 50–51.

85. William James to Henry James, March 10, 1887. Whitehead mentions this quote at the beginning of *Science and the Modern World* (Alfred North Whitehead, *Science and the Modern World* [New York: Free Press, 1925]). I found it through Bell, who quotes the Whitehead passage as an epigraph in Daniel Bell, *The Reforming of General Education* (New York: Columbia University Press, 1966). For the dating of the letter, see Robert D. Richardson, *William James: In the Maelstrom of Modernism* (Boston: Mariner/Houghton Mifflin, 2007), 297 and 562n18.

86. My description of personal styles as patterns of disturbance is inspired by Lydia Davis, *Varieties of Disturbance: Stories* (New York: Farrar, Straus, and Giroux, 2007).

87. Ruth Bader Ginsburg, quoted in Jane Sherron De Hart, *Ruth Bader Ginsburg: A Life* (New York: Knopf, 2018), 27.

88. Hope Edelman, *Motherless Daughters: The Legacy of Loss* (Reading, MA: Addison-Wesley, 1994), 272.

89. Lithwick, in Dahlia Lithwick and Jeffrey Rosen, "Jeffrey Rosen on *Conversations with RBG*," *Live at the National Constitution Center* (podcast), November 12,

2019 (https://constitutioncenter.org/news-debate/podcasts/jeffrey-rosen-on-con versations-with-rbg), 3:06.

90. Bush v. Gore, 531 U.S. 98 (2000); Gonzales v. Carhart, 550 U.S. 124 (2007); Ledbetter v. Goodyear Tire & Rubber Co., Inc, 550 U.S. 618 (2007); Shelby County v. Holder, 570 U.S. 529 (2013); Burwell v. Hobby Lobby Stores, Inc., 573 U.S. 682 (2014).

91. Lithwick, in Lithwick and Rosen, "Jeffrey Rosen on *Conversations with RBG*," 4:30.

92. Jeffrey Rosen, *Conversations with RBG: Ruth Bader Ginsburg on Life, Love, Liberty, and Law* (New York: Henry Holt and Co., 2019), 150 and 15.

93. Ginsburg, quoted in Rosen, *Conversations with RBG*, 138. In 2007, both Ginsburg and John Paul Stevens went on record about the court's rapid rightward shift. In her dissent, Ginsburg notes that no new legal principle emerged in the fifteen years since Casey, only now the court "is differently composed" (Gonzales v. Carhart, 550 U.S. 124 [2007]). Stevens concludes his dissent in the consolidated resegregation cases with this testimony: "It is my firm conviction that no Member of the Court that I joined in 1975 would have agreed with today's decision" (Parents Involved in Community Schools v. Seattle School District No. 1, 551 U.S. 701 [2007]).

94. This is Lithwick's characterization of the picture of RBG's judicial approach that emerges in Rosen's book, in Lithwick and Rosen, "Jeffrey Rosen on *Conversations with RBG*," 4:46.

95. This is Rosen relaying a statement of Ginsburg's from a prior interview in Jeffrey Rosen and Ruth Bader Ginsburg, "RBG on Life, Love, Liberty, and Law," *We the People* (podcast), December 19, 2019 (https://constitutioncenter.org/news -debate/podcasts/rbg-on-life-love-liberty-and-law), 6:08.

96. Ginsburg, in Rosen and Ginsburg, *RBG on Life, Love, Liberty, and Law*, 6:26.

97. See Rosen, *Conversations with RBG*, 223–224. I am quoting from Rosen's recounting of this exchange in Lithwick and Rosen, "Jeffrey Rosen on *Conversations with RBG*," 6:43.

98. Ginsburg, quoted in Rosen, *Conversations with RBG*, 224.

99. Notwithstanding the recent setback represented by Dobbs v. Jackson Women's Health Organization, 597 U.S. ___ (2022).

100. James McCosh, *The New Departure in College Education: Being a Reply to President Eliot's Defence of It in New York, Feb. 24, 1885* (New York: Charles Scribner's Sons, 1885), 4.

101. Eugene Lyle Seeley, Todd Goddard, and Ronald Mellado Miller, "Ge-Whiz! How Students Choose Their General Education Classes," *Journal of Applied Research in Higher Education* 10, no. 3 (2018): 326–327. To be fair, scheduling convenience

was essentially tied with "personal interest." There were two items, one asking students to rank methods of selecting courses and another to "choose all that apply." On the ranking item, the four most popular responses, summing the frequencies that were top-ranked and second-ranked, were, "What best fits my schedule" (62.4%); "Personal interest" (59.7%); "Recommendations from my academic advisors or professors" (29.5%); and "I check internet sites to find the best professors" (24.7%). However, "Personal interest" was top-ranked more often than "What best fits my schedule" (32.3% vs. 28.5%) and was also more frequently selected on the "choose all that apply" item (68.8% vs. 66.8%). Depressingly, a small but not insignificant number of students (3.15%) could not recall a principle of selection; another portion (2.66%) admitted to choosing randomly.

102. Clarissa A. Thompson, Michele Eodice, and Phuoc Tran, "Student Perceptions of General Education Requirements at a Large Public University: No Surprises?" *Journal of General Education* 64, no. 4 (2015): 285.

103. Elizabeth A. Armstrong and Laura T. Hamilton, *Paying for the Party: How College Maintains Inequality* (Cambridge, MA: Harvard University Press, 2013).

104. I served on the UIUC faculty from 2006 to 2019, where I participated in the faculty senate and Campus Faculty Association, served on the Gen Ed Board and various initiatives to strengthen the humanities, and was one the faculty leaders of the Campus Conversation in Undergraduate Education (CCUE) that led to the creation of an experimental integrative track within Gen Ed. It is an institution I know well, and for which I have a great deal of respect. The problems I go on to point out are shared by most comprehensive research universities. That humane learning continues to flourish in such a massive and, it must be said, technicist university is thanks to the living example and endless efforts of specific individuals. I was fortunate to be in Urbana during a period when the late Nancy Abelmann served as associate vice chancellor for research in the arts, humanities, and related fields; when Lauren Goodlad was heading up the Unit for Criticism and Interpretive Theory and then CCUE; and when Antoinette Burton, now director of the Humanities Research Institute, was tirelessly rallying us to defend the humanities in their own terms even while securing conditions for dynamic, new, interdisciplinary and public-oriented humanistic work.

105. 7 U.S.C. 301, §4. In discussing the Morrill Act, it is important to remember that land grants were predicated on land seizures through forced removal of native nations. The land that was "granted" from the federal government to the State of Illinois was first taken from the Peoria, Kaskaskia, Piankashaw, Wea, Miami, Mascoutin, Odawa, Sauk, Mesquaki, Kickapoo, Potawatomi, Ojibwe, and Chickasaw Nations. See the UIUC land acknowledgement statement here: https://chancellor.illinois.edu/land_acknowledgement.html. In the fall of 2021, UIUC enrolled thirteen Native American students among its 33,851 undergraduates (see https://nces.ed.gov/ipeds/datacenter/FacsimileView.aspx?surveyNumber =15&unitId=145637&year=2021).

106. *First Annual Report of the Board of Trustees of the Illinois Industrial University: From Their Organization, March 12, 1867, to the Close of the Academic Year, June 18, 1868* (Springfield: Bakee, Bailhache & Co., 1868), 20–21, https://digital.library.illinois .edu/items/600975d0-5cd8-0132-3334-0050569601ca-2. The quotations in the remainder of this paragraph and the following one are all drawn from p. 49 of this report. "Pierian fount" refers to the Macedonian spring said to be the source of inspiration for the Muses, and specifically to the famous couplet from Alexander Pope's "Essay on Criticism": "A little learning is a dang'rous thing; / Drink deep, or taste not the Pierian spring."

107. This language was updated sometime between 2015 and 2017. The older language is preserved at https://web.archive.org/web/20150218222514/https://courses .illinois.edu/gened/DEFAULT/DEFAULT.

108. Plato, *Republic*, 208–223 (513e–519d); Tara Westover, *Educated* (New York: Random House, 2018).

109. In later essays, I explore two counterexamples: Oakeshott's (re)orientation remarks at the London School of Economics in 1961 ("New Student Orientation") and John Rice's initial advisement of a Black Mountain College student in 1933 ("Wide Awake," pp. 124–128).

110. This is the cover image of the paperback edition of David Shrigley, *What the Hell Are You Doing? The Essential David Shrigley* (Edinburgh: Canongate, 2012).

111. This is what we have set out to provide in the Transformative Educational Studies program in the Lynch School of Education and Human Development at Boston College. Interrupting instrumentalism is the topic (and point) of "New Student Orientation."

112. See https://courses.illinois.edu/gened/DEFAULT/DEFAULT. The old language is retained in slightly modified form as the tagline for the Gen Ed link on the course explorer page (https://courses.illinois.edu//), which reads, "Browse core requirements students must satisfy in order to graduate."

113. For a nice close-reading of another case of discursive decay from founding ideals to modern mission-speak, see the opening of William Deresiewicz, "The Neoliberal Arts: How College Sold Its Soul to the Market," *Harper's* (September 2015).

114. Indeed, in the famous examples of robust programs of general education, we tend to see the founding of a new institution (Black Mountain College; St. Johns College) or of a new autonomous division within a university (The Hutchins College at the University of Chicago).

115. Here I develop further the critique of Responsibility Center Management (RCM) broached in "Campus Tour" (see pp. 9–10 and 269n21).

116. This is from an explanation of RCM budgeting from the CFO of Indiana University. The page no longer exists but a screenshot (from August 8, 2012) is preserved in the IUPUI archives at https://archives.iupui.edu/handle/2450/6269.

117. Clark Kerr, *The Uses of the University*, 5th ed. (Cambridge, MA: Harvard University Press, [1963] 2001). The term "university" derives from the Latin word "universus" meaning whole or entire. However, the term did not originally refer to a "universality of learning," but rather to an incorporated guild of scholars (teachers, students, or both), able to bargain collectively with townspeople prone to rent gauging and other profiteering. See Charles Homer Haskins, *The Rise of the Universities* (Ithaca, NY: Cornell University Press), 9.

118. Abraham Flexner, *Universities: American, English, German* (New Brunswick, NJ: Transaction Publishers, [1930] 1994), 178–179; quoted in Kerr, *Uses of the University*, 5.

119. Flexner, *Universities*, 235, 231–232. Here, Flexner is contrasting the University of London with the "unity of spirit and design" still evident at Oxford and Cambridge (Flexner, *Universities*, 234). However, as Kerr notes, what Flexner says of London echoes his critique of "Harvard and American universities" (Kerr, *Uses of the University*, 5). Flexner sees US universities as increasingly disjointed, equating modernization with expansion in every direction at once: "The result is plain: the American universities are open to innovation; that is excellent; but, alas, they have been invaded indiscriminately by things both good and bad" (Flexner, *Universities*, 221).

120. Quoted in Kerr, *Uses of the University*, 15.

121. Kerr, *Uses of the University*, 6.

122. Kerr, *Uses of the University*, 15.

123. David B. Truman, "Foreword," in Bell, *Reforming of General Education*, vii.

124. See http://catalog.illinois.edu/undergraduate/.

125. This book's closing essay, "Job Prospects," begins with a closer look at these interdepartmental hunger games.

126. Oakeshott, "A Place of Learning," 30.

127. I did this count in 2019. See https://courses.illinois.edu/gened/2019/fall, which links to each category's list of courses.

128. This is a rough calculation. Some cross-listed courses appear twice on a list, once under each department. If we reduce each number by 10%, we get $3 \times 51 \times 130 \times 140 \times 192 \times 444 \times 443 \times 83 \times 82 \times 28 \times 69 \times 178 \times 177 = 4.36 \times 10^{25}$ permutations. However, many courses meet multiple requirements (at UIUC these are known as "double dippers" and "triple dippers"). Assuming a student who takes no more Gen Ed courses than necessary, this greatly reduces the number of thirteen course pathways. At the same time, it adds new shorter pathways, ranging from seven to twelve courses, each with a huge number of variants.

129. Because astronomers must make a series of highly debatable assumptions in counting stars, estimates range widely from 1×10^{20} to 1×10^{24}.

130. The dates 1828 and 1885 serve as useful bookends for a period of rapid change in US higher education. From the founding of Harvard in 1636, into the early republic, we find small denominational colleges—Frederick Rudolph's "temples of piety and intellect"—offering a prescribed curriculum (Frederick Rudolph, *The American College and University: A History* [Athens: University of Georgia Press, (1962) 1990], 3.) Already by 1828, the rumblings of an expanded, more egalitarian, and more research-oriented university had reached New Haven, prompting Yale to issue its famous defense of a unified, Greco-Roman-Christian curriculum (The so-called Yale Report is available online. It was first published as *Reports on the Course of Instruction in Yale College; By a Committee of the Corporation, and the Academical Faculty* [New Haven, CT: Hezekiah Howe, 1828]. For the key opening essay with helpful notes, see Jeremiah Day, "Course of Instruction in Yale College," in *The Liberal Arts Tradition: A Documentary History*, ed. Bruce A. Kimball [Lanham, MD: University Press of America (1828) 2010]). Though it advocated "*gradual* changes," opposing only the notion that the traditional college should be "broken up" and "*new-modelled*," the Yale Report was long read as a rearguard action (Day, "Course of Instruction," 265, emphasis original). "Obviously the Yale Report was no invitation to the future," Rudolph writes, going on to conclude that it had forestalled modernization through the civil war, consigning "thousands of students to thousands of days of boredom" (Rudolph, *American College and University*, 134, 135). Historians disagree over just how homogeneous, rigid, and rote the antebellum colleges were; for a thoughtful appraisal of this debate, see Bruce A. Kimball, *Orators and Philosophers: A History of the Idea of Liberal Education* (New York: Teachers College Press, 1986), Appendix 1.

More recently, historians have tended to view the Yale Report as doing exactly what Rudolph denies, issuing an invitation to the future. As Jack Lane argues, by defending the traditional curriculum on the grounds that it promotes mental discipline, the Yale Report fatefully casts liberal learning not as an integral part of the search for wisdom or civic virtue, but as an instrument for acquiring what is itself another flexible instrumentality. As Lane plays out the story, it goes like this: The writers wanted to save the classical curriculum, and mental discipline justified that course of study. This was a grave mistake because it played into the hands of the enemy, those clamoring for an instrumental collegiate education. They now had only to sever the umbilical connection that the report had established between the classics and mental discipline, or they could discredit mental training and thus collapse the arch of classical liberal education. Actually, they did both. Although forced to the fringes of American higher education by the Yale Report, new fields and disciplines slowly but surely made their way into the college curriculum during the nineteenth century. Late in the century, when psychologists discredited faculty psychology and the natural and social sciences won academic respectability, most of them entered the curriculum as discrete professional disciplines bereft of larger moral/public ends. (Jack C. Lane "The Yale Report of 1828 and Liberal Education: A Neorepublican Manifesto," *History of Education Quarterly* 27, no. 3

(1987): 337; cf. Jurgen Herbst, "The Yale Report of 1828," *International Journal of the Classical Tradition* 11, no. 2 [2004]).

Thus, by the time we arrive at the famous Eliot-McCosh debate of 1885, the question has already shifted from how to evolve the prescribed curriculum to how to rein in Eliot's ascendant and "revolutionary philosophy of virtually total curricular freedom for undergraduates" (George M. Marsden, *The Soul of the American University: From Protestant Establishment to Established Nonbelief* [New York: Oxford University Press, 1994], 199). Far from harking back to eighteenth-century Oxbridge, McCosh's objections to Eliot's position already anticipate the compromise position under which we still operate, with free election hedged by concentration and distribution requirements. While McCosh shows some rhetorical flair, the contrast he draws is relatively modest one. "I hold that in a college with the variety there should be a unity," he declares (McCosh, *The New Departure*, 16). "In Harvard," McCosh explains, "everything is scattered like the star dust out which worlds are formed" (16). By contrast, his Princeton organizes its diverse subjects into three "compacted heads," representing the "Trinity of studies: in Language and Literature, in Science, and in Philosophy" (11n1, 11). While our "compacted heads" differ somewhat, already evident are the basic rationale and architecture of the breadth requirements that would be put in place by Eliot's successor, A. Lawrence Lowell, in 1909. As Lowell was fond of saying, an educated person should "know a little bit of everything and one thing well." (For this version of Lowell's adage, see Arthur Stanwood Pier, *The Story of Harvard* [Boston: Little, Brown, and Company, 1913], 202; cf. Abbot Lawrence Lowell, "Inaugural Address of the President of Harvard University," *Science, New Series* 30, no. 772 [1909]: 502; and Charles Johnston, "A New Experiment: How President Lowell Is Modifying the 'Elective System' at Harvard," *Harper's Weekly*, July 2.)

131. I picked these courses more or less at random, quickly scanning for courses that met the right requirements, just as research tells us that students pick. I was looking for neither a cohesive nor an intentionally eclectic set. I did steer away from classes likely to evoke the usual polemics about the decline of standards or politicization of the university. Though I will raise questions about how such an assortment of classes helps us face up to our formative tasks, I consider each of these topics to be interesting and important in its own right. None of these is offered as the butt of a joke.

132. Rorty, "Education as Socialization and as Individualization," 122.

133. Michael S. Roth, *Safe Enough Spaces* (New Haven, CT: Yale University Press, 2019), 103.

134. Thanks to Jessica Harless and Eboni Zamani-Gallaher for an interesting discussion of this point.

135. William T. Foster, *Administration of the College Curriculum* (Boston: Houghton Mifflin, 1911), 190, quoted in Bruce A. Kimball, *The Liberal Arts Tradition: A Documentary History*, 377. I do not know how common this exact phrase was but

we have already seen two variants: McCosh's (1885) "scattered like . . . star-dust" (just quoted in note 130) and Burton's (1920) "scattering and smattering" (Preface, p. viii). Here is one more, later instance: Harvard President James Conant remarked that the aim of Gen Ed must be more than "collecting in one's mind a wide scattering of factual information, however helpful such information may be in a quiz program" (James Conant, "Some Aspects of Modern Harvard," *Journal of General Education* 4, no. 3 [1950]: 181).

136. William G. Perry, *Forms of Ethical and Intellectual Development in the College Years: A Scheme* (San Francisco: Jossey-Bass, [1968] 1999), 33.

137. *Schopenhauer as Educator* (§6). See Friedrich Nietzsche, *Unmodern Observations: Unzeitgemässe Betrachtungen,* ed. William Arrowsmith (New Haven, CT: Yale University Press, [1873–1876] 1990), 204. I have modified Arrowsmith's translation in one place. He had rendered *Knochenmenschen* as "human skeletons."

138. Scott Carlson, "A Crusade against Terrible Advising," *Chronicle of Higher Education* (August 4, 2020).

139. One recent study of faculty time found that faculty at a state university spend about 2.8% of their sixty-plus-hour workweek mentoring, and 4.7% of their time advising (the distinction is not explained). See Ziker et al., "Time Distribution of Faculty Workload at Boise State University" (2014), https://scholarworks .boisestate.edu/sspa_14/22. For a description of the study, see John Ziker, "The Long, Lonely Job of Homo Academicus," *Blue Review,* March 31, 2014, https:// www.boisestate.edu/bluereview/faculty-time-allocation/.

140. Ellen Bara Stolzenberg et al., *The Freshman Survey: National Norms Fall 2019* (Los Angeles: Higher Education Research Institute, UCLA, 2020), 46. This is the most recent year for which UCLA received enough data to create a weighted, nationally representative sample.

141. William Arrowsmith, "The Shame of the Graduate Schools: A Plea for a New American Scholar," *Harper's Magazine* 232, no. 1390 (1966): 55–56.

142. Arrowsmith, "Shame of the Graduate Schools," 55.

143. I am referring to Franz Kafka, "A Hunger Artist," trans. Willa Muir and Edwin Muir, in *The Metamorphosis and Other Stories* (New York: Shocken, 1948). The second quote is from Arrowsmith, "Shame of the Graduate Schools," 56.

144. Arrowsmith, "Shame of the Graduate Schools," 56.

145. Walker Percy, *The Moviegoer* (New York: Vintage, [1961] 1998), 13; William Arrowsmith, "Teaching and the Liberal Arts: Notes toward an Old Frontier," in *The Liberal Arts and Teacher Education: A Confrontation,* ed. Donald Bigelow (Lincoln: University of Nebraska Press, 1971), 12.

146. On the tenure track as shaper of identity, see William G. Tierney and Estela Mara Bensimon, *Promotion and Tenure: Community and Socialization in Academe*

(Albany: State University of New York Press, 1996); and Nathan F. Alleman, Justin J. Nelson, and Cara Cliburn Allen, "The Stigma of Tenure Denied: An Exploration of Individual and Institutional Implications," *Research in Higher Education* 60, no. 7 (2019). For fuller explorations of scholarly formation, see Bruce Wilshire, *The Moral Collapse of the University: Professionalism, Purity, Alienation* (Albany: State University of New York Press, 1990); and David Damrosch, *We Scholars: Changing the Culture of the University* (Cambridge, MA: Harvard University Press, 1995).

147. On this point, see Higgins, *The Good Life of Teaching*, especially, chap. 1.

148. This is a rough average. I am assuming the standard six years at the rank of assistant professor (ignoring the facts that some go up early or late, others reset some or all of their clock when changing institutions, and others still have to repeat the whole process after a negative decision). I am assuming an average of eight years at the rank of associate professor. I know of no broad national data on average time in rank for associate professors. A 2009 MLA study of language and literature professors found an average 7.4 years for the 145 full professors who responded to their survey. The average was 8.2 years for women, 8.2 years for faculty at Carnegie-designated doctoral institutions, 9.6 years for women in doctoral institutions, and 10.2 years for female professors of foreign languages in doctoral institutions (Committee on the Status of Women in the Profession, "Standing Still: The Associate Professor Survey" [Modern Language Association, 2009], https://www.mla.org/About -Us/Governance/Committees/Committee-Listings/Professional-Issues/Committee -on-Women-Gender-and-Sexuality-in-the-Profession/Standing-Still-The-Associate -Professor-Survey, 5-6).

149. Maxine Greene, *The Dialectic of Freedom* (New York: Teachers College Press, 1988), 14.

150. Deresiewicz, "The Neoliberal Arts," 26, summarizing the thesis of William Deresiewicz, *Excellent Sheep: The Miseducation of the American Elite and the Way to a Meaningful Life* (New York: Free Press, 2014).

151. Deresiewicz, "The Neoliberal Arts," 26.

152. Steven Pinker, quoted in Deresiewicz, "The Neoliberal Arts," 26.

153. Richard Rorty, *Contingency, Irony, and Solidarity* (Cambridge, UK: Cambridge University Press, 1989), 87n8.

154. This is what Jonathan Lear's calls "Kierkegaard's fundamental ironic question" (Jonathan Lear, *A Case for Irony* [Cambridge, MA: Harvard University Press, 2011], 12). Lear also offers a second, blunter form: "Among all Christians, is there a Christian?" These are distillations, not direct quotations, drawing not only on Kierkegaard but also on Plato who raises the "among" question repeatedly in relation to various vocations (I return to this in "Job Prospects" [see pp. 246–248 and p. 372n135]). Compare this line in Kierkegaard's papers: "in the midst of Christendom we seem to have forgotten what Christianity is" ("Selected Entries from Kierkegaard's Journals

and Papers Pertaining to *Philosophical Fragments*" in Johannes Climacus [Søren Kierkeg-aaard], *Philosophical Fragments* [c. 1842-1843], ed. and trans. Howard V. Hong and Edna H. Hong [Princeton, NJ: Princeton University Press, 1985], 220). Interestingly, a line in Emerson comes even closer: "In Christendom where is the Christian?" (Emerson, "Self-Reliance," 280).

155. This interpretive rendering of *Analects* §13.3 draws on a number of transla-tions as follows.

The master must be joking, as surely there are more pressing things to take care of. In a gloss of §13.3 in his introduction, Leys has Zilu ask, "Rectify the names? And that would be your first priority? Is this a joke?" (Confucius, *The Analects*, trans. Simon Leys, ed. Michael Nylan, Norton Critical Edition [New York: Norton, 2014], xvii [henceforth: Leys, *Analects*]). Similarly, Muller has "Are you serious? Why is this so important?" (*Analects of Confucius*, trans. A. Charles Muller [1990], §13.3, http://www.acmuller.net/con-dao/analects.html).

Zilu as a blundering associate and bumpkin. As Halberstad explains, while the Mas-ter "betrays some affection for" this disciple described in the *Analects* as "wild" (§11.18) he also scolds the "worldly, ambitious, and blundering Zilu" as inatten-tive (§11.25) and rash (§5.14 and §11.22) (Luke Halberstad "The Sage and His Associates: Kongzi and Disciples across Early Texts," in Leys, *Analects*, 179-180). I take "Bumpkin" from Ezra Pound's earthy translation: "You Bumpkin! Sprout!" (*Confucian Analects*, trans. Ezra Pound [London: Peter Owen Limited, 1933], 79 [henceforth: Pound, *Analects*]). The most common translation of the epithet is "boorish." I also like Brown's contemporary, "How Dense can you get!" (See Richard Brown, "The Analects of Confucius Book 13 New English Translation" [May 20, 2021], https://brownbeat.medium.com/the-analects-of-confucius-book -13-new-english-transla-585b9db725e8; [henceforth: Brown, *Analects*]).

A Junzi—an exemplary person—should keep his trap shut when he's out of his depth. This translation of *Junzi*, often rendered as "gentleman," comes from *The Analects of Confucius: A Philosophical Translation*, trans. Roger T. Ames and Henry Rose-mount Jr. (New York: Ballatine Books, 1998), 162 and passim [henceforth: Ames and Rosemount, *Analects*]. My free "should keep his trap shut when he's out of his depth," is inspired by Pound's earthy vernacular and the playful aggressiveness of Brown's "How dense?". Some translations bury the sting of rebuke in politesse, for example, Leys' stuffy and wordy, "Whereupon a gentleman is incompetent, thereupon he should remain silent" (Leys, *Analects*, 37). Eno is much more direct: "A junzi keeps silent about things he doesn't understand" (Robert Eno, "The Analects of Confucius: An Online Teaching Translation," Version 2.21 [2015], https://scholarworks.iu.edu/dspace/handle/2022/23420, pp. 66 [henceforth: Eno, *Analects*]).

When speech does not accord with reality, actions misfire . . . This is a condensed version of the Master's closing chain of reasoning, in which each conclusion is restated as the antecedent of the next conditional. I take "speech does not accord with reality" and "miss their mark" from Slingerland (Confucius, *Analects: With Selections from Traditional Commentaries*, trans. Edward Slingerland [Indianapolis: Hackett, 2003], 139 [henceforth, Slingerland, *Analects*]), "laws and punishments" from Ames and Rosemount (Ames and Rosemount, *Analects*, 162), and "wither" and "do not know where they stand" from Leys (Leys, *Analects*, 37). "Actions misfire" is my attempt to capture succinctly and dynamically the calamitous dyspraxia that results from the corruption of our vocabularies of meaning and purpose, praise and blame. Most renderings of this line are too passive, banal, bureaucratic, wordy: "nothing gets accomplished" (Confucius, *Analects*, trans. Annping Chin [New York: Penguin, 2014], 197 [henceforth: Chin, *Analects*]); "matters are not taken care of" (Ames and Rosemount, *Analects*, 162); "no affair can be effected" (Leys, *Analects*, 37); "cannot be followed out, or completed in action according to specifications" (*Pound, Analects*, 79). "If the names . . . do not match reality," Leys suggests in his gloss, "all human affairs disintegrate and their management becomes pointless and impossible" (Leys, *Analects*, xvii). In the closing line, the idiom Leys translates as "do not know where they stand" can also be rendered more literally as not knowing "where to place hand or foot" evoking a palpable experience of disorientation and disintegrity (for variations on the literal version, see Confucius, *The Analects (Lun Yü)*, trans. D. C. Lau [New York: Penguin, 1979], 118; Chin, *Analects*, 197; Eno, *Analects*, 66; and Brown, *Analects*).

156. On changing how you see rather than worrying about how you look, and for the line about "unflappable pretence," see Leys, *Analects*, 35-36 (§12.20). §4.9 says that the true "scholar sets his heart on the Way" (Leys, *Analects*, 11). §6.13 makes it clear that the term *shi* can range from the "noble scholar" to the "vulgar pedant" (Leys, *Analects*, 16). The contrast drawn in §6.18 comes through clearly in Eno's translation: "When patterned refinement prevails over substance, you have a clerk" (Eno, *Analects*, 27). The two terms used to describe the teachable student in §7.8 suggest not only desire but desperation to understand and articulate. Pound speaks of "zeal," Leys of fervor, Slingerland of struggle, Eno of agitation, Moran of "pent-up excitement," and Chin of "frenzy." See Pound, *Analects*, 42; Leys, *Analects*, 18; Slingerland, *Analects*, 66; Eno, *Analects*, 30; Patrick Moran, "Lun Yu, the *Analects* of Confucius A translation, divided by topic, of some of the more noteworthy passages," http://users.wfu.edu/moran/zhexuejialu/Analects_PEM.html, hyphen added to "pent-up"; and Chin, *Analects*, 100.

157. For further discussion of MacIntyre's theory of practice and account of bureaucratization, see "Job Prospects" (see pp. 225–228 and 365n58).

158. Nietzsche, *Unmodern Observations*. Nietzsche explores the thanatotic tendencies of the new scientized historicism in "History in the Service and Disservice of Life" (87–145). The critique of *Homo academicus* is developed especially in the two *Betrachtungen* translated by Arrowsmith. "We Classicists" is Nietzsche's notes toward a never completed "book on *the scholar's way of life*" (V, §187, p. 385, emphasis

original). And in one electric section (203–208) of "Schopenhauer as Educator," Nietzsche offers a devastating thirteen-point indictment of the scholarly type born of the new research university. Throughout his writings, Nietzsche continues to develop this distinction between deathly academicism and joyful wisdom. For example, he picks up his examination of "We Scholars" in §6 of *Beyond Good and Evil*, and extends his critique of the wissenschaftlicher's deadly seriousness in his discussion of asceticism in *On the Genealogy of Morals* (§3). In his introduction to "We Classicists" (in Nietzsche, *Unmodern Observations*, 315), Arrowsmith mentions the concentrations of "brilliant aphorisms" on classics and classicists in *Daybreak*, *Twilight of the Idols*, and *Human, All Too Human*.

159. "We Classicists" (V, §31), in Nietzsche, *Unmodern Observations*, 352.

160. Emerson, *Selected Journals: 1820–1842*, 312. Delbanco discusses this passage, which he quotes in two parts, in Andrew Delbanco, "The Decline and Fall of Literature," *New York Review of Books* 46, no. 17 (1999): 34.

161. Delbanco, "Decline and Fall of Literature," 34.

162. Delbanco, "Decline and Fall of Literature," 34.

163. Goethe to Schiller, December 19, 1798: "[Übrigens] ist mir Alles verhasst, was mich bloss belehrt, ohne meine Tätigkeit zu vermehren, oder unmittelbar zu beleben." Note that in the English translation of the correspondence, *unmittelbar* is mistranslated as "indirectly," a mistake that persists in many requotations (see Johann Wolfgang Goethe and Friedrich Schiller, *Correspondence between Schiller and Goethe, from 1794 to 1805*, trans. L. Dora Schmitz, vol. 2, 1798-1805 [London: G. Bell, 1890], 182).

164. "We Classicists" (V, §25), in Nietzsche, *Unmodern Observations*, 351, emphasis original.

165. Allan Bloom, *The Closing of the American Mind: How Higher Education Has Failed Democracy and Impoverished the Souls of Today's Students* (New York: Simon and Schuster, 1987).

166. Wilshire, *Moral Collapse of the University*, 66 and passim.

167. Quoted in Wilshire, *Moral Collapse of the University*, xix.

168. Wilshire, *Moral Collapse of the University*, 184.

169. Plato, *Republic*, 208 (514a).

170. Bruce Wilshire, "Body-Mind and Subconsciousness: Tragedy in Dewey's Life and Work," in *Philosophy and the Reconstruction of Culture: Pragmatic Essays after Dewey*, ed. John J. Stuhr (Albany: State University of New York Press, 1993), 261, 260. These are distinct passages, a full page apart. I have reversed their order.

171. For an interesting defense of this arrangement, see McClintock, *Homeless*. I have taken this formulation, that the university represents each major domain of

human experience twice, from him (see esp. p. 12). Not only does McClintock not seek to overcome this distinction between academic ("disinterested") and professional ("interested") knowledge, but also his argument is directed against one notable exception to this scheme, namely the university's failure to provide a separate home for the disinterested study of educational experience. In colleges of education, McClintock convincingly demonstrates, the academic and professional study of education have been fused, to the detriment of each. This approach, McClintock writes, "conflates the trappings of academic scholarship with substantial professional learning. As a result, schools of education too often nurture well neither excellence in scholarship nor prepossessing competence among licensed practitioners" (30). The best work in education combines intellectual rigor with the impetus of live social problems and a grounding in the texture of lived experience. But McClintock is right to suggest that there is too much "pseudo scholarship" (34) in education. The academic study of education is hamstrung by being cut off from the arts and sciences and from the constant pressure to produce studies that will solve immediate practical problems. The conflation also warps the preparation of practitioners as they orient their efforts to the acquisition of "a professional peacock-tail" (31n23). Though McClintock's premise, that the distinction between interested and disinterested inquiry is salutary, seems to clash with the Deweyan position I am developing here, his diagnosis of the Ed School muddle does not. As I will discuss shortly in the text, Dewey was clear that even worse than separating liberal and vocational studies is the sort of worst-of-both-worlds curricular compromises that temper the unimaginative with injections of the useless (see, e.g., Dewey, *Democracy and Education*, 257-8). Nor is it entirely clear to what extent McClintock's premise does ultimately clash with Dewey. McClintock wants to distinguish his pairing dis/interested from the common pure/applied binary and suggests that disinterestedness is not a steady state by which one implausibly floats above the fray but is rather a targeted refusal of the control of "inquiry by external interests, however putatively normative others may claim those to be" (McClintock, *Homeless*, 9n2). McClintock admits that further work is needed to distinguish his conception of disinterestedness from notions of purity and objectivity (2n5). In the end, his distinction may sidestep the dichotomies we are here considering: mind/body, thought/action, culture/utility, liberal/vocational.

172. John Dewey, "From Absolutism to Experimentalism" (1930), in *The Later Works of John Dewey, 1925–1953,* ed. Jo Anne Boydston, vol. 5, Electronic Ed. (Charlottesville, VA: Intelex Corp., [1985] 2003), 156. To be precise, what Dewey says is that "*Democracy and Education* was *for many years* that in which my philosophy, such as it is, was most fully expounded" (emphasis added). It is likely that it is *Experience and Nature* (the final revised version of which appeared in 1929) that Dewey thinks has since come to represent his fullest statement. For the argument that overcoming the liberal/vocational dichotomy is the central project of *Democracy and Education* see Higgins, *The Good Life of Teaching*, 140n3.

173. Dewey, *Democracy and Education*, 258.

174. Dewey, *Democracy and Education*, 259, 250.

175. John Dewey, *Art as Experience*, Perigee Trade Paperback ed. (New York: Penguin [1934] 2005), 54–55; cf. 169, 182–184, and 266–267.

176. This obviously assumes a single frame of reference. The earth is large compared with Boston and small compared to the Milky Way.

177. In a short essay from 1929, Dewey explores the limits of the law of the excluded middle when extended from formal ontology to the realm of actual existence. The claim that the door is either open or not open, Dewey points out, "overlooks two facts." First, closed (i.e., airtight) is an ideal limit; practically, closed always means "closed enough." Second, the best description of the door will often be that it is in the process of changing from one state to the other, that is, opening or closing. See John Dewey, "The Sphere of Application of the Excluded Middle," in *The Later Works of John Dewey, 1925–1953*, vol. 5, 201.

178. Dewey, *Democracy and Education*, 257, 259, 326, 255, 348, 133. One must be careful here, since Dewey develops four related concepts: the liberal, the vocational, the pseudo-liberal, and the pseudo-vocational. (And this applies to related dichotomies, such as culture/utility.) The first two are the true, compatible meanings. The latter two are the denatured, oppositional meanings. While he occasionally uses scare quotes to distinguish the pseudo concepts, he typically leaves it to the reader to infer from context which is which. And while Dewey devotes a whole chapter (Chap. 23) to teasing apart the vocational and pseudo-vocational, his remarks on liberal learning are scattered and often indirect. From context we can infer when he would count a trait as a genuine liberal value. For example, the quote about "deeper levels of meaning" (326) comes from Dewey's description of the "philosophical attitude." It is consonant with other characterizations of liberal aims, such as "deepening of intellectual insight" (258) and "personal appreciation of . . . meaning" (259). The argument for reading this as a description of liberal education is not only that the discipline of philosophy is one of the liberal arts. Dewey is referring to a broad disposition, one closer to a definition of liberal education itself: "thinking what the known demands of us, what responsive attitude it exacts" (326).

The last passage I quote is the only reference to "the cultivation of the self" in *Democracy and Education*. It occurs in a discussion of the rhetorical power of the word "disciplinary," which Dewey says has "screened and protected" curricular subjects from scrutiny. It would not even disqualify disciplines if one showed "that they were of no use in life or that they did not really contribute to the cultivation of the self" (133). Here we find Dewey applying his twofold test: vocational *and* liberal; utility *and* culture. We can thus add self-cultivation to our list of liberal education descriptors. While it is true that Dewey sometimes uses *self*, *refinement*, and *culture/cultural/cultivation* to signal the pseudo-liberal, he signals this with qualifiers. For example, in pseudo-liberal education "culture" is "associated with a purely private refinement, a cultivation of certain states and attitudes of consciousness, separate from either social direction or service" (306).

179. Dewey, *Democracy and Education*, 309–310. For a detailed discussion of this Deweyan idea of vocation as (mis)educative environment, see Higgins, *The Good Life of Teaching*, 113–130. The final two sections of "Job Prospects" explore how vocations widen and narrow experiential worlds.

180. In *Art as Experience*, Dewey uses the terms "anesthetic" five times (mixed in with five uses of "non-esthetic" and four of "unesthetic"). While he never explains his novel use of this term normally reserved for numbing agents (though he does use a visit to a dentist's chair as one of his examples of anesthetic experience [206]), the intention is clear. The term signals his intent to move art out of the museum, resituating the aesthetic in broader experiential terms. He describes our everyday experience as insensible, as unconscious as a stone bouncing down a hill (41). He introduces the idea of aesthetic experience through images of alertness and sensitivity, comparing us unfavorably to the animal that is "fully present, all there, in all of its actions: in its wary glances, its sharp sniffings, its abrupt cocking of ears. All senses are equally on the *qui vive*" (18).

181. This network of dichotomies is introduced in Chapter 19 of Democracy and Education. Dewey then examines specific dichotomies in greater detail in later chapters. Chapter 20, "Intellectual and Practical Studies," is devoted to the false opposition between knowing and doing (variously known as "theory and practice, intelligence and execution, knowledge and activity" [262]). Chapter 21 explores the curricular tension between humanism and naturalism that stems from the mind/world dichotomy. Chapter 22 focuses on the pitting of the individual against society. The "Opposition of Duty and Interest" is the subject of the second section of Chapter 26 (350–354).

182. Dewey, *Democracy and Education*, 253.

183. Rorty, "Education as Socialization and as Individualization," 121.

184. Jonathan Kozol has dedicated his career to chronicling such conditions, from *Death at an Early Age: The Destruction of the Hearts and Minds of Negro Children in the Boston Public Schools* (Boston: Houghton Mifflin, 1967) and *Savage Inequalities: Children in America's Schools* (New York: Crown, 1991) to *The Shame of a Nation: The Restoration of Apartheid Schooling in America* (New York: Crown, 2005). For example, on the neo-behaviorist pedagogy, the vacuous (no-collar) vocational curriculum, and the anesthetic architecture of high-poverty, majority minority schools, see Kozol, *Shame of a Nation*, chaps. 3, 4, and 7, respectively.

185. Erica Frankenberg, Chungmei Lee, and Gary Orfield, *A Multiracial Society with Segregated Schools: Are We Losing the Dream?* The Civil Rights Project, Harvard University (2003), 28, https://www.civilrightsproject.ucla.edu/research/k-12-education /integration-and-diversity/a-multiracial-society-with-segregated-schools-are -we-losing-the-dream/frankenberg-multiracial-society-losing-the-dream.pdf. The

situation has only grown worse since the time of this report. In 2021, 39.9% of Black students (2.9 million) and 40.9% of Hispanic students (5.7 million) attended schools enrolling 90% or more non-White students. See NCES Table 216.50, "Number and percentage distribution of public elementary and secondary school students, by percentage of non-White enrollment in the school and student's racial/ethnic group: Selected years, fall 1995 through fall 2021," https://nces.ed.gov/programs/digest/d22/tables/dt22_216.50.asp.

186. College Board, "Total Group SAT Suite of Assessments Annual Report (2022), https://reports.collegeboard.org/media/pdf/2022-total-group-sat-suite-of-assessments-annual-report.pdf.

187. David F. Labaree, "The Winning Ways of a Losing Strategy: Educationalizing Social Problems in the United States," *Educational Theory* 58, no. 4 (2008): 459.

188. Dewey, *Democracy and Education*, 257.

189. Dewey, *Democracy and Education*, 258.

190. Plato, *Republic*, 46 (368c–d).

191. The phrase "liberal arts" is a misleadingly literal translation of *artes liberales*, which would be more accurately rendered as "the disciplined practices befitting a free person." The Latin *ars* (and this also applies to its Greek conceptual cousin, *techne*) encompassed a wide range of practices, including some of what we would call arts, crafts, trades, professions, disciplines, and sciences. Despite the range of *ars*, some thinkers in the liberal arts tradition who wanted to emphasize the formal nature of these subjects instead choose the terms *disciplina* or *studium*. Thus, while Cicero and Varro are both talking about the same sort of practices, the former calls them *artes* and the latter *disciplinae*. Initially, there was also disagreement over which practices (and how many) ought to be counted as *liberales*. However, as the concept works its way from Hellenistic Rome to the Christian middle ages, a final roster of seven is derived. These *septem artes liberales* were famously divided into a group of three *artes sermocinales* pertaining to language and expression (the "trivium" of grammar, rhetoric, and dialectic) and a group of four *artes reales* dealing with mathematical subjects (the "quadrivium" of arithmetic, geometry, music, and astronomy). At some point, the equivocation between *artes* and *disciplinae* settles into a distinction between the *artes* of the trivium and the *disciplinae* of the quadrivium. Thus, the roots of the phrase "liberal arts and sciences" go back at least to Cassiodorus's *De Artibus ac Disciplinis Liberalium Litterarum* (c. 560 CE), though it now refers to a collection of nonapplied disciplines very different from the original seven.

192. Drama, theatrical performance, belongs here. My mention of dramatic literature as relatively disembodied referred to the practice of treating the play as text in literature classes.

193. Many have observed this fact. See for example, Lakoff and Johnson, *Metaphors We Live By*, 48.

194. Dewey, "From Absolutism to Experimentalism," 153.

195. This echoes a line of Dewey's describing the character of the compartmentalizer—who seeks to avoid "the strain of thought and effort needed to bring competing tendencies into a unity"—as "marked by stigmata resulting from this division" (Dewey, *Human Nature and Conduct*, 38).

196. Plato, *Republic*, 209 (515e).

197. John Dewey, *Psychology* (1887), in *The Early Works of John Dewey, 1882–1898*, ed. Jo Anne Boydston, vol. 2, Electronic Ed. (Charlottesville, VA: Intelex Corp., [1972] 2003), 43.

198. See, for example, Dewey, "Culture and Industry in Education" (1906); "The Bearings of Pragmatism upon Education" (1908); *Ethics* (1st ed., 1908), chaps. 17–18; *How We Think* (1st ed., 1910), chap. 15; and Dewey's contributions to the *Cyclopedia of Education* (1912–1913) on "Humanism and Naturalism," "Liberal Education," and "Theory and Practice" (these essays may be found in the *Middle Works of John Dewey*, vols. 3, 4, 5, 6, and 7 respectively).

199. Wilshire, "Body-Mind and Subconsciousness," 257.

200. John Dewey, "Statements to the Conference on Curriculum for the College of Liberal Arts" (1931), in *The Later Works of John Dewey, 1925–1953*, ed. Jo Anne Boydston, vol. 6, Electronic Ed. (Charlottesville, VA: Intelex Corp., [1985] 2003), 417.

201. Steven C. Rockefeller, *John Dewey: Religious Faith and Democratic Humanism* (New York: Columbia University Press, 1991), 312, 335. The characterization of this episode as a "breakdown" comes from F. M. Alexander's story of a client of his, an author who "after finishing his latest book . . . passed through a crisis described as a 'breakdown.'" As I describe in the discussion that follows, Dewey began bodywork with Alexander in 1916 just after the publication of *Democracy and Education*. Rockefeller's conjecture that the client in this story is Dewey seems a safe one.

202. See Rockefeller, *John Dewey*, 303–356; Thomas Dalton, *Becoming John Dewey: Dilemmas of a Philosopher and Naturalist* (Bloomington: Indiana University Press, 2002), chap. 5; Jay Martin, *The Education of John Dewey: A Biography* (New York: Columbia University Press, 2002), 285–293; Alan Ryan, *John Dewey and the High Tide of American Liberalism* (New York: W.W. Norton, 1995), chap. 5; Wilshire, "Body-Mind and Subconsciousness"; Jo Ann Boydston, "Introduction," in *The Poems of John Dewey*, ed. Jo Ann Boydston (Carbondale: Southern Illinois University Press, 1977). Boydston's research suggests that most of Dewey's poems were written between 1910 and 1918.

203. Max Eastman, "The Hero as Teacher," quoted in Dalton, *Becoming John Deweyde*, 113. Eastman writes that, after the polemics over the war, Dewey had "got into a state of tension that in most people would have been a state of illness." Eastman's hesitation to simply admit that Dewey was unwell physically and emotionally during this time is likely explained by his lionizing approach.

204. Ryan, *John Dewey and the High Tide of American Liberalism*, 187.

205. Sigmund Freud, "Mourning and Melancholia," trans. Shaun Whiteside, in *The Penguin Freud Reader*, ed. Adam Phillips (London: Penguin Books, [1917] 2006).

206. Again, this is Rockefeller quoting Alexander. See Rockefeller, *John Dewey*, 335.

207. John Dewey, "The Child's Garden" (#27), in *The Poems of John Dewey*, 19. In the discussion that follows in the text, I concentrate on the forty-six personal poems Boydston designates as "lyric." I should also note that I am allowing myself exceptions to two ordinarily wise methodological principles: (1) avoid psychobiography; (2) read lines in the context of their poems. Though Dewey had some talent and dedication to the craft of poetry, his brief burst of poetic activity can be profitably read as, in effect, a series of distilled, artful diary entries, and thus as windows into Dewey's mental state during the period. My aim is merely to adduce evidence of broad themes running through this group of poems as a whole.

208. John Dewey, Untitled (#8) ("Is this the End?") and Untitled (#6) ("I wake from the long, long night"), in *The Poems of John Dewey*, 6–7, 5–6.

209. John Dewey, "The Child's Garden" (#27), *The Poems of John Dewey*, 19. Other images of cold and ice appear in poems #3, #5, #13, # 14, and #25.

210. John Dewey, "Two Weeks" (#22), *The Poems of John Dewey*, 14–17. Thorny, desiccated landscapes also appear in poems #2, #3, #6, and #28.

211. John Dewey, "Two Births" (#46), *The Poems of John Dewey*, 30–31. Other images of duty, renunciation, and drudgery appear in poems #6, #13, #22, #40, and #43.

212. John Dewey, "Pulse in an Earthen Jar" (#38), *The Poems of John Dewey*, 25. The imagery of confinement, smothering, and suffocation reappears in poems #4, #6, #22, #23, and #28.

213. John Dewey, "Unfaith" (#89), *The Poems of John Dewey*, 66–67. For an account of the intertwined story of Dewey's poetry and his relationship with Yezierska, see Boydston, "Introduction."

214. Wilshire, "Body-Mind and Subconsciousness," 257. This is a revised and extended version of Wilshire, *Moral Collapse of the University*, chap. 8. He reworked this material again as Bruce Wilshire, *The Primal Roots of American Philosophy* (University Park: Pennsylvania State University Press, 2000), chap. 7. All three versions are worth consulting for their different emphases. It was Wilshire's daring and underappreciated *The Moral Collapse of the University* that first led me to the topic of Dewey's encounter with Alexander. As I have come to learn, we have others to thank for rescuing this important episode in Dewey's development from the consensus corpophobic narrative of Dewey's life and work that had ignored or trivialized it. Wilshire was building on a body of work beginning with the crucial early efforts of Frank Pierce Jones and Eric McCormack and continuing in the work of others such as Jo Ann Boydston and Alexander Murray. See Frank P. Jones, "The

Work of F. M. Alexander as an Introduction to Dewey's Philosophy of Education," *School and Society* 57 (1943); Eric David McCormack, "The Neglected Influence: Frederick Matthias Alexander and John Dewey" (PhD diss., University of Toronto, 1958); Frank P. Jones, "Letters from John Dewey in the Wessel Library, Tufts University," *Educational Theory* 17, no. 1 (1967); Frank P. Jones, "Dewey and Alexander," in *Freedom to Change: The Development and Science of the Alexander Technique* (London: Mouritz Books, [1976] 1997); and Jo Ann Boydston, "John Dewey and the Alexander Technique," *Alexander Review* 1 (1986). This piece by Boydston appeared in the third installment of a four-pamphlet series, *John Dewey and F.M. Alexander*, edited by Murray and published by the American Society for the Alexander Technique (AMSAT). See also Alexander Murray, "John Dewey and F.M. Alexander: 36 Years of Friendship" (The 1982 F.M. Alexander Memorial Lecture), published as an appendix to the book version of the McCormack thesis (Eric David McCormack, *The Neglected Influence: Frederick Matthias Alexander and John Dewey* [London: Mouritz, 2014]).

About the dating of Dewey's first session with Alexander: according to Jones, Dewey's lessons with F. M. Alexander continued "intermittently" throughout the 1920s and into the 1930s. From 1935 to 1941, he took lessons from the founder's brother, A. R. Alexander (see Jones, "Dewey and Alexander," 103–104). Dewey wrote to Jones that he had met Alexander as early as 1915, but this seems to be a misrecollection. McCormack has dated their first meeting to a dinner hosted by the Columbia Philosophy Department in 1916 (McCormack, "The Neglected Influence," 47).

215. Jones, "Dewey and Alexander," 97–98.

216. See Martin, *The Education of John Dewey*, 286.

217. Craig Cunningham takes a similar position, quoting from a letter to Joseph Ratner in which Dewey credits Alexander with "one of the most important discoveries that has been made in practical application of the unity of the mind-body principle" (John Dewey to Joseph Ratner [July 24, 1941], Letter #07140, in Harriet F. Simon et al., eds., volume 3: *1940–1953, The Correspondence of John Dewey, 1871–1952*, Electronic ed. [Charlottesville, VA: InteLex Corporation, 2008], quoted in Craig A. Cunningham et al., "Dewey, Women, and Weirdoes: Or, the Potential Rewards for Scholars Who Dialogue across Difference," *Education and Culture* 23, no. 2 [2007]: 51). Cunningham fixes on the phrase "practical application" in reaching his conclusion that Alexander had only a "marginal influence on Dewey's philosophy, more in the way of confirmation than in causal influence" (51). In the end, the most Cunningham will say about the Alexander technique is that it helped Dewey to "solidify," "ground," or "concret[ize]" ideas of Dewey's "already in place" (51). For Cunningham, the credit redounds not to Alexander (as Dewey himself would have it), but rather to Dewey, demonstrating the openness to new experience that he had "always displayed," showing his willingness to listen to those outside the academy and engage with heterodox ideas (51). Cunningham misses the mark here in two ways.

First, we might retort, "Where were these ideas 'in place' before they became grounded in concrete experience?" That is, Cunningham seems to lapse into an idealism precisely as he attempts to assess the role of Alexander in helping Dewey complete his overcoming of mind/body dualism! As Dewey will go on to say in *Art as Experience*, ideas require a medium. Dewey himself supplies a better word than "application," "confirmation," or even "grounding" when he says (in the collaborative auto/biography he prepared with his daughters for the 1939 Library of Living Philosophers volume in his honor), "My theories of mind-body, of the coordination of the active elements of the self and of the place of ideas in inhibition and control of overt action required contact with the work of F.M. Alexander and in later years his brother, A.R., to transform them into *realities*" ("Biography of John Dewey," ed. Jane M. Dewey, in *The Philosophy of John Dewey*, The Library of Living Philosophers, vol. 1, 50th anniv. ed., ed. Paul A. Schilpp and Lewis E. Hahn [New York: Open Court (1939) 1989], 45, emphasis added). Incidentally, it is striking how Martin edits this to read, "My theories of mind-body, of the coordination of the active elements of the self and of the place of ideas in inhibition and control of overt action required [for confirmation] contact with the work of F.M. Alexander" (Martin, *The Education of John Dewey*, 286).

Second, I think Cunningham misses the key point that it is, in significant part, the work with Alexander that restores Dewey's openness to new experience during a period in which the flow of his experience had become clogged, in which he had become a "choked up fountain" and experienced a "hunger . . . to be" (John Dewey, "Two Weeks" [#22] and Untitled [#4] ["Generations of stifled worlds reaching out"], in *The Poems of John Dewey*, 14–17, 4–5). The Dewey who meets Alexander in the late teens is the Dewey who describes himself as "penned" in a narrow present between "a past with a closing door" and the "tight shut door of the future," begging God for "A little hope that things which were / Again may living stir—/ A future with an op'ning door" (see John Dewey, Untitled [#8] ["Is this the End?"], in *The Poems of John Dewey*, 6–7).

218. Rockefeller, *John Dewey*, 343.

219. Rockefeller, *John Dewey*, 313, 339.

220. Rockefeller does perpetuate the myth of a kind and gullible Dewey taken in by a huckster when he says that Dewey "latches" onto Alexander's theories as an answer to the world's problems. See Rockefeller, *John Dewey*, 341.

221. This was the reaction of Ella Flagg Young, who had not seen Dewey for over a decade. See Martin, *Education of John Dewey*, 286.

222. Jones, "Dewey and Alexander," 97.

223. John Dewey to Joseph Ratner [July 24, 1941].

224. Regarding Alexander's breakthrough, Dewey writes, "The act must come before the thought, and a habit before an ability to evoke the thought at will. Ordinary psychology reverses the actual state of affairs" (Dewey, *Human Nature and Conduct*, 30–31). For the full Alexander-inspired section, see 28–35.

225. McCormack, "The Neglected Influence," 159–160. Jones begins his account of Dewey and Alexander with passages from *Art as Experience* (1934) and *Experience and Education* (1938) that also show a subtle but clear Alexandrian residue (Jones, "Dewey and Alexander," 94).

226. John Dewey, *Experience and Nature* (Lasalle, IL: Open Court, 1929). Though Dewey significantly revised and expanded his Carus lectures (December 1922) for publication in 1925, he was not satisfied, especially with the book's opening chapter, which is completely revised in the 1929 edition.

227. Dewey, *Experience and Nature*, 246.

228. John Dewey, "Introduction," in F. M. Alexander, *Use of the Self* (London: Orion Books, [1932] 2001), 11.

229. Wilshire, "Body-Mind and Subconsciousness," 259.

230. John Dewey, "The Child and the Curriculum" (1902), in *The Middle Works of John Dewey, 1899–1924*, ed. Jo Anne Boydston, vol. 2, Electronic Ed. (Charlottesville, VA: Intelex Corp., [1978] 1996), 273; Dewey, *Democracy and Education*, 257. In this 1902 essay, Dewey had already laid down the pattern for his later treatment of the liberal/vocational dichotomy. Instead of enduring the "effort of thought" needed to rework the terms of the debate between the "child" (freedom, relevance, initiative, progress) and the "subject matter" (discipline, rigor, guidance, conservation), we argue the extremes until finally retreating into a "maze of inconsistent compromise" (Dewey, "The Child and the Curriculum," 273 and 277). Fourteen years later, Dewey will speak of the curriculum as an "inconsistent mixture," a worst-of-both-worlds compromise between the pseudo-liberal and the pseudo-vocational (Dewey, *Democracy and Education*, 257).

231. Wilshire, "Body-Mind and Subconsciousness," 260.

232. Plato, *Republic*, 209 (515e).

233. Dewey, *Art as Experience*, 37. This is the passage I mentioned in note 225, used by Jones as an epigraph.

234. Wilshire, *Moral Collapse of the University*, 178.

235. Wilshire, *Moral Collapse of the University*, 182.

236. Jones, "Dewey and Alexander," 97. Jones is relating what Alexander told him about Dewey's debut. "Drugged with thinking" is a direct quote; the other bit a paraphrase.

237. Wilshire, "Body-Mind and Subconsciousness," 260.

238. John Dewey, "Introduction," 10.

239. John Dewey, "Introduction," 10.

240. John Dewey, "Introduction," 10.

241. John Dewey, "Preoccupation with the Disconnected," *Alexander Journal* 3 (1964): 12. This is described as "reprinted from a talk that Dewey gave to the NY Academy of Medicine." The typescript for this 1927 talk, "Body and Mind," is lost. However, it was published in three close variations (see "Textual Commentary," in *The Later Works of John Dewey*, vol. 3, 444-445). "Preoccupation with the Disconnected" contains both abridgments and material not appearing in any of these three versions, including the shout out to Alexander that I quote in the text. It is not clear what version of Dewey's talk the *Alexander Journal* worked from.

242. Wilshire, *Moral Collapse of the University*, 183. Cf. Bruce Wilshire, "The Moral Collapse of the University," *Kettering Review* 30, no. 1 (2012): 20, where he credits C. S. Lewis' recovery of this ancient Greek idea.

243. John Dewey, "Introduction," 12. The concept of the "means whereby" is central to the Alexander Technique. For Alexander's definition, see Alexander, *Use of the Self*, 41n. Richard Shusterman offers this useful gloss:

> Alexander concluded that a systematic method of careful somatic awareness, analysis, and control was needed for improving self-knowledge and self-use: a method to discern, localize, and inhibit the unwanted habits, to discover the requisite bodily postures or movements (the indispensable "means whereby") for best producing the desired action or attitude, and finally to monitor and master their performance through "conscious control" until ultimately a better (i.e. more effective and controllable) habit could be established to achieve the willed end of action. The elaborate method he developed—emphasizing heightened somatic awareness and conscious control through inhibition, indirection, and focus on "the means whereby" as crucial, provisional ends—became the famed Alexander Technique. (Richard Shusterman, "Dewey's Somatic Philosophy," *Revue Internationale de Philosophie* 245, no. 3 [2008]: 301; parenthetical citations removed).

244. Charles Sanders Peirce, "Private Thoughts—Principally on the Conduct of Life," *The Writings of Charles S. Peirce—A Chronological Edition*, Electronic Edition, ed Nathan Houser et al., vol. 1: 1857-1866 (Charlottesville, VA: InteLex Corporation, 2003), 6 (§XLI [September 16, 1856]). Peirce then answers his question with a single word: beauty.

245. The Pugh translation of the Exercises is available online at http://spex .ignatianspirituality.com/SpiritualExercises/Puhl. This quotation is from the first of the "Introductory Observations" (or "Annotations" as they are known in other versions). Pugh also supplies the *Monumenta* marginal numbers. This is §001.

246. Ignatius (Pugh trans.), *Spiritual Exercises*, §020. It is worth noting that one is recommended to undertake Ignatian spiritual exercises with a guide.

247. Peirce, "Private Thoughts," 6 (§XLI).

248. In "Wide Awake," I explore the brilliant life of Black Mountain College, an educational community built around just such a reunion between general and aesthetic education.

249. Murray Sperber, *Beer and Circus: How Big-Time College Sports Has Crippled Undergraduate Education* (New York: Henry Holt and Company, 2001).

250. I have trustworthy secondhand knowledge of a recent small gathering of philosophers (and historians) of education, in which one philosopher (let's call him V) had the temerity to suggest that philosophy might still be linked in some way to its etymological meaning, the love of wisdom. At this, several of his colleagues broke into derisive snorts and clubby laughter, leading the kind one in the group to smooth things over by remarking, "You know we love you, V, but you're crazy."

NEW STUDENT ORIENTATION

1. Oakeshott, "The Idea of a University," in *The Voice of Liberal Learning: Michael Oakeshott on Education*, ed. Timothy Fuller (New Haven, CT: Yale University Press, [1950] 1989), 100.

2. Michael Oakeshott, "On Arriving at a University," in *What Is History? And Other Essays*, ed. Luke O'Sullivan (Exeter, UK: Imprint Academic, 2004). Based on press clippings found in the same file, O'Sullivan dates the text, speculatively, to 1961. A reproduction of the typescript, available online (https://manwithoutqualities .files.wordpress.com/2019/08/scanned20from20a20xerox20multifunction20prin ter-85.pdf), shared with Leslie Marsh by Frank Minogue, shows that the title was supplied by Oakeshott. Minogue dated it 1963.

3. I return to the theme of reorientation in An Allegory of Arrival in "Wide Awake."

4. Oakeshott, "On Arriving at a University," 333.

5. Oakeshott, "On Arriving at a University," 333.

6. Oakeshott, "A Place of Learning" [1975], in *The Voice of Liberal Learning*, 24.

7. Oakeshott, "On Arriving at a University," 334.

8. As Skeffington relates, immediately upon his arrival in 1950, Oakeshott consolidated the loose political science faculty into a functioning Department of Government (only formally instituted in 1962), remaining the formal or de facto head until his retirement in 1968 (see Daniel Skeffington, "The Orator and the Conversationalist: From Laski to Oakeshott, 1921–1965," in *Political Science at the LSE: A History of the Department of Government, from the Webbs to Covid*, ed. Cheryl Schonhardt-Bailey and Gordon Bannerman [London: Ubiquity Press, 2021], 64, 68).

9. I refer to the concepts of the "learning society" and "lifelong learning" which spitshine with an ounce of eduspeak the turds of late capitalism (globalization, "human capital," reification, governmentality, the gig economy). For an Arendtian critique of "the learning society," see Jan Masschelein, "The Discourse of the

Learning Society and the Loss of Childhood," *Journal of Philosophy of Education* 35, no. 1 (2001). For a Lukacsian critique of lifelong learning, see René V. Arcilla, *Wim Wenders's Road Movie Philosophy: Education without Learning* (London: Bloomsbury, 2020), chap. 5. For a Foucauldian critique of the entrepreneurial self and the university of human capital, see Wendy Brown, *Undoing the Demos: Neoliberalism's Stealth Revolution* (Brooklyn, NY: Zone Books, 2015).

10. David Blacker, *The Falling Rate of Learning and the Neoliberal Endgame* (Winchester, UK: Zero Books, 2013), 53. Michael Walzer, *Spheres of Justice: A Defense of Pluralism and Equality* (New York: Basic Books, 1983). I unpack Walzer's value-pluralistic account in "Job Prospects" (see pp. 228–233).

11. Oakeshott, "On Arriving at a University," 336.

12. Oakeshott, "On Arriving at a University," 333–334.

13. From 1957 to 1967, LSE's director was Sydney Caine: "Sydney Caine, a civil servant who had decidedly positive views about the market" (Michael Cox, "Red Flag over Houghton Street? The Radical Tradition at LSE—Myth, Reality, Fact," *LSE History* blog, January 16, 2019, https://blogs.lse.ac.uk/lsehistory/2019/01/16/red-flag-over-houghton-street-the-radical-tradition-at-lse-myth-reality-fact/).

14. For a critique of the connoisseur, see my discussion of Gadamer in "Soul Action" (pp. 33–35). In "Job Prospects," I discuss how liberal learning can degenerate into the hoarding of treasure (see pp. 218–220). My dig at the graduate student is certainly not to disparage critical museum studies and Marxian cultural theory. Who could deny the force of Benjamin's famous, searing indictment:

> Whoever has emerged victorious participates to this day in the triumphal procession in which current rulers step over those who are lying prostrate. According to traditional practice, the spoils are carried in the procession. They are called "cultural treasures," and a historical materialist views them with cautious detachment. For in every case these treasures have a lineage which he cannot contemplate without horror. They owe their existence not only to the efforts of the great geniuses who created them, but also to the anonymous toil of others who lived in the same period. There is no document of civilization which is not at the same time a document of barbarism. And just as such a document is never free of barbarism, so barbarism taints the manner in which it was transmitted from one hand to another (Walter Benjamin, "On the Concept of History," in *Selected Writings*, vol. 4, 1938–1940, ed. Howard Eiland and Michael W. Jennings [Cambridge, MA: Harvard University Press, 2003], §VII, 391–392).

Nonetheless, I stand by my claim that a purely suspicious stance forecloses aesthetic experience. Following Said, I favor a "contrapuntal" approach that braids hermeneutics of retrieval and suspicion (Edward W. Said, *Culture and Imperialism* [New York: Vintage Books, 1994], 66 and passim; compare the closing line of the section on *Mansfield Park* [97]).

15. Fishman and Gardner would approve of Oakeshott's intervention. Among their recommendations to address the cynical transactional mindset prevalent among today's students is a process of continuous "onboarding" that explains "this is what college is about" (Wendy Fishman and Howard Gardner, *The Real World of College: What Higher Education Is and What It Can Be* [Cambridge, MA: MIT Press, 2022], 246, emphasis removed).

16. Timothy Fuller, "Introduction," in Oakeshott, *The Voice of Liberal Learning*, 10; Oakeshott, "A Place of Learning," 27.

17. Oakeshott, "A Place of Learning," 26.

18. Oakeshott, "A Place of Learning," 25, 26, 26.

19. Michael Oakeshott, "Learning and Teaching," in *The Voice of Liberal Learning*, 62.

20. Oakeshott, "A Place of Learning," 25.

21. In this respect, Oakeshott's theory of practice anticipates MacIntyre's. On MacIntyre's theory of practice, see "Job Prospects" (pp. 225–228 and 365n58).

22. Oakeshott, "Learning and Teaching," 62.

23. Oakeshott, "A Place of Learning," 24.

24. Michael Oakeshott, "The Definition of a University," *Journal of Educational Thought* 1, no. 3 (1967): 130.

25. Michael Oakeshott, "The Voice of Poetry in the Conversation of Mankind," in *Rationalism in Politics and Other Essays*, ed. Timothy Fuller (Indianapolis, IN: Liberty Press [1959] 1991), 496.

26. Oakeshott, "Voice of Poetry in the Conversation of Mankind," 496.

27. Maxine Greene, "Teaching for Openings," in *Releasing the Imagination: Essays on Art, Education, and Social Change* (San Francisco: Jossey-Bass, 1995), 115.

28. Oakeshott gestures toward this problem of circularity in lines such as, "the learner is animated, not by the inclinations he brings with him, but by intimations of excellence and aspirations he has never yet dreamed of" (Michael Oakeshott, "Education: The Engagement and Its Frustration" [1972], in *The Voice of Liberal Learning*, 69). "Intimation" is an important term for Oakeshott, signaling his view that ethical and political understanding is largely tacit (see Michael Oakeshott, "Political Education," in *Rationalism in Politics* where he first staked out this position, and especially his postscript about his use of the term).

However, the question is not merely whether we can verbalize the novel value structure but how it is exactly that we can coherently value a new structure of value, how we can aspire to a life animated by different aspirations. This question is at the center of several recent rich books: Talbot Brewer, *The Retrieval of Ethics* (Oxford: Oxford University Press, 2011); L. A. Paul, *Transformative Experience* (Oxford: Oxford University Press, 2014); and Agnes Callard, *Aspiration: The Agency of Becoming* (Oxford:

Oxford University Press, 2018). There is also a line of interesting recent work on the possibility of epiphanic moral conversion: Mark E Jonas, "Education for Epiphany: The Case of Plato's *Lysis*," *Educational Theory* 65, no. 1 (2015); Kristján Kristjánsson, "Epiphanic Moral Conversions: Going beyond Kohlberg and Aristotle," in *Flourishing as the Aim of Education: A Neo-Aristotelian View* (London: Routledge, 2020); Douglas W. Yacek and Kevin Gary, "Transformative Experience and Epiphany in Education," *Theory and Research in Education* 18, no. 2 (2020); and Kevin Gary and Drew Chambers, "Cultivating Moral Epiphanies," *Educational Theory* 71, no. 3 (2021).

As I discuss in A New Organ in "Job Prospects," vocational discernment is a species of this problem. Like Oakeshott (and Brewer), my strategy is the hermeneutic one of embracing the circularity: intimations lead to an initial superficial engagement, which deepens our understanding of the practice's animating goods, which deepens our engagement, and so on.

29. I explore these difficulties in "Wide Awake" (see pp. 124–145). On the ethics of transformative education, see Douglas W. Yacek, "Should Education Be Transformative?" *Journal of Moral Education* 49, no. 2 (2020).

30. Plato, *Republic*, trans. C. D. C. Reeve (Indianapolis, IN: Hackett, [c. 380 BCE] 2004), 209 (515c–516a).

31. Plato, *Republic*, 209 (515e).

32. Jerome S. Bruner and Leo Postman, "On the Perception of Incongruity: A Paradigm," *Journal of Personality* 18, no. 2 (1949).

33. Bruner and Postman, "On the Perception of Incongruity," 221. Nearly all of the participants (27 out of 28) demonstrated this strategy of "perceptual denial" at least once (213).

34. Bruner and Postman, "On the Perception of Incongruity," 216. Fifty percent of the participants displayed a compromise reaction to the trick red cards; 11% to the trick black ones (216, 217). One of the compromise reactions elicited from a trick black card was that the card was alternately black and red (217).

35. Bruner and Postman, "On the Perception of Incongruity," 214. This experience of "disruption" occurred in 4% of the prerecognition responses of sixteen out of twenty-eight participants (218).

36. Bruner and Postman, "On the Perception of Incongruity," 218.

37. John Donne, "Eclogue. 1613. December 26," in *The Complete Poetry and Selected Prose of John Donne*, ed. Charles M. Coffin (New York: The Modern Library, 2001), 183–184.

38. In the Transformative Educational Studies Program in the Lynch School of Education and Human Development at Boston College, we devote an entire course, The Educational Conversation, to the sort of reorientation Oakeshott attempted in 1961, assigning, among other things Oakeshott's "On Arriving at a University."

Given the nature of his themes (1961 going on 1861) and his style (simultaneously conversational, learned, and lyrical) we have been pleasantly surprised by the enthusiasm of our student's response to Oakeshott's anti-orientation speech.

39. Oakeshott, "Work and Play" [c. 1960], in *What Is History?*, 313.

40. Oakeshott, "Education: The Engagement and Its Frustration," 69.

41. Oakeshott, "On Arriving at a University," 337.

42. Oakeshott, "On Arriving at a University," 336.

43. Oakeshott, "Work and Play," 308.

44. Oakeshott, "Work and Play," 308.

45. Oakeshott, "Work and Play," 309.

46. Oakeshott, "Work and Play," 308.

47. Oakeshott, "The Idea of a University," 102. (The same line appears in the longer work, of which this is a distillation and extension (Michael Oakeshott, "The Universities" [1949], in *The Voice of Liberal Learning*, 128). Oakeshott's terminology shifts over time as he draws this tripartite distinction: (A) the grind, (B) mere release from the grind, and (C) escape from the false binary into a third space. In these early essays (1949–1950), he uses (A) work, (B) play, and (C) *skholê*/leisure/interval. A decade later, in "Work and Play" (c. 1960), he uses (A) work, (B) rest/recreation/holiday/"corruptions of play" and, (C) play/*skholê*/leisure (Oakeshott, "Work and Play," 313). A year or so later, as we saw, Oakeshott decided that "leisure" was a "lame" translation for *skholê*. In "Education: The Engagement and Its Frustration" (1972), Oakeshott now not only reinforces the contrast between *skholê* and leisure, but play has been downgraded back to the B-term (Oakeshott, "Education: The Engagement and Its Frustration," 69).

Thinkers such as Oakeshott who want to retrieve ideas that fall between the cracks of our current concepts have no perfect rhetorical option. Ancient terms may be overly defamiliarizing—sealing the author's meaning in a display case at the Bodleian—and risk hiding the fact that the term represents not the displaced worldview itself but our present understanding of what we think we have lost. That said, to eschew foreign/technical terms is to risk that the reader too quickly assimilates the untimely idea to current thinking; and it forces authors to juggle multiple meanings of the same term (as we see in Oakeshott's ambiguous uses of "leisure" and "play"). John Dewey, Josef Pieper, and Michael Walzer faced the same rhetorical dilemma. Dewey avoids archaic terms but then offers the reader the confusing task of disambiguating two meaning of "liberal," when defined in opposition to or as complementary with the "vocational" (see John Dewey, *Democracy and Education: An Introduction to the Philosophy of Education* (New York: Macmillan Company, 1916), chaps. 19 and 23). Pieper does not hesitate to incorporate archaic terms (e.g., *ratio/intellectus, artes liberales/serviles, banausos, acedia*). However, after introducing the ancient distinctions *a/skholia* and *neg/otium*, he uses "leisure" to name both the concept he seeks to retrieve and its modern debasement, bringing out the untimeliness of the older meaning by repeating Aristotle's dictum that "we are not-at-leisure in order to be at-leisure" (see Josef Pieper, "Leisure, the Basis of Culture," trans. Gerald Malsbary, in *Leisure: The Basis of Culture* [South Bend, IN: St. Augustine's Press, (1948) 1998], esp. chap. 1). By contrast, even while Walzer notes their roots in older notions of *skholê* and sabbath, and in ambiguities in the meaning of "rest," Walzer sees the two main, modern structurations of free time, the vacation and the holiday, as spheres in which genuine goods are distributed and pursued (see Walzer, *Spheres of Justice*, chap. 7).

48. Oakeshott, "The Idea of a University," 101, emphasis added. Oakeshott uses a variety of terms to evoke this key concept in his educational writings: interval, interim, *skholê*, leisure, play, detachment. For his variations on this theme, see Oakeshott, "The Universities," 126–129; Oakeshott, "The Idea of a University," 101–103; Oakeshott, "Work and Play," 309–310; Oakeshott, "On Arriving at a University," 334–337; Oakeshott, "The Definition of a University," 140–141; Oakeshott, "Education: The Engagement and Its Frustration," 69, 71–72, and 93; Oakeshott, "A Place of Learning," 24, 41.

49. Oakeshott, "The Universities," 125.

50. Oakeshott, "The Idea of a University," 101.

51. Oakeshott, "The Idea of a University," 102; cf. Oakeshott, "The Universities," 128.

52. Oakeshott, "On Arriving at a University," 335.

53. Oakeshott likes to stress the continuity between the modern primary schools and older institutions such as monastery schools. He says, for example, that the primary school near his rural Dorset home "had a continuous history from the 12th century" (Michael Oakeshott, Letter to Kevin Williams [June 23, 1983], published as "A Letter from Michael Oakeshott," *Newsletter*, Philosophy of Education Society of Great Britain [June 2016]: 11; cf. Oakeshott, "Education: The Engagement and Its Frustration," 71). Or compare his remark that, despite the apparent "experimentalism" of the school he attended, his headmaster's "intention was to centre himself pretty firmly in the sort of grammar school that had been knocking around England for centuries and from which the Victorian public schools emerged" (quoted in Robert Grant, *Oakeshott*, Thinkers of Our Time [London: Claridge, 1990], 120). However, the discontinuities are more instructive. Schools of various sorts have existed for millennia, but mass, compulsory *schooling* is a novel educational modality, arising in the late eighteenth/early nineteenth centuries, born of and contributing to a period of rapid social change marked by the spread of literacy, changing conceptions of childhood, the rise of the nation-state, and the advent of industrialization. Thus, Kieran Egan observes the irony in naming this modern institution "school" (*Schule*; *école*, *escuela*, *scuola*, etc.), a word derived from the Greek *skholê*, meaning freedom from the grind. The irony is that "the

new school was a place to which all children had to go in order to be equipped for productive work." "Calling the new institutions 'schools,'" Egan suggests, "helped to disguise their important differences from the older *skholê*-inspired institutions" (Kieran Egan, *The Future of Education: Reimagining Our Schools from the Ground Up* [New Haven, CT: Yale University Press, 2008], 6). As E. P. Thompson nicely illustrates, the shift in capitalist production from an artisan-merchant to an industrial mode required inculcating new relationships to time and work, a task explicitly handed to the new schools (see E. P. Thompson, "Time, Work-Discipline, and Industrial Capitalism," *Past and Present* 38, no. 1 [1967]: 84–85).

54. Oakeshott, "On Arriving at a University," 333.

55. Oakeshott, "The Definition of a University," 140.

56. Oakeshott, "Work and Play," 309. With the phrase "getting and spending," Oakeshott is referring to the Wordsworth poem, "The World Is Too Much With Us," which I discuss in "Job Prospects" (see pp. 253 and 256).

57. Oakeshott, "The Idea of a University," 101.

58. Oakeshott's earliest published piece on education was "The Universities" (1949). His last was "A Place of Learning" (1975). There is also a manuscript tentatively dated to 1948 that appeared only posthumously (see Oakeshott, "The Voice of Conversation in the Education of Mankind"). There was also a short article he coauthored in high school: Michael Oakeshott and H. Howe, "An Experiment in the Teaching of History," *Georgian (the magazine of St. George's School)* 14 (1919).

59. Oakeshott, "The Definition of a University," 139.

60. On detaching/detachment, see Oakeshott, "The Universities," 130; Oakeshott, "The Definition of a University," 140; Oakeshott, "Education: The Engagement and Its Frustration," 69; and Oakeshott, "A Place of Learning," 24, 39. On "seclusion," see Oakeshott, "A Place of Learning," 24, 26, 34, 41, 42. On places of learning as "sheltered," see Oakeshott, "A Place of Learning," 24, 27.

61. Oakeshott, "A Place of Learning," 24. That the tower is not ivory does not mean that universities are passive puppets of political-economy. As Sheldon Rothblatt shows in his interesting study of the evolution of the University of Cambridge in the Victorian era, a university "may draw upon its own history, heritage and ideals to interpret the demands upon it in a unique and unexpected way" (see Sheldon Rothblatt, *The Revolution of the Dons: Cambridge and Society in Victorian England* [Cambridge, UK: Cambridge University Press (1968) 1981], 26). Indeed, that universities serve social functions is compatible with the claim that universities differ from other segments of society. On one reading, their function is precisely to serve as exceptions, as hedges against our typical amnesia, myopia, and monomania. Thus, universities might be thought to preserve what would otherwise be forgotten, nurture alternate modes of seeing and describing, reanimate goods lost in the pursuit of business as usual. This points to a central ambivalence in the literature

on the corporatization of the university. Are we living through an era in which we finally recognize that the university is essentially an instrument of power and privilege? In this case, the university's aspiration to these forms of independence is simply dangerous false consciousness. Or are we living through the transformation of the university from one set of social functions (including perhaps the nurturing of what Nietzsche called "untimely considerations") to a new portfolio (socializing the costs and risks, but not the profit, of corporate R&D; laundering the inequities of educational tracking; etc.)? I return to these questions in "Public Hearing." Nietzsche originally planned to write thirteen *Unzeitgemässe Betrachtungen*. For the four he completed and a set of careful notes for a fifth, see Friedrich Nietzsche, *Unmodern Observations: Unzeitgemässe Betrachtungen*, ed. William Arrowsmith (New Haven, CT: Yale University Press, [1874] 1990).

62. I return to the question of scale in "Wide Awake" (see pp. 112–113).

When Oakeshott began college in 1920, there were 33,004 undergraduates enrolled full time in the UK. By 1950, when Oakeshott began writing on education, that number had increased 136%, to 78,064. By the time he published his final statement on education, "A Place of Learning," in 1975, the number had increased another 168%, to 209,078. At the time of his death in 1990, the full-time undergraduate enrollment in the UK was 290,285, representing a 780% increase from the time Oakeshott began college (see Vincent Carpentier, "Historical Statistics on the Funding and Development of the UK University System, 1920–2002" [UK Data Service, 2004], http://doi.org/10.5255/UKDA-SN-4971-1). For comparison, the UK population grew only 29% (44 million to 57 million) during these same seventy years. Another point of comparison: in the US, in 1920, 4.7% of eighteen-to-twenty-four-year-olds were enrolled in institutions of higher education; in 1950, 14.3%; in 1975, 40.3%; in 1990, 51.1% (Thomas D. Snyder, ed., *120 Years of American Education: A Statistical Portrait* [Washington, DC: National Center for Education Statistics, US Department of Education, 1993], 76–77, table 24).

63. Oakeshott, "The Definition of a University," 139.

64. Oakeshott, "Education: The Engagement and Its Frustration," 67.

65. Oakeshott, "The Idea of a University," 102; cf. Oakeshott, "The Universities," 128.

66. Oakeshott, "The Universities," 125.

67. Oakeshott's class anxieties bubble up in a series of troubling tropes in which he likens the widening of college admissions to invasion, flooding, and looting. On flooding and looting, see Oakeshott, "The Universities," 129–130. On invasion/invaders, see Oakeshott, "Education: The Engagement and Its Frustration," 71, 76; and Oakeshott, "The Definition of a University," 141.

Oakeshott's elusive, category-defying views make him notoriously difficult to place on the political map. He has been claimed not only by conservatives but also by progressives (Richard Rorty), radicals (Chantal Mouffe), and would-be anarchists

(Richard Flathman). He is "a refusenik of modern life" (Fawcett), defends modernity (Podosik), and anticipates postmodernism (Rorty again). He is said to combine: a celebration of the experience of individuality with a critique of individualism (Franco); both Whig and romantic elements of liberalism (Podosik again); and "a communitarian account of the agent with a liberal account of the republic" (Rabin). The supposed "high priest of modern Conservatism" (Fairlie) was, in 1938, the first Cambridge don to lecture on Marx, with whom he went on to have a critical but far from dismissive relationship. See Richard Rorty, "Review (Michael Oakeshott, *On Human Conduct*; Roberto Mangabiera Unger, *Knowledge & Politics*)," *Social Theory and Practice* 4, no. 1 (1976): 114; Rorty, *Contingency, Irony, and Solidarity*, 57–60; Chantal Mouffe, "Radical Democracy: Modern or Postmodern," in *The Return of the Political* (London: Verso, 1993), 16; Richard E. Flathman, *Reflections of a Would-Be Anarchist: Ideals and Institutions of Liberalism* (Minneapolis: University of Minnesota Press, 1998); Edmund Fawcett, *Liberalism: The Life of an Idea*, 2nd ed. (Princeton, NJ: Princeton University Press, 2018), 314; Efraim Podoksik, *In Defence of Modernity: Vision and Philosophy in Michael Oakeshott* (Exeter, UK: Imprint Academic, 2003), 159; Paul Franco, *The Political Philosophy of Michael Oakeshott* (New Haven, CT: Yale University Press, 1990), 205–206; M. Jeffrey Rabin, "The Idea of Freedom in Michael Oakeshott and the Contemporary Liberal-Communitarian Debate" (PhD diss., University of London, 1999), 19n21; Henry Fairlie (*Spectator* 209 [1962]: 644–645), quoted in Bernard Crick, "The Ambiguity of Michael Oakeshott," *Cambridge Review* 112 (1991): 66. On Oakeshott's teaching Marx in 1938, see Paul Franco, *Michael Oakeshott: An Introduction* (New Haven, CT: Yale University Press, 2004), 188n16. For a detailed recounting of Oakeshott's changing, but far from dismissive, relationship to Marx, communism, democratic socialism, and anarchism, see Luke O'Sullivan, "Michael Oakeshott and the Left," *Journal of the History of Ideas* 75, no. 3 (2014).

Nonetheless, many have been content to ignore such subtleties, reducing Oakeshott to a "cheerleader for the British aristocracy" (Steven Wulf, "Oakeshott's Politics for Gentlemen," *Review of Politics* 69, no. 2 [2007]: 246). His evident disdain for party politics—culminating in his refusal to accept the Companion of Honor award from Margaret Thatcher—did not stop Bernard Crick from memorializing Oakeshott as "a brilliant Tory pamphleteer" (Crick, "The Ambiguity of Michael Oakeshott," 68). This picture did begin to shift with the posthumous publication of Oakeshott's early writings and a new generation of non-polemical Oakeshott scholarship, leading Elizabeth Corey to conclude in a review essay in 2006 that "it is no longer possible . . . to dismiss Oakeshott as merely an ideological defender of the Tory party or an English gentleman out of touch with reality" (Elizabeth Corey, "The World of Michael Oakeshott," *Modern Age* 48, no. 3 (2006): 266). But then came Corey Robin's *The Reactionary Mind*, which seats Oakeshott "at the same table" not only with Hobbes and Burke but also with, among others, Ayn Rand, Antonin Scalia, Margaret Thatcher, and Donald Trump (Corey Robin, *The Reactionary Mind: Conservatism from Edmund Burke to Donald Trump*, 2nd ed. [Oxford: Oxford University Press, 2018], 29).

68. Oakeshott, "The Definition of a University," 141. Compare this with Oakeshott's disturbing claim, from two decades earlier, that "anyone who has worked in a contemporary overcrowded university knows it to be an illusion that there was any large untapped reserve of men and women who could make use of this kind of university but who never had the opportunity of doing so" (Oakeshott, "The Universities," 129).

69. Oakeshott, "A Place of Learning," 28. In "Job Prospects," I both offer a sympathetic reading of our desire to avoid this ordeal and a further development of Oakeshott's argument that it is impossible to do so (see pp. 251–253).

70. Oakeshott, "A Place of Learning," 23.

71. Oakeshott, "A Place of Learning," 40.

72. Oakeshott, "Education: The Engagement and Its Frustration," 93.

73. See Martin Hollis, "Education as a Positional Good," *Journal of Philosophy of Education* 16, no. 2 (1982): 236; drawing on Fred Hirsch, *The Social Limits to Growth* (Cambridge, MA: Harvard University Press, 1976), esp. chap. 3.

74. I develop this idea further in "Public Hearing" (see pp. 189–193).

75. I document this in "Job Prospects" (see p. 203, table 4).

76. For the film, see Bong Joon Ho, dir., *Snowpiercer* (CJ Entertainment, 2013). For the TV adaptation, see Ho, Erickson, et al., executive producers, *Snowpiercer* (CJ Entertainment, 2020–2022). The term "tailies" comes from the series. For the educational equivalent of the tail section, see p. 273n49.

77. For an argument of this sort, see Anthony P. Carnevale and Jeff Strohl, "How Increasing College Access Is Increasing Inequality, and What to Do About It," in *Rewarding Strivers: Helping Low-Income Students Succeed in College*, ed. Richard D. Kahlenberg (New York: Century Foundation Press, 2010). If Thomas Piketty is right, then increased social mobility in the fifties and sixties was a product of a historical aberration (within modern capitalism), a resetting of wealth inequality to near zero by two world wars and specific redistributive policies from FDR and Beveridge to the GI Bill. Since then, while college access has only widened (in the United States, the percentage of eighteen-to-twenty-four-year-olds attending college rose from 25.7% in 1970 to 40% in 2020), economic inequality has returned to pre–World War I levels—making midcentury an exception to the general rule that when return on capital outperforms general economic growth, social mobility decreases and inequality widens over time (see Table 302.60, "Percentage of 18- to 24-Year-Olds Enrolled in College, by Level of Institution and Sex and Race/Ethnicity of Student: 1970 through 2020," ed. National Center for Education Statistics [2021], https://nces.edu.gov/programs/digest/d21/tables/dt21_302.60.asp; Thomas Piketty, *Capital in the Twenty-First Century*, trans. Arthur Goldhammer [Cambridge, MA: Belknap/Harvard, 2014]).

78. See John Marsh, *Class Dismissed: Why We Cannot Teach or Learn Our Way Out of Inequality* (New York: Monthly Review Press, 2011). For further bibliography on the myth that education reduces poverty, see Marsh, *Class Dismissed*, 220n20.

79. David Blacker, *What's Left of the World: Education, Identity and the Post-Work Political Imagination* (Winchester, UK: Zero Books, 2019).

80. I respond to this invitation in "Public Hearing."

81. I take the idea of a "conservatory" from Eduardo Duarte, "Educational Thinking and the Conservation of the Revolutionary," *Teachers College Record* 112, no. 2 (2010), 488–508.

WIDE AWAKE

1. Mary Caroline Richards, *Centering: In Pottery, Poetry, and the Person*, 2nd ed. (Middletown, CT: Wesleyan University Press, [1962] 1989), 15–16. As I will demonstrate, Black Mountain College (BMC) was a community devoted to the virtue of "wide-awakeness" that I introduced in "Soul Action" (pp. 32 and 282n63). The lone documentary about BMC, *Fully Awake* (Cathryn Davis Zommer and Neeley House, dirs., *Fully Awake: Black Mountain College* [Documentary Educational Resources, 2008]), takes its title from the words of an unnamed student: "Every moment at Black Moment seemed alive in a way that few have since. This had to do with being asked to be fully awake, to be at a new threshold of perception" (2'24").

2. Michael Rumaker, *Black Mountain Days* (New York: Spuyten Duyvil, 2003), 4.

3. John Andrew Rice, the leading figure in Black Mountain's early years, not only knew (at least the outlines of) Dewey's educational philosophy but would also have appreciated Dewey's efforts to overcome psycho-physical dissociation through the Alexander Technique (see "Soul Action," pp. 81–88), at one point observing that, "The constant admonition of a college should be not 'Be intellectual!' or 'Be muscular!' (in both cases the dividing line is the neck) but 'Be intelligent!'" (Rice, quoted in Louis Adamic, "Black Mountain: An Experiment in Education," in *My America, 1928–1938* [New York: Harper and Brothers, 1938], 615).

Dewey was on the BMC board and visited the college three times, twice in the 1934-5 academic year and again for two weeks in March, 1936 (see https://deweycenter.siu.edu/publications-papers/chronology.php). Finding Dewey to be a "wonderful listener" and student of "the process of learning," with a deep respect for every "individual's right to be alive," Rice declared Dewey "the only man I have ever known who was completely fit and fitted to live in a democracy" (Rice quoted in Katherine C. Reynolds, "Progressive Ideals and Experimental Higher Education: The Example of John Dewey and Black Mountain College," *Education and Culture* 14, no. 1 [1997], 3, 6, 5, 6). Dewey had similar things to say about what he witnessed at BMC: "The work and life of the College (and it is impossible in its case to separate the two) is a living example of democracy in action. . . . The College exists at the very 'grass roots' of democratic life" ("1940.07.18 (13269): John Dewey to Theodore Dreier," in *The Correspondence of John Dewey (I-IV), 1871-2007*, Electronic Edition, gen. ed. Larry Hickman, vol. 3: 1940-1953, eds. Harriet Furst Simon et al [Charlottesville, VA: InteLex Corporation]).

4. Though Black Mountain officially closed in 1957, the college's last true year in operation was 1955–1956. Only a few returned in the fall of 1956, and in spring 1957 everyone had departed save Charles Olson, the college's final rector, who remained to settle accounts.

5. Here I include students, regular faculty, summer faculty, and others who participated in the life of the college. The reader should not put too much weight on these categorizations. I might just as well have put Albers in education, Cage in music, or Rauschenberg in painting. Other categories, such as performance or collage or sculpture, would have led to further reshuffling. For examples of successful graduates beyond the arts, see Mary Emma Harris, *The Arts at Black Mountain College* (Cambridge, MA: MIT Press, 1987), 52.

6. For a blow-by-blow account of its endless schisms and excommunications, see Duberman, *An Exploration in Community*. For a critique of its educational philosophy from one of the excommunicated, see Eric Russell Bentley, "Report from the Academy," *Partisan Review* 12, no. 3 (1945).

7. Josef Albers, "Art at Black Mountain College (1946)," in *Josef Albers. An Anthology 1924–1978*, ed. Laura Martínez de Guereñu, María Toledo, and Manuel Fontán, 236, emphasis removed. This edited collection of Albers writings and some appreciative texts about him (henceforth *Albers Anthology*) forms one part of a larger exhibition catalogue, *Josef Albers: Minimal Means, Maximum Effect* (Madrid: Fundación Juan March, 2014). It is not clear if the catalogue had editors beyond the anthology editors.

8. Richards was the first to bring Artaud into English, and her translation of *The Theater and Its Double* remains well regarded. (See Antonin Artaud, *The Theater and Its Double*, trans. Mary Caroline Richards [New York: Grove Press (1938) 1958]). Tellingly, Richards relates that it was initially rejected by a theater magazine as too "sophomoric" (Mary Caroline Richards, *Opening the Moral Eye: Essays, Talks, and Poems*, 2nd ed., ed. Deborah Haynes [Hudson, NY: Lindisfarne Press (1962) 1996], 35). For glimpses into her journey of integration, see Richards, *Centering*; and the documentary, Richard Kane and Melody Lewis-Kane, dirs., *M. C. Richards: The Fire Within* (Kane-Lewis Productions, 2004).

9. Aimee Levitt, "Fielding Dawson: The Best St. Louis Writer You've Never Read," *Riverfront Times*, August 18, 2010, https://www.riverfronttimes.com/newsblog/2010 /08/18/fielding-dawson-the-best-st-louis-writer-youve-never-read.

10. The context of Dawson's remark deepens the point:

When Fielding (Fee) Dawson was at ECU [Eastern Carolina University] for a residency, shortly before Jonathan Williams' in the fall of 1994, a student asked him what famous people had attended Black Mountain College. Fee had a just wrapped up a 40-minute colloquy that was an impassioned, personal history and description of all that made BMC uniquely outside the parameters of our media-generated notion of fame that so easily confuses personality and marketability with art. Visibly stunned and for a few moments speechless as he no doubt considered how little of what he'd said had been heard by the questioner, Fee finally chuckled and muttered, "We were all famous. You just never heard of us" (Alex Albright, "We Were All Famous—You Just Never Heard of Us," *Appalachian Journal* 44/45, no. 3/4–1/2 [2014]: 226).

11. These attachments are tangible in works such as Jonathan Williams, *A Palpable Elysium* (Boston: David R. Godine, 2002); Fielding Dawson, *The Black Mountain Book: A New Edition* (Rocky Mount: North Carolina Wesleyan College Press, [1971] 1990), and Fielding Dawson, *An Emotional Memoir of Franz Kline* (New York: Pantheon, 1967).

12. Once we acknowledge this fact, that an institution of higher education should be judged according to its contribution to the flourishing of its graduates, we confront an acute methodological problem. It is easy to list famous alumni, and not too hard to collect statistics on the earnings of graduates. What is extremely difficult to determine is whether an institution aided its graduates in making discoveries and forming dispositions that helped them go on to craft good and meaningful lives. How does one peek in on these lives? What standards are used to assess them? How could one possibly sift out the influence of the college years from the myriad confounding variables? Exit interviews are useful, but many of the effects of college, for better or worse, will only reveal themselves in later life. While all HEIs confront this problem, the fact that BMC has been an object of fascination since its founding means that we have better than average access to portraits of its graduates. Though retrospective accounts focus on the undergraduate years, the impact of those years in later life is evident in the humanity of the person doing the recounting. For BMC, sources for this sort of longitudinal-existential reckoning (the word "assessment" seems out of place) include individual memoirs (see, for example, Dawson, *The Black Mountain Book*; and Rumaker, *Black Mountain Days*); an anthology of shorter retrospections (Mervin Lane, ed., *Black Mountain College: Sprouted Seeds, an Anthology of Personal Accounts* [Knoxville: University of Tennessee Press, 1990]); an exhibition at a reunion forty years after the closing of the college featuring ninety-four panels of visual and verbal remembrance (*Remembering Black Mountain College*, Catalogue of an Exhibition Curated by Mary Emma Harris [Black Mountain, NC: Black Mountain College Museum and Arts Center, 1996]); video oral histories (https://www.blackmountaincollege.org/oral-histories/); and a documentary film (Zommer and House, *Fully Awake*).

13. For example, Stankiewicz begins her review of Harris by asking, "Why should an unaccredited college which lasted only twenty-four years (1933–1957), enroll[ing] fewer than 1,200 students total . . . be the subject of a history?" (Mary Ann Stankiewicz, "[Review of Mary Emma Harris, the Arts at Black Mountain College]," *History of Education Quarterly* 28, no. 1 [1988]: 146). The review ends without her really answering this question.

14. Estimates vary. For most years, we do have data on how many students were enrolled but, especially when you add in summer session enrollments, it becomes difficult to determine the total number of unique students who passed through BMC. Fewer than 1,200 is the most common figure cited (see Stankiewicz above, and, e.g., Naomi Blumberg, "Black Mountain College," *Encyclopedia Britannica*, https://www .britannica.com/topic/Black-Mountain-College). One influential source puts the figure a bit higher at "fewer than 1300" (Harris, *The Arts at Black Mountain College*, 244). Díaz estimates the average enrollment over the twenty-four years at forty students per year, which would mean a total of only 960 (Eva Díaz, "Summer Session 1948," in Helen Molesworth, ed., *Leap before You Look: Black Mountain College, 1933–1957* [Boston: Institute for Contemporary Art, 2015], p. 219). I think the average may be a bit higher than that, based on reasonable interpolations among the figures found in Duberman, *An Exploration in Community*, 167, 228, 282, 323, 344, 361–362, 387, 410, 423, 430, and 465n2; Harris, *The Arts at Black Mountain College*, 52, 175; and Albert William Levi, "The Meaning of Black Mountain," in Lane, *Sprouted Seeds*, 183.

15. Charles Olson, "On Black Mountain (I)," in *Muthologus: Lectures and Interviews*, ed. Ralph Maud (Vancouver: Talon Books, [1968] 2010), 285.

16. Conventionally, BMC is said to have had three phases, corresponding with each of its leading figures: Rice in the 1930s, Albers in the 1940s, and Olson in the 1950s. While Rice is usually described as the founder and first rector of Black Mountain College (BMC), neither claim is strictly true. BMC was founded by a small group centered on Rice and inspired by his dismissal from Rollins College and by the vision of an ideal college he had extolled there. Technically, Rice was BMC's second rector, though its first, Frederick Georgia, served for only a year before Rice took over. As Duberman explains, "Though Rice was the acknowledged leader, it was thought best he not be so designated, since the official AAUP report on the Rollins affair hadn't yet appeared and there was an off chance it might contain some censure of him" (Martin Duberman, *Black Mountain: An Exploration in Community* [Evanston, IL: Northwestern University Press (1972) 2009], 20). Rice, then served as rector from 1934 to 1938. Albers joined the faculty during the college's first year and stayed through AY 1948–1949, serving as rector only for the final six months of his tenure. After visiting in the fall of 1948 and teaching in the summer sessions of 1949 and 1950, Olson joined the faculty in 1951 and served as rector from 1953 to 1956. While sound as a generalization, this focus on charismatic leaders obscures both the dialectical nature of leadership at Black Mountain College (e.g., Albers serving as counterpoint to Rice, and Bill Levi serving as counterpoint to Albers) and the leadership of quieter figures such as Robert Wunsch and Ted Dreier (Wunsch served as rector from 1938 to 1944; Dreier from 1944 to 1947).

17. Quoted in "Ninth Year Begins in New Quarters," in *Black Mountain College Newsletter* 15 (October 1941), https://digital.ncdcr.gov/digital/collection /p249901coll44/id/702/rec/12.

18. Donald M. Frame, ed. and trans., *The Complete Works of François Rabelais* (Berkeley: University of California Press, 1991). This volume contains the five Gargantua and Pantagruel books and some miscellaneous writings.

19. Levi, "Meaning of Black Mountain," 182. Levi served on the BMC faculty from 1945 to 1950, serving as rector from 1947 to 1948.

20. Levi, "Meaning of Black Mountain," 182.

21. Levi, "Meaning of Black Mountain," 181.

22. Levi, "Meaning of Black Mountain," 182. With the Covid-19 pandemic, we have just experienced a version of this phenomenon. With students forced into remote learning, campuses stood empty. Suddenly, the lavish facilities—dorm rooms, food courts, rock climbing walls, professional-level sports arenas—went from money makers to loss leaders. Without denying the educational importance of living and learning together on campus or suggesting that campus leaders were indifferent to health concerns, I think it is fair to say that the decision to bring students back to campus in the fall of 2020 was one that, one way or another, had to be made.

23. Duberman, *An Exploration in Community*, 26.

24. Buckminster Fuller taught at Black Mountain in the summers of 1948 and 1949. Scalability is obviously central to the work of Fuller, author of *Operating Manual for Spaceship Earth* (New York: Simon and Schuster, 1969). In its own way, the concept of scale was just as important for Olson. Consider this description of Olson from Guy Davenport: "His attention was constantly changing focus, from rods and cones in a pigeon's eye to the drift of continents. . . . Olson wanted his students to achieve vertically the entire horizon of human knowledge" (Guy Davenport, "Olson," in *The Geography of the Imagination: Forty Essays by Guy Davenport* [San Francisco: North Point Press, 1981], 82).

25. Olson, "On Black Mountain (I)," 285. The quotations that follow are from the same source and page.

26. Richard Buckminster Fuller, "Josef Albers 1888–1976 (1978)," in *Albers Anthology*, 350.

27. Rice, quoted in Adamic, "An Experiment in Education," 645.

28. Cf. Duberman, *An Exploration in Community*, 432; on the closure of the college, see chap. 14. While the summer art institutes of 1952 and 1953 were "the most remarkable ever held," the year-round community dwindled in the fifties (362). Nor were conditions ripe, as Duberman relates, for yet one more of BMC's recoveries. Having always relied on having a mix of leaders, from the pragmatic to the ecstatic, leadership was now concentrated in the single figure of Olson, a man whose leadership style can only be described as shamanic. In this final phase, there developed an anything-goes, hard-drinking, tortured-artist culture. Some students were injured

in a horrible car crash. There was a looming morals charge involving an adulterous student. Impressed neither by Olson's leadership nor his Beat-poetic style of correspondence, BMC's chief patron, Stephen Forbes, finally pulled the plug.

29. Duberman, *An Exploration in Community*, 18.

30. Levi, "Meaning of Black Mountain," 179.

31. I introduced this idea of bureaucratization in "Soul Action" (see pp. 65–67); I develop MacIntyre's account in "Job Prospects" (see pp. 225–228).

32. For an explication of Arendt's concepts of natality and action, see Chris Higgins, *The Good Life of Teaching: An Ethics of Professional Practice* (Oxford: Wiley-Blackwell, 2011), 92–99. I return to this concept at several points in "Wide Awake." Compare my discussion of natality and banality in "Job Prospects" (see pp. 252–253).

33. See my discussion of Oakeshott's conception of *skholê* in "New Student Orientation" (pp. 100–102). I return to the phenomenology of *skholê* later in this essay (see pp. 127–128).

34. Duberman, *An Exploration in Community*, 24; Duberman is stitching together, with his own interpolations, quotations from notes that Rice made in 1934 (see p. 452n33).

35. Quoted in Duberman, *An Exploration in Community*, 168.

36. Duberman, *An Exploration in Community*, 65.

37. The Lake Eden property was purchased in 1937. The studies building was erected during the final year at Blue Ridge (1940–1941). Finish work continued during the first year at the new campus.

38. May Sarton, "Excerpt from Unpublished Letter to Rosalind Greene," November 1940, in Lane, *Sprouted Seeds*, 81.

39. See Duberman, *An Exploration in Community*. The picture that emerges from his group-dynamics-focused history of BMC is of a community where "creativity and tension [were] bedmates" (281), and tension was managed through the periodic expulsions that organize Duberman's account: Rice in 1939 (chap. 5); Bentley and followers in 1944 (chap. 7); Wallen and followers in 1948 (chap. 9); Dreier, the Alberses, and others in 1949 (chap. 10). While personal failings and conscious ideological differences partly explain each purge, this repetitive "search-and-destroy mission" is suggestive of projective identification and scapegoating, the archaic, unconscious, processes by which groups deal with "anxiety and unwanted parts" (Leroy Wells, Jr., "The Group as a Whole: A Systemic Socioanalytic Perspective on Interpersonal and Group Relations," in *Groups in Context: A New Perspective on Group Dynamics*, ed. Jonathon Gilette and Marion McCollum [Reading, MA: Addison-Wesley, 1990], 72, 73). For some of the deep cultural roots of sacrifice and scapegoating, see Mary Douglas, *Purity and Danger: An Analysis of Concepts of Pollution and Taboo* (London: Routledge, [1966] 2002); Mary Douglas, "The Go-Away Goat," in *The*

Book of Leviticus: Composition and Reception, eds. Rolf Rendtorff and Robert A. Kugler (Leiden: Brill, 2003); and René Girard, *The Scapegoat* (Baltimore: JHU Press, 1986).

40. Olson was interviewed at Beloit College in 1968 (Olson, "On Black Mountain [I]"), and in his Gloucester home in 1969 (Charles Olson, "On Black Mountain [II]," in *Muthologus*).

41. Olson, "On Black Mountain (II)," 347

42. Olson, "On Black Mountain (I)," 276.

43. Olson, "On Black Mountain (I)," 276.

44. While I go on to emphasize Olson's attraction to the idea of a distributed or mobile college, he is clearly ambivalent about whether BMC has a necessary or contingent connection to its mountain home. On the one hand, Olson says that BMC is a society not an institution (Olson, "On Black Mountain [II]," 327–328). He enthusiastically cites Ed Dorn's judgment that BMC was ultimately not a rooted structure, only people passing through an arbitrary location:

> I think the value of Black Mountain was that very able people and very alive people were there off and on and through it. And that's what made it a very important place to be. I don't see any superstructure that existed there which would relate people and what they subsequently did, although there might be one, and a case could be made for it. But I don't think that's so important. It was literally a place, and it was very arbitrary. North Carolina is a very unlikely place . . . There was no important logic connected with why it should be there (quoted in David Ossman, "Edward Dorn," in *The Sullen Art: Interviews with Modern American Poets* [New York: Corinth Books, 1963], 83).

Olson applauds Dorn's take in two interviews (see Charles Olson, "Filming in Gloucester," in *Muthologus*, 208–209; and Olson, "On Black Mountain (II)," 321–322 and 322n6).

On the other hand, Olson, the "poet of Gloucestor," was deeply attuned to place, to land, and to the local. (For an in-situ portrait of Olson's site-specific practice, see the documentary, *Polis Is This: Charles Olson and the Persistence of Place* [Henry Ferrini, dir., Ferrini Productions, Inc, April 2007]. See also Eric Riewer, "A Sense of Locality: Olson in Gloucester," *Cahiers Charles V*, no. 5 [1983]). Unsurprisingly, then, Olson was also drawn to a site-specific understanding of BMC, one he began to articulate in his very first visit to Black Mountain (see Charles Olson [attributed], "Black Mountain College as Seen by a Writer-Visitor, 1948," *Credences* [New Series] 2, no. 1 [1982]; the rationale for the attribution appears on p. 87, the piece itself on pp. 89-90). Over the years, Olson became further attuned to this genius loci, "this strange spot, this first town on the plateau of the Alleghenies starting west," this "little shallow ladle of a spoon at the bottom of a valley" in the shadow of a mountain of "Cherokee legend" (Olson, "On Black Mountain [I]," 278).

Olson tries to collect this ambivalence in an avian trope, as evident in these two moments from the Gloucester interview:

Go to the farms where you get back to simpler things! Go where you are boss, go where you isolate yourself! Go into holes . . . like in "The Kingfishers," which I wrote just at the time I was at Black Mountain. That's the point of the kingfisher: he lays his eggs in holes dug in banks. I mean lay some eggs, for god's sake! Be fecund!

    In the end, like a bird that had to fly, I had to fly from that nest as John [Rice] had originally conceived her as flying from a rented nest. (Olson, "On Black Mountain [II]," 328, 339).

45. On Olson's Poundian imperative, see Francine du Plessix Gray, "Charles Olson and an American Place," *Yale Review* 76, no. 3 (1987): 345. For Olson's pathbreaking intervention in poetics, see Charles Olson, "Projective Verse," in *Collected Prose: Charles Olson*, ed. Donald Allen and Benjamin Friedlander (Berkeley: University of California Press, [1950] 1997). In this essay, Olson cites the opening line of his poem, "The Kingfishers": "What does not change / is the will to change" (Charles Olson, "The Kingfishers," in *The Selected Writings of Charles Olson*, ed. Robert Creeley [New York: New Directions (1949) 1967]; quoted in Olson, "Projective Verse," 246).

46. This is not to suggest, of course, that Olson was drawing on his contemporary, Arendt. Olson drew his inspiration from Pound, the transcendentalists, and other sources.

47. Charles Olson, "The Present Is Prologue," in *Collected Prose*, 206–207.

48. Olson, "The Present Is Prologue," 205.

49. In January, 1955, BMC student Ed Dorn asked Olson what he should read in order to understand the American West. Some days later Olson delivered to Dorn an overflowing, diagrammatic, epistolary essay—projective verse meets student-centered pedagogy—which began by stating two assumptions, the second of which is "that *sociology*, without exception, is a lot of shit—produced by people who are the most dead of all . . . this dreadful beast, some average and statistic" (since published as Charles Olson, "A Bibliography on America for Ed Dorn" (1964), in *Collected Prose*, 297, emphasis in original; for the backstory, see the editors' note on p. 435).

50. See Charles Olson, "Plan for the Operation of Black Mountain College after 1956" (c. 1954), in Molesworth, *Leap before You Look*, 50. This title, which seems to have been supplied by Molesworth, awkwardly suggests that Olson somehow knew in 1954 that the college would close in 1956. No explanation is given of the tentative dating of the diagram. The diagram itself has two all-caps, underlined headers. In the upper left, under "The Corporation of Black Mountain College," we find a governance structure and "principle of operation," glossed by the medieval phrase "*societas magistrorum et discipulorum*," a variant of the phrase "*universitas magistrorum et discipulorum*" (the corporation or union of masters and pupils) from which we derive the term "university." Then the main image is placed under a header that reads "The Federated Operations of Said Corporation." For Molesworth's helpful reading of this image in the context both of impending closure and of the college's embrace

of instability, see Helen Molesworth, "Imaginary Landscape," in *Leap Before You Look*, 51.

51. While Olson was not a visual artist per se, under his projective program, the poetic page becomes a space for a kind of "visual performance" (for this argument, see Eleanor Berry, "The Emergence of Charles Olson's Prosody of the Page Space," *Journal of English Linguistics* 30, no. 1 [2002]; building on Johanna Drucker, "Visual Performance of the Poetic Text," in *Close Listening: Poetry and the Performed Word*, ed. Charles Bernstein [New York: Oxford University Press, 1998)]). And there is a clear continuum from projective verse through full-blown concrete poetry to word art. Olson was fascinated by pictorial writing, particularly Mayan glyphs. (For a rich exploration of the ways in which art and non-art images satisfy and frustrate our cross-cutting impulses to look, read, and decipher, see James Elkins, *The Domain of Images* [Ithaca, NY: Cornell University Press, 1999]). Olson also felt a kinship with the young Cy Twombly, the BMC student who would go on to achieve fame as a painter of graffiti-like abstractions, whose canvases—like the chalked diagrams of a fevered instructor—feature words (visible, struck through, erased), diagrams, and cursive-like, looping skeins. In a letter to Robert Creeley (November 29, 1951), Olson shares that he had the "the pleasure, of talking to a boy as open & sure as this Twombly, abt *line*, just the goddamned wonderful pleasure of *form*, when one can talk to another who has the feeling for it—and christ, who has?" (see George F. Butterick, ed., *Charles Olson & Robert Creeley: The Complete Correspondence*, vol. 8 [Boston: Black Sparrow Press, 1987], 199). A year later, Olson wrote, for a show of Twombly's, a glowing "preface" that suggested that both men were moved by the same archeological impulse (Olson, "Cy Twombly," in *Collected Prose*). This diagrammatic impulse is found not only in Twombly but throughout modern art, from Marcel Duchamp and Francis Picabia through Ad Reinhardt's commentaries on the artworld to Jean-Michel Basquiat, Gabriel Orozco, and Mark Lombardi (a nice place to jump into art historical debates around this impulse is Margaret Iversen, "Desire and the Diagrammatic," *Oxford Art Journal* 39, no. 1 [2016]).

If all of Olson's poetry has a diagrammatic aspect, full-fledged diagrams play an important role in Olson's promethean writing practice, a practice that blurs the boundaries between poetry and prose, research and creative writing, the letter and the lesson plan (on the overlap between Olson's poetics and pedagogy, see Alan Golding, "From Pound to Olson: The Avant-Garde Poet as Pedagogue," in *Ezra Pound and Education*, ed. Steven Yao and Michael Coyle [Orono, ME: National Poetry Foundation, 2012]; Michael Kindellan, "Projective Verse and Pedagogy," in *Staying Open: Charles Olson's Sources and Influences*, ed. Joshua Hoeynck [Wilmington, DE: Vernon Press, 2018]; and Jeff Gardiner, "Olson's Poetics and Pedagogy: Influences at Black Mountain College," in Hoeynck, *Staying Open*). His "Plan for a Curriculum of the Soul" is at once a poem, a diagram, and a work of educational philosophy (Charles Olson, "A Plan for a Curriculum of the Soul," *Magazine of*

Further Studies 5 [1968]). His aforementioned "Bibliography on America for Ed Dorn" at one point suddenly announces, "OK. I want to make a drawing," after which follows a piece of projective, diagrammatic pedagogy (Olson, "A Bibliography on America for Ed Dorn," in *Collected Prose*, 305). Olson's other diagrammatic prose works include "Proprioception" (1961–1962), "The Vinland Map Review" (1969), and "Continuing Attempt to Pull the Taffy off the Roof of my Mouth" (1969) (all three are found in Olson, *Collected Prose*).

52. Olson, "On Black Mountain (I)," 268.

53. Olson, "On Black Mountain (II)," 316, 319.

54. On the traveling seminar, see Olson, "On Black Mountain (II)," 345. On the university of the airwaves, see Olson, "On Black Mountain (I)," 275; cf. Olson, "On Black Mountain (II)," 328.

55. Olson, "On Black Mountain (II)," 328, 346.

56. Olson, "On Black Mountain (I)," 271.

57. Olson, "On Black Mountain (II)," 344.

58. Olson, "On Black Mountain (II)," 344.

59. M. C. Richards, "Black Mountain College: A Golden Seed," *Craft Horizons* (June 1977), 70. A half century after this declaration and we indeed find new exhibitions and books on BMC appearing annually. In the last two decades, there have been four major exhibitions devoted to BMC in

- Spain: *Una Aventura Americana*, curated by Vincent Katz, Museo Nacional Centro de Arte Reina Sofia, Madrid, October 2002–January 2003. Catalogue, Vincent Katz, ed., *Black Mountain College: Experiment in Art* Paperback reissue ed. (Cambridge, MA: MIT Press, 2013).
- The United Kingdom: "Starting at Zero: Black Mountain College 1933–1957," curated by Caroline Collier and Michael Harrison, Arnolfini, Bristol (November 2005–January, 2006), Kettle's Yard, University of Cambridge (January–April 2006). Catalogue, Caroline Collier and Michael Harrison, eds., *Starting at Zero: Black Mountain College 1933–57* (Bristol and Cambridge: Arnolfini and Kettle's Yard, 2005).
- Germany: "Black Mountain: An Interdisciplinary Experiment, 1933–57," curated by Eugen Blume and Gabriele Knapstein, National-galerie im Hamburger Bahnoff, Museum für Gegenwart, Berlin, June–September 2015. Catalogue, Eugen Blume et al., eds., *Black Mountain: An Interdisciplinary Experiment 1933–1957*, 2nd ed. (Leipzig: Spector Books, 2019). See also *Black Mountain Research*, a book project by Annette Jael Lehmann, with the assistance of Verena Kitteland and Anna-Lena Werner (Bielefeld: Kerber Verlag, 2016).
- The United States: "Leap Before You Look Molesworth: Black Mountain College, 1933–1957," curated by Helen Molesworth and Ruth Erikson, Institute

of Contemporary Art/Boston, October 2015–June 2016 (traveling to the Hammer Museum and Wexner Center for the Arts). Catalogue, Molesworth, *Leap before You Look*.

Other recent books include Eva Díaz, *The Experimenters: Chance and Design at Black Mountain College* (Chicago: University of Chicago Press, 2015); Anne Chesky Smith and Heather South, *Black Mountain College (Images of America)* (Charleston, SC: Arcadia, 2014); Julie J. Thomson and Michael Beggs, *Begin to See: The Photographers of Black Mountain College* (Asheville, NC: Black Mountain College Museum + Arts Center, 2017); Jonathan Creasy, ed., *Black Mountain Poems* (New York: New Directions, 2019).

60. Alfred Schutz, *Collected Papers*, vol. 1, *The Problem of Social Reality*, ed. Maurice Natanson (Dordrecht: Kluwer [1962] 1982), 213.

61. Henry David Thoreau, *Walden: A Fully Annotated Edition*, ed. Jeffrey S. Cramer (New Haven, CT: Yale University Press, [1854] 2004), 88.

62. Though most are careful to describe Black Mountain as a liberal arts college with a fine arts emphasis, the legend of BMC as an art school persists. For example, the Royal Academy just ranked it as a world-changing art school (see Sam Thorne, "Eight Art Schools That Changed the World," *RA Magazine* [Spring 2019], also published on the Royal Academy blog [March 28, 2019], https://www.royalacademy.org.uk /article/eight-art-schools-that-changed-the-world-bauhaus-anniversary). The documentary *Fully Awake* strikes a balance with its opening pair of captions: (1) "Founded in 1933, Black Mountain was an influential experiment in education"; and (2) "During its short existence, the school inspired collaboration and innovation, ultimately shaping 20th century modern art." However, a search of JSTOR (keyword "Black Mountain College"; all fields; articles only; 1956–) yields 162 articles in art and art history journals, 25 in education journals, and 26 in overlapping journals (art education, music education, aesthetic education).

63. Olson, "On Black Mountain (II)," 318, cf. 316. "Bindu" is a Sanskrit term meaning "drop," "dot," "point," or "spot," with specialized meanings in a range of Buddhist sects. Bindu is variously the vanishing point that organizes an image, the driving impulse, the essence, seed, or source. A moment earlier in the interview, Olson described BMC's logo, designed by Josef Albers, as "that crazy *bindu*, we would say today, the pureness of that *bindu*, which was pure target, black and white target" (316). A moment before that, he characterizes BMC's founding impulse by saying that Rice's "agitation was really pedagogy."

64. We can situate Black Mountain (1933) in the line that extends from the early experiments at Antioch (1852) and Berea (1855), through the founding of Reed (1908), Deep Springs (1917), the Experimental College at the University of Wisconsin (1927), and St. John's (1937), to the massive wave of experimentation in the sixties. Higginson identifies no fewer than thirty-six noteworthy experiments from

1957 to 1972 (Reid Pitney Higginson, "When Experimental Was Mainstream: The Rise and Fall of Experimental Colleges, 1957–1979," *History of Education Quarterly* 59, no. 2 [2019]: Table 1, pp. 204–205). The best book on the experimental tradition remains Gerald Grant and David Riesman, *The Perpetual Dream: Reform and Experiment in the American College* (Chicago: University of Chicago Press, 1978).

65. John A. Rice, "Foreword to the First *Black Mountain College Catalogue*, 1933/34," in Blume et al, *Black Mountain: An Interdisciplinary Experiment*, 38.

66. This is how Reynolds characterizes Rice's departures from the University of Nebraska and the New Jersey College for Women (Reynolds, "Progressive Ideals and Experimental Higher Education," 3). The founding of BMC followed directly on the heels of Rice's third attempt to fit into an institution, Rollins College, which ended not only in the firing of Rice but in the exit of an entire group of faculty and students sympathetic to him.

Given Rice's counterdependence—his reflexive disdain for authority figures, institutional structures, and social mores—it is surprising how long he did last in academia. The ultimate non-department-man, Rice somehow left Nebraska as an associate professor and chair in the Classics Department. Here was a professor known for ignoring disciplinary boundaries and even course content to follow dialogues where they led. And his own scholarly trajectory shows how little he fit the model of disciplinary specialization: he received first honors in jurisprudence as a Rhodes Scholar at Oxford, pursued a PhD in classics at the University of Chicago (which he never completed), and returned to England on a Guggenheim to study eighteenth-century literature.

Indeed, Rice might well have served as a case study of the tensions between formative education and scholarly formation that I explored in A Skeleton Faculty in "Soul Action." At Chicago, Rice found graduate school to be mere training for "technicians" and graduate students simultaneously immature ("older in years [but] in no other way") and "hardened" (John Andrew Rice, *I Came out of the Eighteenth Century*, Southern Classics [Columbia: University of South Carolina Press (1942) 2014], 272). During his Guggenheim, though he sometimes enjoyed being a "detective," he found research to be somehow necrophilic, concluding that "I could not spend my life apart from life" (297). Rice's topic was the (then) contested authorship of "A Tale of the Tub," which meant wading into the relationship between Jonathan Swift and Samuel Johnson. But Rice struggled with adopting the distantiated stance of the researcher. He sensed that walling off the eighteenth century or choosing sides between Swift and Johnson would be to erect walls within himself:

> I was living in another century, and my own. Jonathan Swift was my author and Swift was half of the eighteenth century—Doctor Johnson was the other— and Swift was half, or more than half, of me. The trouble was, that I was both of them, minimum editions—and they were enemies.

> Research is the report of what one has found out rather than of what one knows. The area of exploration is outside oneself, and, if not already dead, must be deadened. (296)

Rice did not want to accumulate "findings" about dead specimens but to achieve (what we called in "Soul Action") "chest knowledge" through hermeneutic encounter with living voices. He would disavow neither his Swiftian nor his Johnsonian side, neither his eighteenth century loyalties nor his twentieth century sensibilities: he refused to edit himself down to a "minimum edition." In his decade at Black Mountain, Rice did find his way back from instruction to teaching and from department meetings to intentional educational community. And in writing his autobiography and in his final decades as a writer of short stories, he found his way back from research reports to humane letters. I say more about Rice's formation in the text below (see pp. 149–151).

67. Lane, *Sprouted Seeds*, 1–2. Lane oversimplifies in speaking of the group rallying around Rice's plan to found a new college. Rice had led the critique of Rollins, but, in aftermath of the firings and departures from Rollins, it was the group that led the charge toward Black Mountain. It took a while to convince Rice to make it a go (see Duberman, *An Exploration in Community*, 11–13).

I will not rehearse the entire story of Black Mountain College (BMC), which has already been richly narrated and illustrated. Duberman's remains the definitive history. Notably, he not only chronicles the trials, tribalism, and triumphs of this community devoted to facing oneself, but takes the writing as occasion to confront his own beliefs and loyalties, sometimes even imaginatively projecting himself into BMC debates. All historians reach out to the past from interests rooted in the present, negotiating the familiar-strangeness of that which both shapes us and eludes us. As a historian at Princeton in the late sixties, Duberman is writing both from within the academic system that BMC sought to displace and amid a flowering of educational and communal experimentation that BMC can be said to have anticipated. To my mind, it is an uncommon virtue to foreground the conditions and stakes of one's inquiry as Duberman does. It would be something of a performative contradiction if Duberman were to leave himself out of the history of a community that challenged the divorce of living and learning, knowing and becoming. For those who find Duberman too pointed and interlocutory, there is Mary Emma Harris's more conventional, richly illustrated chronicle, *The Arts at Black Mountain College*. If both histories are framed by the three core BMC concepts—art, education, community—Harris concentrates on the first two of these and Duberman the final two. For a beautiful unpacking of the BMC archives, see Blume et al., *Black Mountain: An Interdisciplinary Experiment*. This is only one of several exhibition catalogues that, through both image and text, help us get a feel for the texture of life at BMC.

68. Rice, quoted in Adamic, "An Experiment in Education," 624, 623.

69. From a group dynamics perspective, the life of a splinter group is interesting. One of the core lessons of psychodynamic, group-as-a-whole theory is that groups evoke, collect, and redistribute our human ambivalences around belonging, dependence, and authority. We long for inclusion and dread engulfment; we desire autonomy and fear exclusion; we want to be taken care of and deny our dependence; we wish to be relieved of the burden of directing our own actions and resent being told what to do. To help us sort out and contain these messy, conflictual feelings, groups typically spawn dependent and counter-dependent subgroups. (On the role of ambivalence, projective identification, and subgrouping in group life, see, e.g., Warren G. Bennis and Herbert A. Shepard, "A Theory of Group Development," *Human Relations* 9, no. 4 [1956]; and Wells, "The Group as a Whole"). As long as the splinter group is still nested within the larger system, it is unified in its counterdependence; and it need only look across the aisle or quad to keep tabs on its split-off desires for belonging, dependence, and heteronomy. However, if the rebels successfully oust the old guard, they must now find ways to contain these all-too-human ambivalences. Paradoxes ensue. The former factional leader is elevated to rebel-in-chief. Now each must decide what it means to be loyal to the insurrection, to follow the leader or maintain the spirit of counterdependence. Ejecting the other is an unstable strategy. The split-off part comes home to roost.

70. Rice, "Foreword," 38.

71. John Dewey, *The Public and Its Problems* (Athens: Swallow Press/Ohio University Press [1927] 1954), 183.

72. Like Dewey, Rice was a progressive educator with qualms about progressive education as a program. Instead of meeting the pedagogical present with open minds, as Dewey had recommended, Rice found that many progressive educators "were running on something that happened a good while back"; instead of living an experimental, dialogical ethos, "they've got the thing laid out. This is the way to do it. And by God if you don't do it that way you're not It" (Duberman, *An Exploration in Community*, 24). For the classic defense of this Deweyan ethos and critique of the reduction of progressivism into canned epitomes, see Joseph J. Schwab, "The 'Impossible' Role of the Teacher in Progressive Education," *School Review* 67, no. 2 (1959).

73. For detailed transcripts of these fall 1936 meetings, see Duberman, *An Exploration in Community*, 102–113; the quotations are from pp. 104 and 109.

74. Charles Perrow, "Drinking Deep at Black Mountain College," *Southern Cultures* 19, no. 4 (2013): 93. The meeting took place in 1948.

75. See the exchange from a 1951 meeting, quoted in Kindellan, "Projective Verse and Pedagogy," 9–11. On p. 11, Adams remarks "that he doubts if anybody here knows what Mr Olson is talking about!"

76. The open educational question is the subject of Higgins, *The Good Life of Teaching*, chap. 8. For a discussion of teaching as a practice, whose community is drawn together by their ongoing agreement to disagree over how best to understand the goods of that practice, see chaps. 2 and 6, for example, pp. 68–69 and 189.

77. Eva Díaz develops this theme, arguing that, in the pedagogy of Josef Albers, Buckminster Fuller, and John Cage, we find three different models of experimentation (see Díaz, *The Experimenters*).

78. John A. Rice, "Fundamentalism and the Higher Learning," *Harper's Monthly Magazine*, May 1937. To reiterate, Rice was equally troubled by the progressive's lack of rigor as by rigor mortis of the great books crowd. Indeed, Rice sounded off in one BMC meeting that "'progressive education' when it is stupid, is much more stupid than the other kind" (Duberman, *An Exploration in Community*, 24). It was Rice's ambition to build a college that would let go of the usual formula (lecturing, cramming, regurgitation, grading, credentialing) without grabbing on to a new one, whether it be "read these books" or "follow the student's interest."

79. See, for example, Charles Olson, "A Later Note on Letter 15," in *Selected Poems* (Berkeley: University of California Press, 1997), 155.

80. I discuss this in "Soul Action" (pp. 3–6 and 270n23).

81. For a critique of the pseudo-progressive rhetoric that MOOCs focus on the "learning experience" by enabling "just in time learning," see Rashid Robinson, "Learning On-Demand: Massive Open Online Courses and the Privatization of the Educational Experience," PhD diss., University of Illinois at Urbana-Champaign, 2021).

82. Oakeshott, "A Place of Learning," in *The Voice of Liberal Learning: Michael Oakeshott on Education*, ed. Timothy Fuller (New Haven, CT: Yale University Press, 1989), 27.

83. Pound, *A B C of Reading* (Reading, UK: Faber and Faber Limited, [1934] 1961), 40.

84. Socrates compares himself to a gadfly in *Apology*. Regarding the midwife and matchmaker metaphors, for a guide to the Platonic references, see Avi Mintz, "The Midwife as Matchmaker: Socrates and Relational Pedagogy," in *Philosophy of Education 2007*, ed. Barbara Stengel (Urbana, IL: Philosophy of Education Society, 2008). The *Phaedo* offers a vision of the teacher figure accompanying students on the search for truth.

85. Olson, "On Black Mountain (II)," 319.

86. Alphonse de Lamartine, quoted in Dolores Hayden, *Seven American Utopias: The Architecture of Communitarian Socialism 1790–1975* (Cambridge, MA: MIT Press, 1976), 348.

87. Here in "Wide Awake" I take this claim as axiomatic, having devoted "Soul Action" and "New Student Orientation" to its motivation and explication. This

subsection of "Wide Awake" also consolidates the critique, which runs throughout *Undeclared,* of the exchange-value logic that has captured the contemporary multiversity (see "Campus Tour," "Public Hearing" (pp. 194–195), and "Job Prospects" (pp. 206–207).

88. On this point, see Katherine Ki-Jung Jo, "Making the Examined Life Worth Living: The Ethics of Being a Liberal Educator" (PhD diss., University of Illinois, 2019), http://hdl.handle.net/2142/105850.

89. For one version of the red pill, see Marc Bousquet, *How the University Works: Higher Education and the Low-Wage Nation* (New York: NYU Press, 2008), especially chap. 4.

90. Louis Althusser, "Ideology and Ideological State Apparatuses (Notes toward an Investigation)," trans. Ben Brewster, in *Lenin and Philosophy and Other Essays* (New York: Monthly Review Press, 1971), 162.

91. Plato, *Republic*, trans. C. D. C. Reeve (Indianapolis, IN: Hackett, [c. 380 BCE] 2004), 212 (518d).

92. In 2015, the YMCA Blue Ridge Assembly, "after a great deal of research . . . prayer and reflection," changed the name of the building from Robert E. Lee Hall to Eureka Hall (a new name inspired by the exclamation made by the Assembly founder, Willis D. Weatherford, when he first came upon the site where the building now stands). The YMCA Blue Ridge Assembly's statement is preserved here: https://kadampa-center.org/blue-ridge-assembly-statement-lee-hall, accessed October 30, 2021.

93. "Blue Ridge Assembly Historic District," National Register of Historic Places Inventory—Nomination Form, https://files.nc.gov/ncdcr/nr/BN0005.pdf.

94. Duberman, *An Exploration in Community*, 36, quoting from the typed manuscript Cramer sent him, "I went to Black Mountain College" (see p. 450n16, and p. 453n63; misspelling of Doughten corrected). Cramer would go on to have a complicated relationship with Rice as I note below (p. 335n121) and as described in Katherine Chaddock Reynolds, *Visions and Vanities: John Andrew Rice of Black Mountain College* (Baton Rouge: Louisiana State University Press, 1998), 128–129 and 134-135.

95. Lane, *Sprouted Seeds*, 46.

96. Here we pick up several of the key themes—*skholê,* reorientation, arrival—of "New Student Orientation." We will turn to Rousseau's *sentiment de l'existence* to thicken our phenomenology of *skholê*; to Rice's allegory of the doubled self to deepen our sense of what it takes to turn the soul; and to Rumaker's narrative of finding his voice to concretize the idea of arrival as a protracted process.

97. It was called the "painted porch" because it doubled as an art gallery. Though no paintings were hung on the façade of Lee Hall, the centrality of the arts at Black Mountain further links its porch to the Stoa Poikile.

98. Dewey offered this anecdote about his difficulty in finding decent chairs for the Lab School: "We had a great deal of difficulty in finding what we needed, and finally one dealer, more intelligent than the rest, made this remark: 'I am afraid we have not what you want. You want something at which the children may work; these are all for listening'" (John Dewey, "The School and Society," in *The School and Society/the Child and Curriculum* [Chicago: University of Chicago Press (1900) 1990], 31). Proving again that Whitehead was right about all philosophy being a footnote to Plato, philosophy of education is just catching up to Plato's stress on posture in his famous allegory of miseducation and transformation (see the epigraph on p. 71). Black Mountain was a place where learners were constantly shifting their literal and learning postures. This section thus links back to the discussion of Dewey's postural re-education with Alexander (see "Soul Action," pp. 82–88). It was Chris Moffett who first got me thinking about the educational importance of chairs and posture. My thinking in recent years has been enriched by dialogue with Samantha Ha DiMuzio about the educational and epistemological implications of walking.

99. This idea that it was ingenious branding to name the modern institution after the ancient idea of *skholê* comes from Kieran Egan (see 311–312n53).

100. Jean-Jacques Rousseau, *Reveries of the Solitary Walker*, trans. Peter France (London: Penguin, 1979), 89.

101. Eve Grace, "The Restlessness of 'Being': Rousseau's Protean Sentiment of Existence," *History of European Ideas* 27 (2001): 140. As Grace explores, there are apparently conflicting versions of the *sentiment de l'existence:* the Rousseau of the Discourses and *Emile* stresses energetic action; the Rousseau of the *Reveries*, calm repose. Here is how Grace captures the active version: "The plenitude of life would seem to be felt when, like a race horse running at top speed, we stretch our every power, our every faculty, to its utmost" (140). In contrast, the Rousseau of the *Reveries* describes an equilibrium between our powers and our desires, a pleasure in simply being, with no need for striving. Grace concludes, and I concur, that we need not read these as rival accounts. Though the quiescent version is clearly ateleological, I see no implied teleology in the active version. The active principle seems to be an overflowing, "the natural expansiveness of life seeking exercise" not a needy filling of a void (140). As Grace points out (136), Rousseau himself held that the sentiment of existence was contingent upon shifting conditions, and described his *Reveries* as records of "daily fluctuations," as "barometer readings of my soul" (Rousseau, *Reveries of the Solitary Walker*, 33). It seems best then to read Rousseau as offering not rival conceptualizations of the experience, but an open-ended phenomenology of our access to it, a record of the variable conditions under which we may become present to ourselves (it may be on a vigorous hike rather than in sitting meditation) and take pleasure in our aliveness (it may be a moment of loafing blessed by a breeze rather than at a gallop).

102. Rousseau, *Reveries of the Solitary Walker*, 88.

103. Rice, quoted in Adamic, "An Experiment in Education," 626.

104. Friedrich Nietzsche, "Schopenhauer as Educator," trans. William Arrowsmith, in *Unmodern Observations: Unzeitgemässe Betrachtungen*, ed. William Arrowsmith (New Haven, CT: Yale University Press, [1874] 1990); 165–166.

105. This idea has recently been compellingly restaged by René Arcilla. For his critique of educational reification, see René V. Arcilla, "Is There Really Such a Thing as Philosophy of Education?," *Philosophical Studies in Education* 45 (2014). For his theory of education as being led out, see René V. Arcilla, *Wim Wenders's Road Movie Philosophy: Education without Learning* (London: Bloomsbury, 2020). For an appreciative critique of Arcilla's view of education as destiny, see Chris Higgins, "The Hermeneutic Straightaway," *Journal of Philosophy of Education* 55, No. 4-5 [2021]). For an autobiographical and conversational introduction to Arcilla's thinking, see René V. Arcilla, Chris Higgins (respondent), and Samantha Ha (guest host), "How Can Education Be about Acquiring Nothing?," *Pulled Up Short* (podcast), May 3, 2021, https://www.bc.edu/content/bc-web/sites/pulled-up-short/episodes/season-one.html#006.

106. For a discussion of the kitschification of education, see Higgins, *The Good Life of Teaching*, 252–253.

107. Duberman, *An Exploration in Community*, 36.

108. While Rice wrote no systematic treatise on education, a fairly clear picture of his views emerges in his autobiography, *I Came out of the Eighteenth Century* (for an interesting addendum, see John A. Rice, "Black Mountain College Memoirs, with an Introduction by William C. Rice," *Southern Review* 25, no. 3 [1989]), and especially in Louis Adamic's Rice-centered, indeed essentially co-authored, portrait of BMC. After an extended visit in the fall of 1935, Adamic brought the college to the world's attention with a glowing piece in Harper's (Louis Adamic, "Education on a Mountain," *Harper's Monthly Magazine*, no. 172 [April 1936]). After a series of further, shorter visits, he published an updated version (Adamic, "An Experiment in Education"). Significant portions of these largely overlapping portraits are given over to long conversational but polished quotations from Rice. Rice explains their working method: "Louis took a cottage in the village and came up at night with a list of questions, to be answered by me before the next night. What was the college trying to do, and how? That was the burden and I spent many late hours trying to answer" (Rice, *I Came out of the Eighteenth Century*, 337).

Incidentally, it seems that both Duberman and Rice himself misdate Adamic's initial visit. Adamic opens the *Harper's* piece, published in April 1936, explaining that he visited BMC "early last autumn," that is, fall 1935, a fact confirmed in the opening line of his revised chapter. Rice dates Adamic's arrival impossibly to "the late autumn of 1936," months after the article was out (Rice, *I Came out of the Eighteenth Century*, 335). Duberman's date, though less implausible, is still erroneous. He has Adamic arriving in January of 1936 and staying for three months (Duberman, *An Exploration in Community*, 116). Even if *Harper's* could turn a submission around in a month, it is absurd to suppose that Adamic would return to New York with an article written in March, describing experiences from January and February, thinking they had happened in the fall. Besides, Duberman himself cites correspondence between Rice and Adamic from that January and February, when they supposedly would have been together at Black Mountain (see Duberman, *An Exploration in Community*, 473n7).

Some of Rice's responses to Adamic were drawn from his "Foreword" to the first BMC *Bulletin* and from two articles that built on it (see Rice, "Foreword"; John A. Rice, "Black Mountain College," *Progressive Education* 11 [1934]; and John A. Rice, "Black Mountain College," *School and Home* 16 [April 1935]). Thanks to Lopa Williams of the Boston College Library for tracking down the month of publication for the *School and Home* piece so that I could verify whether Rice had completed it before Adamic arrived.

Two other windows into Rice's views are his aforementioned critique of Hutchins (Rice, "Fundamentalism and the Higher Learning") and the early chapters of Duberman's history, a key source for which is a 1967 interview with Rice.

109. Rice develops his parable of the true and false self in Adamic, "An Experiment in Education," 629–633. I have chosen to attribute the entirety of this allegory of the doubled self to Rice, despite some ambiguity in Adamic. The *Harper's* version features two long stretches of blocked text about the decline of village life, rise of the nuclear family, creation of the superficial self, and BMC as a new sort of village that feeds the true self and winnows away the false one—introduced respectively via "To condense what several people have said to me" and via "BMC people explain this as follows" (Adamic, "Education on a Mountain," 522, 524). However, in the chapter version, the first of these block-quotation-condensations is now attributed to Rice and the important first paragraph from the second *Harper's* block now appears without quotation marks (though featuring ellipses where Adamic removed a phrase from the *Harper's* block) and introduced only as "That is explained as follows" (Adamic, "An Experiment in Education," 631).

110. This was central in the so-called communitarian correction of liberalism in the eighties. See for example, Alasdair MacIntyre, *After Virtue: A Study in Moral Theory*, 3rd ed. (South Bend, IN: University of Notre Dame Press, [1981] 2007), especially chaps. 3 and 15; Michael J. Sandel, "The Procedural Republic and the Unencumbered Self," *Political Theory* 12, no. 1 (1984).

111. Adamic, "An Experiment in Education," 627, 626.

112. Adamic, "An Experiment in Education," 630. On webs of interlocution, see Charles Taylor, *The Sources of the Self: The Making of the Modern Identity* (Cambridge, MA: Harvard University Press, 1989), 35–40.

113. Adamic, "An Experiment in Education," 630.

114. Paul Simon, "Kodachrome" (1973), Universal Music Publishing Group.

115. I draw attention to the importance and difficulty of pedagogical beginnings in Chris Higgins, "Turnings: Towards an Agonistic Progressivism," in *Philosophy of Education 2008*, ed. Ron Glass (Urbana, IL: Philosophy of Education Society, 2009), https://educationjournal.web.illinois.edu/archive/index.php/pes/article/view/1358.pdf.

116. Adamic, "Education on a Mountain," 524.

117. Duberman, *An Exploration in Community*, 116.

118. Adamic, "Education on a Mountain," 524.

119. Duberman, *An Exploration in Community*, 117.

120. Duberman, *An Exploration in Community*, 118. While it is easy to hear this as blaming the victim, I think Rice is correctly sensing the group's own ambivalence around being ruled. Evarts suggests some of these relational dynamics when he says of Rice, "He was loved, feared, and sometimes hated. A real father figure" (John Evarts, quoted in Reynolds, *Visions and Vanities*, 129).

121. "The most profound influence" comes from Duberman, who is quoting one remark as representative of what he heard from "many" of Rice's former students (Duberman, *An Exploration in Community*, 4). The other testimonials are all drawn from Reynolds, *Visions and Vanities*: Nat French on finally using his mind (87); Sue Spayth Riley on Rice as empathetic and respectful (134); Betty Young Williams on learning to question and on her internal dialogue with Rice (134). It is Doughten Cramer, whom we met earlier on the porch, who both acknowledges and endorses Rice's ego-bruising methods: "Mr. Rice succeeded in beating me down to a pulp. He was an inspiration to me" (135).

122. Adamic, "An Experiment in Education," 630.

123. Adamic says that the method of "group influence" had been "continually revised" in response to his article and the criticism it elicited from DeVoto, who had opined that the group dynamics described by Adamic were "vicious" and "downright dangerous" (Adamic, "An Experiment in Education," 630; Bernard DeVoto, "Another Consociate Family," *Harper's Monthly Magazine*, no. 172 [April 1936]). Accordingly, whereas many portions of Adamic's 1938 chapter are identical to the *Harper's* article, the section on group influence clearly receives some attention. Indeed, Adamic softens the passage I quoted earlier (see p. 131), removing "bitter" before "enemy," adding "often" before "starved," and changing "must be attacked without mercy" to "must be allowed to recede and disappear" (Adamic, "An Experiment in Education," 632).

124. Adamic, "An Experiment in Education," 631. This is my spin on Adamic's description of the heady opening days of term, with its feeling of a "grand

week-end party." All of the quotations in my rehearsal of Adamic's views on freedom, candor, etcera are drawn from p. 632 of this text.

125. We are focusing on a teacher's agonistic efforts to help students work through their ambivalence about authenticity, but what if the purveyors of liberal learning are themselves still hobbled by a fear of freedom. Rice worried that "some of those who had joined the Black Mountain experiment didn't even want freedom for themselves—though they were the last to know it" (Duberman, *An Exploration in Community*, 28). Their love of freedom was only abstract, Rice insisted, the "intellectual structure they had built up in defense of freedom was quite at variance with [their] own emotional needs" (29). The practice of teaching requires a simultaneous practice of self-examination.

126. For the shadow side of interpellation/recognition, see Althusser, "Ideology and Ideological State Apparatuses (Notes toward an Investigation)"; and Jessica Benjamin, *The Bonds of Love: Psychoanalysis, Feminism, and the Problem of Domination* (New York: Pantheon Books, 1988).

127. Duberman, *An Exploration in Community*, 26.

128. Adamic, "An Experiment in Education," 632. It was precisely this aspect of Black Mountain that most offended DeVoto, who called out Adamic for praising a college that looked "a good deal less like an educational institution than a sanitarium for mental diseases" (DeVoto, "Another Consociate Family").

129. Adamic, "An Experiment in Education," 641.

130. Adamic, "An Experiment in Education," 641.

131. Harris, *The Arts at Black Mountain College*, 38. Harris mentions only casting-against-type, the less radical of Wunsch's two methods (though thinking about the effect a role will have on an actor is already unorthodox).

132. Adamic, "An Experiment in Education," 641. The ellipsis is Adamic's, though I have also elided a redundant phrase in this same spot.

133. Hannah Arendt, *The Human Condition*, 2nd ed. (Chicago: University of Chicago Press, [1958] 1998), 176–177.

134. In his account of educational exemplarity, Warnick is mainly worried about what he takes to be the default view that we simply choose our role models. However, I think he would agree that we do not want to swing to the opposite view that erases the agency in influence. For his communitarian corrective to our voluntaristic bias and interesting perception-based account of emulation, see Bryan Warnick, in *Imitation and Education* (Albany: State University of New York Press, 2008). For more on the dialectic of agency and influence, see "Soul Action," pp. 16–17 and 277n13.

135. Rumaker, *Black Mountain Days*, 60.

136. Rumaker, *Black Mountain Days*, 60.

137. See Rumaker, *Black Mountain Days*, 60, 264, and 347. Actually, Olson never said this to Rumaker directly. After his first public reading, Rumaker was standing near Stefan Wolpe, who remarked to Olson in a stage whisper that "the trouble with Rumaker is that he doesn't know how to *lie* yet" (264, italics original). Grinning delightedly, Olson made sure Rumaker took in Wolpe's remark. It took a year, and multiple talks with Olson, who "hammered away at Wolpe's insight," before Rumaker could "grasp and make use" of the idea (264). And it was year's after this that Rumaker finally "got to the core of Stefan's meaning," by formulating it in the maxim that "The lie of the imagination creates the truth of reality" (264).

138. Rumaker, *Black Mountain Days*, 25. To be exact, Rumaker and his three friends were first greeted by Olson's wife, Connie, who showed them around the campus. Rumaker did not meet Olson until the second day of his visit.

139. Arendt, *The Human Condition*.

140. Arendt, *The Human Condition*.

141. Donald W. Winnicott, *Playing and Reality* (New York: Routledge, [1971] 1989), 150. This section of "Wide Awake" picks up the main themes of "Soul Action."

142. I develop this account of imagination in Chris Higgins, "Modest Beginnings of a Radical Revision of the Concept of Imagination," in *The Imagination in Education: Extending the Boundaries of Theory and Practice*, ed. Sean Blenkinsop (Cambridge, UK: Cambridge Scholars Press, 2009).

143. For Orwell's descent down the mineshaft, see George Orwell, *The Road to Wigan Pier* (Orlando, FL: Harcourt Brace Jovanovitch, 1958), 25–28.

144. Oakeshott, "A Place of Learning," 28. "The sole cause of man's unhappiness," Pascal famously ventured, "is that he does not know how to stay quietly in his room" (Blaise Pascal, *Pensées*, tr. A.J. Krailsheimer [London: Penguin, (1670) 1995], 37 [§136]). This recent study offers a chilling confirmation of our abiding inability to be alone with our own thoughts: https://www.ncbi.nlm.nih.gov/pmc/articles/PMC4330241/.

145. I developed this point earlier, in "Soul Action" (pp. 14–15).

146. For a detailed defense of this proposition, that education is inseparable from a thick background conception of what it means to be, and to flourish as, a human being, see Higgins, *The Good Life of Teaching*, 254–273. This position is compatible with my claim above (pp. 121 and 330n76) that a vibrant educational community will nurture open questions about our becoming, rather than settling on a fixed anthropology, pedagogy, and ethics.

147. Indeed, we find two discourses, neither doing justice to the costs and dangers of transformative experience. Influenced by positive psychology, much school and curriculum talk simply pretends that students need give nothing up.

Transformative learning is a gentle climb on a sunny day. Meanwhile, most academics, at least most in the humanities, assume that the whole point of college pedagogy is to "trouble" students' assumptions. And perhaps it is, but there is something ethically troubling about our blithe embrace of disruption when we give so little thought to supporting students through disorientation and disillusionment, let alone to the constructive phase of transformative education. There is good philosophical work challenging both discourses. As an antidote to the former, see Mark E. Jonas, "When Teachers Must Let Education Hurt: Rousseau and Nietzsche on Compassion and the Educational Value of Suffering," *Journal of Philosophy of Education* 44, no. 1 (2010); Avi I. Mintz, "The Happy and Suffering Student? Rousseau's Emile and the Path Not Taken in Progressive Educational Thought," *Educational Theory* 62, no.3 (2012): 249–265; and Avi I. Mintz, "Helping by Hurting: The Paradox of Suffering in Social Justice Education, *Theory and Research in Education* 11, no. 3 (2013). Yacek and Gary document the swing toward disruption (Douglas W. Yacek and Kevin Gary, "Transformative Experience and Epiphany in Education," *Theory and Research in Education* 18, no. 2 [2020]). Stillwaggon probes how young people mourn the selves they are asked to give up (James Stillwaggon, "'A Fantasy of Untouchable Fullness': Melancholia and Resistance to Educational Transformation," *Educational Theory*, 67, no. 1 [2017]); Yacek asks whether we can justify transformative learning ethically (Douglas W. Yacek, "Should Education Be Transformative?" *Journal of Moral Education* 49, no. 2 [2020]). And Jo considers how higher education and the professoriate would have to evolve were we truly to devote ourselves to helping students reintegrate after disruption (Katherine Ki-Jung Jo, "Making the Examined Life Worth Living: The Ethics of Being a Liberal Educator" [PhD diss., University of Illinois, 2019], http://hdl.handle.net/2142/105850).

148. After Kant (see *Uber Pädagogik*, §29), it is common to speak of the "paradox of education," referring to the tensions between freedom and restraint. I was introduced to the idea by Helmut Peukert (in a seminar on Levinas and Education at Columbia University in the mid-nineties), who, if I remember correctly, credited to Martin Buber his preferred form of the paradox, that one needs the influence of another to become oneself. I am not sure where, if anywhere, Peukert discusses this in print. Bernhard Grünwald similarly recalls that Peukert "once qualified" the dialectic of leadership and autonomy as a pedagogical paradox (see Bernhard Grümm, "Religious Education Teacher between Biography, Habitus and Power: Professional Ethical Perspectives," *Journal of Christian Education in Korea* 61 [2020]). For an interesting discussion of the paradox, see Lars Løvlie, "Does Paradox Count in Education?" *Utbildning & Demokrati* 16, no. 3 (2007).

149. Higgins, "Turnings: Towards an Agonistic Progressivism."

150. Nietzsche, "Schopenhauer as Educator," 66.

151. Walker Percy, *The Moviegoer* (New York: Vintage, [1961] 1998), 13.

152. Adamic, "An Experiment in Education," 616, 615, emphasis original.

153. Adamic, "An Experiment in Education," 621, 615.

154. This koanic Q&A was inspired by the pugnacious ending of John Cage, "Experimental Music: Doctrine," in *Silence: Lectures and Writings*, 50th anniv. ed. (Middletown, CT: Wesleyan University Press, [1961] 2011).

155. For a classic statement of the relational imperative in education, see Martin Buber, "Education," trans. Ronald Gregor Smith, in *Between Man and Man* (Boston: Beacon, [1926] 1955). What I am calling the hermeneutic stance is closely related to the German concept of *Bildung* which, in the Hegelian/Gadamerian variant I favor, involves a twofold mediation: individual self-formation (*bilden*: to form) is mediated by cultural images (*Bilden*), texts, and ideals; cultural re-formation is mediated by the particular ways in which individuals come into their own (for the beginnings of a rehabilitation of the concept, see Hans-Georg Gadamer, *Truth and Method*, trans. rev. by Joel Weinsheimer and Donald Marshall, 2nd rev., Continuum Impacts ed. [New York: Continuum, (1960) 2004], 8-16). What I mean by the "existential imagination" is well represented by those critics—Erich Auerbach comes to mind—who, despite their erudition, are less interested in what they can show us about literary works and more interested in how the works involve us in a struggle to comprehend reality (see Erich Auerbach, *Mimesis: The Representation of Reality in Western Literature*, Fiftieth anniv. ed., trans. Willard R. Trask [Princeton: Princeton University Press, (1953)] 2003).

156. Franz Kafka, "Letter to Oskar Pollak (27 January, 1904)," in *Letters to Friends, Family, and Editors* (New York: Schocken, 1977), 15–16.

157. This is the key premise of Higgins, *The Good Life of Teaching*.

158. Jonathan Lear, "Preface: The King and I," in *Open Minded: Working Out the Logic of the Soul* (Cambridge, MA: Harvard University Press, 1998), 4.

159. Quoted in Adamic, "An Experiment in Education," 634, ellipses original. Though not everyone makes this distinction, I think Rice is correct to distinguish cynicism (a simplifying deflation) and irony (a complexity-acknowledging embrace of contraries).

By stressing the difficulty and necessity of asking authentic questions in teaching, Rice locates himself in a Socratic tradition. As Hans-Georg Gadamer puts it,

> Among the greatest insights that Plato's account of Socrates affords us is that, contrary to the general opinion, it is more difficult to ask questions than to answer them. When the partners in the Socratic dialogue are unable to answer Socrates' awkward questions and try to turn the tables by assuming what they suppose is the preferable role of the questioner, they come to grief. Behind this comic motif in the Platonic dialogues there is the critical distinction between authentic and inauthentic dialogue (Gadamer, *Truth and Method*, 356).

I discuss the importance of the live question to the life of the teacher and practice of teaching in Higgins, *The Good Life of Teaching*, 130–140, 254–278. On pp. 135–137, I introduce Gadamer's typology of pseudo-questions, including the pedagogical question, or question with no questioner.

160. Albers belonged to this tradition as well. In his first Trinity lecture, he writes,

> This is to remind us that the example, the indirect and unobvious influence, is the strongest means of education, that the unintentional influence of the teacher's being and doing is more effective than many like to believe.
>
> Therefore, we as teachers help develop others best through developing ourselves. In the end all education is self-education. And we as teachers have no right to demand from our students what we are unable or unwilling to do ourselves.
>
> As development means growth, how can we develop others if our own growth is arrested? As growth is the aim and measure of development for the teacher as well as for the student, it is also its excitement and therefore its most effective stimulus. Without it, teaching is only a hard job and sour bread (Josef Albers, "Search Versus Re-Search: Three Lectures at Trinity College (1965)," in *Albers Anthology*, 294).

161. Alfred North Whitehead, *The Aims of Education, and Other Essays* (New York: The Free Press, [1927] 1967), v. For more on this minor tradition and the conception of teaching it contests, see A Skeleton Faculty in "Soul Action," and Higgins, *The Good Life of Teaching*, 2–9, and chap. 5.

162. Richard Rorty, "Education as Socialization and as Individualization," in *Philosophy and Social Hope* (New York: Penguin, 1999), 125.

163. Rorty, "Education as Socialization and as Individualization," 126.

164. Rice, *I Came out of the Eighteenth Century*, 205. In the discussion of John Webb, I cite from this text parenthetically, by page number.

165. Hannah Arendt, "On Hannah Arendt," in *Hannah Arendt: The Recovery of the Public World*, ed. Melvyn Hill (New York: St. Martin's Press, 1979), 336–337.

166. Adamic, "An Experiment in Education," 615.

167. Adamic, "An Experiment in Education," 617, 616.

168. Adamic, "An Experiment in Education," 643; Rainer Maria Rilke, *Letters to a Young Poet*, trans. M. D. Herter Norton, rev. ed. (New York: W.W. Norton & Co., 1954), 54. I develop this idea of poetic calling further in "Job Prospects" (see pp. 238–240 and 369n95).

169. Rice, *I Came out of the Eighteenth Century*, 272.

170. Rice, *I Came out of the Eighteenth Century*, 272.

171. As I discuss in "Soul Action" (see pp. 87 and 305n242), this is Bruce Wilshire's term for embodied awareness of ourselves in relation to the good.

172. Rice, *I Came out of the Eighteenth Century*, 296.

173. Adamic, "An Experiment in Education," 619.

174. William Arrowsmith, "Teaching and the Liberal Arts: Notes toward an Old Frontier," in *The Liberal Arts and Teacher Education: A Confrontation*, ed. Donald Bigelow (Lincoln: University of Nebraska Press, 1971), 12.

175. For an answer to this question, see Arcilla, *Wenders's Road Movie Philosophy*, 134–140.

176. On the sophomore as ideal, see "Soul Action," pp. 60–62.

177. Duberman, *An Exploration in Community*, 38. Duberman is quoting from BMC's first catalogue.

178. BMC Catalog #1, quoted in Duberman, *An Exploration in Community*, 38.

179. Duberman, *An Exploration in Community*, 38.

180. Richards, *Centering*, 120. For example, Rice, and just about everyone else, attended Albers's courses, and Xanti Schawinsky attended Rice's classes (Schawinsky describes one of Rice's class sessions in Duberman, *An Exploration in Community*, 110).

181. Though this does not rule out, of course, that they sometimes took up the stance of students of each other's teaching.

182. Victor Kestenbaum, *The Grace and the Severity of the Ideal: John Dewey and the Transcendent* (Chicago: University of Chicago Press, 2002), passim, 84.

183. Kestenbaum, *The Grace and the Severity of the Ideal*, 88.

184. Kestenbaum, *The Grace and the Severity of the Ideal*, 79–83, passim, 89.

185. James, "Pragmatism and Humanism," quoted in Kestenbaum, *The Grace and the Severity of the Ideal*, 97.

186. I offer a more multidimensional conception of open-mindedness in Chris Higgins, "Open-Mindedness in Three Dimensions," *Philosophical Inquiry in Education* 18, no. 1 (2009).

187. Kestenbaum, *The Grace and the Severity of the Ideal*, 96.

188. Kestenbaum, *The Grace and the Severity of the Ideal*, 96.

189. The structure was actually invented in Germany in 1922. Fuller reinvented and popularized it, developing in dialogue with BMC student, Kenneth Snelson, the key structural principle of "tensegrity" (Fuller's term) or "floating compression" (as Snelson called it). In the summer of 1948, a large sphere constructed from venetian blind scrap that failed to rise was dubbed "the supine dome." In 1949, a smaller sphere built from aircraft tubing was successfully erected, Fuller's "Autonomous Dwelling Facility with a Geodesic Structure."

190. BMC student, Jerrold E. Levy, quoted in Duberman, *An Exploration in Community*, 295.

191. This is Duberman, embedding a quotation from Penn, in Duberman, *An Exploration in Community*, 302.

192. Duberman, *An Exploration in Community*, 302.

193. Duberman, *An Exploration in Community*, 302.

194. *Fully Awake* (35:40–35:50).

195. *Fully Awake* (35:58–36:20).

196. *Fully Awake* (36:21–36:27).

197. Duberman, *An Exploration in Community*, 303.

198. Both DeKooning and Cunningham are quoted in Duberman, *An Exploration in Community*, 296.

199. A bookend to this story of Bucky's acting debut is that of the verbal and literal giant, Olson, deciding to study dance with Cunningham. According to one review of the documentary *Polis Is This,* Olson comes off "as a great, clumsy-looking bear of a man, resembling an out-of-shape offensive lineman" (https://www.popmatters.com/72586-polis-is-this-charles-olson-and-the-persistence-of-place-2496032018.html). The point, Cunningham explains, was not that Olson was "going to be a dancer": he was seeking a "kind of physical experience" (quoted in Duberman, *An Exploration in Community*, 380). Olson worked hard and to Cunningham's surprise he was, in his own way, "marvelous" (380). "I *enjoyed* him," Cunningham recalls, "he was something like a light walrus" (380, emphasis original).

200. This paragraph not only draws together threads from the preceding sections of "Wide Awake" but also rehearses some of the major conclusions of "Soul Action."

201. Josef Albers, "Combinative Form (1935)," in *Albers Anthology,* 230. Compare two related formulations: "education is first self-education" and "in the end, all education is self-education" (Josef Albers, "On Education (1945)," in *Albers Anthology,* 261; Albers, "Search Versus Re-Search," 294).

202. Arendt, *The Human Condition*, 180.

203. Hannah Arendt, "The Crisis in Education," trans. Denver Lindley, in *Between Past and Future: Eight Exercises in Political Thought* (New York: Penguin, [1958] 1977), 186. The passage continues in an interesting vein. A half century before the rise of social media influencers, Arendt made this observation:

> This may indeed be the reason that children of famous parents so often turn out badly. Fame penetrates the four walls, invades their private space, bringing with it, especially in present-day conditions, the merciless glare of the public realm, which floods everything in the private lives of those concerned, so that the children no longer have a place of security where they can grow.

204. Julia Connor, "Living a Making: Source in the Literary Work of M.C. Richards," *Journal of Black Mountain Studies* 7 (2015). Connor mentions in particular the

Living Theater and the Open Theater. I do not know whether Peter Brook read Artaud in French or was also introduced to Artaud by Richards's translation. Pawlik notes that the founders of the Living Theater, Julian Beck and Judith Malina, met with Richards in April 1958 to discuss Artaud (Joanna Pawlik, "Artaud in Performance: Dissident Surrealism and the Postwar American Literary Avant-Garde," *Papers of Surrealism* 8 [2010]).

205. See https://digital.ncdcr.gov/digital/collection/p249901coll44/id/622.

206. This is Tudor's description of the new state of "musical perception" he needed to acquire (which he did in part by reading Artaud's *Theater of Cruelty* with Cage and M. C. Richards) in order to perform Boulez's "2nd Sonata." See Eric Smigel, "Recital Hall of Cruelty: Antonin Artaud, David Tudor, and the 1950s Avant-Garde," *Perspectives of New Music* 45, no. 2 (2007): 173. On the BMC Artaud reading group, see Duberman, *An Exploration in Community*, 370.

207. Duberman, *An Exploration in Community*, 300.

208. John Cage, "Defense of Satie," in *John Cage*, ed. Richard Kostelanetz (New York: Praeger, 1970): 81; quoted in Mary Emma Harris, "John Cage at Black Mountain: A Preliminary Thinking," *Journal of Black Mountain Studies* 4 (2013), https://www.blackmountaincollege.org/mary-emma-harris-john-cage-at-black-mountain-a-preliminary-thinking/.

209. Duberman, *An Exploration in Community*, 300.

210. Indeed, Wunsch, who inaugurated BMC's drama program, also saw "dramatics as an educational discipline" and "as a meeting place for all of the arts" (quoted in Harris, *The Arts at Black Mountain College*, 38).

Duberman makes the point that *Dans Macabre*, a participatory, mixed-media production in the round anticipates *Theater Piece No. 1*. On this point, Mary Emma Harris demurs, stressing that while the Schawinsky pieces, like Cage's proto-happening, were nonnarrative and mixed media, the former were "carefully planned and rehearsed, with nothing left to chance" (see Duberman, *An Exploration in Community*, 90; Harris, *The Arts at Black Mountain College*, 40).

211. Harris, *The Arts at Black Mountain College*, 40.

212. Duberman, *An Exploration in Community*, 89–90.

213. Quoted in Harris, *The Arts at Black Mountain College*, 40.

214. Albers, "Search Versus Re-Search," 294.

215. From one of Robert Sunley's interviews, curated by the Black Mountain College Project. See http://blackmountaincollegeproject.org/Features/SUNLEY/SUNLEYpartII/OutsidetheClassroomDRAMA.htm.

216. The pithy description of Arendt's space of appearance comes from Kimberly Curtis, *Our Sense of the Real: Aesthetic Experience and Arendtian Politics* (Ithaca, NY: Cornell University Press, 1999), 71.

217. Arendt, *The Human Condition*, 178.

218. See Arendt, *The Human Condition*, 208–220.

219. For an explication of Arendt's concepts of action, the deed, and the space of appearance, see Higgins, *The Good Life of Teaching*, 92–99.

220. In this respect, and not only this one, Arendt's view resonates with that of Simone Weil, who imagines the needs of the soul arranged in antithetical pairs. See Simone Weil, "The Needs of the Soul," trans. Arthur Wills, in *The Need for Roots: Prelude to a Declaration of Duties toward Mankind* (London: Routledge, [1949] 2002).

221. Arendt, *The Human Condition*, 175.

222. John Ruskin, *Modern Painters*, vol. 3 (containing Part IV, "Of Many Things"): chap. 16, §28, emphasis original, available at https://www.gutenberg.org/files/38923/38923-h/38923-h.htm). Albers knew and liked this Ruskin passage (though he apparently attributed it to Emerson at first). For example, he ends his first and begins his second Trinity College lecture by quoting the last line (Albers, "Search Versus Re-Search," 295). Though it appears only once more in the Albers anthology, in "Concerning Abstract Art," in her postscript to that essay, Guereñu say that the quote recurs "in many of Albers' later texts" (Josef Albers, "Concerning Abstract Art (1939)," in *Albers Anthology*, 246).

223. Quoted in Duberman, *An Exploration in Community*, 41. I have deleted an interpolation from Duberman.

224. Adamic, "An Experiment in Education," 617.

225. Adamic, "An Experiment in Education," 637.

226. Adamic, "An Experiment in Education," 637. Emphasis in the original. Here Rice's analysis of the educative power of the arts dovetails with the idea of "practical *Bildung*" as developed by Hegel via Gadamer; for a précis, see Higgins, *The Good Life of Teaching*, 6–7.

227. Rice, "Foreword," 40.

228. Francis Alÿs, *Paradox of Praxis 1 (Sometimes Making Something Leads to Nothing)*, 1997. See https://francisalys.com/sometimes-making-something-leads-to-nothing/.

229. Richards, *Centering*, 19. Though Albers fully shared this philosophy, he recommended against a ceramics program on the implausible grounds that clay lacked this resistant property (Harris, *The Arts at Black Mountain College*, 188).

230. Duberman, *An Exploration in Community*, 41.

231. John Rice, "Organization and Procedure at Black Mountain College," quoted in Jason Miller, "The Arts and the Liberal Arts at Black Mountain College," *Journal of Aesthetic Education* 52, no. 4 (2018): 50; Adamic, "Education on a Mountain," 519.

232. Rice, *I Came out of the Eighteenth Century*, 330. The second and third quotations are both from Adamic, "Education on a Mountain," 519.

233. Rice, *I Came out of the Eighteenth Century*, 328, 329.

234. Adamic, "An Experiment in Education," 616–617.

235. In fact, Rice had found not one but two educators who resonated with this ideal of a rigorous-progressive general education rooted in studio classes. Josef's wife, Anni, a former student of Paul Klee who had just begun to direct the Bauhaus weaving workshop when the couple was forced to leave Germany, was to become an important member of the BMC faculty, not to mention a highly regarded textile artist.

236. Duberman, *An Exploration in Community*, 46. Duberman's source for this is Albers himself, in his 1967 interview with the Alberses. Díaz refers to this quote as a "frequent refrain" in the Albers literature, citing only this source, which she describes as Albers quoting himself (Eva Díaz, "The Ethics of Perception: Josef Albers in the United States," *Art Bulletin* 90, no. 2 [2008]: 282n2).

We do find independent verification in Horowitz, who cites his 1996 interviews with Ted and Bobbie Dreier (Frederick A. Horowitz, "Albers the Teacher," in *Josef Albers: To Open Eyes. The Bauhaus, Black Mountain College, and Yale*, ed. Frederick A. Horowitz and Brenda Danilowitz [London: Phaidon, 2006], 261n1). However, on the Dreiers' version, the remark occurred even earlier, with Albers answering a question from student Norman Weston, when first walking up to Lee Hall. And they quote Albers in broken English, saying, "To make open the eyes."

Albers describes the moment twice more in the mid-sixties, both times recalling that he answered even more succinctly, "to open eyes." In the first Trinity lecture, he describes this as "his first educational sentence in English," adding that even in his later years at Yale he found that he had only more reason to stand by "his first educational promise on this continent" (Albers, "Search Versus Re-Search," 292; cf. Josef Albers, "March 1965 Interview," in Lane, *Sprouted Seeds*).

While it is true that Albers had studied English for only three weeks when he made this remark, its brevity is better explained by his lifelong devotion to economy, his preference of showing over telling, and his penchant for distilling ideas into as few well-chosen words if not a wordless action). Thus, at one point he writes that we

> overvalue acoustical education, which means the oral and aural communication, [such that] . . . many classes attract only idle curiosity or offer only ephemeral entertainment.
>
> Words may attract, but examples inspire and fire. The example is the strongest medium of education. The indirect influence of being and doing is more effective than many may believe. (Josef Albers, "A Second Foreword [1936]," in *Albers Anthology*, 235)

In this same unpublished piece (234), Albers writes, "Let us open eyes and minds more than books." Duberman (46) also adds this gem: "'I had to be careful,' [Albers] once shrewdly remarked, 'not to learn English too well because it would have interfered with my communication.'"

237. Josef Albers, "Concerning Art Instruction (1934)," in *Albers Anthology,* 218–219.

238. Albers, "Search Versus Re-Search," 294; Paulo Freire, *Pedagogy of the Oppressed,* trans. Myra Bergman Ramos, 30th anniv. ed. (New York: Continuum, [1970] 2000), 71. Written in Portuguese in 1967–1968, the English translation appeared first; the Portuguese version came out in 1972.

239. Albers, "Search Versus Re-Search," 293, 294. Indeed, already in the mid-thirties we find Albers protesting that "committing [facts] to memory [had] been overvalued" (Albers, "A Second Foreword (1936)," 234). "Why don't we promote more experiences," Albers asks at the outset of his Havana lectures, "instead of continuing or collecting our own or other people's experiences? Why make people learn things by memory, instead of teaching them to see inwardly?" (Josef Albers, "Constructive Form (1934)," in *Albers Anthology,* 223).

240. Albers, "Search Versus Re-Search," 291.

241. Albers, "Art at Black Mountain College (1946)," 264; Josef Albers, "Dimensions of Design (1958)," in *Albers Anthology,* 282.

242. Albers, "Search Versus Re-Search," 291.

243. See, for example, Josef Albers, "Op Art and/or Perceptual Effects (1965)," in *Albers Anthology,* 315.

244. Josef Albers, "[the Artist's Voice: Josef Albers] (1962)," in *Albers Anthology,* 287.

245. Albers, "Search Versus Re-Search," 295.

246. Albers, "Search Versus Re-Search," 295.

247. Albers, "Search Versus Re-Search," 298. Regarding the sensitivities of soul, Albers writes, "every person has all the senses of the soul (e.g., sensitivity to tone, color, space)" (Albers, "Concerning Art Instruction (1934)," 218).

248. "An big artist," Albers would say disparagingly when the subject of professional artists came up (Duberman, *An Exploration in Community,* 46).

249. Josef Albers, "Creative Education," in *The Bauhaus: Weimar, Dessau, Berlin, Chicago,* ed. Hans Maria Wingler (Cambridge, MA: MIT Press, [1928] 1969), 142. The second part of this quote appears as an epigraph in Molesworth, *Leap before You Look,* 33.

250. Josef Albers, "Speech at Black Mountain College Luncheon, New York City Cosmopolitan Club (1938)," in *Albers Anthology,* 240.

251. On Dewey's use of "anesthetic" see "Soul Action," pp. 74 and 298n180.

252. Díaz, "The Ethics of Perception," 263.

253. Anni Albers, "Work with Material," in *Black Mountain College Bulletin 5* (1938), http://toto.lib.unca.edu/findingaids/mss/BMCMAC/01_bmcmac_publications

/bmcmac_pub_05_1937-38/bmc_05_bulletin_1938/default_bmc_05_bulletin
_05_1938.htm. Reprinted as Anni Albers, "Work with Material," *College Art Journal* 3 (January 1944): 51–54.

254. Albers, "Search Versus Re-Search," 294.

255. Albers says that precision is a "decisive" factor "in art, as in all communication," in Albers, "Art at Black Mountain College (1946)," 264. Economy was central to Albers understanding of art and aesthetic education. In a piece written shortly after arriving at Black Mountain, Albers declares that "We stress the economy of form: ratio of effort to effect" (Albers, "Concerning Art Instruction (1934)," 220). This latter phrase appears repeatedly in Albers's writings and is incorporated into his fourfold definition of art (origin, content, measure, aim) as the measure of art (see Josef Albers, "The Origin of Art (Ca. 1940)," in *Albers Anthology*, 253; Search Versus Re-Search," 291). Albers also stressed care for one's materials and space. For example, his Yale colleague, Robert Engman, reports that "Albers would grow 'furious' when people abused property. 'If he saw you with your knee bent and your foot against the wall, it was almost like a ticket home'" (quoted in Horowitz, "Albers the Teacher," 79).

256. Duberman, *An Exploration in Community*, 46.

257. Albers, "Speech at Black Mountain College Luncheon," 242.

258. Albers, "Speech at Black Mountain College Luncheon," 241.

259. "School of intentions": Albers, "Constructive Form (1934)," 222. "Cultivate human relatedness": Albers, "Search Versus Re-Search," 294. What I am calling "situational responsiveness," Albers calls "thinking in situations" (which he also defines as "imagination" or "flexible imagination") (see, e.g., Albers, "Search Versus Re-Search," 303, 310).

260. The phrase "spiritual constitution" appears twice: Albers, "Speech at Black Mountain College Luncheon," 235; Albers, "A Second Foreword (1936)," 240.

261. Albers, "Concerning Abstract Art (1939)," 245.

262. Though Albers and Arendt draw a similar distinction, they mark it with different terms. For Arendt "self-expression" is the lesser thing, the intentional sharing of our what-ness. She uses "disclosure" and "revelation" interchangeably to name the way in which our who-ness is temporarily uncloaked when we act in the public realm. Albers also likes the term "revelation" for this latter activity. Where he differs is in using "self-disclosure" to name the lesser thing. Meanwhile, Albers vacillates on "self-expression," often using it as an equal term of abuse while occasionally using it to name the genuine article. In the end, Albers's preferred terms are "revelation" and "realization."

For "self-expression" as the valorized term, see Albers, "Art at Black Mountain College (1946)," 264; Josef Albers, "My Courses at the Hochschule Für Gestaltung at Ulm (1954)," in *Albers Anthology,* 275; and Josef Albers, "Albers Answers:

'What Is Art?,' 'Can Art Be Taught?,' 'What Would You Say to the Young Art-ist?' (1958)," in *Albers Anthology,* 283. For the leveling of "self-expression and/or self-disclosure," see Albers, "Search Versus Re-Search," 312. See also his statement that he is "unable to accept self-expression either as the beginning of art studies or as the final aim of any art" (Albers, "Search Versus Re-Search," 291). In one interview, Albers notes with pleasure that Cezanne, whom he admires, only used the word "expression" once, opting instead for the term "realize" (Albers, "[the Artist's Voice: Josef Albers] (1962)," 287). In what would eventually become the motto for the Albers Foundation, Albers defined the aim of art as "the revelation and evocation of vision."

No doubt differences between their views remain. It is possible that Albers's sense of working over time to cultivate the vision that is revealed chafes against the way in which, for Arendt, self-disclosure cannot be willed. And certainly, the fact that Arendt classifies art under work, not action, is a major stumbling block in assimilating their views. On whether art should be so classified, see Higgins, *The Good Life of Teaching,* 102-104.

263. Arendt, *The Human Condition,* 180, 179–180.

264. Josef Albers, untitled poem, *Origin 8* (Third Series), January 1968, Celebrat-ing Josef Albers, 24. Originally in Josef Albers, *Poems and Drawings* (New Haven, CT: Yale University Press, [1958] 2006, unpaginated).

265. See, for example: https://black-mountain-research.com/photography/#jp -carousel-503; the first image in Harris, "John Cage at Black Mountain" (https:// www.blackmountaincollege.org/mary-emma-harris-john-cage-at-black-mountain -a-preliminary-thinking/); Horowitz and Danilowitz, *To Open Eyes,* 97 and 77; Harris, *The Arts at Black Mountain College,* 82; and Molesworth, *Leap Before you Look,* 187.

266. "Insight into soul-action," Dewey declares, "is the supreme mark and criterion of a teacher" (John Dewey, "The Relation of Theory to Practice in Education," in *John Dewey on Education,* ed. Reginald D. Archambault [Chicago: University of Chicago Press, (1904) 1974], 319). But just as it is central to teaching to notice what students notice, so it is central to learning to attend to the teacher attending. For a discussion of these points see Higgins, *The Good Life of Teaching,* 241–248.

267. Horowitz, "Albers the Teacher," 228.

268. Josef Albers, "Truthfulness in Art (1937)," in *Albers Anthology,* 236.

269. Horowitz, "Albers the Teacher," 74. For some examples of Alber's antics, see p. 76.

270. Horowitz, "Albers the Teacher," 76.

271. Horowitz, "Albers the Teacher," 78.

272. Horowitz, "Albers the Teacher," 131. I hope this brief sketch of Albers's pedagogy does not seem hagiographic. Even an appreciative former student such

as Horowitz includes disturbing details about Albers pinching female students on the rear end (80), temper "tantrums" (78–79), and crits so "devastating" and "merciless" that some students "allegedly required days or weeks to recover after he had laid waste to their work, and even considered dropping out of school altogether" (78).

273. Albers, "Search Versus Re-Search," Lecture II.

274. Josef Albers, "On My Work (1958)," in *Albers Anthology, 284.*

275. Josef Albers, "Teaching Form through Practice (1928)," in *Albers Anthology,* 214. For a discussion of congeniality in the context of vocation, see "Job Prospects," pp. 237–240.

276. It is worth looking at the stunning, marvelously diverse leaf studies produced in Albers's classes, for example Horowitz and Danilowitz, *To Open Eyes*, 233–235. Four of the thirty-six examples of student work displayed by the Albers Foundation are leaf studies (see https://www.albersfoundation.org/alberses/teaching /students). For eight of Albers's own leaf studies, see https://www.albersfoundation .org/art/highlights?artists=josef-albers&mediums=collage&page=1.

277. Albers, "Teaching Form through Practice (1928)," *214.*

278. Albers, "Search Versus Re-Search," 291.

279. This sounds like anthropomorphization only if we assume that humans alone have a theatrical impulse, a premise contested by Gadamer who argues that "self-presentation is a universal ontological characteristic of nature" (Gadamer, *Truth and Method*, 108). The idea that recognition of an other occasions a fuller self-enactment yielding "an increase of being" is also Gadamerian (while this animates the whole of *Truth and Method*, see in particular 135–152).

280. Horowitz, "Albers the Teacher," 76.

281. Albers, quoted in Horowitz, "Albers the Teacher," 232. Horowitz is quoting from a lecture Albers delivered in 1966 at the University of Bridgeport, of which there are audiotapes. The first elision and the interpolation are Horowitz's. The sentence I removed is truncated by another elision of Horowitz's, making it a bit hard to parse. Albers refers to some subset of the twenty compositions as so diverse that they practically hail from "from different countries, different races." It is unclear how problematic this metaphor proves to be.

282. Ralph Waldo Emerson, "Self-Reliance," in *Essays and Lectures*, ed. Joel Porte (New York: Library of America, [1841] 1983), 259–260.

283. Alfred North Whitehead, "The Rhythm of Education," in *The Aims of Education*, 17.

284. See Zommer and House, *Fully Awake* (25:06). Two former students speak about the importance of these private spaces, one using the term "studio" and the other "study."

285. This is Arendt's translation of the Latin aphorism that forms both the closing of *The Human Condition* and the opening of *The Life of the Mind*. For this exact version, see Hannah Arendt, *The Life of the Mind*, One Volume Edition (San Diego, CA: Harcourt Brace & Company), 7–8. Note that Arendt incorrectly attributes the aphorism to Cato who, as Cicero reports, himself attributed it to Scipio Africanus.

286. Søren Kierkegaard, *Papers and Journals: A Selection*, trans. Alastair Hannay (London: Penguin Books, 1996), 161.

287. David Blacker, *Democratic Education Stretched Thin: How Complexity Challenges a Liberal Ideal* (Albany: State University of New York Press, 2007), 127.

288. See my earlier discussion of *skholê* and Oakeshott's concept of the interval in "New Student Orientation," pp. 99–102.

289. Duberman, *An Exploration in Community*, 37.

290. Arthur Penn, in Zommer and House, *Fully Awake* (32:13–32:38).

291. Perrow, "Drinking Deep at Black Mountain College," 88.

292. Hannelore Hahn, in Zommer and House, *Fully Awake* (33:08–33:29).

293. Perrow, "Drinking Deep at Black Mountain College," 88–89.

294. Duberman, *An Exploration in Community*, 92.

295. Sarton, Excerpt from Letter to Greene, 81.

296. Hahn, in Zommer and House, *Fully Awake* (33:56–34:28).

297. Sarton, Excerpt from Letter to Greene, 81.

298. Fielding Dawson, "Talk for Saturday, March 7, 1992: Education at Black Mountain," *Appalachian Journal 44/45* (2017-18): 573.

299. Levi, "Meaning of Black Mountain," 184.

300. John Dewey, *Democracy and Education: An Introduction to the Philosophy of Education* (New York: Macmillan Company, 1916), 80.

301. In the passage quoted, Dewey lists the four forms of hypostasization in a slightly confusing order: first that of the future, then that of the internal and the external, and finally that of the past.

302. See, for example, Jürgen Habermas, *Knowledge and Human Interests*, trans. Jeremy Shapiro (Boston: Beacon Press, 1971), 223; and, Jürgen Habermas, *The Theory of Communicative Action*, vol. 1, *Reason and the Rationalization of Society*, trans. Thomas McCarthy (Boston: Beacon Press, 1984), 92.

303. On the distinction between environment and surroundings, see Dewey, *Democracy and Education*, 11–12. Dewey writes, "The things with which a man *varies* are his genuine environment. Thus the activities of the astronomer vary with the stars at which he gazes or about which he calculates" (11, emphasis original).

304. Dewey, *Democracy and Education*, 76.

305. In *Truth and Method*, Gadamer takes the well-known interpretive principle—that one needs both to understand a text as a whole in order to notice its salient particulars and to understand its particulars to gain insight into its overall meaning—and gives it historical dimension and existential depth. See Gadamer, *Truth and Method*, Part II. It is possible to read Aristotle's account of practical wisdom as a common ancestor of both Gadamer's hermeneutics and Dewey's theory of reconstruction.

306. Oakeshott, "A Place of Learning," 29.

307. Dewey, *Democracy and Education*, 76. Emphasis original.

308. Compare René V. Arcilla, *Mediumism: A Philosophical Reconstruction of Modernism for Existential Learning* (Albany: SUNY Press, 2010).

309. If the arts and education are not externally related, one making the other into its instrument, but definitionally interconnected, then we should find concepts at Black Mountain that are simultaneously pedagogical and aesthetic. And that, I want to argue, is just what we find in the concepts of medium and happenings and stage, in the concepts of centering in pottery and breath in poetry.

310. Rauschenberg and Cernovitch were students; Cage, Cunningham, and Tudor were summer faculty; and Olson and Richards were regular faculty.

The variations in recollections, kaleidoscopic to begin with and then frayed by time, are comically far-flung. *The date*: one attendee has it in early summer; most have it in August but cannot recall the exact date. A BMC calendar lists a concert by John Cage on August 16, but this may have been a different event. *The personnel*: most agree on the list above, though Caroll Williams has Cunningham accompanied by members of the company he had not yet assembled; and she has someone named Jay Watt, not David Tudor, performing a sound piece with radio and duck calls. *The arrangement*: Francine du Plessix Gray and Cage himself put Cage up on the ladder. M. C. Richards and David Weinrib put Cage at a lectern. Duberman offers five rival accounts from attendees on the basis of his interviews, concluding with this summary:

> We now know there was a ladder—or at least a lecturn—and if MC wasn't on it (and she probably wasn't, since she was riding a horse, or in a basket) then Rauschenberg or Olson was. Except that Olson was also in the audience. But possibly that was after he delivered his poem; or maybe he came down and sat in the audience in order to deliver his poem, since that, as you'll recall, was broken into parts and it may be that he himself delivered only one of those parts (the part that was in French, perhaps). As for Rauschenberg, we know he exhibited something, either as backdrop or foreground—and something that he had made. Except of course the gramophone: clearly he couldn't have made that—nor those discs, which were something from the twenties, or thirties, or Piaf. (Duberman, *An Exploration in Community*, 377–378).

311. It is also sometimes referred to as *Untitled Event (1952)*. Some consider it the first happening; others an important "proto happening." I think Greg Allen probably gets the hermeneutic logic right when he observes—apropos of the remark by Nicholas Cernovitch, the event's projectionist, that "nobody knew we were creating history"—"and they weren't, at least until Cage began teaching the event at his legendary New School classes several years later to students who would be among the first performance artists" (see https://greg.org/archive/2009/08/10/you-didnt -have-to-be-there-and-even-if-you-had.html).

312. On Wolpe's relationship to Cage's Dadaistic turn, see Duberman, *An Exploration in Community*, 368.

313. Quoted in Duberman, *An Exploration in Community*, 375.

314. Michael Kirby and Richard Schechner, "An Interview with John Cage," *Tulane Drama Review* 10, no. 2 (1965): 51.

315. Kirby and Schechner, "An Interview with John Cage," 52.

316. This is based on the drawing that M. C. Richards made for William Fetterman in 1989 (William Fetterman, *John Cage's Theater Pieces: Notations and Performances* [Amsterdam: Harwood Academic Publishers, 1996], 100). No doubt, others remember the layout differently. Richards sketch seems clearly off on one point, since she shows Cunningham's "dance path" outside the seating, whereas multiple attendees, including Cunningham himself, have him traversing the aisles (his only preparation, he says, was to practice in the aisles to see "how much I could manage without kicking somebody" [Duberman, *An Exploration in Community*, 377]).

317. John Cage, "Julliard Lecture," in *A Year from Monday: New Lectures and Writings* (Middletown, CT: Wesleyan University Press, [1952] 1967), 106, 106, 110. Recollections differ over what Cage read during *Theater Piece No. 1*. In 1961, Cage himself identified the text as his Julliard Lecture, and this accords with many of the testimonials, which recall him reading something about the relation of Zen and music, with a quotation from Meister Eckhart (John Cage, "Foreword" in *Silence*, x). The duration of the lecture also fits the timing of *Theater Piece No. 1*, as suggested by its sole remaining score. On this point, see Fetterman, *John Cage's Theater Pieces*, 100.

318. Ruth Erikson, "Chance Encounters: Theater Piece No. 1 and its Prehistory," in Molesworth, *Leap before You Look*, 299. Some remember the projections starting on the ceiling and moving down the wall. The paintings were suspended from the ceiling.

319. See the epigram that opens John Cage, "On Robert Rauschenberg, Artist, and His Work," in *Silence*, 98. Cage refers to 4'33 as his "silent piece." All of the following Cage quotes come from this essay.

320. On this distinction, see Chris Higgins, "Instrumentalism and the Clichés of Aesthetic Education: A Deweyan Corrective," *Education and Culture* 23, no. 3 (2008).

321. Compare Rauschenberg's own characterizations of his work, for example: "I don't want the piece to stop on the wall. And it has to somehow document what's going on in the room and be flexible enough to respond" (quoted in Barbara Rose's *Rauschenberg* [New York: Vintage, 1987], 110); and "I had to make a surface which invited a constant change of focus and an examination of detail. Listening happens in time. Looking also had to happen in time" (quoted in G. R. Swenson, "Rauschenberg Paints a Picture," *Art News* [1963]: 45; requoted in Jonathan Fineberg, "Robert Rauschenberg's 'Reservoir,'" *American Art* 12, no. 1 [1998]: 87).

322. Dorothy Gees Seckler, "The Artist Speaks: Robert Rauschenberg," *Art in America* (1966): 76; quoted in Fineberg, "Robert Rauschenberg's 'Reservoir,'" 86.

323. Cage, "Experimental Music," 12.

324. Duberman, *An Exploration in Community*, 371; Kirby and Schechner, "An Interview with John Cage," 52.

325. Duberman, *An Exploration in Community*, 372. For photographs of Cunnningham (with Albers and Cage) and of Richards (with Tudor) holding what are likely the same white coffee cups as those used in *Theater Piece No. 1*, see Harris, "John Cage at Black Mountain" (https://www.blackmountaincollege.org/mary-emma -harris-john-cage-at-black-mountain-a-preliminary-thinking/).

326. A. V. Grimstone, ed., *Two Zen Classics: Mumonkan and Hekiganroku* (New York: Weatherhill, 1977), 44.

327. Duberman, *An Exploration in Community*, 376.

PUBLIC HEARING

1. John M. Gregory, "Inaugural Address," in *First Annual Report of Board of the Trustees of the Illinois Industrial University: From Their Organization, March 12, 1867, to the Close of the Academic Year, June 18, 1868* (Springfield: Bakee, Bailhache & Co., 1868), 174. Gregory was the first regent (the term president was adopted in 1894) of what is now known as the University of Illinois. Gregory addresses his remarks to "fellow citizens of Illinois." In the elided sentences, he explains that the founders will have to build this new kind of university even as they are running it.

2. Thomas Jefferson, "December 2, 1806: Sixth Annual Message," US National Archives. Transcript available at https://millercenter.org/the-presidency/presidential -speeches/december-2-1806-sixth-annual-message.

3. President's Commission on Higher Education, *Higher Education for American Democracy*, vol. 2 (New York: Harper, 1947), 23, quoted in Nancy Folbre, *Saving State U: Fixing Public Higher Education* (New York: The New Press, 2010), 38.

4. David F. Labaree, "Consuming the Public School," *Educational Theory* 61, no. 4 (2011): 394.

5. Labaree, "Consuming the Public School," 394.

6. David F. Labaree, *The Making of an American High School: The Credentials Market and the Central High School of Philadelphia, 1838–1939* (New Haven, CT: Yale University Press, 1988), xiv, and see chap. 6.

7. Labaree, "Consuming the Public School," 393.

8. In both cases, these are Labaree's figures: high school enrollment rose from 200,000 in 1890 to two million in 1920; college enrollment rose from 1.5 million in 1940 to 11.6 million in 1980 (David F. Labaree, *A Perfect Mess: The Unlikely Ascendancy of American Higher Education* [Chicago: University of Chicago Press, 2017], 104, 106).

9. Labaree, *A Perfect Mess*, 106.

10. This is the title of a track from Paul Simon's album, *There Goes Rhymin' Simon* (1973). See Labaree, *A Perfect Mess*, 97.

11. As reported in Gregor Aisch et al., "Some Colleges Have More Students from the Top 1 Percent Than the Bottom 60. Find Yours," The Upshot, *New York Times*, January 18, 2017, https://nyti.ms/2jRcqJs. This article is based on the much-discussed Chetty study (see https://opportunityinsights.org/paper/undermatching/).

12. I compiled this table from the data provided in Nick Hillman, "Why Rich Colleges Get Richer & Poor Colleges Get Poorer: The Case for Equity-Based Funding in Higher Education," Third Way (2020), https://www.thirdway.org/report/why-rich -colleges-get-richer-poor-colleges-get-poorer-the-case-for-equity-based-funding-in -higher-education. Hillman uses data from IPEDs and the Chetty study.

13. Generated using the *Times* interactive tool (https://www.nytimes.com /interactive/projects/college-mobility/) which is based on the Chetty data.

14. See Table IX, "Percentile Cutoffs in 2015 Dollars for Parent and Child Income by Birth Cohort," in Chetty's online data repository (https://opportunityinsights .org/data/?geographic_level=0&topic=0&paper_id=3084#resource-listing). The cutoff for the 99.9% for the 1991 cohort in 2015 dollars is $3,028,600; in 2023 dollars, that is $3,881,715. The cutoff for the 99% is $630,500; in 2023 dollars, that is $808,103.

15. Ozan Jaquette, *State University No More: Out-of-State Enrollment and the Growing Exclusion of High-Achieving, Low-Income Students at Public Flagship Universities*, Jack Kent Cooke Foundation, UCLA (2017), https://www.jkcf.org/research/state -university-no-more-out-of-state-enrollment-and-the-growing-exclusion-of-high -achieving-low-income-students-at-public-flagship-universities/.

16. Quoted in Jaquette, *State University No More*.

17. When I do not cite a source, the information offered is readily available on university websites. When a university lists a range, I take the average cost. When I refer to "tuition," I am referring to the total annual estimated costs.

18. The webpage has since changed. Here is a historical link: https://web.archive
.org/web/20180101121507/https://www.admissions.illinois.edu/invest/tuition.

19. See http://admissions.indiana.edu/cost-financial-aid/tuition-fees.html.

20. The website has since changed. Here is a historical link: https://web.archive
.org/web/20170312081554/https://admissions.indiana.edu/cost-financial-aid/roi
.html.

21. See https://www.admissions.umd.edu/costs/ (accessed October 2015). The
webpage has since changed and unfortunately there is no archived version.

22. IPEDs Table 330.10, "Average undergraduate tuition, fees, room, and board
rates charged for full-time students in degree-granting postsecondary institutions,
by level and control of institution: Selected years, 1963–64 through 2020–21,"
https://nces.ed.gov/programs/digest/d21/tables/dt21_330.10.asp. In 2020 dollars, the average annual cost at four-year publics was as follows: 1980 ($7747); 2000
($13,005); 2020 ($21,520).

23. The stratification evident in our New Jersey grid can be replicated in any state,
looking only at public strata. In Illinois, for example, using the Times/Chetty college mobility tool, we find

- UIUC: median family income, $109,000; grad income (at thirty-four),
  $59,700; 50% of students from top quintile, 6% from the bottom.
- Southern Illinois University, Carbondale: family income, $75,700; grad
  income, $42,000; 31% from top quintile, 9.2% from the bottom.
- Chicago State University: family income, $32,100; grad income, $31,900;
  4.7% from top quintile, 20% from the bottom.

24. Compare the eight-stage "devolutionary cycle" offered in Christopher New-
field, *The Great Mistake: How We Wrecked Public Universities and How We Can Fix
Them* (Baltimore, MD: Johns Hopkins University Press, 2016). Figure 1 (p. 36)
shows the cycle at a glance.

25. One much-discussed cause is administrative bloat. On this, see "Campus Tour"
(pp. 10 and 274–275n64–66).

26. Quoted in Folbre, *Saving State U*, 46. This was a favorite remark of Duderstadt's, quoted in various forms. Folbre cites James J. Duderstadt, *The View from the
Helm: Leading the American University during an Era of Change* (Ann Arbor: University of Michigan Press, 2007), 145. Here, though, Duderstadt paraphrases his own
oft-quoted remark somewhat differently, adding two more stages of the devolu-
tion of State U, inserting "state-related" in the progression from state-assisted to
state-located, and citing approvingly a colleague's quip that, while no longer state-
supported, publics are still "state-molested" by "opportunistic state politicians."

27. Kristen Cummings et al., *Investigating the Impacts of State Higher Education Appropriations and Financial Aid*, State Higher Education Executive Officers Association

(2021), Appendix A, p. 82, https://sheeo.org/wp-content/uploads/2021/05/SHEEO
_ImpactAppropationsFinancialAid.pdf.

28. According to the Government Accounting Office, in 2012, 25% of public college revenue came from tuition, 23% from state funds. See http://www.gao.gov
/assets/670/667557.pdf. Regarding four-year publics, see Kich, "A Real Numbers-
Cruncher Weighs in on the Campos Article."

29. See "Where does our money come from?" at https://cfo.berkeley.edu/budget
-101.

30. Naomi Schaefer Riley and James Piereson, "Reimagining the Public University," *National Affairs*, no. 42 (2020).

31. Mary Ellen Flannery, "State Funding for Higher Education Still Lagging,"
NEA Today, October 25, 2022.

32. See https://www.washington.edu/opb/uw-data/fast-facts/ and https://public
affairs.ku.edu/budget#:~:text=KU%20Revenues,18%20percent%20of%20KU's%20
revenues.

33. See https://finance.umd.edu/budget/facts-and-figures/operating-budget;
https://bpir.uconn.edu/wp-content/uploads/sites/3452/2019/06/FY20-Budget
-Presentation-Fin-Affairs-6.10.19.pdf; https://www.rutgers.edu/about/budget
-facts; https://budget.wisc.edu/content/uploads/Budget-in-Brief_2021-22_V15
-1.pdf; https://budget.utexas.edu/about/budget; https://publicaffairs.vpcomm
.umich.edu/key-issues/tuition/general-fund-budget-tutorial/; https://sc.edu/about
/offices_and_divisions/budget/documents/fy20_budgetdoc.pdf; https://budget
.psu.edu/BOTJuly/BoardDocuments%2022-23/incomepie.aspx. For the Chapel
Hill figure, see Jane Calloway, "Carolina's Money: Where We Get It; How We
Spend It," *The Well*, March 11, 2021, https://thewell.unc.edu/2021/03/11/. For
the UC Boulder figure, see Flannery, "State Funding for Higher Education Still
Lagging."

34. Thomas Mortenson, "State Funding: A Race to the Bottom," *The Presidency*
15, no. 1 (2012): 29.

35. See http://www.cbpp.org/research/state-budget-and-tax/years-of-cuts-threaten
-to-put-college-out-of-reach-for-more-students.

36. David Blacker, *The Falling Rate of Learning and the Neoliberal Endgame* (Winchester, UK: Zero Books, 2013), chap. 4.

37. This page was up for at least five years. It is mentioned in an OpEd in September 2014, and here is an archived link from September 2019: https://web.archive
.org/web/20190212015155/https://admissions.berkeley.edu/cost-of-attendance.

38. Berkeley's figure is misleading since it is in line with concurrent estimates of the
average pay bump for any BA. Indeed, in 2018, the Federal Reserve calculated the college earnings advantage at $31,800/year (as reported by CNN Business: https://www

.cnn.com/2019/06/06/success/college-worth-it/index.html). Meanwhile, these figures obscure the disturbing fact that poorer students see only a fraction of this gain. One study found that students whose families make less than 185% of the Federal Poverty Level get a 91% earnings boost over high school graduates, while those from families above this income level line get a 162% boost (Brad Hershbein, *A College Degree Is Worth Less If You Are Raised Poor* [Washington, DC: Brookings, 2016]).

39. Karl Marx, *Capital: A Critique of Political-Economy*, trans. Ben Fowkes, vol. 1 (New York: Vintage, 1977), 125.

40. Marx, *Capital*, vol. 1, 125.

41. Ralph Waldo Emerson, "The Conduct of Life," in *Essays and Lectures*, ed. Joel Porte (New York: Library of America, 1983), 1060. In "New Student Orientation," I say more about the existential use-value of liberal learning, which helps us stay in touch with the fugitive question, what is worth wanting? (see pp. 96–99).

42. Marx, *Capital*, vol. 1, 128.

43. Wendy Fishman and Howard Gardner, *The Real World of College: What Higher Education Is and What It Can Be* (Cambridge, MA: MIT Press, 2022), Fig. 5.3, p. 130.

44. Jobbification: an ugly word for an ugly phenomenon. "Vocationalization" is more common, but, as I argue in "Job Prospects," the jobbified university is not truly devoted to vocational education.

45. As I discuss in "Job Prospects," there is a bitter irony here. Even as credentials, degrees in the arts and humanities are underrated. And as soon we expand our view beyond credentialing and job preparation, the arts and humanities emerge as the key contributors to vocational education writ large.

46. This data is drawn from the Humanities Indicator Project (https://www.amacad.org/humanities-indicators) as reported by Nathan Heller, "The End of the English Major: Enrollment in the Humanities Is in Free Fall at Colleges around the Country. What Happened?," *New Yorker*, March 6, 2023.

47. Steven Johnson, "Colleges Lose a 'Stunning' 651 Foreign-Language Programs in 3 Years," *Chronicle of Higher Education* 65, no. 20 (2019).

48. See https://www.collegeart.org/news/2018/11/08/colleges-facing-cuts-to-arts-and-humanities/.

49. See https://dailynous.com/category/cuts-and-threats-to-philosophy-programs/.

50. See http://www.esubulletin.com/news/emporia-state-suspends-academic-programs/article_e997ead2-3eca-11ed-a4ec-7703a48a5527.html.

51. Paul A. Samuelson, "The Pure Theory of Public Expenditure," *Review of Economics and Statistics* 36, no. 4 (1954): 387.

52. I say more about the land-grant tradition in "Soul Action" (see pp. 46–48 and 286n105).

53. Sarah Vowell, "A University of, by and for the People," *New York Times*, February 15, 2018.

54. Here I am dealing swiftly with a question—the nature and value of public education—that I have explored in detail in other work: Chris Higgins and Kathleen Knight Abowitz, "What Makes a Public School Public? A Framework for Evaluating the Civic Substance of Schooling," *Educational Theory* 61, no. 4 (2011); Chris Higgins, "The Possibility of Public Education in an Instrumentalist Age," *Educational Theory* 61, no. 4 (2011); Chris Higgins, "The Public and Private in Education," in *International Handbook of Philosophy of Education*, vol. 2, ed. Paul Smeyers (Dordrecht: Springer, 2018); and Chris Higgins, "From the Editor: Educational Philosophy as the Vanguard of the Public Humanities," *Educational Theory* 68, no. 3 (2018).

55. Robert F. Kennedy, "Remarks at the University of Kansas," March 18, 1968, available at https://en.wikisource.org/wiki/Remarks_at_the_University_of_Kansas.

56. Charles Taylor, "Cross Purposes: The Liberal-Communitarian Debate," in *Philosophical Arguments* (Cambridge, MA: Harvard University Press, 1995), 190–191.

JOB PROSPECTS

1. Jean-Jacques Rousseau, *Emile, or on Education*, Introduction, Translation, and Notes by Allan Bloom, 2nd ed. (New York: Basic Books [1762] 1979), 201.

2. Hart Research Associates, "Falling Short? College Learning and Career Success," survey conducted on behalf of the Association of American Colleges & Universities (2015), 1, https://www.aacu.org/sites/default/files/files/LEAP/2015employerstudent survey.pdf.

3. The employers were asked to rate their employees' preparedness in each area on a 1–10 scale. The percentages refer to the portion of employers who rated their employees 8–10 in the given area. I have averaged subcategories in two cases. Communication was divided into oral (28%) and written communication (27%). There are several categories related to diversity: "Awareness/experience of diverse cultures in US" (21%); "Working with people from diff. backgrounds" (18%); "Proficient in other language" (16%); and "Awareness/experience of diverse cultures outside US" (15%).

4. The Hamilton Project, "Career Earnings by College Major," Interactive Chart (May 11, 2017). See http://www.hamiltonproject.org/charts/career_earnings_by _college_major/. Of the two business options, I chose "Business Management and Administration." I checked both optional boxes, "Include Full-Time Workers Only" and "Include Graduate Degrees." Among those who hold only a bachelor's degree, business majors do consistently outearn history majors.

5. Hamilton Project, "Career Earnings by College Major." I calculated career figures by averaging earnings at at ten, twenty, and thirty years post degree. I took

the average earnings of four engineering majors: aerospace, civil and architectural, computer, and electrical. Again, I selected both "Include Full-Time Workers Only" and "Include Graduate Degrees."

6. Hamilton Project, "Career Earnings by College Major." Again, I selected "Include Full-Time Workers Only" and "Include Graduate Degrees" and averaged the figures at ten, twenty, and thirty years. In this database, philosophy and religious studies majors are combined in a single category.

7. Adapted from Table 6 in Dirk Witteveen and Paul Attewell, "The Earnings Payoff from Attending a Selective College," *Social Science Research* 66 (2017): 165. Witteveen and Attewell's analysis is based on data from the first cohort of NCES' Baccalaureate and Beyond longitudinal study, which tracked the labor market experiences of 1993 college graduates through 2003. The ten-year data on the second cohort, of 2008 graduates, should soon be available (there is a four-year snapshot available now).

8. See Ruth Walker, Christopher Moore, and Andrew Whelan, eds., *Zombies in the Academy: Living Death in Higher Education* (Bristol, UK: Intellect, 2013).

9. Megan J. Laverty, "There Is No Substitute for a Sense of Reality: Humanizing the Humanities," *Educational Theory* 65, no. 6 (2015): 642–643. Laverty takes the phrase "managerial newspeak" from Raymond Gaita, who himself is building on George Orwell. When Laverty says that "we *now* know," I take it that she is referring to the broadly hermeneutic, anti-behavioristic turn of the eighties, when thinkers such as Rorty, Taylor, and MacIntyre brought Diltheyan, Oakeshottian, and Gadamerian arguments to bear in Anglo-American philosophy of action. As MacIntyre puts it, "There is no such thing as 'behavior,' to be identified prior to and independently of intentions, beliefs and settings" (Alasdair MacIntyre, *After Virtue: A Study in Moral Theory*, 3rd ed. [South Bend, IN: University of Notre Dame Press, (1981) 2007], 208).

10. Philip W. Jackson, in "The Mimetic and the Transformative: Alternative Outlooks on Teaching," in *The Practice of Teaching* (New York: Teachers College Press, 1986).

11. Laverty, "There Is No Substitute for a Sense of Reality," 641n22; glossing Jackson, "The Mimetic and the Transformative," 138n23.

12. The first strategy does not reduce everything to the bottom line, but it does leave work stranded there.

13. Let me here address three methodological questions. First, while I see these six tasks as necessary conditions of full vocational enactment, I take no stand on whether they collectively constitute a sufficient condition. This list may be incomplete.

Second, I am treating undergraduate education as the beginning of a process of vocational formation that extends beyond the university and across the lifespan. I speak of *formation* and *enactment* to distance my account from our default assumptions about the what, where, and when of vocational education. Only a sliver of vocational learning amounts to preparatory didactics, as in "here are the tools and how to use them." In order to learn to do the work well, we need not only instruction but formation of habits of thinking and doing, seeing, and valuing. Here we must heed John Dewey's warning that the results of formal instruction are "superficial" and short-lived compared to the "sharing in actual pursuit" through which knowledge is "transmuted into character" (John Dewey, *Democracy and Education: An Introduction to the Philosophy of Education* [New York: Macmillan Company, 1916], 8). It is only after we engage the work, as apprentices in a community of practice, that we truly begin to fathom the how and why of it. And at this point, the causal arrow becomes bidirectional: we are not only forming ourselves for practice but forming ourselves through it. In pursuing the idea of vocation as a medium of one's general education, I am building on previous work and earlier essays in this book. For a MacIntyrean and Deweyan theory of vocational formation and enactment, see Higgins, *The Good Life of Teaching: An Ethics of Professional Practice* (Oxford: Wiley-Blackwell, 2011), chap. 2 and pp. 111-130. In "Soul Action" (pp. 73–74), I introduced Dewey's theory of vocation as medium. In "Wide Awake" (pp. 163–164), I further developed the idea of medium in relation to the arts and the concept of positive freedom.

Third, the language of "task" is meant to signal not steps in a linear process but enduring challenges to which we continually return. (Thanks to Jake Fay for pressing me to clarify this point.) There is a logic to the order which begins with finding a calling and ends with leaving it. At the same time, I have already indicated some of the nonlinear progressions in vocational life. For example, while credentialing is based in part on technical know-how, the richest technical education usually occurs on the job. Or consider two of the further knotty circles I will go on to explore. You cannot explore the ethical geography in and around your work if you have not yet chosen a line of work (task 3 depends on task 1); but you cannot fully understand how a line of work will connect you with what is important until you have begun to discern the goods internal to the practice (task 1 depends on task 3). Similarly, you cannot grow in and through a vocation if you have not chosen one (task 5 depends on task 1); but, vocations shape our abilities, sensibilities, and aspirations (task 1 depends on task 5).

14. For an analysis of the prestige market, see Frank Donoghue, *The Last Professors: The Corporate University and the Fate of the Humanities* (New York: Fordham University Press, 2008), chap. 5.

15. Elizabeth A. Armstrong and Laura T. Hamilton, *Paying for the Party: How College Maintains Inequality* (Cambridge, MA: Harvard University Press, 2013).

16. As noted above, I am not here assuming a one-way relation between one's makeup and one's choice of vocation, as if our talents were all ready-made and fully formed. The phrase, hopes and talents, is meant to evoke this productive circular logic of vocations as simultaneously an expression of and formative influence on who we are. I explore one example of this vocational spiral of experience in my

discussion of Dr. John Sassall. For a theoretical exploration of vocational circles of experience, see Higgins, *The Good Life of Teaching*, esp. chaps. 4 and 8.

17. Dewey, *Democracy and Education*, 308.

18. William Deresiewicz, "The Disadvantages of an Elite Education: Our Best Universities Have Forgotten That the Reason They Exist Is to Make Minds, Not Careers," *American Scholar* 77, no. 3 (2008): 28–29.

19. See "Public Hearing" on the vicious circle of instrumentalization and jobbification.

20. For Oakeshott's idea of the interval, see "New Student Orientation" (pp. 100–102). On the culture of "total work," see Josef Pieper, "Leisure, the Basis of Culture," trans. Gerald Malsbary, in *Leisure: The Basis of Culture* [South Bend, IN: St. Augustine's Press, (1948) 1998].

21. Walker Percy, *The Moviegoer* (New York: Vintage, [1961] 1998), 13.

22. There are many factors foreclosing vocational dialogue. Contemporary students feel a tremendous pressure to hit the ground running on a clearly defined career path (indeed, most students are already juggling school and work). And there is the stigma attached to being undeclared. Universities offer less and less resistance to the general culture of busyness, distraction, and overwork. Faculty are constantly asked to do more. Tight budgets lead to big classes, discouraging individual relationships. Students think that office hours are only for course-related questions.

Even if the student does show up and broach these vocational/existential questions, the typical faculty member is unprepared to help (on the miseducation of the professoriate, see A Skeleton Faculty in "Soul Action"; on the "pastoral" dimension of higher education, see Katherine Ki-Jung Jo, "Making the Examined Life Worth Living: The Ethics of Being a Liberal Educator" [PhD diss., University of Illinois, 2019], http://hdl.handle.net/2142/105850).

To the argument that Gen Ed serves this function: in a recent survey of students at a state flagship, only 28% agreed (and only 2% of these, strongly) that "General Education courses have helped me or will help me choose a major" (Clarissa A. Thompson, Michele Eodice, and Phuoc Tran, "Student Perceptions of General Education Requirements at a Large Public University: No Surprises?" *Journal of General Education* 64, no. 4 [2015]: 285).

I was drawn to work at Boston College in part because of their commitment to vocational discernment. For example, Halftime retreats are organized around Michael Himes' three-part version of what I am calling the great vocational question: What gives you joy? What taps your talents and expands your abilities? What does the world need you to be? Father Himes' iconic video elaborating the three questions can be found online at https://www.youtube.com/watch?v=P-4lKCENdnw.

23. Maxine Greene, "The New Freedom and the Moral Life," in *Landscapes of Learning* (New York: Teachers College Press, 1978), 152.

24. On this point, see Arcilla's interesting discussion of the social importance of the dialogue between adolescent melodrama and adult cynicism in René V. Arcilla, *For the Love of Perfection: Richard Rorty and Liberal Education* (New York: Routledge, 1995), 134–148.

25. Thomas Piper, dir., *Five Seasons: The Gardens of Piet Oudolf* (2017).

26. Oudolf was born in October of 1944. I have taken this timeline—first nursery work at age twenty-six, design firm launched in 1976, farmhouse in Humelo purchased in 1982—from Sally McGrane, "A Landscape in Winter, Dying Heroically," *New York Times*, January 31, 2008, https://www.nytimes.com/2008/01/31/garden /31piet.html.

27. I explore the overlaps and divergences between the modern humanities and humane learning in Chris Higgins, "Waist High and Knee-Deep: Humane Learning Beyond Polemics and Precincts," *Educational Theory* 65, no. 6 (2015).

28. In "Soul Action," I send out a rescue party to hunt for the living formative ideals buried underneath the bureaucratic business that is Gen Ed.

29. Indeed, I have contributed to that study in previous work and two sections of this book. See Chris Higgins, "Turnings: Towards an Agonistic Progressivism," in *Philosophy of Education 2008*, ed. Ron Glass (Urbana, IL: Philosophy of Education Society, 2009); "New Student Orientation"; and "Wide Awake," pp. 124–145.

30. Oakeshott, "A Place of Learning," in *The Voice of Liberal Learning: Michael Oakeshott on Education*, ed. Timothy Fuller (New Haven, CT: Yale University Press, 1989), 28–29. I should explain two of my elisions.

The first removes Oakeshott's qualification that a culture is "the whole of what an associated set of human beings have created *beyond the evanescent satisfaction of their wants.*" This is confusing given that Oakeshott clearly holds that cultures are centrally defined through their particular constructions of "wants" and the arts through which to attain them. "To be human," Oakeshott writes, is "to have wants and try to satisfy them" (25). In liberal learning, we may be "invited to pursue satisfactions [we] has never yet imagined or wished for," but it is still satisfaction at issue (24). Oakeshott is not setting thinking against desiring. Culture for him is the elaboration of desire through imaginative conversation. True, man cannot live by bread alone: we need focaccia, right out of the oven, dripping with a good olive oil. The key word here is "evanescent" which in Oakeshott is typically code for shrinking your ambitions down to the fad of the moment.

My second elision removes a chauvinistic remark. Oakeshot says that it is "particularly [a culture] such as ours" that displays this rich variegation and dynamic internal tension. I do not mean to hide Oakeshott's ignorance, his apparent belief that other cultures are more homogeneous than ours. However, I worried that this moment of reflexive condescension would distract from what overall seems a successful acknowledgment of the contingency within and across cultures.

31. For a fuller catalogue of imaginative registers, see "New Student Orientation," p. 97). Here is another of Oakeshott's lists: culture is "an inheritance of feelings, emotions, images, visions, thoughts, beliefs, ideas, understandings, intellectual and practical enterprises, languages, relationships, organizations, canons and maxims of conduct, procedures, rituals, skills, works of art, books, musical compositions, tools, artefacts and utensils - in short, what Dilthey called a *geistige Welt*" (Michael Oakeshott, "Learning and Teaching," in *The Voice of Liberal Learning*, 45).

32. For Oakeshott's critiques of child-centered education and relevance see, for example, Michael Oakeshott, "Education: The Engagement and Its Frustration," in *The Voice of Liberal Learning*, 71–77; and Oakeshott "A Place of Learning," 31. I argue that Oakeshott nonetheless counts as a (novel kind of) progressive educational theorist in Higgins, "Turnings: Towards an Agonistic Progressivism."

33. Oakeshott, "A Place of Learning," 29.

34. Oakeshott, "A Place of Learning," 29.

35. The first phrase comes from John Stuart Mill, the second from contemporary art historian Jonathan Fineberg. See John Stuart Mill, *On Utilitarianism* (1859), chap. 3, §1, various editions; and, Jonathan Fineberg, *Art Since 1940: Strategies of Being* (New York: Prentice Hall, 1994).

36. Oakeshott, "The Voice of Poetry in the Conversation of Mankind," 501.

37. Michael Oakeshott, "The Study of Politics in a University," in *Rationalism in Politics*, 187.

38. Oakeshott, "The Voice of Poetry in the Conversation of Mankind," 493.

39. "The Study of Politics in a University," 187. The term "conversability" comes from "The Voice of Poetry in the Conversation of Mankind" (492), where Oakeshott contrasts it with the tendency toward bullying or "eristic," and with the congealing of a discourse into "dogmata," appearing as "as set of conclusions reached."

40. Oakeshott, "The Voice of Poetry in the Conversation of Mankind," 493–494.

41. Oakeshott, "The Voice of Poetry in the Conversation of Mankind," 494.

42. Oakeshott, "The Voice of Poetry in the Conversation of Mankind," 494.

43. J. D. Salinger, *Franny and Zooey* (Boston: Little, Brown and Company, 1961), 146, emphasis original.

44. The short "Franny" serves as a sort of prologue. The heart of *Franny and Zooey* is the long second novella, "Zooey," which picks up the action at home with Zooey's attempt to help Franny. We know that Lane attends Princeton because Franny is there for "the Yale game," which suggests Princeton or Harvard, and Lane takes her to a restaurant favored by students who, "had they been Yale or Harvard men, might rather too casually have steered their dates away from Mory's or Cronin's" (Salinger, *Franny and Zooey*, 10).

45. Matthew Arnold, "Preface to Culture and Anarchy" (1869), in *Culture and Anarchy and Other Writings*, ed. Stefan Collini (Cambridge: Cambridge University Press, 1993), 190. For a discussion of this passage and a critique of the tendency to celebrate or denounce such humanist epitomes rather than engage the thought behind them, see Higgins, "Waist High and Knee-Deep," *Educational Theory* 65, no. 6 (2015): 703–708.

46. Salinger, *Franny and Zooey*, 146–147, emphasis original.

47. William Wordsworth, "The World Is Too Much with Us," in *Selected Poems and Prefaces*, ed. Jack Stillinger (Boston: Houghton Mifflin, [1807] 1965).

48. Max Weber, *The Protestant Ethic and the Spirit of Capitalism*, trans. Talcott Parsons, Routledge Classics ed. (London: Routledge, 2001), 128. I have followed Sung Ho Kim (in the Weber entry of *Stanford Encyclopedia of Philosophy*) in restoring Weber's Nietzschean allusion by translating "*letzten Menschen*" as "last man" rather than "last stage" and "*Menschentums*" as "humanity" rather than "civilization." For alternate translations of Weber's "*Fachmenschen ohne Geist*" (Parson's "specialists without spirit") and more on the Nietzschean flavor of this sentence, see "Soul Action" (pp. 35–36 and 282–283n73). I have left Parson's "cage" even though two more recent translators, Baehr and Kalberg, convincingly argue that the "iron cage" is a mistranslation of "stahlhartes Gehäuse," the famous phrase that appears earlier in this paragraph. Weber describes a process in which the "lightly worn cloak" of calling ossifies into a "shell as hard as steel" (Baehr) or a "steel-hard casing" (Kalberg). The Gehäuse is not an external enclosure but an internalization of ideology, a sclerotic habitus. Nonetheless, here the Gehäuse seems to enclose all of us moderns, so Parsons' classic "cage" seems preferable. See Peter Baehr, "The 'Iron Cage' and the 'Shell as Hard as Steel': Parsons, Weber, and the *Stahlhartes Gehäuse* Metaphor in the *Protestant Ethic and the Spirit of Capitalism*," *History and Theory* 40, no. 2 (2001); Max Weber, *The Protestant Ethic and the Spirit of Capitalism: The Revised 1920 Edition*, trans. Stephen Kalberg (New York: Oxford University Press, 2011), 177.

49. It is an exaggeration to suggest that standard approaches to professional ethics entirely collapse into ordinary morality. There is often a stress on role-specific moral obligations (e.g., client confidentiality) and on practice-specific moral dilemmas (e.g., whether to promote a very weak student or force him to repeat a grade). I nonetheless maintain that on the whole professional ethics favors questions of right over questions of good, duty and proscription over purpose and significance, and that indeed this deontic focus tends ultimately toward general principles. As I have argued elsewhere, following MacIntyre and others, the aretaic turn in recent ethics implies a shift in professional ethics. We turn to practices not to apply moral principles worked out elsewhere but to investigate the nature of the good. We do so not simply to curb self-interest but to better understand how practices help practitioners cultivate admirable selves and worthwhile lives. See Higgins, *The Good Life of Teaching*.

50. MacIntyre, *After Virtue*; Michael Walzer, *Spheres of Justice: A Defense of Pluralism and Equality* (New York: Basic Books, 1983); Michael J. Sandel, "The Procedural Republic and the Unencumbered Self," *Political Theory* 12, no. 1 (1984).

51. For a reconstruction of the renaissance in substantive ethics, building on Bernard Williams, Charles Taylor, and MacIntyre, see Higgins, *The Good Life of Teaching*, 21-35 and 42–43nn1–4.

52. There were actually three major critiques of liberalism in a span of three years. Beating MacIntyre and Walzer to the punch by a year was Michael J. Sandel, *Liberalism and the Limits of Justice* (Cambridge, UK: Cambridge University Press, 1982). Another communitarian-leaning critic of liberalism is Taylor who helpfully intervened with Charles Taylor, "Cross Purposes: The Liberal-Communitarian Debate," in *Philosophical Arguments* (Cambridge, MA: Harvard University Press, 1995).

53. See Walzer, *Spheres of Justice*, 12.

54. Though MacIntyre doesn't mention zombies, what I say here echoes the thought experiment with which he opens *After Virtue*.

55. See David Blacker, *The Falling Rate of Learning and the Neoliberal Endgame* (Winchester, UK: Zero Books, 2013), 53. I like Blacker's coinage, which, as he says, echoes the idea of "regulatory capture." Walzer himself refers to this process with the overly broad term "domination." "Colonization" might be apt, but Jürgen Habermas has made this (*Kolonizierung*) his term of art for the co-opting of the "lifeworld" (local, living, symbolic worlds, animated by communicative action) by "system" (instrumental rationality, market logic, and strategic action), a process that is closer to what I am calling "bureaucratization."

56. MacIntyre, *After Virtue*, 194.

57. MacIntyre, *After Virtue*, 194.

58. For a detailed explication and extension of MacIntyre's theory of practice, see Higgins, *The Good Life of Teaching*, chap. 2. For discussion of its basic architecture, showing how goods and virtues are shaped at each levels of ethical life (practice, individual life narrative, and tradition), see pp. 48–55. For a detailed typology of internal goods, see pp. 55–63. The remainder of the chapter is devoted to a close examination of what differentiates practices from other activities. For a review of the criteria separating practices from other activities, see pp. 63–80. For the relationship between practices and institutions, with a closer look at the distinction between internal and external goods, see pp. 73–78. For a brief discussion of the moral virtues that enable practitioners to resist the corruption of their practices, see p. 78.

59. Cf. MacIntyre, *After Virtue*, 188.

60. I composed this thought experiment in 2015. *The Queen's Gambit* has an ending just like this. MacIntyre appears nowhere in the credits.

61. Jeffrey Brenner, MD, as interviewed by Stephen J. Dubner in "How Many Doctors Does It Take to Start a Healthcare Revolution?," *Freakonomics* podcast, April 9, 2015. The transcript is available at *https://freakonomics.com/podcast/how -many-doctors-does-it-take-to-start-a-healthcare-revolution-2/*.

62. Michael J. Sandel, *What Money Can't Buy: The Moral Limits of Markets* (New York: Farrar, Straus and Giroux, 2012).

63. For this translation of Weber's "*stahlhartes Gehäuse*" (famously translated as "iron cage"), I am drawing on the translations of Baehr and Kalberg (see above, note 48).

64. Walzer, *Spheres of Justice*, 75.

65. Walzer, *Spheres of Justice*, 10. That the boundaries between practices need to be neither too porous nor impermeable is also a concern of MacIntyre's, as I show in my discussion of para-practices and the public role of practices. See Higgins, *The Good Life of Teaching*, 71–73 and 78–80.

66. Walzer, *Spheres of Justice*, 10.

67. Walzer introduces the concepts of convertibility and dominance and the distinctions between simple and complex equality, and between monopoly and tyranny, in *Spheres of Justice*, chap. 1. In the preface (p. xv), Walzer describes distributive justice as "an art of differentiation." For a discussion of liberal society as "a world of walls," each of which "creates a new liberty," see Michael Walzer, "Liberalism and the Art of Separation," in *Thinking Politically: Essays in Political Theory* (New Haven, CT: Yale University Press, [1984] 2007), 53.

68. He does, however, acknowledge, in the recognition chapter, that "no substantive account of self-respect will also be a universal account," since there are particular forms of dignity attached to different lines of work. See Walzer, *Spheres of Justice*, 274–275.

69. The subjects of chapter 9 are kinship, love, sex, and marriage. While friendship does make several cameos in *Spheres of Justice*, for example, "love and friendship cannot be bought" (102), it is not treated as a good pursued within its own sphere nor emphasized in Walzer's discussion of affective ties. In a discussion of the limits of desert as a distributive principle, Walzer briefly turns to art appreciation as an example (24), but again this seems to call for no expansion or reorganization of his list of spheres.

70. Walzer, *Spheres of Justice*, 8.

71. Walzer, *Spheres of Justice*, 8.

72. Walzer, *Spheres of Justice*, 8.

73. Presumably, Walzer himself would locate this good in the sphere of security and welfare, which he initially defines as communal arrangements to secure first our "survival and then [our] well-being" against the "indifference and malevolence

of nature" (65). However, while shelter as security fits here, the broader relation of dwelling and flourishing is taken up in later chapters. It comes up in one way in Walzer's discussion of family and the domestic sphere in chapter 9. It then receives what might be its fullest expression in chapter 12, in Walzer's discussion of the spherical corruption in Pullman, Illinois:

> *A man's home is his castle.* I will assume that this ancient maxim expresses a genuine moral imperative. . . . But what the maxim requires is not political self-rule so much as the legal protection of the domestic sphere—and not only from economic but also from political interventions. We need a space for withdrawal, rest, intimacy, and (sometimes) solitude (300, emphasis original).

74. Ronald Dworkin, "Review of M. Walzer, *Spheres of Justice* (New York, NY, 1983)," *New York Review of Books* 14 (1983).

75. Michael Walzer and Ronald Dworkin, "'Spheres of Justice': An Exchange," *New York Review of Books* 21 (1983).

76. Walzer and Dworkin, "'Spheres of Justice': An Exchange."

77. R.H. Tawney, quoted in Walzer, *Spheres of Justice*, 209. Walzer differentiates the first two types of schooling on pp. 206-207, adding general education on pp. 208–209.

78. Walzer, *Spheres of Justice*, 196.

79. Walzer, *Spheres of Justice*, 193.

80. Den Hartogh finds four distributive principles at work in *Spheres*: desert, free exchange, to ensure that individual needs are fulfilled by collective provision, and to ensure full membership. See Govert Den Hartogh, "The Architectonic of Michael Walzer's Theory of Justice," *Political Theory* 27, no. 4 (1999): 498.

81. Den Hartogh denies that Walzer finds any spheres in which, starting from a distinctive good, we then find a corresponding distinctive principle of distribution. Some of Walzer's spheres (membership, security and welfare, honor) are *defined* by the range of application of a particular distributive principle, and so it is only "trivially" true that we find in them an autonomous distributive logic (Hartogh, "The Architectonic of Michael Walzer's Theory of Justice," 501). With other spheres, Walzer does start with a particular good, but in these cases, as I have already noted with reference to education, he often finds multiple distributive principles at work. Another problem with Walzer's account is that, while his key message is to protect the integrity of the spheres, to avoid convertibility and domination, he builds some forms of domination into his system. Membership is a controlling good, a kind of moral trump suit, since the theory is about distribution, which presumes a bounded political community. There is the further question of whether Walzer was right to include money (and commodities) as a separate sphere, since money is not a good in its own right but a symbol of convertibility. Whereas domination by membership over other spheres is

acceptable, much of Walzer's book is about identifying limits to exchange logic, drawing limits around "what money can buy" (see pp. 103–107). Because Walzer makes money a separate sphere of value and a particular threat to the integrity of the other spheres, this blurs the distinction I am making between MacIntyrean and Walzerian accounts of corruption and integrity. Preserving the distinction between internal and external goods and defending the integrity of spheres start to amount to the same thing if money is central among external goods and chief among dominating spheres. That said, there are generative differences in their accounts. For example, Walzer's focus on distributive justice presumes a degree of scarcity and competition, a hallmark of MacIntyre's external goods. (In my discussion of MacIntyre, I show why this competitiveness criterion is too strict and also why he is mistaken to categorize recognition, which Walzer sees as a core sphere, as an external good. See Higgins, *The Good Life of Teaching*, 73–75). Rather than attempt to close the distance between the two theories, I am content to let MacIntyre stand for the threat that goods in any practice/sphere can begin to hollow out, devolving into formalism, expediency, and cost-benefit analyses while letting Sandel stand for the threat of convertibility on which some genuine good is instrumentalized to serve another genuine good.

82. Walzer, *Spheres of Justice*, 295.

83. Oft-quoted, seldom cited, the first appearance I have found so far is in Ray Ginger, *Eugene V. Debs: The Making of an American Radical* (New York: Collier Books, 1949), 125.

84. Walzer, *Spheres of Justice*, 297.

85. Jeremy W. Peters and Jackie Calmes, "Road Shows Get Rolling for Romney and Obama," *New York Times*, September 1, 2012, https://www.nytimes.com /2012/09/02/us/politics/next-to-native-status-claimed-by-ryan-in-the-drive-for-oh io.html.

86. Harry Boyte and Nancy N. Kari, *Building America: The Democratic Promise of Public Work* (Philadelphia: Temple University Press, 1996).

87. Alasdair MacIntyre, *Three Rival Versions of Moral Enquiry: Encyclopaedia, Genealogy, and Tradition* (Notre Dame: University of Notre Dame Press, 1990), 62.

88. Higgins, *The Good Life of Teaching*, 55.

89. In fact, for Dewey, it is impossible to have but one vocation, as I explain in "Soul Action" (see pp. 31ff.). Dewey uses the words "vocation" and "occupation" interchangeably.

90. Dewey, *Democracy and Education*, 309, emphasis original.

91. Dewey, *Democracy and Education*, 310.

92. In this and the following two paragraphs in the text, I am reprising the central themes of my book, *The Good Life of Teaching*, which examines the general relation

between work and self-cultivation before turning to the specific question of self-ful teaching.

93. John Dewey, "The Relation of Theory to Practice in Education," in *John Dewey on Education*, ed. Reginald D. Archambault (Chicago: University of Chicago Press, [1904] 1974), 318–319.

94. Dewey, *Democracy and Education*, 309–310. In "Soul Action," I quoted the entire passage from which this line is drawn (see p. 74).

95. Rainer Maria Rilke, *Letters to a Young Poet*, trans. M. D. Herter Norton, rev. ed. (New York: W.W. Norton & Co., 1954), 54. Written between 1903 and 1908, the letters were first published, in German, in 1929. Herter Norton's English translation first appeared in 1934. The context here is Kappus's love life, but Rilke's general point is that we should approach life (work, relationships, and the rest) as a poetic calling and thus as an education in the broadest sense.

96. Rilke, *Letters to a Young Poet*, 46, 40.

97. Rilke, *Letters to a Young Poet*, 47, 78.

98. Rilke, *Letters to a Young Poet*, 47.

99. Interview by Anderson Cooper, with Paris Denard, August 6, 2018, *Anderson Cooper 360*, http://transcripts.cnn.com/TRANSCRIPTS/1808/06/acd.01.html. Speaking to Denard about President Trump, West observed that what makes Trump immoral is not that he has a gangster element in his makeup—we all do—but that he gives his free rein:

> I know there's gangster in me. There's gangster in you. There's gangster in Trump. There's gangster in Anderson. The challenge is how do we get control of those gangster elements such that we live a life of some decency and a slice of integrity? That's what we're talking about. It's all about accountability. Accountability. Accountability.

100. Rilke, *Letters to a Young Poet*, 47.

101. Salinger, *Franny and Zooey*, 167–8.

102. See https://www.oed.com/view/Entry/39063?redirectedFrom=congenial#eid.

103. See https://dictionary.cambridge.org/us/dictionary/english/congenial.

104. Hannah Arendt, *The Human Condition*, 2nd ed. (Chicago: University of Chicago Press, [1958] 1998), 179.

105. Arendt, *The Human Condition*, 179–180.

106. Robert Farris Thompson, *Flash of the Spirit: African and Afro-American Art and Philosophy* (New York: Vintage, 1984). I was lucky enough to have my college experience shaped by "Master T" (as Thompson was known to the students of Timothy Dwight College), whose study of Yoruba and other influences on Black Atlantic art, culture, and spirituality taught him to reject this psychologism and individualism

of the modern West and to foster a community capable of summoning and paying witness to these flashes of the spirit (whether we call it àshe or daimon).

107. Talbot Brewer, *The Retrieval of Ethics* (Oxford: Oxford University Press, 2011). For more on the question of how we come to value a new structure of value, see my note in "New Student Orientation" (p. 308n28).

108. On the waning of the older tradition and the rise of a narrowly scientific conception of medicine, see Robert M. Veatch, *Disrupted Dialogue: Medical Ethics and the Collapse of Physician/Humanist Communication, 1770–1980* (Oxford: Oxford University Press, 2004).

109. Anthony Grafton and Lisa Jardine, *From Humanism to the Humanities: Education and the Liberal Arts in Fifteenth- and Sixteenth-Century Europe* (London: Duckworth, 1986), 1–2.

110. That such civic roles, and thus seats in formal humanistic education, were reserved for men alone is true, but there were learned female humanists in the Renaissance. Grafton and Jardine use this fact to show the anachronism of our view of humanities education as general, nonvocational education. They show how teachers such as Guarino Guarini, Lauro Quirini, and Angelo Poliziano had to rework their understanding of humanistic education when corresponding with accomplished humanists Isotta Nogarola, Cassandra Fedele, and Alessandra Scala, women who were barred from such civic roles by the sexism of the day. These educators struggled to makes sense of such aims as eloquence and erudition, personal virtue and self-cultivation, once detached from professional practices and civic functions. See Grafton and Jardine, *From Humanism to the Humanities*, chap. 2.

111. William Carlos Williams, quoted in James K. Gude, "Reflections from the History of Medicine," *Sonoma Medicine: The Magazine of the Sonoma County Medical Association*, http://www.nbcms.org/AboutUs/SonomaCountyMedicalAssociation /Magazine/TabId/747/language/en-US/PageId/201/sonoma-medicine-reflections -from-the-history-of-medicine.aspx.

112. Walker Percy quoted in Gude, "Reflections from the History of Medicine."

113. Percy quoted in Gude, "Reflections from the History of Medicine."

114. Williams, quoted in Gude, "Reflections from the History of Medicine."

115. John Berger, *A Fortunate Man: The Story of a Country Doctor (with Photographs by Jean Mohr)* (New York: Vintage, [1967] 1997), 24. I am so grateful to Megan Laverty for her gift of the perfect book at the perfect time.

116. Berger, *A Fortunate Man*, 55.

117. Berger, *A Fortunate Man*, 54–55.

118. Berger, *A Fortunate Man*, 55.

119. Berger embodies this virtue of imaginative perception whether he is writing about art, animals, Spinoza, or the predations of petrocapitalism. See, for example,

John Berger, *Selected Essays*, ed. Geoff Dyer (New York: Vintage, 2003); John Berger, "Why Look at Animals?", in *About Looking* (New York: Vintage, 1991), John Berger, *Bento's Sketchbook* (London: Verso, 2015); and John Berger, "How to Resist a State of Forgetfulness," in *Confabulations* (London: Penguin, 2016).

120. Dewey, *Democracy and Education*, 288.

121. Ludwig Wittgenstein, *Philosophical Investigations*, trans. G. E. M. Anscombe, Reissued German-English ed. (Oxford: Blackwell, [1953] 1997), 48e (§115).

122. See Hans-Georg Gadamer, *Truth and Method*, 2nd rev., Continuum Impacts, ed. and trans. Joel Weinsheimer and Donald Marshall (New York: Continuum, [1960] 2004), 267–382, especially pp. 340–354. For an exploration of Gadamer's theory as it applies to vocational experience, see Higgins, *The Good Life of Teaching*, chaps. 4 and 8.

123. See Gadamer, *Truth and Method*, 270 and 350–352.

124. Berger, *A Fortunate Man*, 55.

125. Berger, *A Fortunate Man*, 55.

126. Berger, *A Fortunate Man*, 57.

127. Berger, *A Fortunate Man*, 57.

128. Freud describes psychoanalysis as a *Nacherziehung* in a number of places. See the *Standard Edition of the Complete Psychological Works of Sigmund Freud*, trans. and ed. James Strachey (London: Hogarth Press, 1953), vol. 7, p. 267; vol 14, p. 311; and vol. 15, p. 450.

129. "*Mihi quaestio factus sum.*" "*Quaestio*" here is also sometimes translated as "puzzle" or "enigma," or, as R. S. Pine-Coffin has it, "problem." See Augustine, "*Confessiones*" (397–401 CE) in Opera Omnia Cag, Electronic Edition, Opera: Part 2, ed. Cornelius Mayer (Charlottesville, VA: InteLex Corporation, 2000), 182ln40 (Bk. 10, §50); Augustine, *Confessions* (397–401 CE), trans. R. S. Pine-Coffin (London: Penguin, 1961), 239 (Bk. 10, chap. 33).

130. Berger, *A Fortunate Man*, 143.

131. Jonathan Lear, "Preface: The King and I," in *Open Minded: Working Out the Logic of the Soul* (Cambridge, MA: Harvard University Press, 1998), 4.

132. Andrew Abbott, *The System of Professions: An Essay on the Division of Expert Labor* (Chicago: University of Chicago Press, 1988).

133. Sigmund Freud, "Analysis Terminable and Interminable," in *The Standard Edition of the Complete Psychological Works of Sigmund Freud, Volume XXIII (1937–1939): Moses and Monotheism, an Outline of Psycho-Analysis and Other Works*, ed. and trans. James Strachey (London: Hogarth, [1937] 1961), 248.

134. For an appreciation of one such lovably absurd dwelling, the one that we educational philosophers have built precisely by chewing it over, see Higgins,

"Educational Philosophy as the Vanguard of the Public Humanities," *Educational Theory* 68, no. 3 (2019).

135. See Jonathan Lear, *A Case for Irony* (Cambridge, MA: Harvard University Press, 2011), 23. Compare my critique of Steven Pinker's functionalism in "Soul Action" (see pp. 64–68 and 292n154).

136. Kenneth Burke, "Literature as Equipment for Living," in *The Philosophy of Literary Form* (Berkeley: University of California Press, [1941] 1974).

137. Karl Marx and Friedrich Engels, "Manifesto of the Communist Party" (1848), trans. Samuel Moore in cooperation with Engels (1888), https://www.marxists .org/archive/marx/works/1848/communist-manifesto/index.htm, chap. 1.

138. Milan Kundera, *The Unbearable Lightness of Being*, trans. Michael Henry Heim, Perennial Classics ed. (New York: HarperCollins, [1984] 1999), 2.

139. F. H. Bradley, "My Station and Its Duties," in *Ethical Studies* (Oxford: Clarendon Press, [1876] 1988).

140. Iris Murdoch, "Metaphysics and Ethics" [1957], in *Existentialists and Mystics*, ed. Peter Conradi (New York: Penguin, 1998), 75.

141. Charles Taylor, "Self-Interpreting Animals," in *Human Agency and Language: Philosophical Papers*, vol. 1 (Cambridge, UK: Cambridge University Press, 1985).

142. Oakeshott, "A Place of Learning," 19, 23. This discussion of Oakeshott's theory of our ambivalent relationship to our freedom as self-interpreting animals builds on my earlier discussion in "New Student Orientation" of liberal learning and the ordeal of consciousness (see pp. 96–99 and 103–104).

143. Oakeshott, "A Place of Learning," 18.

144. Simone Weil, *The Need for Roots: Prelude to a Declaration of Duties toward Mankind*, trans. Arthur Wills (London: Routledge, [1949] 2002).

145. Arendt, *The Human Condition*, 11. Compare my discussion of natality as an educational principle at Black Mountain College in "Wide Awake" (see pp. 115–118 and 141).

146. *Arche* is a Greek term meaning beginning, origin, source, principle, rule. "Anarchic" is Birmingham's term, nicely capturing how Arendt sees natality as both the arising of a new principle, a principle of beginning, and disruption of ruling conventions. See Peg Birmingham, "The an-Archic Event of Natality and the 'Right to Have Rights,'" *Social Research: An International Quarterly* 74, no. 3.

147. Arendt, *The Human Condition*, 247; Hannah Arendt, *The Origins of Totalitarianism* (San Diego: Harvest/Harcourt, 1973), 478–479.

148. Hannah Arendt, *The Life of the Mind*, One Volume Edition (San Diego, CA: Harcourt Brace & Company), 4, quoted in Stephanie Mackler, *Learning for*

Meaning's Sake: Toward the Hermeneutic University (Rotterdam: Sense Publishers, 2009), 27. Mackler offers the gloss that it would "be an exhausting existence if we had to understand everything for the first time."

149. Pound, *A B C of Reading* (Reading, UK: Faber and Faber Limited, [1934] 1961), 13.

150. Søren Kierkegaard, *The Sickness unto Death: A Christian Psychological Exposition for Upbuilding and Awakening*, ed. and trans. Howard V. Hong and Edna H. Hong, Kierkegaard's Writings (Princeton, NJ: Princeton University Press, 1983), 32–33 (SV 11:146).

151. Wordsworth, "The World Is Too Much with Us."

152. Elizabeth Bishop, "In the Waiting Room," in *The Complete Poems, 1927–1979* (New York: Farrar, Straus and Giroux, 1983). The poem has a long first section, followed by four further stanzas. I will cite parenthetically by stanza.

153. I offer a detailed discussion of Jinny's experience of rooted flow in "Soul Action" (see pp. 36–39).

154. William James, *Psychology: A Briefer Course*, vol. 14, The Works of William James, Electronic Edition (Charlottesville, VA: InteLex Corporation, [1892] 2008), 21.

155. We find ourselves in the garden of forking paths and interestingly it may be from this Borges story from which Ishiguro drew his title:

> It was under English trees that I meditated on that lost labyrinth. . . . I imagined a labyrinth of labyrinths, a maze of mazes, a twisting, turning, ever-widening labyrinth that contained both past and future and somehow implied the stars. Absorbed in those illusory imaginings, I forgot that I was a pursued man; I felt myself, for an indefinite while, the abstract perceiver of the world. The vague, living countryside, the moon, the remains of the day did their work in me; so did the gently downward road, which forestalled all possibility of weariness. The evening was near, yet infinite. (Jorge Luis Borges, "The Garden of Forking Paths" [1941], in *Collected Fictions*, trans. Andrew Hurley [London: Penguin, 1998], 122)

Hats off to Dennis Shirley who, when I told him the title of Ishiguro's novel, immediately recalled the phrase from (the translation) of Borges' "Garden of Forking Paths." Though some have compared Ishiguro to Borges, I can find no discussion of the possibility that Ishiguro's title is taken from Borges.

156. Alasdair MacIntyre, *Three Rival Versions of Moral Enquiry: Encyclopaedia, Genealogy, and Tradition* (Notre Dame: University of Notre Dame Press, 1990), 62.

157. "Sclerotic habitus" is a gloss of Weber's *"stahlhartes Gehaüse,"* famously translated as "iron cage." (see above, note 48).

158. Jonathan Lear, *Freud* (New York: Routledge, 2005), 152–153.

159. From Rushdie's blurb on the back cover of the Vintage International edition. See Kazuo Ishiguro, *The Remains of the Day* (New York: Vintage, 1993).

160. Selina Todd, "Domestic Service and Class Relations," *Past and Present* 203, no. 1 (2009): 183–184.

161. See https://web.archive.org/web/20060825134010/http://www.vam.ac.uk /collections/architecture/past/save/index.html.

162. Now extinct in the wild (Britain), English butlers are apparently now in demand by the new superrich of Russia, China, and the Middle East.

163. Marx and Engels, *Manifesto of the Communist Party*, chap. 1.

164. The issue of whether a series of small errors are trivial or significant is overdetermined for Stevens. Later, we learn that Miss Kenton struggled to get Stevens to see that the errors his aged father was making were a sign of his father's inability to continue to do the work (see Ishiguro, *The Remains of the Day*, 55–60).

165. Sigmund Freud, "Drives and Their Fates," trans. Graham Frankland, in *The Unconscious* (London: Penguin Books, [1915] 2006). The specific mechanisms I go on to mention are described on pp. 20–21.

166. Oakeshott, "A Place of Learning," 24. For a gloss of this passage, see "New Student Orientation," pp. 96–97.

167. Marx and Engels, *Manifesto of the Communist Party*, chap. 1.

168. I am referring to Mark Fisher, *Capitalist Realism: Is There No Alternative?* (Winchester, UK: Zero Books, 2009). The observation about the end of the world, which inspires Fisher's first chapter, has been attributed to both Fredric Jameson and Slavoj Žižek. Though Žižek does say something along these lines in the 2005 documentary bearing his name, it appears that Jameson got there first. In *Seeds of Time*, his 1994 book (based on his 1991 Wellek Lectures), he offers a less quotable version (xii). The version I quoted appears in Fredric Jameson, "Future City," *New Left Review*, May/June, 2003, https://newleftreview.org/issues/ii21/articles /fredric-jameson-future-city, though Jameson himself introduces it as something "someone once said."

169. Charles Taylor, *The Sources of the Self: The Making of the Modern Identity* (Cambridge, MA: Harvard University Press, 1989), chaps. 3-4. He defines the concept on p. 63.

170. Ishiguro, *The Remains of the Day*, 184–190, 206–211, 240–245.

171. Taylor, *Sources of the Self*, 68.

172. Later that night, Stevens will recall an episode when Lord Darlington allowed a friend to show up Stevens's knowledge of foreign affairs to prove the proposition that "democracy is something for a bygone era" and that "the world is too complicated a place for universal suffrage" (Ishiguro, *The Remains of the Day*, 198).

After admitting that Darlington's views "will seem today rather odd—even, at times, unattractive," he appeals to duty (199). For Stevens, while a butler's loyalty must be "*intelligently* bestowed," once he finds someone "noble and admirable" he cannot be in the business of "forever reappraising his employer" (201, emphasis original; 200). In practice," Stevens reasons, it is "simply not possible to adopt such a critical attitude towards an employer and at the same time provide good service" (200).

173. Rousseau, *Emile*, 193.

INDEX

Abbott, Andrew, 247

Academic mal/formation, ix–x, xii, 55, 60–65, 68–70, 79, 90, 146, 148, 151, 154, 294–295n158

Adamic, Louis, 132–135, 137, 142, 145

Administrative bloat, 10, 355

Advisement, 60–61, 109, 124–128. *See also* Black Mountain College (BMC), mentoring at

Aesthetic education. *See also* Albers, Josef, on formative aesthetic education; Black Mountain College (BMC), arts/aesthetic education at
  and general education, x, 88–89, 111, 160, 162, 164–167, 180
  and liberal arts curriculum, 73–74, 78–80, 88–89, 109

Aesthetic experience
  vs. aesthetic consciousness, 32–35
  vs. anesthetic experience, 14, 74, 251, 298n180
  and holistic formation, 30–32, 151–152, 155, 158, 197, 229 (*see also* Formative experience, theatrical dimensions of)
  in vocational enactment, 73–74, 210–211, 254 (*see also* Vocation, as poetic calling)

Agency of the learner. *See also* Formative education, as quest; Freedom awakening, 18, 64, 68–69, 93–96, 140–141, 144, 174–176, 208–210

(*see also* Pedagogical beginnings; Search, the)
  and dialectic of influence, 16–17, 138, 277n13, 336n134, 338n148, 340n160
  as driving formative education, 16–18, 19, 48, 148, 157, 340n160
  and major selection, 49, 128, 208–210
  as sparked by that of teacher, 64, 340n160, 148–150, 152, 154

Agonistic dimension of education. *See* Transformative education, as agonistic

Albers, Anni, 110, 165, 168, 345n235

Albers, Josef, xi–xii, 110–112, 118, 159, 175, 340n160
  on formative aesthetic education, 111, 122, 157, 160, 165–172, 176
  as leader at Black Mountain College, 319n16, 321n39
  as teacher, 162, 168–172, 348–349n272

Alexander, F. M. (Frederick Matthias)
  Alexander Technique, 82, 86–87, 305n243
  as influence on John Dewey's philosophy, 83–88, 302–303n217, 303n224
  and treatment of John Dewey, 82–84, 86, 89, 300n201, 302n214

Althusser, Louis, 5–6, 124

Alÿs, Francis, 164